Earl the Pearl

MY STORY

EARL MONROE

with QUINCY TROUPE

FOREWORD BY SENATOR BILL BRADLEY

SPORTS
PUBLISHING

To my mother, Rose; my sisters, Ann and Theresa; my father, Vernon;
my aunts, Nicey and Mary; Mr. Sam; my grandmother, Mom;
my cousins, Joe, Bobby, Jimmy, and Margie; my heart, Marita;
my children, Sandy, Rodney, Danielle, and Maya;
my grandchildren, Harvey (Champ), Carlia, Darian, and Monroe;
and my relatives, the Allens, the Halls, and the Chapmans

—Earl Monroe

To Margaret Porter Troupe

—Quincy Troupe

Copyright © 2013, 2019 by Earl Monroe

First Skyhorse Publishing edition 2019. Published by arrangement with Rodale Books,
an imprint of the Crown Publishing Group, a division of Penguin Random House LLC.

Sports Publishing books may be purchased in bulk at special discounts for sales
promotion, corporate gifts, fund-raising, or educational purposes. Special editions can
also be created to specifications. For details, contact the Special Sales Department,
Sports Publishing, 307 West 36th Street, 11th Floor, New York, NY 10018 or
sportspubbooks@skyhorsepublishing.com.

Sports Publishing® is a registered trademark of Skyhorse Publishing, Inc.®, a Delaware
corporation.

Visit our website at www.sportspubbooks.com.

10 9 8 7 6 5 4 3 2 1

Library of Congress Cataloging-in-Publication Data is available on file.

Book design by Christopher Rhoads
Cover design by Brian Peterson
Cover photo from the lens of George Kalinsky

ISBN: 978-1-68358-329-5

Printed in the United States of America

CONTENTS

Part Three
MY HUNGER FOR NBA RESPECT AND A CHAMPIONSHIP RING

FOREWORD

THERE HAS NEVER BEEN a basketball player like Earl Monroe. He wasn't the quickest guy in the league or overpowering physically, standing six foot three with a minimum of musculature on his frame, yet he was a uniquely great player. What set him apart was his control of the ball, his sense of the court, and his uncanny ability to gauge the distance between himself and anyone who could block his shot. When he had the ball, each part of his body seemed to move independently, controlled by a single command center. Among his manifold skills, his spin move became unstoppable. He drove toward the defensive man only to turn his back on him at the last possible second before collision, pivot with his left foot, and head away at a forty-five-degree angle. What was different from any other player's spin was Earl's one-handed control; it was as if the ball were attached by a short string to his fingers. When he was in a playful mood, he spun, let the ball hang suspended in air, crossed his hands like an umpire calling a runner safe, looked one way and touch-passed it in the opposite direction. At such moments, a murmur would ripple through the crowd and burst into an explosion of shouting, clapping, laughing, and stamping of feet. It was thus that Earl became "The Pearl," and, more appropriately, "Black Magic," because he made things happen with the ball that defied explanation.

Someone once asked Earl how he decided what to do on the court.

He replied that he didn't know what he was going to do until he'd done it. Like a great jazz artist, he created in the moment.

When Earl was traded from Baltimore to New York in the early seventies, people said that the Knicks would need two basketballs to satisfy the scoring ambitions of its new backcourt duo, Earl Monroe and Walt Frazier. It didn't turn out that way. What people didn't know was the strength of Earl's dedication to winning. In New York Earl changed his game. In a sense, he sacrificed superstardom for his team. He learned to play within a much more structured offense and demanding team defense. He never complained; he made himself fit in. Still, there were nights when the magic could not be contained.

I remember a game against Milwaukee in the 1972–1973 season. The Knicks were behind by 19 points with about 6 minutes to go. The fans were already starting to leave Madison Square Garden. Then suddenly Earl took over the game and scored repeatedly. At one point in those closing minutes, he jumped, changed the position of the ball three times, and floated it over the outstretched hand of Milwaukee's center, seven-foot-two Kareem Abdul-Jabbar. On his next two forays he drove directly at his man, then spun left, took two more dribbles, and made each shot from the baseline. The same thing happened in the final game of the 1973 NBA Finals against the Los Angeles Lakers. When our stalwart forward, Dave DeBusschere, went down with a badly sprained ankle, Earl would not let us lose. We took energy from his play and elevated our game that night down the stretch, winning our second NBA title in four years and giving Earl what every player, deep down, yearns for—a championship.

For all of Earl's athletic achievements, what sets him apart is his character: He grew up in a tough Philadelphia neighborhood, but without becoming "a tough" himself; he encountered persistent racism, but he never turned bitter; he was well aware that he had special basketball skills, but he never gave in to arrogance. There is a remarkable peace at the core of his personality. The flamboyance of "The Pearl" exists right alongside the gentleness of "off-court Earl." People are always glad to see him. He never complains. He smiles easily. Even as he went through five hip operations, five back operations, eleven sinus operations, and countless stomach problems from all the ibuprofen he took in his playing days, he exuded his own brand of joie de vivre. His quiet strength made him unselfish as a player and continues to make him cherished as a friend. In my twenty years in politics, I asked Earl to come to many of my political events and share the memory of his magic with my supporters. He never once refused.

At the end of the day, Earl seems to know that kindness is more important than on-court heroics and that those who love him count for more than those who applauded him. He accepts life's ups and downs; neither overwhelm him. Balance on the court and balance in life—this seems to be his motto. In *Earl the Pearl*, you will read his story in his own voice. The quiet man has finally spoken. It is a story worth reading, as his life has been a life worth leading.

Bill Bradley
New York City

PROLOGUE

WHEN I WAS 17 YEARS OLD, during the summer of 1962, after my senior year at John Bartram High School, there was a certain guy a couple of years older than me that I played against in a one-on-one game for the title of best young basketball player in all of South Philadelphia.

During my junior year in 1961, Matt Jackson, a senior at Bok Technical High School, was considered hands down the top basketball player in the city. That year he was the top high school scorer in all of Philadelphia, and after graduating he left the city to go play at South Carolina State College. Matt was a forward with a great body—about six feet five, six feet six inches tall and 220 pounds—a close-cropped, *quo vadis* haircut, and a light brown complexion. He was what some would call a classic basketball player, you know, because he would back you down, shoot a turnaround jump shot over his opponent, or a little right-handed or left-handed hook shot in the lane or on either side of the basket. Though he wasn't fast or quick, he was a deadly shooter when he got his shot off, and he looked like a pro when he played the game.

On the other hand, I was six three and skinny, had long arms, and weighed around 170 pounds. My game was honed in the schoolyard, playground style, you know. I had slick moves and a crossover dribble in my bag of tricks, plus a pretty good jump shot from anywhere on the floor from 20 feet in and a lightning-quick spin move that got me anywhere on the floor and to the rim for layups or for tricky spin shots high off the backboard. But I had a game in the paint, close to the basket, too, because I played center, with my back to the basket, in high school. I had learned and honed my craft on playgrounds with the best opponents Philadelphia had to offer, and I felt I was ready to play anyone from anywhere, any place, anytime. In other words, my confidence level was very high at this time.

But my confidence hadn't always been this great. In fact it was during the summer before this showdown, in 1961, that I began to put the building blocks into place that would help me elevate my game to another plateau. At first, when I was growing up, I was a baseball and soccer player. Basketball didn't become my great love until I was 14 years old, when I was attending Audenried Junior High School. I was already six three by then, and I started playing with a group of guys from Audenried that included Steve "Smitty" Smith, George Clisby, "Leaping" John Anderson, Ronald Reese, and Edwin "Wilkie" Wilkinson. Later, on the 30th and Oakford Street playground, we formed a team called the Trotters. Not that we played like the Globetrotters, because we actually fashioned our team game style after the Boston Celtics.

Soon we had a stellar five, and we learned to play the game together. Smitty was my main man, my best friend to this day. We went through junior high, high school, and college together. He was five foot nine. Wilkie was also five nine and could dunk. George Clisby, "Clis" to us, was about six two. Leaping John was about six four and could really jump. Then there was Ronald Reese, who was smaller, about five eight. Everyone on our team was really a guard back then. Leaping John played center, I played center and forward, Clis was a forward, and the other three guys were guards, but everybody played interchangeable positions.

I credit the guys I played with on the Trotters with helping me improve my game. Wilkie was the catalyst, though, because he was the guy who dreamed up certain shots. He'd go home and come back to the playground with things like right-handed and left-handed jump hooks, or a fake to the right and shoot with the left hand move. We didn't get what he was doing at first, but after a few days we'd all get it. Then he'd go home and dream up something else. He was very creative, very innovative. I got a lot of stuff from just watching him and trying to imitate the moves he made.

Wilkie taught me never to be afraid to try something different, because unless you tried things, you'd never know whether you could do them or not. So I started interjecting a lot of new moves and shots into my game, like double-pump hanging shots in the lane and twisting layups with either hand. And it got to the point where I had perfected a lot of those moves, like coming down and putting a little dipsy-doo move on my opponent, then crossing him over, putting a spin move on him, and going to the basket hard to make a floating layup, or spinning the ball in off the backboard with my left or right hand. I always tried these moves in practice first so when I was in a game it just came natural to me, rather than trying something for the first time in a game when I might not be comfortable doing it.

But even my friends on the Trotters were able to get picked to play in games before me, and at one point they were all better ball handlers, rebounders, and shooters than I was. They just knew how to play the game and I didn't yet. So I decided I was going to be a star while I was sitting on the sidelines watching them and all those other players get all the runs. I was 15 or 16 when I decided I was going to be as good as or better than any player getting picked ahead of me. Getting looked over made me want to succeed really badly, so I practiced harder until I got better. But the guys I played with and against from my neighborhood got better, too, and that just meant I had to work even harder on my game.

My game really started to come together when I started playing against college guys, when I was around 16. Everyone on the Trotters got better around the same time, too, but I just made more progress. On the playground we never had a coach, so we coached and taught ourselves to understand how to play. That was one of the main things in Philadelphia: to understand how to play the game. When we started playing against college guys and beating them, that gave all of us a lot of confidence, especially me.

But I still had to really work on my dribbling, because I played forward and center, and I already knew that no college coach was looking to recruit a six-foot-three center. I understood I would have to play guard at the next level, which meant I wasn't going to be able to play unless I improved my ball handling. So I went to the courts at Oakford Street playground and started dribbling all around it with my left hand. Then I would turn around and do the same thing with my right. Then I would dribble in circles, dribble the figure eight, left-handed and right-handed. I practiced like this for hours. When I was finished with this, I would shoot. Dribble and shoot, all kinds of shots, all summer, all day, from 10 in the morning until 10 at night, when the lights went out on the street and on the playground. Then I would go home. My mother, the rock in my life, who would do anything for me, rubbed me down and gave me a massage each and every day that summer. I did this routine 12 hours a day, every day, until I began seeing signs of improvement in my outside shooting and my dribbling.

Because I shot so much, my shoulders got all this tension and knots in them, and they hurt really bad, too. But I knew the only way to get better and to reach my goal was through constant practice. By then I had also realized I had to become a special basketball player. This fact became clear to me during my final year in high school when my coach, Tony Coma, sent out footage of me to various colleges.

After looking at my tapes, the coach at Southern Illinois University—where Walt Frazier went after high school—wrote back and said I "couldn't handle the ball." That wasn't true because I could do that very well by then! But I was playing center, with my back to the basket and making my moves from down low, close to the basket, and couldn't show that I could dribble and shoot like a guard, and there was no footage of my ability to do all these things. Had I played guard and had to drive to the basket for layups, or shoot pull-up jump shots on my high school team—like I did when I played on the playgrounds—there would have been evidence that I could dribble and "handle the ball." But there was no film of me playing on the playground, so I was just out of luck.

Then racism raised its ugly head when a white coach from a white southern school who had heard of me asked Coach Coma for my transcript. Now, John Bartram was an integrated school and Coach Coma was white, as were three of the starting players on our team. So maybe the southern white coach thought I was white, too. But when he asked for my picture and Coach Coma sent him one and he saw I was black, we never heard from him again. That was in late spring 1962, and during that time, there weren't a lot of black players playing basketball for southern white schools. That incident just made me more determined than ever to succeed.

After I got my dribbling handle together, I knew I could get to any spot on the floor for whatever shot I wanted to take. And that's what it's all about in basketball: being able to get from one spot to another on the court. Then I was able to come out and play better. After that, it was just a matter of playing all the time and executing the repetition in games like I did in practice. I also improved my overall game and my passing to help my teammates score more points. I knew these were skills I had to practice hard at to improve, to be able to do them all the time against top-flight competition, to execute in real time, you know, in games, in order to be better than my opponents.

I have this thing about just being practical. Seems like I've always had it. I've always felt that if I put my mind to something, I could do it, that if I could see it in my mind, in my imagination, I could accomplish it. I believe you have to visualize what it is you want to do, and once you see it in your mind, you can do it. That's just the way I feel. I have always felt that's where I was ahead of a lot of guys during my time, because I saw myself succeeding, knew how to get there, saw the game in my head, and saw myself being better than the guys I was playing with and against.

Plus, I'd always known I needed to understand what my own physical gifts and limitations were, you know, my mental attitude toward the game; this was always important for me. Then, I had to compensate for the deficiencies I found in my game. For example, I always knew I wasn't a fantastic leaper. I could jump, but not out of the gym like some other guys. So I didn't try to do those kinds of leaper things that guys who could really jump did, like high-flying windmill dunk shots à la Dr. J or Michael Jordan. I never attempted any shots like that. My game was closer to the floor, making magical, mind-bending moves with the ball.

When you play a game like basketball—or any other game, for that matter—you might not be the best all the time, because there's always somebody out there that's as good as or better than you some of the time. On any given day, someone can be better. But you've got to understand what you have, what you can do best against that player to be effective. If that person is a good defensive player and you know you can't get around him, then what is your recourse? You've got to understand what you can do against him that will keep him back on his heels and allow you to be effective. Maybe it's shooting jump shots, or dipsy-doo spin shots off the backboard, little left-handed shots instead of right-handed ones around the basket. Maybe it's twisting your body while hanging in the air under the basket and shooting off the glass on the other side, with the rim acting as the protector for your shot. You know what I mean? A little magic and a little creative dipsy-doo can take you a long way. Maybe you become a thinking player if you can't jump over a guy. So what do you do? What's your recourse? Maybe out-think him is what you can do. Basketball, for me, is like playing a game of chess: You have to stay several moves ahead of your opponent if you're going to be successful.

I learned a lot of things playing on the playgrounds, but the only problem was that I was from South Philadelphia, and when I was grow-ing up, players from there still weren't getting a lot of runs on most playgrounds outside of our neighborhood. Most of the best-known players were from some other neighborhood, like West or North Philadelphia. My home playground court was at 30th and Oakford in South Philadelphia, which was the black playground court in that area. The court where the white players ran was on 30th and Tasker, and me and my guys used to travel down there sometimes to play. A guy named Jerry Rullo was the playground director at Tasker, and he orga-nized those games. He played with the Philadelphia Warriors in 1946 and had a lot of guys playing for him at Tasker.

Their games were great competition, and a lot of times, if we black guys won, we'd have to fight our way out of there going home. When race riots broke out in the area in those days, everybody would say, "It must be March," because that was the month we'd play against each other, when it was getting warm outside. (I've never heard of a race riot anywhere when it was cold. If you fight when it's cold, you hurt your knuckles.)

When I understood all of this, my game improved by leaps and bounds, and very quickly. When I understood what the game of basket-ball was all about—that it was scientific—I passed a lot of players who had been ahead of me. In my senior year of high school I scored about 21 points a game. That was the first year I played the whole varsity sea-son. I kept written notes about all the guys who dogged me as a player, and as I got better and beat them I would cross their names off my list in the little blue notebook my mother gave me. Eventually I made sure

I beat all the guys whose names I wrote in that notebook. That gave me satisfaction, let me know just how good I was getting, after I beat certain top-notch players.

Matt Jackson came back to Philly from college and heard my name dropping from everyone's lips. I guess this pissed Matt off because he had been top dog in South Philadelphia basketball a year before. One day, after Matt and his people had been going around dissing me and my game to everyone who would listen, calling me a "hotdog" and a "show-boat, playground player," suddenly all of South Philly was abuzz about which of us was the best player, especially since I had also been the leading scorer in the city during my last year in high school. I think all of this got up under Matt's skin, because he really didn't think I was better than him, as some of my supporters were going around saying.

So we met at the David Landreth Elementary School schoolyard to settle the whole matter. On the day of the one-on-one matchup, the whole place was jam-packed, people packed like sardines into and around the playground. The place was overrun with basketball fanatics, you know, men and women, old, young, and middle-aged, sitting on benches, plopped down on the ground, hanging on the chain-link fences by their fingers and toes, folks all up in the trees like bats hanging from branches, so many people's faces looking through the wire mesh fences. I remember thinking I was seeing nothing but eyes as wide and round as the shining silver dollars my father once gave me, eyes staring at us in wonder, and all to watch Matt and me play for the title of best young basketball player in South Philadelphia. Before the game I told Matt, "Let's bet five dollars on the game." Now that was a lot of money to lose in those days, but I felt it would make me play better, and it did. That game was memorable, a match made in roundball heaven, the classic traditional player against the playground hotdog showboat, the flashy, imaginative, creative baller against the steady, do-it-by-the-book, old-fashioned player out on the blacktop.

The whole scene was like a spectacle. You could cut the excitement and tension that were hanging in the air with a knife or a razor. It was something else. It was one of the most exciting things—if not *the* most exciting thing—to happen to me in my life up to that moment. Matt and me played to 21 points and the first one there won. But hey, I'm getting ahead of myself and my story, so let me go back to where it all began.

Part One

GROWING UP IN SOUTH PHILLY:
1944 TO 1959

Chapter 1

—

EARLY LIFE IN SOUTH PHILLY

I WAS BORN AT 2:15 IN THE MORNING on a wintry day, November 21, 1944, at the University of Pennsylvania Hospital. My mother, Rose, named me Vernon Earl Monroe Jr., after my father. Being born on that day makes me a Scorpio, and the biggest significance about that is the fact that I'm pretty perceptive about a lot of things, at least I think so. One thing is certain: I don't forget a lot of things and I'm very vindictive, which some say is a trait of Scorpios. Generally, though, I look at how people treat me and then I treat them the same way. See, I'm a big advocate of the old saying that you do unto others as they do unto you.

Anyway, they tell me the day I was born was a very cold day and after my older sister Ann came to see me, she told people I was about 23 or 24 inches of nothing but skin and bones. She also said I was "the ugliest thing she'd ever seen." At least that's what she told me she said over the years. But, you know, she loved me so much when I was coming up that later on I kind of forgave her for that comment, though not altogether.

My mother's last name changed to Smith when she married again after my father left, but while my father was around she was Rose Monroe. Before that she was just Rose Hall, which was her family name. She was one of 18 kids, born somewhere in the middle of my grandmother's children. By the time I was born, all of my mother's brothers and sisters except three had passed away: There was just my mother and her two sisters, Aunt Nicey and Aunt Mary, and Uncle Jim. But Uncle Jim died on the 22nd of November, the day after I was born. Ma—that's what I called my mother—told me later that Uncle Jim had died relatively young, at around 40, after he swallowed a red-hot potato that burned up his insides. I don't know if that's the real truth, but there's no one around to refute it. So people in my family always said things like "when God takes something away, God brings you something back," and that "something," I guess, was me.

Ma was born September 14, 1914, in New Bern, North Carolina, and my father, Vernon Earl Monroe, was born on Christmas Day, 1912, in Columbia, South Carolina. They were married in the early 1940s but didn't stay together very long: I think he left when I was five or six years old. She was 30 years old when she had me, and my parents brought me home to a row house located at 2524 Alter Street in South Philadelphia (it's no longer there), where I lived until I was 11 years old.

Philadelphia is famous for its row houses, which line the streets of the inner city for block after block. I think row houses were first built in Philadelphia, or at least that's what I remember some people telling me when I was growing up. Anyway, row houses are attached to each other at the sides and most are not too big in size. They have white stone steps that lead up to the entrance of the house from the sidewalks called stoops, and you find people sitting on them, especially during the hot summers. I lived in that row house on Alter Street with my mother, my sister Ann, and my father, until he left. John Smith, my stepfather, moved in a couple of years later. A year or so after my stepfather moved in, my baby sister, Theresa, was born. But we all, at one time or another, lived in that two-story house I was brought home to when I was born.

That house had a basement with a furnace, and it also served as a place that we stored a lot of stuff in, including coal for the furnace. On the first floor there was a living room, dining room, and a kitchen. Behind it was a small yard that had an outhouse nobody used. Behind the yard was an alleyway piled high with a lot of trash (some stinking garbage, too), and it ran the length of one city block. We sometimes used to play hide and go seek back there in the daytime (but never at night), and when we ran through the alley it would be like running up and down small hills, with low-lying flat stretches between each hill of trash.

At night—and sometimes even during the day—criminals used to run through this alley to try to escape from cops who were after them for whatever crimes they had committed—mostly small-time stuff. Many times they would get away, because the cops were afraid to really search for them back there. Plus, the crooks were guys from the neighborhood and they knew where all the hiding places were, which route to take to get away—you know, the tricks of the trade of being escape artists. But sometimes they would get caught by the cops and go to jail, though this didn't happen often.

In the front of the house, on the first floor, there was a small vestibule you had to go through to get to the front door, which led outside to Alter Street. Then you went down four whitewashed steps to cross the sidewalk and then you were on the street, which was dirt and cobblestone. On the second floor of the house were a small bedroom for my sister Ann and a larger master bedroom that my mother and father (and later, my stepfather) slept in, along with me. I slept in a baby crib until I outgrew it and bunked down on a cot. It was cozy up there, a little tight, but no one ever complained.

Around the time I was four or five years old, I remember Ann—who was 15 years older than me—was going with a man named Andrew "Big Jimmy" James, who later became her husband. Anyway, when Big Jimmy would come over to the house in the daytime during the summer to see Ann, they would be trying to make out in the front room, because Ma and my father were away working. So they would be on the couch,

trying to be romantic, you know, kissing and whatnot, and I'd come into
the front room, put two chairs together and lay there looking at them.
They never said anything, but I knew they were pissed off by the way
they looked at me. Big Jimmy probably thought I was part of the CBA,
you know, the Cock Blockers Association! Maybe he even thought I was
the king of it, you know what I mean? (When I spoke at Ann's funeral
in 2007, I said, "I know Andrew must have been thinking back then
when he and Ann first met that I was the king of the CBA.")

My maternal grandmother, who we all called "Mom," ran a speak-
easy next door to our house, at 2522 Alter Street, from the time I was
born. And, at the same time, my mother ran card games in our house on
weekends, when people got off work. They would come over to my
mother's house and play card games like bid whist, pitty pat, and tonk,
and they played for money. As I grew older, I would stay up late just to
watch what was going on. Sometimes someone—I can't remember who
they were, though it might have been a man named J.D.—would carry
me on their shoulders over to Mom's place and I'd watch the people
gambling and playing the numbers, because my grandmother did this,
too. Then someone would say, "Hey Earl, what number should I play?"
And I would give them a number and they'd play it. Or, somebody
would be shooting dice and my grandmother would say to me, "Earl, call
the number." And I would call it. And if they won she would say, "See,
I told you. Earl's a good luck numbers guy."

But my mother didn't like me being there, around this kind of stuff.
So she'd be monitoring what was going on and she'd tell me sometimes,
"Go on home, Earl. Stay upstairs, boy, and go to bed."

During the day my grandmother had a store where she sold candy
and food all year round and shaved-ice cones drenched with different-
colored sweet syrups we called "water ices" (they called them "snowballs" or "snow cones" in other places) during the summer, when it was
hot. At night Mom would sell liquor for 50 cents a shot—you know,

bourbon, scotch, and gin—and glasses of wine, beer, and whatnot in her house.

She also sold pork sandwiches, pickled pigs' feet from a big old jar full of them, chitlins, anything fried. Just slap some bread on whatever it was to absorb some of the liquor and people could drink more because they had a base of grease in their bellies. So she'd be selling fried porgy sandwiches—with all the bones left in the fish—that people ate like there was no tomorrow. Sometimes, all of a sudden someone would start choking and coughing because they had a bone caught in their throat. Then somebody would have to run and get a loaf of bread so they could wash the bone down their throats with water. (I never liked greasy food like pigs' feet or chitlins, myself. I just couldn't get down with it, especially chitlins, because the smell just turned me off.)

Everybody who came by gambled, shot craps, drank, played the numbers, things like that. All of this went on in my grandmother's house. Later, as I grew older, I watched people dancing and listening to the music of Ray Charles, Sam Cooke, the Platters, and James Brown.

The first real lasting image I can recall of my father was him pulling me aside one day and telling me he was going away. I remember this day vividly, because before he left he told me to hold out both my hands, and I did. Then he poured two handfuls of shiny silver dollars into my cupped hands. When my father gave me all those shiny silver dollars, I thought it had to be all the money in the world. That made me real happy, even though I never really cherished money too much—although I always knew I needed to make some—when I was growing up. But I thought after my father gave me those silver dollars that I could always make do in my life, because the actual fact that my father gave me all those shiny silver coins could really carry me through to accomplish whatever it was I wanted to do in my life. Now, whether that's true or not, I have never forgotten that moment. After all, I was only five.

Back then those silver dollars really meant something special to me.

My mother kept them for me for safekeeping and she would give me one every now and then, whenever I really needed something. Maybe that's why later on, after I hooked up with my father again, I always saw him as a source of money until I got to know him much better. I don't know, I never thought about it. But when he gave me all those silver dollars that day, that was the last time I remember seeing him until we were reunited 14 or 15 years later, when I was 19 years old and in my first year of college. That was an important, eventful day for me and I will talk more about it later. But I didn't know anything about my father when I was growing up. As a matter of fact, I told everybody he was dead, even though I knew he wasn't. I guess I might have been ashamed of the fact that I didn't have a real father around, so I lied. Plus, I really didn't know where he was, so it was almost as if he was dead.

In 1951, when I was six, I remember my mother started living with John Smith, who I called Mr. John. Suddenly, he was just there. My sister Ann, who was living with us at the time, left the house after she married Andrew James in March 1951. Big Jimmy was in the army, stationed out in Colorado Springs, Colorado, so Ann moved out there with him and I moved into her room and laid claim to her bed.

My sister Theresa was born September 11, 1951. Her father was John Smith. I remember Ann bought Ma a TV set for her birthday, which corresponded with Theresa's homecoming from the hospital. That was great timing! Because it was the first TV set on our block, that was when a lot of neighborhood people started coming by our house, especially young kids, to sit up and look with wonder at the black-and-white images coming out of what was then considered a magical little box with a screen.

It was something else just watching people's faces as they craned their necks, leaned forward to watch that rectangle with a flickering small screen and those rabbit ears sitting up on top. My grandmother used to talk to the set, saying, "don't you go there, don't you see people are waiting for you!" People would be staring in amazement—and disappointment, too—at all that weird-looking white and gray flickering and listening to the buzzing fuzz sounds coming from the TV, until somebody had the sense to get up and turn the set off. Then the people visiting our house would file out the front door looking bewildered and dazed and our family would go upstairs and go to bed.

When "Mr. John" first came to live with us, I was very young and really didn't have any thoughts about him one way or the other. I mean, he was just somebody else there, and I can't recollect drawing any kind of conclusion about him beyond the fact that he had come to live with us. After Theresa was born we became a family, and that stood for something. But as time went on and I grew older, my stepfather started to get on my nerves and I began to dislike him, especially the way he treated my mother. Still, I must admit, he always had a good job—he was a butcher at A&P Market—and he made really good money, which took care of us and all the bills very well.

Mom—her name was Nicey—lived next door to us (her daughter, Aunt Nicey, was named after her) and her last name was Hall, or Allen—she was an Allen, too. Because back in those days a woman might have a husband, then she wouldn't have a husband—you know what I mean? So she was all those names at once. Mom was something else, a different kind of woman, real strong. There were empty lots next to her house, and she grew fresh vegetables on some of them, you know, stuff like collard greens, tomatoes, string beans, and other vegetables.

On the other side of Alter Street, a lady named Miss Mabel Wilson lived. Miss Wilson ran the Vacation Bible School I attended during summer months, and she kept a garden where she grew a lot of vegetables and had peach trees, too. A lot of kids in the neighborhood—including me—loved to pick those peaches off the tree branches and eat them during summer and fall. Man, those peaches were sweet and really good. Miss Mabel was a very industrious and caring person. She was also very religious and had four sons, Carroll (who I went to school with), Harvey, Stanley, and Jerry—who was the oldest—and a daughter named Lily.

Anyway, Miss Mabel started to teach Bible studies there in the summer, but not when it rained because the school didn't have a roof. It was a little lot across the street from Miss Mabel's place, between two houses. It just had some tables and chairs with a wood-and-wire fence around it and a small gate that swung back and forth to let you in. People in the neighborhood respected that place because no one ever went in and vandalized it, you know, like took the wooden chairs or the tables. After her death, to honor her for the community work she did all of her life, the political bigwigs in the area renamed the block we all lived on Mabel Wilson Way.

I wasn't playing any kind of basketball at the time, but when we didn't have a basketball I used to shoot socks stuffed with rags, beach balls, soccer balls, or baseballs at milk crates. These crates were substitutes for a real basketball rim and were nailed to a wooden post holding up the gate outside Miss Mabel's school. We just made ourselves a court to play on. Nearly every young person in the neighborhood—including girls, like my sister Theresa—shot baskets there and were a part of these games. We would shoot at this milk-crate basket most summer days when it didn't rain from the time I was four until I was 13.

That's where I made my first basket, in the milk crate nailed to the wooden post in the vacant lot outside Vacation Bible School. Later we graduated from a milk crate to a kind of rim of sorts. We'd just measure out 10 paces back from the crate, and that's where people shot from. Whoever made a basket from the 10 spot would win. I'd win some and lose some, but I always had fun, though I wanted to win all the time. Later on, after I started playing basketball seriously, I always thought my game would have some kind of divine intervention because I had shot so many baskets at Vacation Bible School when I was young. Deep down, I always thought something good was going to happen because I shot and played there. I don't know why I thought this way, but I did. Maybe because I thought shooting at a basket in a religious place would put me one up on everyone else. Who knows, maybe it did.

I don't remember a lot of details about my first eight or nine years on this planet, but I do recall having a lot of fun playing with the other kids in the neighborhood as I grew up there, despite the poverty, violence, pain, and sadness all around me. I grew up on that one block on Alter Street, and for much of my early childhood it was like a cocoon or small bubble, and it was my whole world. It was almost like living in the rural part of the country, but in the city. Overall, however, I would definitely say the good times outweighed the bad times in my life by a wide margin. I do remember, though, that the neighborhood smelled really bad sometimes, stunk like rotten fish because of all the trash and garbage piled up in the alleys and on some of the vacant lots. People didn't like it, but the authorities didn't do anything about it, so we had to live with it, because it was what it was. We didn't have air-conditioning back in those days—I don't know if it had been invented, but I do know nobody living where I lived had it—so everyone's houses would be steaming hot in the summertime. We had fans to cool everything down.

I can't remember anyone in our neighborhood who had an electric refrigerator back in those days, either—I know we didn't have one until later. Everyone had iceboxes that they stored their meat, fish, and vegetables in so they wouldn't spoil. So people needed ice to keep the iceboxes cool and that's where the name "icebox" came from. (Even today, a lot of older people call electric refrigerators by that name.) So there were icemen who went around the neighborhoods selling blocks of ice and shouting out chants to influence customers to buy their product. They would come around with ice piled high in their horse-drawn wagons or on little trucks, calling out that they were there, saying, "Get your fresh ice here," or something like that.

The icemen also carried steel ice tongs around with them that had two loop handles and two curved tongs with sharp ends that looked like elephant tusks; this is what they used to pick up the blocks of ice to carry them into their customers' houses. Everyone had ice picks they used to chip the ice (or to stab someone with in a fight—they, like the ice tongs, were fearsome weapons!). When people heard the iceman's chant, they would rush out of their houses to buy a few blocks of the square cold stuff. The blocks of ice might sell for 25 or 50 cents or even a dollar to people who had the money to buy it, and fortunately my family did.

But the blocks of ice were used for more than just keeping food cool; they were also used for helping to cool down houses during the summer heat. Ma would put the block—or blocks—of ice in a tub. Then she would turn the fan on and the spinning blades created a wind that blew over the ice and sent a cool breeze over us. It was slick and cool at the same time, you know what I mean? Black people were always creative about a lot of things, and this was one of the ways that we made do.

Those people who didn't have electric fans would sit out on their stoops—you know, the three or four little stone steps fronting their houses—and fan themselves by hand. They would use whatever would circulate a breeze—a cardboard fan from church, a magazine, a rolled-up newspaper—and they would talk, drink, gossip, and laugh about whatever funny story was circulating in the neighborhood on any given day. And listening to my neighbors growing up there, they seemed to be having a lot of fun, despite the heat.

Winters were different, if only because people didn't sit outside when the weather turned cold. And when the snow came, especially if it was heavy, entire streets would be covered with the white stuff that looked so peaceful and pretty when it first fell. Then, after a few days the pristine-looking heaps of snow would become ugly, with dirt, trash, cigarette butts, and empty cans and bottles turning the once-serene-looking scene into a horrible mess. When the snow was really heavy, because we had such narrow streets around where I lived, cars would get snowed in and sit covered top to bottom by the curb, some even out in the middle of the street. No snowplows came around to clean the streets where I lived, so me and some other kids would charge a nickel or a dime, or sometimes as much as 25 cents, to dig out people's cars. Even though I made a little money sometimes, man, was that hard work.

The weird thing about growing up in Philadelphia back in the day (especially for me), though, was that all the neighborhoods were like small, insulated communities. They were like little cities within a city, or a small town within a small town, and seldom did people venture out of those little isolated areas to meet other folks. So these communities were like little bubbles that we all lived in, and to get to know people who lived maybe only a couple of blocks—maybe even one block—away was very difficult and sometimes even dangerous. It was even worse for me, because I mostly only knew, trusted, and hung out with people in my own immediate family. (This was to change, however, as I grew older and started to get out into other communities through playing basketball, though it didn't change my personality all that much; I still mostly dealt with my immediate family and with friends I knew from a long way back.)

I remember Mom had a big, black dog named Jack—he might have been a terrier, but he was definitely a street dog. Jack would just lay around Mom's house, never bothering anybody, until a car came by. Then he would jump up and chase that car down the street, barking like crazy, until he disappeared. Then he would come back a little later, his tongue hanging out, his eyes all wide and bright, and everybody would pat him on the head and say, "Good dog, Jack. Good dog." Then he would lay back down and doze off until another car came by and then he would repeat the same thing all over again. A few times he jumped up and chased those cars and didn't come back for maybe a week or so and nobody knew where he went, though we didn't worry too much about him because he always came back.

Then one day, when he was about 14 or 15 years old, Jack jumped up and chased a car and never came back and we never knew what happened to him. It was only after he was missing for a month or so that everyone started to worry about him. Finally, everybody grew sad because we realized he might never come back, and he didn't. It was a downer not having Jack around anymore. Everybody missed him, especially seeing him chase those cars down the street, barking like crazy. Jack was really something.

Mom was a very independent woman, and although she didn't go to church, she always kept her Bible close by and would read from it whenever she could. She cooked all the time, though I never liked her cooking because it was different—just like she was different from everyone else in my family—so I never ate her food. But the real reason I never ate her food was that I liked the way my mother cooked so much better; I just preferred her food over Mom's. Mom's cooking was for a large group of people and my mother cooked specifically for us.

Now, she never liked this, but over time it was something Mom accepted and we got along real well. On the other hand, everybody in our family gained a lot of knowledge from her, including me, despite her being very different in the way she spoke. When she talked she would use all these Southern black words, like she would call me "Oil" instead of "Earl." I don't know why she called me that and I never asked why (maybe it was because she couldn't pronounce "Earl" correctly). But it never bothered me and over time I just got used to her calling me by that weird name. But other than being different in her use of language, she was a fountain of wisdom for all of us.

My mother worked at a factory until I was older—around 17—and she and my stepfather owned a grocery store. I remember her being on her knees a lot at home, scrubbing floors because she was such a hard worker and she liked for everything to be clean. Ma was always there for my family and she was always trying to make everything right for everybody, and she did whatever it took to keep things running smoothly. I was the middle child, but it was almost like I was the baby of the family because I had two sisters, and so I grew up basically being the only young male in a house full of women. I think having all these females around really spoiled me, because I got my way about almost everything, especially from my mother, who thought I could hardly ever do anything wrong. But everything wasn't peaches and cream for me growing up—everything wasn't roses—because I saw some really violent things.

I remember once two guys started fighting right on Alter Street next to my house. I was across the street with some other kids when this started to happen. I must have been about five or six years old. These guys were grown men, 30 years old, maybe—everybody looked older to me back then, you know? So I don't know exactly how old they actually were. But they were really well-dressed guys, sharp, with straw hats, hip, probably some numbers cats, you know, men in what we called back then "the life," meaning they were on the fringe of criminal activity.

Like I said, I was across the street from my house, playing by the garden next to the Vacation Bible School, when all of a sudden I heard the voices of these two men rising to shouts. That's when I started paying attention to them. I heard one of them saying to the other guy, "You motherfucker, I'll kill you, motherfucker!"

All of a sudden they started pushing each other, then they started fighting each other with their fists, hitting each other upside the head and on their bodies, swinging wildly, tearing at each other's shirts and

cursing. Then one of the guys took out this big knife and started stabbing the other one. And he didn't just stab him once, he kept stabbing
him, over and over again, and screaming, "I'll cut your fucking heart
out! I'll cut your fucking heart out!"

Then the man being stabbed fell back on the fence around the yard
next to our house, and the guy doing the stabbing started cutting into
the man's chest, trying to carve the other guy's heart out! By this time
the guy was bleeding profusely, all over himself and the street. Then the
other man started digging into the man's chest again, this time with his
bloody hands, trying to pull his heart out! Suddenly he stopped, took a
step back, and looked at his bloody hands. Then he looked at me and a
bunch of other kids who had gathered there on the street after the fight
started. All of a sudden he seemed to panic, started walking toward me,
his face a mask of fury and shock, and I remember this scared the shit
out of me. Then he ran by me and the other kids, went up on Cowboy
Hill, and I never saw him again after that. It was horrible, really scary
and crazy and I think I was traumatized for a long, long time after that
by the memory of it all.

The man being stabbed never said anything except for making a few
grunts. He didn't scream or yell out in pain or fear. He just had this
stunned look on his face the whole time, like he couldn't believe what
was happening to him. Maybe he might have already been dead! Then
he slid off the fence and fell on the ground, flopped around awhile
twitching, with blood coming out of his mouth and nose, until he was
still. It was a terrible, awful, bloody scene. There was a lot of blood
everywhere, thick pools of it that left red stains after people in the
neighborhood brought out hoses and washed all the blood away.

Now, I had seen the two men many times in the neighborhood,
because they lived around there somewhere. They were regulars,
seemed to be friends maybe, at least when I saw them. I don't know, but
I remember seeing them talking to each other a few times, smiling, you

know, being friendly with each other. Then this shocking madness happened, and it was so weird and unexpected.

When the cops came, they didn't question anybody in the neighborhood (they didn't question me, and I saw it all), maybe because it happened a lot back then, you know? People fighting with fists and knives. There were a lot of horrible, bloody scenes and the police probably saw a lot of them. Maybe that's why they didn't question anybody. This killing happened before guns were everywhere, and so the fights back then would be mano a mano with fists or knives, and the fights would be very bloody, though I never saw another one quite like this one.

When it was all over I think I was in shock, even though I didn't know what shock was back then because I was too young to really know what I felt. But I did know that I had never seen anything like that before—or since—so I know I felt real weird, very different, scared even, confused. So to get a handle on my feelings and to get back to some kind of normal routine, I just jumped on my broomstick pony and rode it up to the top of Cowboy Hill, which was where the man who had killed the other man had run. I don't know why I went the same way the killer ran, because I should have been scared to go that way. But I didn't think about that then, probably because I wanted to be somewhere comforting and Cowboy Hill had always been that way for me. So I just rode my broomstick pony up there and tried to forget about what I just saw. It comforted me to be up there and it remained one of my favorite places to play when I was young.

Looking back on it now, that episode was the most terrible thing I ever witnessed in my life. It was so horrifying because it was so vivid and I remember it still today, as if it just happened! As I grew older this savage memory became a touchstone for me whenever I thought about violence and death. It perhaps is why I have always tried to avoid violent situations and why for a long time I was so afraid of death.

We called Cowboy Hill that because it was the place where me and the other young neighborhood kids would go to play and where we would ride our broomstick ponies—some of the other kids had them, too—because we really saw ourselves as cowboys. We went up there also to look at the trains that ran by. Some of the older guys in the neighborhood would hitch rides on the trains. I didn't know where the trains were going, but I knew they were going somewhere, and that really intrigued me. Anyway, I remember another incident that involved my mother and Cowboy Hill.

My mother was tall and fast for a woman. Very fast. That's why I never tried to run away from her. I remember one day when I was about five or six years old, I was riding my broomstick pony in front of the house and these older guys came down the hill, crossed Alter Street, knocked me off my broomstick pony, stole it, and ran back up the hill with it. So I ran into the house to tell my mother, hollering, "Ma! Ma! Some guys just took my pony!"

So she said, "Where'd they go?" and I told her, "Over the hill!"

So she ran out of the house, up the hill, across the tracks, down to the trestle, about a two-block run, and caught them. She took my pony back and brought it back to me. I don't know what she did to those guys, because she never told me, but she came back with my stuff. Ma was a good athlete. I don't know if she played anything, though. I never asked her. She was just Ma to me. All I know is that she came back with my favorite pony and that was real cool!

My mother was also fearless. I remember one time she went into the garden next to Mom's and came out with this black snake, a garter snake, I think. A garter snake isn't poisonous, but seeing it scared the hell out of me, I guess because I was so young at the time. I still don't want to be around any snakes even today, poisonous or not. But Ma had grown up in North Carolina and she just wasn't afraid of many things, including animals and snakes. She would talk to me about going through chests of drawers when she was growing up and finding snakes in there and killing them. Even my older cousins, Jimmy and Joe, didn't ever mess with my mother, and they were very tough guys.

Growing up was really something back then, really a lot of fun, despite all of the violence. I remember on holidays during the summer, grown folks would roast a whole pig on a spit at the bottom of Cowboy Hill, right across from our house. And people would eat barbecued pig and party until the wee hours of the morning. Like I said, the kids would have a ball because when I was young we used to make all kinds of things, all the time. We'd make our own slingshots, wooden guns that we played war with, and wooden skate trucks with roller-skate wheels we attached to the bottoms of two-by-fours instead of buying metal scooters from the store. We had to use our imaginations to make the things we wanted, because our parents didn't have a lot of extra money to spend on us. The only thing I remember we couldn't seem to make was sleds with steel runners that we used to belly flop and slide on in winter when there was tons of snow. So our parents would break down and buy them from the store, even though they were low on money; they just made do to keep us kids happy, and we were.

We also played hide and go seek, games like that. We played a lot of stuff up on the railroad tracks, you know, throwing stones at each other, at passing cars below, and at the white guy in the caboose of the freight train as it passed. He used to get so mad at us for throwing those stones he would shoot a real rifle at us, because we'd hit him sometimes, or the window of his cab, which would go *ping! ping! ping!* and annoy the shit out of him. Then he would pull out his rifle and draw a bead on us and fire. *Bang! bang! bang!* would go his rifle shots. The bullets would be ricocheting all over the place, scaring us to death. But we'd come back whenever we knew the train would be passing, or when we just happened to be up there and it came by. You know, being young kids, we were too silly to be really afraid of anything. We weren't bad, though, just curious and mischievous, but mostly we were just bored.

We never really thought about dying or what would happen if one of those bullets ever hit us. But the sound of those bullets whizzing by our heads and ricocheting *bang! bang! bang!* off walls and concrete did scare us! No question about it. But only for that moment. Plus, we were having fun. Just like all young kids, we knew better than to get in the way of those passing trains or bullets because we could have gotten ourselves killed. Our parents had warned us about those trains, and every kid in the neighborhood knew better, though we still did it.

For most of the time when I was real young, I didn't have a lot of close friends. My sister Theresa hadn't been born yet. So I created this imaginary friend named Tommy, who was my sidekick. Tommy would come along with me when I rode my broomstick pony. Like I said, I saw myself as a cowboy, and every cowboy needs a sidekick. Like the Lone Ranger had Tonto, I had Tommy. He was also my friend, even though he was invisible, and I used to do everything with him. I'd talk to him.

"Hey, Tommy," I'd say. "What do you think we should do here? Let's go in the other room." Or I'd say, "Let's ride up on Cowboy Hill and see what's up there." Things like that. I invented Tommy when I was three or four years old and he stayed with me for a long while.

I outgrew Tommy's usefulness and probably stopped talking to him and riding with him about the time Theresa was born, because then I had somebody else around. Maybe it was a couple of years after she was born that Tommy disappeared from my life. But while he was there, Tommy and I would play horsey on my broomstick pony and have great conversations.

Around this time, besides riding my broomstick pony, I was also learning how to ride the bicycle my mother had bought me. But I kept falling off it and cutting up my legs, arms, and hands until my cousin Jimmy showed me how to ride it. Then, after that—I must have been about seven or eight—I had no problem riding it.

I remember one time in the winter, when I was around that same age, I went on up Cowboy Hill with some friends to ride our sleds down the hill. Anyway, I was belly flopping down on my sled when some older guys started throwing snowballs at us from the trestle. One of them hit me in the eye and I couldn't see. So I crashed into a wall and the back of the sled cut through my pants into my leg. Now, at first I didn't know I was injured because my leg wasn't hurting and I couldn't see where I was hurt. But then when I started walking home I began to limp and I felt a pain in my leg. When I got home I told Ma what had happened and she took down my pants and we saw this big hole in my leg, all the way to the bone, with little pieces of flesh hanging to the sides and whatnot. Anyway, my mother screamed and I started crying. She bundled me up and immediately took me to the hospital—I think it was Philadelphia General, or the University of Pennsylvania Hospital—to get my leg fixed.

After we arrived at the hospital, we just sat there for two hours. Nobody came out to deal with us. Because my leg was hurting really bad by now, I started whimpering from the pain. When Ma heard me whimpering she became enraged and started screaming at people behind the counter, telling them off. Then I remember looking around and seeing this heavyset older black lady, who was probably homeless, with bandages wrapped around her huge legs and feet, just sitting there in a chair. I guess I started looking at her because she looked kind of strange, you know, and had a look on her face I couldn't quite comprehend.

After a while a nurse came over and unwrapped her feet and legs. Maggots started crawling out of her feet, and the nurse jumped back with a look of horror in her eyes. Maggots! I couldn't believe it! I almost threw up! When the nurses saw the maggots they immediately started talking about amputating the lady's feet and legs because they were gangrenous. To this day I don't know how she was walking around. But she was.

Finally, after Ma's ranting and raving, a doctor came over to see me.

When he saw the big hole in my leg, he said, "Oh, we didn't think it was this bad!"

Then they rushed me into a room and stitched me up. But I still, to this day, have a V-shaped scar on my leg.

That woman with the maggots crawling out of her feet always stood out in my memory as being really weird. But I saw some other strange people on Alter Street, and some of them were really funny, like Mr. Sonny Man, who had the longest tongue I have ever seen! When I first started noticing him I was around seven or eight and he was maybe in his forties or early fifties—I don't really know how old he was. I would see him around on weekends, sitting on somebody's steps, licking his long, snakelike tongue out of his mouth, licking it up across his eyebrows, sticking it in one of his ears, or curling it to the back or top of his head. He was a really strange-looking person, kind of like Huggy Bear from *Starsky and Hutch* or one of the other characters Antonio Fargas played in the movies and on TV.

Mr. Sonny Man would be dressed in khakis and a little shirt, with a vest on top of the shirt and a cap on his head. He was kind of thin and he would always be drunk when I saw him, making some unintelligible slurping sounds like *blawo, blawo, blawo, blah*, his mouth wide open as he did all kinds of weird things with that long, snakelike tongue of his. No one in the neighborhood was afraid of Mr. Sonny Man because he was harmless, wouldn't hurt a fly. People just thought he was funny and weird, you know what I mean? People walking by would be looking at him amazed, shaking their heads and calling out his name: "Mr. Sonny Man, goddamn, Mr. Sonny Man, why you be doing your tongue like that!"

Then they would laugh, shake their heads, and walk away. Sonny Man was there until he wasn't there after I moved off Alter Street when I was 11. I never saw him again after I moved, never knew what happened to him, because no one I knew ever mentioned his name.

My Aunt Mary, my mother's sister, lived down on Manton Street, about five blocks from where we lived. The neighborhood where I grew up was on the borderline between Italian and Irish communities. At the time white people were white, and there were no distinctions made between Italians, Irish, or whatever else on my part. But we did know about the Jewish people, because Mr. Rosenberg, our insurance man, was Jewish, and he wore a yarmulke. So there was interaction between Jews, Irish, Italians, and African-Americans, even if it wasn't that much.

In 1952, when I was around eight years old, I remember my mother asking me to go get something from the store that the little Jewish man named Mr. Siegel—I don't remember his first name—owned. (This happened before my parents bought the three-story house that had Mr. Siegel's grocery store on the ground floor, which was down the street from Aunt Mary.)

Anyway, his store was located at 1217 South 26th Street at Manton Street, a few blocks from where we lived on Alter Street. Now, I used to hear some of the older black people at our house and in the neighborhood say, when they sent someone to get some groceries from Mr. Siegel, "Go get me some bread from the dirty Jew."

They used to call him that name because a lot of people thought he was cheap and cheated black customers out of their money. At least that's what I heard them say. So when my mother sent me to buy something from Mr. Siegel—I don't remember if Ma called him "the dirty Jew" or not, but she generally didn't use that kind of language—I just went. But since I had never been there before, when I walked into the store and saw him, I just called him by the name I had heard everyone else use when they talked about him.

"Is this the dirty Jew's store?" I said.

He was a short old man, kind of feisty, and he looked at me real hard, then shook his head.

"How would you like it if I called you a dirty nigger?" he asked.

I looked at him dumbfounded because I didn't know what he was talking about.

"Well, this must be the place then," I said.

He kind of laughed at that. Maybe he thought it was funny. I don't know what he thought. But I did understand. I just didn't realize what I was saying when I called him by that name (neither one of those slurs—"dirty Jew" or "dirty nigger"—registered with me, because I was too young to even know what they meant). So I just stood there until he gave me whatever it was my mother had sent me to get. Then I paid him his money, got whatever change back he owed me, and left.

That was the last time I ever used that term, though, or any derogatory expression like that. I think it was my first lesson in race relations, and it's a realization that I soon came to truly understand. Like I said, growing up in South Philadelphia back in those days, there was no real distinction made between Jewish, Italian, and Irish people, because everyone of those groups were just white people to me. You were either white, black, or Puerto Rican, like Pedro, who lived two doors away from me. That's the only thing I knew, and there weren't too many Puerto Ricans or Chinese people around either, at least not down there where I lived. So for the most part it was black or white and that was that. But after the incident with Mr. Siegel, my mother explained the differences between the races to me. She told how what people say to each other and how they say it could be harmful in this regard. So I began to understand that words were important, that you could insult people from all different races if you used dirty, nasty words to call them by, whether you meant to hurt them or not. So I learned to think about what I said and called people after that; it was a very important lesson.

There were some really bad people around the neighborhood, like the guys in a gang called the Sharks, who were notorious. The same was true of some of the guys in my neighborhood who were members of a gang called The Road, which my cousin Jimmy was the leader of. Most of the folks that lived around there were scared to death of them. Added to the members of Sharks and The Road were hard-nosed neighborhood guys like Jasper, who went off to jail all the time, and when he came out nobody wanted to run up against him or get on his bad side. Jasper never seemed to be able to acclimate himself to living on the outside, so after a while he just stayed in jail and I never saw him again. Then there was a guy named Ostell who had the body of an Adonis. He played football and boxed, and after he went to jail for something—I don't remember what—it became obvious that he was gay. But being gay didn't stop him from being rough and tough; he just liked having sex with men.

We used to go over to Aunt Mary's house a lot, and she and her sons, Jimmy, Bobby, and Joe, would come over to our house often, too. Aunt Mary's last name was Hill, and she had one of the nicest brick houses on Manton Street. She drove a yellow and white 1954 or '55 Chevrolet Bel Air, and she was always dressed to the nines—real sharp. I remember her with furs around her neck, rings and necklaces, expensive dresses and shoes. She was a portly, dark woman, and because she was always so well dressed and seemed to have it all together, she reminded me of some of the women on the *Amos 'n Andy Show* that I later used to watch on TV.

Aunt Mary was a feisty individual, traveled a lot, and always had money because she was the neighborhood's biggest numbers person. Then she had a stroke, and that changed everything. Before the stroke, though, she was like a man, very tough, very competent, and a very strict lady, even though her sons were some of the meanest, most out of control people in the neighborhood. She had people working for her, and even her white male bosses who came by to collect the money respected her. My grandmother, her mother, used to play what seemed like a thousand numbers a day, you know, on the horse races, a penny on each bet. There were always these real long white sheets with numbers on them lying all around Aunt Mary's house. These were the winning and losing numbers.

Like I said, Aunt Mary had a lot of people working for her—men and women—who would run around collecting money and checking the numbers on the sheets to see who had won or lost. Then some people would come by with smiles if they won, or frowns when they didn't. A lot of people played, though, each and every day. I never knew how much a penny won, because I never played. But there was a lot of money around Aunt Mary's house, and no one ever thought to rob her because she had great protection.

She was hooked up with these white guys who were the bosses of all the numbers rackets, the money people who bankrolled and protected her. Word had it they were part of the Italian Mafia, though I didn't know if this was true. But those guys were serious and nobody messed with them. They would come around, wearing nice clothes—but not suits—and smoking big cigars, to pick up their money from Aunt Mary. But the funny thing about those guys was that they couldn't smoke cigars in Aunt Mary's house; they had to put their cigars out before going in her home because Aunt Mary didn't like cigar smoke, didn't like the way they smelled, felt the smell was too strong, so she didn't allow it in her place.

These white men drove nice, new, shiny big cars—Oldsmobiles, Cadillacs, Buicks—and they would park their cars up on the sidewalks because Philly streets were so small—still are. No one ever double-parked on the streets in the neighborhood because they were so narrow you couldn't drive a car through if they did. So people parked on the sidewalk or halfway up on the sidewalk. Anyway, these white guys would come by, pick up their money, and leave, and nobody ever bothered them, nobody, even though a lot of people—real bad people, too—knew they were always carrying a lot of money!

Sometimes when I would be around, some of the gamblers who

hung out at Aunt Mary's thought I was a good luck charm for some reason—I never knew why they thought this. So when they shot dice or played the numbers, some of them would ask me to blow on their dice or give them a number or some numbers they could bet on that day. Like I said, I don't know why they felt this way, but a lot of people used to do that with me. Maybe they felt I was a good luck charm because some of the people won whenever I blew on their dice, or whenever I gave someone a number. But you know what? Not one of them ever gave me a penny when they won—never. Not one time did they give me anything, not even one thank-you.

Aunt Mary changed a lot after she had the stroke and lost the use of her left side, including her left arm; she even had to drag her left leg around. It was hard for me to watch her go through that, because she had been such a compelling individual. After the stroke, she became a bitter person. You could see the pain in her face all the time, because she just couldn't get used to being incapacitated—I guess nobody could get used to being that way. She wasn't outgoing anymore, seemed irritated all the time about any little thing. I used to love being around her because she'd take me for rides in her car and we'd wash it together. But after the stroke it was hard for her to do that anymore. Still, she never stopped running her numbers business. She always had money and made it available to our family to help us take care of each other, and that was something I always greatly admired her for.

Aunt Mary's boys, my cousins Jimmy, Joe, and Bobby Hill, were a lot older than me. They were all big and dark like me; in fact, I looked a lot like Jimmy, and as I grew older and bigger, people—especially the police—would mistake me for him. Jimmy was about six foot four or six foot five. He was the biggest. Bobby was about six three, six four, and Joe was the shortest at about six feet even. Joe was the oldest, maybe 12 years older than me; Bobby was in the middle and maybe 11 years older; and Jimmy was perhaps eight or nine years older than I was. I

loved all my cousins and looked up to them, but Bobby was my favorite
because he was always the coolest one of the three.

Bobby, like his two brothers, wore a slicked-back, processed
hairdo we called a "conk" back then, and he had all the girls. He was
smart, could talk, was real smooth, dressed real nice, and seemed like
he had it all together, so he was my guy. Bobby always went another
way and was never into the gang thing. He never hung with Joe and
Jimmy too much, because they were a part of what we in the neighborhood called "runners of the road," which was a gang. The Road was
the name of one of the gangs in our neighborhood, and Joe and Jimmy
were big-time members—Jimmy was the leader—and I guess because
they were so bad, that was another reason why nobody messed with
Aunt Mary.

When I was little, Joe, Bobby, and Jimmy would come over to my
house—or I'd be over at theirs—for family gatherings. All the older
folks would collect in the dining room, the kitchen, or the front room to
sit around and talk and eat. That's when my cousins would call me out
into the vestibule, away from the adults, and beat me up. They would
punch me on my arms and legs, or slap me upside my head, that kind of
stuff. Bobby wouldn't do it, but Jimmy and Joe would because they
were always mischievous guys. So they would be pinching me on my
arms, punching me in my chest, or thumping me on my head with their
thumbs and middle fingers. When I screamed in pain my mother would
come out and chase them down the street.

Later, as I grew older and understood things, I found out that many
people were scared to death of them. I remember one time, early in the
day, seeing Jimmy walk by our house with two girls that he took up on
Cowboy Hill. Rumor had it that he ran a "train" on the girls—that meant
a group of men would have sex with a woman or a girl—with members
of his gang. Later that day, I thought I saw what seemed like a thousand
other guys go up the hill where Jimmy had gone with the girls, but I

don't remember seeing any of them come down. It was almost like a dream, but I was awake and young. The whole neighborhood was in an uproar for about two days after that.

Like I said, I was young, and although I knew what was going on, was street smart in some ways already, a lot of things just went right by me because I wasn't old enough to understand exactly what was happening. I never really was a part of any gang scene because I wasn't drawn to it, didn't see anything cool about being in that kind of life. But I was protected in the neighborhood, maybe—and it's only my guess, looking back—because I was Jimmy and Joe's little cousin.

They didn't save me from everyone, though. There were bad guys around me all the way through elementary school who would take my money. So bigger, older guys would pick on me and take the money my mother gave me to take to school. I remember a real dumb guy named Whitey who went to elementary school with me (I must have been about 10 or 11, but he was already in his teens), and he used to take my money from me. He was dumb as a piece of wood, so I guess that's why he was in elementary school, but he was mean.

Whitey lived around the corner from me, but I never knew why they called him "Whitey." He was brown skinned and had scars all over his face and hands from gang fighting. He and his guys—some as old and dumb as him—used to catch me and some of my classmates in the bathroom and pee on us if we didn't have any money to give them. One day, though, when I was a little older—not much older—things changed. I remember Whitey walked up and demanded my money, but I had had enough—I really don't know why—and I said, "Naw."

Well, he was shocked to hear this coming from me. So he looked real hard at me and asked, "What's wrong, you ain't got it?"

"Yeah, I got it," I said, "but I ain't giving it to you!"

He was stunned. But maybe because Jimmy and Joe were my cousins, he didn't do anything. I will never know why he didn't. He just turned around and walked away, saying, "Aw right, I'll check you out next time. Later."

I was stunned and relieved, because I was really shaking in my boots when I said "Naw." I said it before I realized I was saying it! But I learned something from that incident. I understood that I had to stand up for myself in order to survive being picked on or losing my money to someone like Whitey. If I went around the block to avoid him and get to school, I just had to go through another crowd of tough guys like him. So I had to learn how to make my way through all that different kind of gangster stuff. Sometimes it was hell, you know what I mean? I found out that if you stood up for yourself, people stopped messing with you out of respect.

One time after I stood up to Whitey, when I was little older, I was playing stickball and there was a little guy we called "Meatball," because he had a big, round head that looked like a meatball in a plate of spaghetti. Anyway, I hit a home run off of him. We were playing on the elementary school playground, and when I was running around the bases, Meatball retrieved the ball and hit me upside the head with it. Now, I always had a bad temper, even if I didn't like to fight. So I chased Meatball until I finally caught him, and I beat his ass real bad. That's the way I started making my statement as I grew older, by going crazy on people. After doing this a couple more times, it got around that I would stand up for myself, wasn't scared, and might be a little bit crazy, too. People stopped messing with me after that, including Whitey.

One of the people I grew up with, Carroll Wilson, lived right across the street from me. I used to go over to his house and hang with him and his brothers and sister sometimes. Down the street was Poochie, my first "girlfriend," who also went from G. S. Benson Elementary School to Charles Y. Audenried Junior High School. A couple of houses down from Poochie lived a boy named Billy. I can't remember his last name, but I knew him because he would come around to Vacation Bible School in the summers to shoot baskets, and I remember him being a real nice kid. One day Billy drowned when he went with another boy named George down to the Schuylkill River. Billy must have been 10 or 11 when this happened, and I must have been around eight or nine. After Billy and George went swimming in the river and Billy drowned, George came back to the neighborhood and didn't tell anyone that Billy had died. It was crazy!

When people found out Billy had drowned and that George had left him in the water and come back without telling anyone Billy was dead, everyone grew leery of him, and it stayed that way for a long, long time. I don't know if it ever really changed. Billy and George were great friends, so people couldn't figure out why he would do that, you know what I mean? Why would he leave Billy there like that and not tell anyone? After the police talked to him, George was never charged with anything, but there was always this lingering doubt about him in the backs of everyone's minds from then on, because no one could understand how George could treat his best friend like he did. I tell this story here to illustrate how tight-knit the neighborhood was.

It was around this time that I started loving music, you know, all kinds of genres. But rock 'n' roll and R&B became the focus of my attention. That music was me, it was what I heard in my heart and soul (although later on I did like some jazz—Miles Davis especially—and some pop music). But R&B had my heart. The great soul singer Solomon Burke used to come through the neighborhood because he knew my cousin Margie. She was from another part of the family and we called her Cousin Margie. She and my sister Ann were close. Solomon would come over to see Margie and Ann, and after I found out he was famous I would go around the neighborhood after he got there and tell people he was in our house. (I guess I knew about selling an image even back then.) Then, people would pay me a nickel to come in our house just to get a short glimpse of the great star. Burke was a nice guy who would speak to everyone. He must have thought I was a budding businessman, because he would smile at me and just shake his head when he saw me collecting my money. I must have been about eight or nine at the time.

It was around this age when I first had "sex" with my girlfriend, Poochie. She was nice looking, a little plump, with light skin and short, nice hair. We'd grind against each other standing up against a wall in the vestibule. I remember we were kissing heavily one night, and I guess we just decided to go the whole nine yards. After that we grinded a lot and I was hooked. All kinds of people from the neighborhood would be coming over to watch TV in our house, since there wasn't another one around that I knew of. Poochie would be there a lot (she was a year younger than me). So when I was nine and while everyone else was watching TV, she and I would be out in the vestibule grinding up against the wall, which is the way I did it then—and I did it a lot—until I got to high school. I guess I was curious about what having sex was, what it felt like, why people like my cousins liked it so much. It wasn't until I was around 11 that two sisters that lived down the street sort of took me under their wing and showed me real sex. It was strange because they were three and four years older than me and they had started to grow pubic hair. So while we were doing it standing up, their pubic hair kept sticking me because I didn't have any.

Now, I don't know why I didn't lie down and have sex until I was in high school. And even in high school, I mostly did it standing up against walls: I guess I have always been a creature of habit. But I know one thing: Having sex made me feel good, and this feeling only increased as I grew older.

Chapter 2

COMING OF AGE, JUNIOR HIGH SCHOOL, AND MY INTRODUCTION TO BASKETBALL: 1956 TO 1959

EVEN THOUGH I GREW UP IN A ROUGH NEIGHBORHOOD, I always did well with my studies in elementary school. I did my homework, read a lot, and didn't ever get into any real trouble, except for little mischievous stuff that every little kid my age got into. When I graduated from G. S. Benson Elementary School in June 1956 and moved on to Audenried Junior High School in September of that year, all of a sudden school started getting very strange for me. Some of the strangeness came as a result of having to adjust to a situation different from elementary school, and it affected my studies and my life. When I came out of elementary school I was one of the top students academically and was voted one of those most likely to succeed. So I was placed in the good, top classes for smart kids when I got to my new school.

Everybody in my neighborhood went to Benson Elementary and Audenried Junior High. I started attending Audenried along with two of my longtime friends, "Leaping John" Anderson, who we later called

"Leap" for short, and Ronald Reese. We played baseball out on the playground together (and basketball later), and after graduating from junior high school, the three of us went outside the neighborhood to attend John Bartram High School, which was in an all-white neighborhood.

Initially I was a good student at Audenried, because one of the things I prided myself on at the time was that I got good grades. I also wanted to become a poet. So in the seventh grade I got into the poetry class as an extracurricular activity and quickly started to write different poems. I worked on our school newspaper also and got involved with publishing poems in it, including one of mine called "Spring":

> *Spring*
> *I love the spring*
> *but it rains*
> *when I go out to play*
> *I always want to stay*
> *the birds hum*
> *the bells ring*
> *the children play*
> *and I sing*
> *I look above in thankfulness*
> *for this is the time*
> *I love best*
> *Spring*

Publishing this poem spurred me on to really want to be an English major. (Later, when I went to college, I wanted to have two majors, English and history. But as it turned out, I ended up majoring in elementary education.)

What was different about going to Audenried was that there were more kids than there had been at Benson, and more of them were white kids, too, as the school was located in a racially mixed neighborhood. At Audenried I was in the top classes in the seventh and eighth grades, and in the ninth grade, too, but that was when somebody at the school decided they were going to experiment with some of the classes. This happened in 1958, when I was 13. I was put in an experimental class, which was supposed to have the school's top pupils in it. But when they placed some of the worst-acting students in that class and transferred some of the good people into the worst classes to see what would happen, I didn't like it. Because all of a sudden I was in classes with people who didn't care about studying, or poetry, or art. It made me real mad. Once I started going to these classes, I knew right away that I wasn't going to be getting the same education and attention that I had been getting, so I rebelled. It just didn't set right with me and it caused me a lot of tension.

Up until this time I had been playing soccer and baseball at Audenried, but after they put me in those lower classes I just stopped really caring about school—and even playing those sports—because I was really pissed off about what had happened. Now, I have always been a little temperamental and stubborn when something happens to me that I don't think is fair, and I definitely didn't think this was right. So I withdrew from school activities and sulked from then on out.

Then this incident happened with one of my teachers, and it was all downhill after that. One day I came into Horatio Smith's class late and I was sulking. I had steel taps on my shoes that were very loud as I walked in. So, here I am tapping loudly to my seat in the back and Mr. Smith said, "Vernon, that's one E."

Mr. Smith used to always call me by my first name, Vernon. Anyway, an E was like a demerit. And if you got three Es in a semester you were in big trouble. I've always had a little temper, so I kept on tapping to the back of the class.

"Vernon, that's two more Es now," Mr. Smith said.

So by the time I reached my seat, I had three Es for the semester. Being a very logical person (that's another thing, I have always been very logical), I surmised that if I had three Es already and had ensured myself of a poor grade for the semester, there was no sense in working hard in Mr. Smith's class, so I didn't. That started a trend. And Mr. Smith's class was an English class, which I really enjoyed. But after that incident I got it in my head that it didn't make much sense to do anything, so I didn't! In the end I got twenty Es for that semester and things kind of kept snowballing downhill from there. Even though I passed, it still wasn't the same. I'd stopped studying. I'd lost interest in being an excellent student. I stopped doing all the things I had done in the past. Instead, I embraced a negative kind of behavior in terms of my academics and it kept rolling on over—snowballing, if you will—until I got into high school and I was left back in the 10th grade.

I must admit junior high was a problem for me, and some of it had to do with the fact that I was spoiled and immature. Still, I did have some fun outside of school during my years at Audenried, especially after I really started getting into music. I remember one song by the Flamingos, "I Only Have Eyes for You," that was special to me in junior high school. I just loved it, especially the lyric "Our love must be a kind of blind love / I can't see anyone but you." After I heard the Flamingos sing this lyric, which kind of got stuck in my head, that's when I started really getting involved with girls and I would use that lyric on them sometimes.

My mother worked at a factory down on Oakford Street for a long time when I was growing up. She was just a regular factory worker who worked the day shift. I don't know how much she made, but obviously it couldn't have been a whole lot. She used to walk to work. It was about seven blocks. I remember her getting up early and always being on time. Then she'd get me ready to go to school and Theresa ready for when Mom came over to watch her. She made sure I was on my way to school and sometimes, if she had time, she'd walk with me, because the way to school was the same route she took to go to work.

Sometimes, before Theresa was old enough to go to school, she would follow behind me and I wouldn't know she had left home, where my grandmother was supposed to be watching her. She would just leave the house without our grandmother knowing it and walk to school. So there were times I'd hear that she was in school looking for me, because she was lost. It was weird! But growing up with my mother and sister was beautiful, even though I had to watch the stupid, violent stuff that was happening with my mother and stepfather at times, which caused me to start disliking him intensely. But despite what was happening in their lives around this time, my life and my sister's life were pretty secure. Our mother was the driving force behind everything, and she was a saint in my eyes. Regardless of all the arguments between my stepfather and my mother, growing up in my neighborhood was always interesting.

There were a few new people I started hanging out with around this time, like Steve "Smitty" Smith (who would later become my best friend and change his name to Sahib Abdulkhabir). I met Smitty at Oakford playground—he attended another elementary school—where we played baseball, soccer, and, later, a few pickup games of basketball, though I wasn't really into basketball at the time. I also met another longtime friend, George Clisby (who later became a policeman) there. Besides Smitty and Clisby and a few others, I have always stayed close to my immediate family, no matter what I did, or what happened for me; I was never too far from those in my Philadelphia family. I never really got into distant cousins, only the people who were right around me, those that affected my life on a daily basis. That was my family and that's basically who I cared for, and that's still the way I am today.

My mother hardly ever whipped me or anything like that, although one day I remember I made her so mad—I have forgotten what I did—

that she told me to go and bring her an ironing cord so she could whip my ass with it. So I ran down to Aunt Nicey's house—which is where all of my young relatives went whenever any of us got into trouble, because she didn't have any children and was very nurturing to us. But after I got there, I was having such a good time I just stayed and didn't go back home. Plus, I was scared of how bad Ma was gonna beat me with that ironing cord because of how angry she was with me! So I just stayed and went home the next day. It was just her and my godfather, Sam Jones, who everybody called "Mr. Sam." Aunt Nicey was like my other mother and Mr. Sam was kind of like a father figure to me, as well as my godfather. So whenever anything happened I would run away from home and go to Aunt Nicey's house, even though everybody knew exactly where I was going.

When I got home the next day I told my mother I had stayed at Aunt Nicey's because I was having such a good time. She already knew this and wasn't as angry with me as she had been the day before, so she just pinched up a piece of the flesh on my arm and twisted it—which was how she usually punished me when she was angry—until I screamed in pain. But her pinch wasn't anywhere close to being as painful as an ironing cord would have been had Ma whipped me with one, and for that I was thankful.

Aunt Nicey was the oldest of my two aunts. Aunt Mary was next to her, and my mother was the youngest. Aunt Nicey was a very thin woman who drank a lot—mostly whiskey. And the interesting thing about her was that she would chew a lot of food, hold it in her mouth while she added some whiskey and Coke, and then swallow everything down. That used to amaze me, you know what I mean? That was something to watch. And she would do this every day, all day long. Aunt Nicey never worked as far as I know. Mr. Sam took good care of her.

Anyway, when he was young Mr. Sam traveled all over the United States working construction on tall buildings, walking those planks way up in the air, high off the ground, putting bricks and steel girders in buildings as they were being constructed. He was a very interesting guy. Mr. Sam used to talk about being down in South Carolina, living on Daufuskie Island with the Gullah people.

Mr. Sam said he worked on Hilton Head Island, which is just off the mainland of South Carolina to the north of Daufuskie, and that he took a boat from Daufuskie to Hilton Head every day, leaving early in the morning when the tide went out and coming back at night when the tide came in. Mr. Sam said he worked construction on Hilton Head, building up all those resorts located down there. He used to say all the islands along the South Carolina coast were basically filled with black people in those days—and still are even today—of pure African descent who spoke a funny strange kind of dialect called Geechee. I never went down there when I was young, but my sister Ann used to tell me about it because she went down south every summer. Aunt Nicey and Mr. Sam were really different from a lot of people, but I loved her—and Mr. Sam, too—very much and learned a lot from both of them.

In 1955 we moved from Alter Street to 1120 South 26th Street, at the corner of Alter Street, and we stayed there until around 1962, the year I graduated from high school, when we moved to 1217 South 26th Street at the corner of Manton Street; that was the three-story building we bought from Mr. Siegel. That building was not only our home, but also the grocery store my parents opened on the ground floor. My mother and stepfather bought the house at 1120 South 26th Street from an Italian family named Puncheanella, one of the very few white families that lived in my neighborhood.

Our new house was a two-story storefront with large windows on both sides of the double-door entrance. The house had three bedrooms in the family area upstairs on the second floor, a bathroom, and a back room next to the bathroom that led to the porch over the garage. We used to sit out there and relax. In the summer we used to lean over the rail and pick pears from the big tree next door; we also used that porch as a storage space. Downstairs there was a large living room, a dining room, and a kitchen, and the garage behind it, but no backyard, which was a drag. The house was much bigger than the one on Alter Street, as was my room—and everybody else's, too—and I really liked that.

When I was a kid I had the same close neighborhood feeling being in church that I did sitting around my home. I remember sitting in Zion Hill Baptist Church down on 39th and Walnut, and Reverend Spence was preaching. I remember feeling something, you know, this surge in my body. I didn't know what it was and I told my Aunt Nicey, who was sitting next to me, about it.

"Well, what do you think it is?" she said.

I told her I didn't know.

"It must be the Holy Ghost," she said.

Whatever it was, it spurred me to go up to the altar when they were calling for candidates for baptism. I think I was 14 or 15, but maybe I was younger. I don't exactly remember when it was because it was like a dream. The funny thing about the day of my baptism was that as I was walking down the aisle in the white sheet they gave me, I started to get very nervous, because the preacher was going to baptize me and I couldn't swim. Maybe I was afraid of death, of drowning like my friend Billy. I don't know exactly what it was, but I know getting baptized really scared me. Especially when I got up to the altar and Reverend Spence guided me up to the baptismal waters behind the pulpit and put his hand on my head and started to dunk me under the water, saying, "Now I baptize you, in the name of the Father, the Son, and the Holy Ghost!"

I got really scared. Then he dunked me under the water again, and it seemed like this time I was down there for an hour, you know? That really scared the shit out of me and I came up gasping for breath. I really thought I was going to drown. After that I started sitting in the back of the church, and it was only a matter of time before I stopped going altogether.

One of the reasons I stopped going to church was that I could never really understand the Bible, you know what I mean? I could never fully understand the language that was used in the Bible when I read certain passages. I had to go back and read them three or four times to get an understanding of what was really being said. I used to always wonder why they couldn't just use simple, straightforward English.

I guess that's the reason why people go to Bible study, to get the interpretation of the words. Maybe that's the reason why I never understood that much of the Bible, because I never went to Bible school in church to get that interpretation. Like I said, I was afraid of death by this time, though I never really knew why. Maybe it had something to do with me seeing that man being stabbed to death in front of my eyes right by my house when I was growing up. Maybe it was because I had no control over death, you know, how or when it came. I've always wanted to be in control of everything that happened in my life, and I knew I had no control over death. Maybe that's why I was so afraid of it. I just don't know and have never been able to explain my fear of dying. Or maybe I was just growing more mature, starting to have my own beliefs about living in the world. Even today, I believe that going to church and reading the Bible does not make you a righteous person. Believing in God and trying to live right is the most important thing to me.

Going to church also bothered me because I could never exactly grasp what the minister was talking about, or why the congregation always believed everything the minister said. But it was mostly reading the Bible that turned me off. Reading it made me feel very self-conscious and I was always afraid afterwards, even of going to see biblical movies like *The Ten Commandments*. Even in school at Audenried, when the teachers would bring up religious subjects around Easter—when they talked about Jesus being nailed to the cross and him dying like that—it just disturbed me, made me feel very weird. All that talk of "fire and brimstone," even in my history classes at school. I do know my mother wanted me to go to see that *Ten Commandments* movie because she was religious, but I never wanted to see it and wouldn't go with her. So she took my sister Theresa instead. And that was one of the first times I went against my mother's wishes and she didn't punish me for doing so. Like I said, it was strange going to church, but I always lived by the old-school teachings, because no matter what my beliefs were I was still basically driven by old-school religion.

Like, for instance, I always believed since I was small that there were certain ways I was supposed to act, certain things I was supposed to do, like not talking about or back to my elders. I believed in opening doors for women, treating them with respect. Just basic things I learned as a kid. I believed there was a certain amount of respect I had to give people, always believed I had to give folks who had accomplished something important their due. I've always tried to live my life by these rules, which are close to the spirit of the teachings of the Bible.

I have also never believed anyone should mistreat other people just because they don't like them. I always thought I had to give people their space to do and be what they wanted to be, because I always wanted to be treated the same way. But we weren't totally a religious family, even though my mother would go to church. As I got older and started playing basketball, that became my religion on Sundays. I was a very shy person when I was growing up, didn't like to express myself by talking too much with people I didn't know, but I would discover later that I was a people person and that I could express myself creatively out on the basketball court.

The driving force in my life behind all of this, everything in my life, was always my mother. Ma would go to church when she could and then come home and we'd have a big, good meal that she'd gotten together before she left to go to morning service. On Sunday mornings, before she left for church, I'd have pancakes. And when I started playing basketball on Sundays I'd have a lot of pancakes, because I knew I would be coming home late. So I'd have a very big meal: pancakes, scrambled eggs and ham, scrapple, maybe some bacon, baked beans, hot dogs and rice left over from Saturday. Then I'd put syrup over everything and eat all of that. My plate would be piled high, but I'd eat all of it and I'd be good for the rest of the day. Sometimes, when I got home later, there'd be chicken or roast beef that I would eat.

I used to love my mother's cooking. She cooked most every day, things like thinly sliced steak smothered in gravy and onions. And because I loved rice it was always served with every meal. There were certain Fridays when she didn't cook. On those Fridays she would just go and pick up already-cooked silver trout and french fries from the fish store. Usually the trout was fried and served in sandwiches. But my favorite meal was on Saturdays when I ate baked beans, hot dogs, and rice with a lot of sugar in it, served with homemade corn bread. That was my favorite meal. Even today, whenever I get sick, the first thing I do is go get me some baked beans—vegetarian beans, though—chicken franks, and white rice. I fix me some Jiffy corn bread and I'm good to go. That's what I eat to combat sickness. We never drank milk in our house. Never. But I drank a lot of sodas—grape, orange, red—back then; any kind of soda, you name it, and I drank it. Later, when we had the grocery store, my mother would say, "Earl, stop drinking up all the sodas, because you're drinking up all the profits."

But I never stopped; I'd sneak and do it. Then I'd drink juices— orange, grape juice, stuff like that—and Kool-Aid. But I never gained weight until my second year in the pros. I guess I had a high metabolism and I just burned all that food and soda off.

It was around this time that organized basketball saved every-thing—including my studies—and gave me a focus for the rest of my life. Up until this time I had loved soccer and baseball, and I wanted to be Willie Mays after I saw him make that great catch in the 1954 World Series. I became a catcher on a team at Oakford playground, though, because all the other positions were filled. My friend Smitty played third base and my other friend, Edwin "Wilkie" Wilkinson, played center field, like Mays. I didn't wear a catcher's mask because it was too heavy for my head, and of course one day this batter hit a foul tip that sailed over my catcher's mitt and nicked me in the eye. Boy, did that hurt, and scared the holy shit out of me, too! That was the end of my career as a catcher. Right then and there I took off all of my equipment, threw it on the ground, dropped my catcher's mitt, and walked off the field. I played first base after that.

I still loved baseball and wanted to become a pro baseball player at the time, and after seeing Willie Mays make that amazing catch I got more serious about that. But I could never root for the Philadelphia Phillies baseball team because I was under the impression that Connie Mack was the owner of the Phillies and it was said that he would never have a black player on his team. It turns out Connie Mack never owned the Phillies (he owned the Philadelphia Athletics), but in the community we assumed the Phillies were his team because the stadium the two teams shared was called Connie Mack Stadium. As a result, I just always rooted for Baltimore, the New York Giants, the Brooklyn Dodgers, or the Milwaukee Braves because of Hank Aaron.

After I had been at Audenried for a while, something happened that changed all of this, my love for soccer and baseball especially (even though I kept playing both sports). What happened was that one day I met Audenried's basketball coach and started playing ball. After that I dropped my dream of becoming a baseball player like a hot potato. It all started in 1958, when I was 14 years old. One day I was walking down the hallway (and I was basically the same height I am today, about six feet three and a half; I hardly grew any as I got older, except I've gained more weight) and the junior high school basketball coach, Monroe Barrett, saw me and asked if I played basketball. I said, "No, sir."

So he said, "Well, you come down to the gym this afternoon,"

And I did. That's where it all started. I don't know, but I think the reason I started to get into the game of basketball so much back then was because all the guys I hung around with played. I wasn't very good at first—in fact I was terrible—so I really started to focus on the game. I wanted to be good, to get revenge on all the people who used to outplay me, beat whatever team I was on, and then laugh at me. And there were a whole lot of those guys, including, at first, some of my friends. So I know revenge was a factor in fueling my determination to get better.

I used to come home after practice complaining because everyone was so much better and far ahead of me. But it was when I started playing on Oakford playground that guys started really making fun of my game. I complained so much about being made fun of that my mother got tired of hearing me whine. So she gave me a little blue notebook and told me to write down all the names of the people who were better than me and were teasing me, and I did. Then she told me that as I started beating those guys I should cross out their names in the book. So I started keeping notes about all those guys who beat and made fun of me. And as I beat them, I crossed their names off my list. The exhilaration of crossing them off the list really motivated me to get better at basketball, and eventually I did.

Around this time I thought back to September 29, 1954, to that day in the Benson Elementary School library when I was watching the New York Giants play against the Cleveland Indians in Game One of the World Series at New York City's Polo Grounds with a bunch of classmates. I remember the game was in the eighth inning and a batter—I think his name was Vic Wertz—hit a long high drive to dead center field that everyone thought was going to be a home run or at least hit the wall. Then I remember watching Willie Mays, who had been playing shallow, take off and run like a bat out of hell after the ball that nobody thought he had a chance of catching. All of a sudden, on the dead run, Mays reached out his arm and his glove and made this astonishing over-the-head catch out on the warning track, in dead center field, 420 feet from home plate.

After Mays caught the ball, he spun around so fast he lost his cap and made this clothesline throw from deep center field to the infield, preventing the runner on second base from scoring on a tag-up play. Everybody—people in the library and even the announcer on television—was shouting and screaming about how Willie Mays caught up with that baseball, let alone made the catch, which after this was known simply as "the Catch." It was the greatest catch I ever saw—I have never seen one as great since then—and one of the most incredible athletic things I have ever seen in my life. After that, Willie Mays became a hero of mine and I really started playing baseball a lot at Oakford playground at 30th and Oakford Streets.

It was only after Coach Barrett asked me to come down to the junior high school gym and I started playing with the team that I started seriously going down to Oakford playground to play basketball and get better. That's where I started playing with Smitty, Wilkie, Clisby, Leaping John, and Ronald Reese. We started playing together all the time, and they were all much better than I was at first. We called ourselves "the Trotters" and nicknamed the playground we played at "Trotters Ground."

We named ourselves the Trotters, short for the Harlem Globetrotters, because they were a famous black team back then—still are today—and played a flashy-style city game we tried to imitate (we patterned our squad after the Boston Celtics, our favorite team back in those days). Although none of us had even ever watched the Globetrotters play (I didn't see them play in person until I was in the pros), older guys on the playground had watched them, styled their games after them, and told us how they played. We wanted to model our game after the style the old heads played, but only on the playground, because Coach Barrett was teaching fundamentals and the traditional game at Audenried and he allowed no flashy playground stuff on his team.

Because I was six three, Coach Barrett made me play center. Having never played organized basketball before, I'd never been in a situation in which someone was trying to tell me what I should or shouldn't be doing, you know what I mean? On the playground we were our own coaches. But Coach Barrett would tell me really little simple things like "Earl, catch the ball with two hands," or "Earl, keep the ball up high, over your head," or "Earl, get the rebound out." He'd say, "Earl, get your hands up so you can catch the ball" or "Catch the ball with your back to the basket." He said these things to me to help me better understand the fundamentals of the game. I didn't like being told what to do at first, but in time I grew to appreciate Coach Barrett and the things he taught me.

I was already big for a 14-year-old, though I was really skinny, just arms and legs. People—including Coach Barrett—thought I was going to get even bigger, maybe grow to be six eight or six nine. So Coach Barrett taught me basic things he thought I needed to know to play against bigger centers, and that's one of the reasons I started developing the little spin shots off the backboard and little moves and whatnot that let me get my shot off against bigger opponents. I learned to touch whoever was defending me, even if they were bigger, so I could create just enough space to get my shot off.

Coach taught me that using my body was very important to get in position to get rebounds, or to back an opponent underneath the basket where he couldn't really jump because his head would be up in the net if he did. So playing center—and guard, too—was all about getting a feel for who's guarding you, being able to get in position to do whatever it was you had to do to be effective. Like in junior high I developed little fadeaway jump shots right in front of the basket, little hooks. I learned to fake my shot to get my opponent up in the air, so when he was coming down I would be going up for my shot. The other thing I learned from Coach Barrett was to go directly at my opponent's body because it was harder for them to block my shot that way without fouling me. He also made me shoot a lot of free throws, so I could score that way, too. And, perhaps most importantly, he taught me to develop good footwork, to always be in a position to take good shots against taller players without walking with the ball, you know, getting a traveling call whistled against me. So these were the things I was learning from Coach Barrett—the fundamentals of the game—and these skills really helped me to better my game.

Still, even if I was beginning to become consumed with playing basketball, I was still just a teenager and I was thinking about other things, too, like wanting to drive cars. So around this time, when I was fourteen years old, I started trying to teach myself to drive through trial and error. Now, I knew I shouldn't have been trying to do this, but I always saw myself being behind the wheel of a car. I remember one time, when I was supposed to just be washing my aunt Mary's car, I took it for a spin and sideswiped a whole bunch of cars on Ellsworth, which is a very narrow street one over from Alter. I did that a lot for a while. I didn't think I was being mischievous or anything; I just wanted to learn how to drive a car and eventually I did, like I said, through trial and error, which meant I would have accidents from time to time. But that's the only way I knew how to do it, even if it pissed Ma off. But because she loved me so much and let me get away with murder—I was really spoiled by my mother growing up—she didn't do anything to me for messing up her sister's car. (When I was older and finally got a car, my driving was still so bad my guys used to almost fight to sit in the back seat. No one wanted to ride shotgun up front beside me, they were so afraid that I'd have an accident.)

In junior high I had a paper route that my mother and I built up until it was profitable. Like I said, my mother did everything to help me when I was growing up. She was so protective of me and used to go around my paper route with me, basically selling my papers, delivering them to the different houses. She really didn't want me being out there by myself. (That's one of the reasons why later on I tried so hard to make something of myself in basketball, so I could do something good for my mother.)

One day we went to a house to deliver a paper and a kid came to the door and called my mother "the paper lady." Hearing the little boy say that about my mother hurt me so bad it left an indelible mark on my mind. I knew right then that there was something more I needed to do for my mother, because I never ever wanted to hear anyone else think that was what she did. I mean, she worked every day and this was what she did with me in the evenings, so I wouldn't be out there alone delivering papers at night. That's just how much she loved me. She was always more than just a mother to me; she was a great friend, as well, and I really always respected her for her commitment to my well-being.

We—all my friends, too—were teenagers now and we wanted to do the things we saw adults doing, you know, like drinking and dancing, making out with each other, kissing and having sex, listening to music, driving cars, getting into clothes and fashion. But we needed a place to hang out, so my mother let us use our basement. We started a boys and girls' club there called the Activity Club while I was going to Bartram. We'd meet in the basement of my house at 1120 South 26th Street and dance and make out. At first, when everyone arrived, the lights would be on, then as things heated up the lights would go out. When they came on, everybody would have white all over the backs of their clothes, because all the walls were whitewashed and that's where we were kissing and doing the do, up against those whitewashed walls.

My sister Theresa, who was about 9 or 10 years old at the time, sold wine in our house for 50 cents a glass like Mom was doing in her house. See, we found out that the Puncheanellas had left these gallons of home-made wine in the basement. So Theresa, being a very enterprising young girl, sold shots of wine to kids in the neighborhood.

Selling stuff was good training for Theresa because later, after we moved to 1217 26th Street—when my stepfather bought Mr. Siegel's house with the grocery store—she would be behind the counter selling candy to the kids in the neighborhood for a penny. Later, when Theresa went to college, she studied accounting and business, which was right up her alley. She had a big jar full of penny candy, and she used to fill it two or three times a day. Theresa was something else, and cold-blooded, too. I remember one day some girl in the neighborhood came to the door of the grocery store, and she had been shot in the arm by somebody. The girl, who was around 16, was trying to escape from whoever shot her. But Theresa, who was by herself, just closed and locked the door in her face so the shooter wouldn't come in the store after her. I never knew what the girl's name was, but I heard she survived. I'll always remember that incident because it showed me that even at a young age, my sister really knew how to handle things and was tough as nails.

Man, we had a great time in that club! We started the Activity Club when I was 16 or 17, in the 11th grade. Looking back, it was all about growing up, trying to find and shape our own identities when we were entering those teenage years. We wanted to separate ourselves from our parents—like all adolescent kids do—and, as always, there's risk in doing that. At the time, however, we didn't mind or know we were really taking chances with our futures. We didn't consider the possibil-ity that we might produce babies by having sex, or do something stupid as a result of drinking. We just didn't think about those dangers because we were having too much fun.

The interesting thing about growing up where and when I did was that I began to see, as I got older, that there was a lot of racial tension between white and black people in Philadelphia, and as a result of this tension we had race riots in the city every spring. Even though I grew up in a mixed neighborhood, I still didn't have any white friends. But I met some at Bartram.

At the time, though, I didn't really know any white people, or how they were in real life. My impressions of them came only from what I saw on television. I used to think most white people were funny because I loved watching Red Skelton, Sid Caesar, Lucille Ball, Milton Berle, and Imogene Coca on television, and they were hilarious to me. So at first I thought most white people were just like them, until I knew the real deal better. But I loved watching those comedians on television. I remember we'd have a houseful of people cracking up over those comedians and their slapstick skits. They were hilarious. I remember some of the older people talking about how funny a lot of black comedians were, but I never saw any on television at that time, and it wouldn't be until much later on that I saw and heard how really funny a lot of black comedians were, like Moms Mabley, Redd Foxx, *The Amos 'n Andy Show*, and, even later, Richard Pryor. But watching those white comedians on television got me thinking somewhere deep in my head about trying to be a comedian myself when I grew up. Later in my life I did try to become a comedian, too, but it didn't work out.

My study habits hadn't improved by this point, either. I still didn't like being in class or with my teachers, so my grades weren't good. That started to upset my mother and stepfather. I considered my time at Audenried one lost year—the 9th grade—because, despite getting into girls and music and also getting my first introduction to organized basketball, I didn't want to be there. By the spring of 1959 and into the summer of that year, after I graduated from Audenried, I really started to play on the playgrounds a lot with the Trotters, against other teams, and my basketball skills improved quickly. It was still, however, a definite learning period for me in terms of absorbing what I needed to know in order to become really good at playing the game.

So that summer after I graduated from Audenried, I practiced a lot and played many pickup basketball games on the Oakford playground—and on other courts around the area, also—with my friends on the Trotters. I felt all this focus, hard work, and practice would serve me well and get me ready for when I entered Bartram High School that coming fall.

Chapter 3

HIGH SCHOOL YEARS:
1959 TO 1962

I BEGAN ATTENDING JOHN BARTRAM HIGH SCHOOL in September 1959. The school was located in Southwest Philadelphia, in an all-white neighborhood, at 67th Street and Elmwood Avenue. But a lot of black kids also attended the school, and the basketball team was mixed. My best friend, Steve Smith, also went to Bartram, as did a bunch of other kids from my neighborhood, like Leaping John Anderson and Ronald Reese. We didn't really want to go to South Philadelphia High School or Bok Technical High School, which were both located in our area of South Philly. But the main reason we decided to go to Bartram was because our fellow Trotters, George Clisby and Edwin "Wilkie" Wilkerson, were going there, and we decided to follow them. They were both ahead of us. Wilkie was a smart kid who skipped a couple of grades in school (eventually he went to Cheyney State Teachers College with Ed Bradley, the *60 Minutes* commentator), so by the time we got to Bartram he was already about to graduate.

I really enjoyed going to Bartram because it was so far away from where I grew up and lived and it probably also had something to do with having a different experience. Like I said, I have always been a practical

person, so I just looked at the situation of going to high school at Bartram as something I had to do, you know, because my boys were going
there. It was what it was. I had to go to high school and the choice I
made was the best choice for me. Plus, when I got to Bartram, I didn't
face any race riot–type stuff out there, although I knew it could happen.
What's important to understand is that when black people find themselves in an integrated situation, we adjust quicker and better to the
circumstances than, perhaps, whites would if the situation was reversed.
Blacks have had to sometimes adjust to living in all-white environments
throughout our history in this country, so it wasn't a big thing for me to
adjust to this new situation; I just rolled with it.

I think I started to compartmentalize my life while I was going to
Bartram, you know, separating what was happening in the black community I had grown up in from what I was beginning to experience in
this all-white community. This would later extend into my experiences
as a basketball player, when I had to reconcile the organized, traditional
way I had to play at Bartram with the more creative, improvisational
game I had to master on the playgrounds in South Philly. I didn't realize
at first when I started doing it, but I embraced this compartmentaliza-
tion of my life as I matured.

The neighborhood around the school wasn't violent in the way my
neighborhood was when I was growing up. In fact, it seemed kind of like
a civilized community, tolerant toward blacks. I didn't see white guys
pointing at me because I was black, or riding on top of cars and calling
me names, like happened in other white neighborhoods in Philadelphia.
That's not to say there weren't racist, violent white people in the neighborhood or at the school; I know there were, but they just didn't bother
me. A lot of racist stuff had been happening all over America for a long
time at this point, like what happened in 1958 out in Little Rock, Arkansas, when governor Orval Faubus blocked those nine young black kids
from going to a white public school out there, you know what I mean?

That kind of ugly stuff was beginning to appear in the local newspapers, and a lot of my family and other black folks in Philadelphia were talking about it all the time. And, you know, I was now at an age where I was beginning to recognize and think about what all this racial stuff meant for me, too, even though I didn't know what I could do about any of it. But it was calm out where I was going to school, so it was cool for me going to Bartram.

In my first year, playing on the junior varsity team in the fall of 1959, I played about the same as everyone else on the team. Coach Klingman, who was white, as most of our players were, emphasized a passing, balanced team approach to the game. So our team scores against other teams were not gigantic, and a guy could be the high scorer with, like, 10, 11, or 12 points in any given game. We were all learning the organized way of playing together as a team, setting screens, passing the ball, and getting better as a unit. Still, things were starting to look up for me in terms of playing the game, both on the playgrounds and in Coach Klingman's system.

I was playing better and starting to get a little recognition at Bartram, though I wasn't where I wanted to be. I still had a lot to learn about playing the traditional team game. I'm sure that had I attended South Philadelphia or Bok Technical I would have encountered black players and coaches there who would have also stressed team fundamentals over individual play. It's just a matter of organized play versus playground. But I was beginning to get there, you know, making baby steps, and that was cool. Unfortunately, I still wasn't studying for my classes like I should have been and in the winter of 1960, disaster struck. I was left back in 10th grade because of bad grades.

I probably had been deluding myself, because I thought I was doing fine with my schoolwork when my homeroom teacher, Mr. Fine, failed me. Looking back, I now realize my failing was a carryover from the bad habits I had developed in my last years of junior high school. Now, failing was bad enough because I knew Ma was going to come down hard on me for it. She had been getting tired of me for a while for not dedicating myself to my studies, and one day she had laid down the law on me. (She didn't curse me out, though. Ma never used foul words on me, although I had been told she knew how to use them.) Now I knew she was going to read me the riot act, and she did, telling me I had better get myself together, or else. This time, though, because I'd failed, I soon discovered I couldn't play basketball anymore, and that really hurt me.

This whole thing was a wake-up call for me, and I remember finding out I couldn't play like it was yesterday. Bartram's junior varsity team was scheduled to play against Edison High's JV team at their gymnasium, so we would have to ride trolleys and trains to the game. To get there the school gave everyone on the team tokens to ride the trolley and the train, and I had just picked up mine when I saw our coach, Mr. Klingman, in the hallway. He called me over with a wave of his hand.

"Earl," he said, "I just got word that you're academically ineligible to play, so you've got to give me your tokens. Also, you have to go down and see your counselor. I'm sorry about this."

I was shocked, stunned. So I gave him my tokens and went to see the counselor and that's when he told me Mr. Fine had failed me, that he had given me the okeydoke, which meant I had to be left back a grade. Man, that hurt me real bad, cut me deep to the bone. But I decided then and there, very quickly, to use that disappointment as motivation. I knew my mother was going to be very angry with me, so what was I going to do? I decided that I would buckle down and work extra hard on my studies during the next semester, and I did. I got a double promotion. I got put back in my regular class, and that meant I could play basketball again.

I played very well once I rejoined the JV. At first everyone on all my teams—the Trotters at Oakford playground and the guys at Bartram—

was better than me, but constant practice changed all that, and eventually I moved ahead of them, both in high school and out on the playground. But I also found out that most of the best players were still out there playing on the playgrounds and that I still had a lot to learn about the game if I was to succeed out there playing against those guys. At first I'd be out there just sitting on the sidelines, watching. I mean, even after I learned to play the game pretty well I still wasn't good enough to compete on the playgrounds with those guys. So, I'd be one of the guys just sitting. They had guys running games out there who'd played college ball, people like Wally Jones, Walt Hazzard, Wayne Hightower, and even Wilt Chamberlain would come out sometimes. These guys were legends already in Philadelphia playground basketball, and they would be out there showing their stuff on the playgrounds and playing hard.

So I'd be sitting on the sidelines hoping to get to play against some of them. And if there was *nobody* else around they'd look over, you know (and it'd be so funny, because they'd be looking me over and I'd be trying to inch up, you know, trying to get a little taller, so they could see me), and then, maybe, at the end of the day, after I'd sat there all day long, somebody might say, "Hey Earl, come on, we need five guys here, so you be the fifth man."

But in my head I used to always say to myself, *I don't want to be the fifth man, I want to be the number one draft choice.* That's what I always said to myself, and I worked at it, worked my way up through hard work until I could not only just play with the big boys, but compete with them at the same high level they played at. That's when I started to feel pretty good about myself. But I got my biggest feeling of revenge when I later started to dominate the playground basketball scene in Philadelphia. To my way of thinking, this was a sign of very good things that were to come.

I was becoming sort of a risk taker playing basketball on the playgrounds; this was happening because of my growing philosophy of doing things through trial and error. I had begun approaching most things I did through trial and error, and it became a practice that would last me the rest of my life, especially in basketball. Doing things through trial and error helped bring me to an approach to the game that I would later call "the science of the game." Now, "the science of the game" basically starts out as trial and error, because a lot of the time back then I wasn't involved in organized basketball, like when I was playing on the playgrounds.

But my real focus at this time was on becoming a really good basketball player both at school and out on the playground. In order to do this I had to compartmentalize myself in that I had to discipline my game at school, yet improvise and play free out on the playground. That was a hard thing to do, but this was the challenge I faced. By this time I had caught up with and then surpassed my friends Smitty, Leap, and Reese in terms of basketball skills. Smitty at one point in time had a really good jump shot, but he lost it when he started trying to play like Elgin Baylor, you know, twitching and shaking his head as he was going to the basket, trying to make all kinds of moves. When he changed his outside game to one in which he was always driving to the hoop, he lost his jumper. Still, he was a good point guard at five foot nine because he could handle the ball, pass, and dribble, so he was like the quarterback of the JV squad. Reese was a steady ballplayer who never did anything spectacular, and Leap just could jump out of the gym, though he wasn't a great shooter.

By this time I was able to play out on the perimeter, or on the side of the court. I had been practicing a lot on the playground, developing moves that would allow me to drive to the basket. In my junior year at Bartram I could not only play with my back to the basket down low, but I could also play facing the basket and make moves out there that would allow me to get my midrange jump shot off, which was also improving by this time. But the fancy, creative stuff I left on the playground because I was playing center for Bartram. My play on the junior varsity team had improved so much by this time they wanted to bring me up to the varsity squad. I had gotten better not only at shooting the ball, but also in my passing skills and my leadership.

My friends and me on the Trotters never had anyone around to coach us on the playground, so we coached each other and learned from the older players. See, in Philadelphia the older guys pass on the history of the game on the playgrounds. That's where basketball wisdom is passed on and where I got most of my knowledge of the game of basketball. Like for instance, players in Philadelphia might not be the best dunkers, but they learn to outthink their opponents out on the court. The playground is where I learned to see the flow of the game. Then I had to focus on what was happening and understand where I was in the game and what I had to do to make myself better. I started to understand this concept when I was around 15 or 16, but it took me a couple of years before I really started putting it all together.

I was around 16, I think, when some people started calling me "Black Ben" because I was dark. I never knew where the name came from, but I didn't like it because it had a derogatory feeling. So I never considered it a nickname because there weren't a lot of people who called me that; just some smart-alecky lighter-skinned people who I had embarrassed on the basketball court. So whenever someone called me by that name I just didn't answer, which became the way I handled it from then on.

See, I had already learned from my sister Ann by the time I was 13 or 14 how people in Philadelphia mistreated and didn't respect dark-skinned black people. And this came from black people themselves who were light skinned, or even brown skinned. Now, Ann was brown skinned, not dark like I am, but light-skinned black people looked down their noses even at her. She told me she had to deal with this attitude

when she was going to West Philadelphia High School, especially with
light-skinned women with so-called good, almost straight or curly hair.
When she told me this I started to pay attention to how people were
treating me with regard to my skin color.

I learned early on that my color set me apart. Plus I was usually
taller than everyone in my class. I began to notice that because I was
dark skinned and tall, women would clutch their bags tighter and look
at me suspiciously when I walked close to them. That left an indelible
impression in my mind. So as I grew older, I had to pull all those negative reactions toward me together and devise plans for how to deal
with them.

When I saw people walking toward me, I could visualize in my
mind what they were thinking about me and I knew instinctively who
distrusted me just by looking into their eyes or by watching their body
language. But I realized that that was the way it was and that it didn't
have anything to do with whether I was a good person or not, whether
I was smart, or deserving, or talented at playing basketball. It just was
what it was, and getting upset about it wasn't going to change anything.
So I just ignored people who treated me badly because I was darker than
they were and refused to answer when they called me a derogatory
name. After I started ignoring anyone who called me "Black Ben" and
when I started to get real good on the playground court, one day someone called me "the Duke of Earl," after Gene Chandler's famous song.
They called me this after I got good. They even made a chant up at
games; whenever I did something great, they would chant, "Duke,
Duke, Duke of Earl."

I responded to that nickname, as I did when they called me "Thomas
Edison" (or "Tommy" for short) because of the way I invented moves and
stuff out on the court. These were nicknames I got in high school, but
none of them stuck.

After practicing hard all summer and playing in pickup games and tournaments whenever and wherever I could, I returned to Bartram in the fall of 1960 with a new attitude about my studies and about play-ing the game of basketball. I was determined to prove myself, both at Bartram and out on the playgrounds. I knew that I loved the game by this time, loved the competition of going up against other really good players, and I knew what I had to do to get better, which was to focus my attention on the game, hone my skills, and practice hard.

I was starting to become aware of a lot of different things by this time, I guess because I was going on 16 years old and growing up. Right before my birthday in 1960, John F. Kennedy was elected president. A lot of black people everywhere supported him over Richard Nixon. Kennedy was the talk of South Philly, and although I hadn't paid too much attention to him up until this point, I saw that a lot of people in my family really liked him and voted for him. He seemed to be cool, had a beautiful, stylish wife named Jacqueline—Jackie for short—so I started paying attention to him after that.

I was practicing my dribbling a lot during the winter of 1961. By this time I was obsessed with playing basketball and getting better, you know, sharpening all my skills. So every day when I came home from school, if it was too cold to go outside to the playground and practice, I'd dribble the basketball in the living room of our house while I was listening to music. I'd dribble with my left hand and then with my right to a beat in my head that went something like, *tah-tah-TAH, tah-tah-TAH, tah-tah-TAH, tah-tah-TAH, tah-tah-TAH.*

I would practice it with different songs. But I started dribbling the ball so hard that the sound of the ball hitting the floor got really loud, and if my mother was home she'd yell, "Earl, stop bouncing that ball so loud in the house!"

I didn't know it at the time, but I was developing a rhythm for drib-bling that filtered up into my head from the music I listened to. I had been taking some piano lessons and was seriously starting to listen to a lot of different kinds of music, like Gladys Knight and the Pips, James Brown, the Platters, even some jazz like Bobby Timmons, a great Philadelphia piano player, and some Miles Davis. So my overall game was starting to fall into a rhythm and all of it—music, risk taking, being creative in inventing shots, my dribbling, passing, the way my body moved—began to develop into a style that was on the verge of being original. The only thing was I couldn't do these moves in a high school game—or practice session—because the playground game wasn't allowed there yet. I would use them off the playground in the future, but not until after I was out of high school.

During the second semester of my junior year of high school, I was promoted to the varsity team from the junior varsity. The varsity was coached by Tony Coma. But Coach Coma cut me from the varsity and I had to play junior varsity again because I was in the 11th grade. The odd thing about being cut from the varsity was that it happened right after I had the greatest day I'd ever had playing basketball. I scored points, made steals, played great defense, blocked shots, made great passes to my teammates, got rebounds, set screens, did all the other things I was supposed to do on the basketball court. Then, I ended up getting cut. I mean, I did everything that was imaginable during that scrimmage. But Coach Coma called me into his office and told me, "You're going to have to play junior varsity."

This really pissed me off! But I didn't say anything because I was too shy. I never questioned why he cut me. I just looked at it as "it is what it is." I knew I couldn't change anything. I guess he already had the varsity team set by then. I mean, there were some good players on the varsity squad. And maybe I would have just rode the bench instead of starting and playing very well (and continuing to develop my game) on the JV squad. Who knows what would have happened? I knew by then that I could be a streaky scorer at times. You know, one day I couldn't miss anything, but the next day my shooting might be off.

I was a center on the JV team but probably would have had to play forward on the varsity, because they had a six-feet-five- or six-feet-six-inch kid named Boyd O'Neal playing center. But getting cut like that just added fuel to the fire burning in my belly to get better and succeed. It made me want to get revenge on those who played above me, which I eventually did.

Even though I was beginning to have some success in developing as a basketball player, some things remained the same. One day, after the season was over, I was on my way to my morning class and I saw this far-out image of my cousin, Jimmy, standing on top of a truck with a machine gun. Now, in order for me to get to school I had to take a bus and the trolley to get there, because it was a long way from where I lived. So that's what I did that day: I took the bus to the trolley. I'm riding the trolley, not thinking of anything, and I look out the window when we come around this turn and there, on top of this truck, in a rival gang territory, is Jimmy with a machine gun and he's just shooting it, just being himself. I never found out what he was shooting at or why because I never asked him about it. I don't even know if he was arrested, but it was him up there all right, sure as shit. It was just unbelievable! But I wouldn't put anything past Jimmy. He was capable of doing anything when he was young, because he was just that crazy. I remember saying out loud, "Oh my God! Oh my God!"

Then I ducked down, covered my head, and hoped nobody knew I was related to him because it was very embarrassing for me to watch Jimmy acting out in that stupid way. Plus, it was also a matter of me being in a rival gang's territory, so I could have gotten shot. Maybe I felt embarrassed also because my outlook on life had been changed by going to high school in a mostly white neighborhood, where things like that didn't happen. Maybe it was because I never liked stupid acts like that, or violence. Or maybe it was because I was maturing, seeing the world through a different lens, and shedding the fact that I might well have approved of this kind of behavior when I was younger but was unwilling to do so now. I don't really know why I was embarrassed at that moment because I can't go back and enter the mind-set of the 16-year-old I was at that time, though I know for certain I would disapprove of Jimmy—or anyone else—behaving that way now.

From that day on I went the opposite way to school, the long way, which took me two hours instead of 45 minutes. I went this way because I didn't ever want to run into that kind of scene again, and I didn't. Like I said, I don't know if Jimmy went to jail for being out there shooting off a machine gun, but both he and his brother Joe went to Graterford State Prison, outside Philadelphia, a few times for something around this time, though I can't remember the exact years. I remember going to visit them in the prison a couple of times during the summer when I was in high school, and they were so different when they were in jail. They looked so humble when I saw them there, dressed all in white, and I felt sorry for them. They both would be talking about getting their lives together when they got out. But as soon as they were paroled and came back home they would fall back into being the same people they were before they went in, doing the same old shit, you know what I mean? And I would say to myself, *Is this the same person I saw in prison?*

They went back and forth over the years, but the last time Joe and Jimmy got out they had both changed for real. But more about that later.

Girls started to become a serious part of my life when I turned 15, and I tried to have one in every part of the city. This lasted until I was 18. But it was a beautiful thing for me, when I started getting into girls. I got into them because I started going to a lot of parties throughout the city and I was a pretty good dancer. Girls liked me because I could dance.

I've never been one of those people who stayed on the telephone and talked a long time. If I called a girl it was generally to say, "Hi, what's going on?" I might stay on for four or five minutes, that's about it.

I would generally talk with them while we both were at home—me at my house and them at theirs—in a relaxed spot. But I found it hard to just talk to anyone for a long time back then because I didn't have a bunch of stuff in my mind. I wasn't talking about too much deep stuff with them, though I was developing a nice, smooth kind of conversational voice, which was probably my biggest asset in terms of trying to get girls to like me back then. I was still shy, but they seemed to like me anyway. They also liked me because I was starting to get a reputation—when I was around 17—for being a pretty good basketball player. So that started to attract them, also. I guess when I got them alone they liked me even better. I don't know. But I never remembered hardly any of their names, because I'm not good at that. I also didn't get to really know them because at the time I was such a hit-and-run artist when it came to women. I was in and out so quickly I couldn't keep all the names in my head. But I do recall a girl named Rosa Lee, who was around 15 and short, and Irene and Juanita, who were sisters, and Gloria and a girl named Claudette, who I took to the prom. I dated all of them, though I don't know why their names stick in my memory; maybe it's because they were sweet. But after them, all the names of the girls I went out with are a blur.

One night sometime during the spring of 1961, my mother sent me to the laundromat up on Wharton Street and 28th, which was close to Benson Elementary School—I think we had moved from 1120 South 26th Street to 1217 Manton at the corner of 26th Street around this time. So I went in there to wash and dry some clothes. After I had put the clothes in the dryer, I was looking out the window when I noticed the zipper on my pants was halfway down. So I took the zipper in my hand and was trying to zip it back up when it got stuck just at the moment when these white women were walking by.

So I got the zipper fixed and headed back to the dryers to finish up when all of a sudden these two white cops came in, shoved me up against the wall, and put handcuffs on me, talking about how I was exposing myself to these white women. I was shocked! I had hardly noticed the women other than to see that they were older than me, kind of plump, and definitely not fine. The cops put me in the meat wagon and they told me on the way down to the police station that they were going to beat my ass, saying, "Who do you think you are, exposing yourself to white women? We'll beat your fucking ass!"

That really scared me.

"I wasn't doing anything to those women," I said. "I was just trying to get my zipper zipped back up because it got stuck."

They just looked at me kind of mean. When we arrived at the police station, they started trying to intimidate me.

"We're going to bust your black ass and send you back to Africa," one said.

But they didn't hit me. They just locked me up and I guess they called my mother, who came down to the station with our congressman Bill Barrett and they bailed me out for about 50 dollars. Congressman Barrett told the policeman that I was a star basketball player, a church-going guy, whatever, and convinced them to throw out the charges and let me go. That was a shocking incident for me, and I think it got me to really start thinking about what it meant to be a black man in this country. I started to become aware of the dangers of that. I hadn't done anything and had a spotless record, so if they could treat me like that, they could do it to anyone who was black—especially a black male—and that was really scary. Still, there was nothing I could do about it; it was what it was and I couldn't change it, at least not back then, in the days before the civil rights movement really took shape.

But it was clear I was growing up, because this wouldn't have happened to me a couple of years earlier. The fact that I was tall and dark
didn't help my situation, either. Still, getting older brought with it other
benefits besides getting better at playing basketball, like really appreci-
ating music more deeply and learning to dance better. The music we
used to dance to back in those days was R&B. We had great disc jockeys
in Philly, like Georgie Woods, Jimmy Bishop, and Joe "Butterball" Tam-
burro. Those guys brought a lot of artists to Philadelphia—the Temptations, Gladys Knight and the Pips, and Smokey Robinson and the
Miracles. We used to have a great time dancing to that music. But Philadelphia was—and still is—a really big small town. A lot of the things
that happen in big cities also happen in Philly, but not on the same scale.
If somebody famous in music came to town, everybody went to see
them at the Uptown Theater.

We also had a lot of gang warfare in Philly around this time, with
people getting shot with zip guns, knifed, all that kind of stuff. Most
of the time, though, it was mano a mano back then. People fought
with their hands, and every now and then somebody had a zip gun.
Even then there weren't a whole lot of killings.

The most important thing to keep in mind when you start talking
about Philadelphia is that it's the way it is because it's comprised of
many little ethnic communities—black, Italian, Irish, Jewish—con-
nected together, and some of the times they can't seem to coexist. But
Philly is a house party town, too, and we have more togetherness than a
lot of other cities. House parties are a big thing in Philly, and I used to
love to go to them. They were something during my generation. Generally what happened was there'd be a house, and you'd go there with two
or three guys. Because you weren't invited to a lot of these parties you
more or less crashed them, and in a lot of instances you might not be
welcome. So there might be fights.

I remember one time some guys came down to our neighborhood

and they had a fella with them named Gangwar Butch. Now, Gangwar was about my size, six three, six four. I remember guys jumping out of a car and going after him, and I've never in my entire life watched a guy that big grow so small. Man, he suddenly got so low to the ground and he was running about a thousand miles a minute. His legs were just going and going, spinning around like bicycle wheels, or the Road Runner in those cartoons. I've never seen anyone run in that position before or since. It was funny! So one group of guys in a gang would come down to a neighborhood and make a sweep and then there'd be retaliation. These were the kinds of things that were going on in my neighborhood, and it seemed like they'd been going on forever. People got beat up, but most of us survived.

You came to house parties to party, you know, to dance, eat cake and food, and to hit on girls—not to fight. But that didn't mean there'd be no fights over something stupid, usually over a girl. Because you might be in another neighborhood and the neighborhood guys might not like you hitting on the girls from their area. So, you might have to fight your way out. A lot of that happened. We fought a lot of the time at house parties, which is why we always traveled to them in groups of three or four—so we could protect each other. But we danced a lot, too, all kinds of dances. It was fun, it was like going to the Palladium Ballroom in New York City, where you had thousands of people. We just had houses full of people at these parties in Philadelphia. It was intimate, but we had just as much fun. See, I wasn't hanging out with anybody at Bartram except with friends I knew from the neighborhood. I was going to school out there, doing what I needed to do, but my energy was consumed by basketball, girls, dressing up, and parties. I wasn't thinking about hardly anything else outside of my own compartmentalized worlds.

It was around this time that I started having serious disagreements with my stepfather. See, he always tried to act like my real father, though I was never as close to him as I guess I could have been. He never beat me or anything like that, but it seemed to me he was always using psychology on me as a way to keep me at bay as I grew up. I remember once when I was about 16 or 17 we got into an argument because I set a glass of water down without putting a coaster under it. That error in my judgment left a mark on top of the wooden console that housed our new Muntz TV and stereo system. Anyway, my stepfather got really mad at me for doing this, and he said to me when he ordered me out of the front room, "Get out of here! You'll never amount to anything!"

He was very angry about what I did, because it might have damaged the surface of the wood for good. Now, I admit I was wrong, but I was about six foot three at the time, much taller than him—he was about five nine—and athletic. Plus, I was street smart by this time and had a couple of large, dangerous cousins, Jimmy and Joe, in my family who might have seriously hurt him if he hit me. So he couldn't even think about physically jumping on me, though I wanted him to, because then I would have had an excuse to beat him up because of the way he was treating my mother.

"I'll kill you!" I shouted.

He was shocked and my mother was afraid someone was going to get hurt, so she jumped between us.

"Git out of the house!" he screamed. "Git out!"

So I left, went down to Aunt Nicey's house to chill out for a minute. After that the psychological mind games he'd always played on me didn't matter to me anymore. They didn't work, because by now people were always trying to use similar mind games on me while playing basketball, or when they didn't want me to succeed. I just didn't listen to that kind of stuff anymore, because I was beginning to know who I was and it didn't make any difference what anybody said about me when they tried to play games with my mind. None of that stuff worked because I'd learned to just block it out.

I never was very close to John Smith, though I didn't hate him or anything like that. He was an okay kind of guy, but, like I said, I just didn't like the way he treated my mother. For example, on occasions my stepfather would stay out late, or go away for a couple of days. Then, when he came home, he and my mother would argue loudly and fiercely about his whereabouts; they would fight sometimes, and he would hit her. I remember one time when this happened, my mother saw me watching, and she looked at me and winked, as if to tell me, "It's okay, I got it. It's under control."

If she hadn't done that, I don't know what would have happened, because I was so angry with him there's no telling what I might have done. I think I probably would have jumped on my stepfather and beat his ass, even though I've always hated violence.

Now, as I have said, my mother wasn't a fat woman, but she was kind of big, being around five foot eleven—which is where I got my height—and she was very strong. She was bigger than my stepfather and could take a punch, too (and she took a lot of them in that relationship). My stepfather, who looked like the actor Courtney Vance (the husband of actress Angela Bassett), was a muscular man who always took care of himself and his body. Those fights I saw between my mother and step-father were one of the things that led me to feel violence was never the answer to any problem even between men, but especially between men and women. That's why I never wanted to get involved in hitting a woman, because I saw a lot of it when I was growing up and I knew what it did to me as a kid watching it happen.

My mother would always do anything she could to try and protect me in those situations. But seeing those fights also taught me what men like to do when they're wrong. My stepfather would come in late and try to have sex with my mother, as if fucking was the cure-all that would solve everything, but it didn't. It never worked on my mother, because they just kept on fighting. I knew that my mother was trying hard just to keep everything together and to make sure we were able to grow up as painlessly as possible. So I grew up under those circumstances with my stepfather. It wasn't a hard life, because he always brought home the bacon, you know, the money.

My stepfather's skill as a butcher came in handy later on, when he and my mother bought the building with the grocery store and renamed it Smith's Grocery Store. The store was on the first floor and we lived on the second and third floors; our kitchen was located on the first floor, behind the grocery store. The building was located at South 26th and Manton Street. My stepfather butchered all the meats there, and that store kept my family—and me—in money, even after I graduated from high school. I could always go into the store and go through the cash register to get myself a little pocket change, fix myself a sandwich to go. Later on, when my guys came over after basketball games, we could eat well. My mother always said I ate up the profits. So having the grocery store was cool. My stepfather was always good financially for the family. It was just that he and I had this strained relationship because of how he treated my mother, and I always loved my mother more than anything in the world.

We also had a certain dress style in the clothes we wore back in Philadelphia during those days, and we thought the clothes we wore reflected the kind of city we were: cool. There was a style called "yock," and if you were a yock that meant you were a cool dresser. Yocks wore brogans that were always shined real high, or quarter vance (a shoeshine that was real high gloss). You wore your pants up a little high, a tad bit over the tops of your shoes. You also wore a little cap, you know, not the Big Apple kind of cap, but just a little straight cap with a little bill and a snap up in the front. When you dressed like this, this said you were cool. You wore coats and button-down shirts with no ties. But if you did wear a tie, you wore it with a button-down shirt. You might have a suit, whatever. But your outfits were always sharp and clean, pressed real well. We called this pressed look "blade," which meant you were sharp as a tack, dressed to the nines, and looking good.

Toward the end of my junior year, in 1961, Coach Klingman told me that Coach Coma was thinking of bringing Smitty, Leap, and me up to the varsity squad to stay and to play in the tournament games, and he did. The varsity already had a really good squad that many thought was one of the best in the city. Boyd O'Neal, who was a senior and one of two black players on the team, was All-City and played the center spot. The other black player was Willie Mobley, six foot two, who went on to be signed by the New York Yankees baseball team. The other three starters were Chris Kefalos, a six four sophomore forward; Bill Spencer, a six foot senior point guard; and Bob Lohse, a senior, who was about six one. With those guys already in place, we knew we might not play too much, but still it was exciting to get called up and I saw it as an opportunity to move closer to my dream of playing at a very high level and on a more public stage.

The star of the varsity team, Boyd O'Neal, was a really good guy and a tenacious rebounder. When he graduated from Bartram, he went on to Southern Illinois University, where he played with Walt Frazier. The other good player on that team was Chris Kefalos, who was a really good shooter. (Chris was Greek, and later, after playing ball for Temple University, he went over to Greece and played for the Greek national team; he stayed over there for years, playing and coaching.)

My two friends and I were overjoyed when we were promoted up to the varsity, even though it happened at the end of the second semester. Coach Coma brought us up because he wanted to have a stronger team to play in the championship tournament, and adding the three of us did make our team better. I became a starter when I was called up, although I didn't score much. I did manage to do a few things that made people notice me, though.

Bartram went on to play in the city championship game at the

Palestra that year, which is where we played all the championship basketball games in Philadelphia back then. We were matched up against
Saint Thomas More High School, a Catholic school, on Saint Patrick's
Day, with two Irish guys, Art McNally and Tom McCollum, serving as
referees. We lost that game 51–50, in a very close back-and-forth, nip-
and-tuck battle.

That championship game was very competitive and the loss hurt
me real bad, because I thought we really had the best team. Some people said the referees impacted the game because Saint Thomas More
was a Catholic team comprised mostly of Irish players. So the loss was
a little controversial. But who was going to say anything? Saint Thomas
More had some good players, even if I don't remember their names,
except for Bobby Zell, who I think scored 11 points in that game. They
also had a guy named Larry White who maybe had about 12 and
another guy named Joe Burton who led them with 14 points. For us,
I think Lohse scored 11 points, O'Neal had 13, and Mobley had 14. I
played for four minutes and scored 4 points, and I think Leap played in
that game but I don't think he scored. In truth, I also thought there
were some questionable calls. But it is what it is and they won and that's
history now. Case closed.

Playing in the city championship game was really memorable for
me, especially because I was playing at the legendary Palestra—the University of Pennsylvania's gym—for the first time and hearing all those
screaming people. It was a shot of adrenaline for me, and it gave me a lot
of confidence going into my senior year.

There was something I noticed about playing with my white teammates at Bartram, and with Boyd O'Neal also, who was black. What I
understood was that the white players hung with each other off the
court, and even when we weren't playing together in the gym. Maybe it
was because they were from the same neighborhood and it was a cultural thing. Maybe it was a racial thing. I don't know and didn't think

too deeply about it at the time. On the other hand, the black guys on the team did the same thing; we hung with each other in the same way, with the exception of Boyd O'Neal, who kind of hung by himself. See, he was from an upper-class black family that lived in integrated West Philly, and me and my other black teammates were all from our section of South Philly, which was almost all black. Maybe that was cultural, too, or a class thing. Again, I don't know, but it was just something I noticed then and would see a lot of on teams I played for over the years—and in society—later on.

I worked harder to get better and that hard work and focus helped me a lot in terms of improving my game over the summer of 1961. By that summer I had developed a lot of different skills—my passing, dribbling, and shooting had all improved significantly—out on the playground with the Trotters, and by this time I was the star of that team. But as we got better individually, we also grew as a team. I had started out with these guys as the low man on the totem pole, but by now I was the top man on that pole. At that time, we were playing on the playground against guys in college and my confidence in my game was growing by leaps and bounds. It's funny because I went from sitting on the sidelines watching other players get to play and hoping to get picked to being the one who got picked all the time. That was very satisfying.

By the time I was going into my senior year in high school, everybody wanted me on their squad in those playground battles, and those games were great. We had a saying on the playgrounds in Philly, "Rise and shine," which meant as long as your team won when you played in a pickup game, the team could keep playing. If you lost you had to sit down and wait until some other team lost; then you might play again. But that losers list was long. So when you were playing, everybody played hard, played their asses off, so they wouldn't have to sit down and wait for another chance to play, which might take all day. Essentially, those people that were beginning to know about me in Philadelphia knew me for being able to go to the basket and do trick shots off of the backboard. Besides, after I lost a game the other team coming onto the court always picked me to run with them.

During that summer, I added a skill that improved my game dramatically. This happened when an older guy named Ron Ford showed me how he did the spin move, which I had watched him do a couple of times out on the playground when I played against him. The move really excited me. So one day he showed me how he executed the move. The way he did it was that he used two hands when he spun, but the hand he had the ball in was held away from his body. For instance, if he was dribbling with his left hand he would transfer the ball to his right hand out on the court and then spin with it in that hand and go to the hole. When he spun, he would do it with the ball in his right hand, but it would be away from his body, and that was too slow for me.

So, the way I taught myself to do it was that I would be facing my opponent out on the court, coming at him at full speed. Then I would stutter-step the defender, fake right, and when he moved to one side or defended me going right, I would spin to the left with the ball in my right hand, close to my body, and get my shoulders past the opponent. Then I would move my head and shoulder by him just as I was spinning with the ball still in my right hand (it could be my left hand, too, because I taught myself to do it with both hands). Then when I was past the defender—the only way he could stop me was to put his arm out and that would be a foul—I'd be on my way to the bucket, and then there really wasn't much anybody could do but just watch me go up and score. That move was a revelation for me. It was also a fluid move, all in one motion, and it had to be executed lightning quick. It was also a devastating move for my opponent to guard, and once I got it all together it raised my game to another level. When I added the spin move to my repertoire, you know, that was the beginning of me being able to hold my own against anyone playing basketball in Philadelphia.

That was the difference between my spin move and Ron's: Mine was quicker than his and got me to the basket faster. But I only did the move out on the playground, never in organized games, until I left Philadelphia to go to college. Still, I give credit to Ron Ford for showing me the move and to my great friend Smitty for letting me know who showed me the move after I had forgotten who it was.

The interesting thing about becoming "the man" in any sport is that when you become a star you start to carry yourself differently. Your walk changes, as does your attitude. And your ears start turning around like those of cats and you can even pick up the whispers that are going around in the crowd when you walk in to play. When you're the man, you hear people whispering your name, almost in awe: "Look, that's Earl Monroe—'Thomas Edison,' 'the Duke of Earl'! Man, he's a bad motherfucker! One of the best around!"

When I started hearing those things being said about me it changed the way I felt about myself and my game. Now, I started wanting the ball in my hands at crunch time out on the playground and in my last year at Bartram, so I would have it in my hands so I could take the last shot if that's what was needed to win a game. I found myself starting to strut a little, even though I was a very shy person. But I found myself getting used to it, even reveling in that role to the point where I was not afraid of taking that last shot because I believed I could make it and, more importantly, my teammates believed I could make it, too.

I remember a girl who was in my homeroom class in 10th grade. Her name was Patricia Holte, and she later became Patti LaBelle. She became the leader of the group Patti LaBelle and the Bluebelles, which was later shortened to just plain LaBelle. Then, she went out on her own and kept right on putting out hits. Patti was just a friend back at John Bartram; we never went out together on a date. I remember her winning the talent show in our junior year of high school with her singing, which was off-the-charts great even back then.

That talent show was organized by a student teacher named Eileen
Brown, who later became the president of Cambridge College in Boston.
Anyway, people were already whispering about how good Patti was
when she just blew all the competition away with her fabulous voice in
that talent show. What happened was, Patti was part of a girl group and
another girl was singing lead and she couldn't cut it, couldn't hit the
high notes. So Patti just kind of pushed her aside and stepped out front
and *bam!* she hit all the notes and everyone went, like, *Whoooooo!* Her
voice was unbelievable and it's been like that ever since. Her voice never
really seemed to change, she's been able to transform herself so many
different times. She's had a phenomenal career and she's just an incredible person. I guess hearing her at that talent show was just a sign of
things to come, because I always knew she had it in her to be very
successful.

Sometime during my senior year I ran into Ollie Chamberlain, the
younger brother of the great Wilt Chamberlain. See, Ollie went to Bartram with me and I had always liked the socks that Wilt wore when he
played. The socks were called "hunter" socks. They were thicker than
regular socks and they had red tops. I wore them because Wilt wore
them and because I had little skinny legs. So the socks were long and
could cover up most of my legs because they extended up to and over
my calves. But I always wanted to get a pair from Wilt because his were
even longer. So one day when I saw Ollie at school, I asked him;

"Ollie, does Wilt have an extra pair of hunter socks laying around?
If he does do you think you could get me a pair?"

So he said, "Yeah, Earl, he's got plenty, I'll get you a pair."

The next day he brought them to school with him and I wore those
socks in practice, in games, on the playgrounds, everywhere I played. I
wore them so much I wore the bottoms out of them. After that I wore
them over other socks when I played, which hid my skinny legs a little
more. Man, I wore those socks my whole senior year and then I retired

them and put them in safekeeping. But there's a final story about these socks that I will tell toward the end of this story, which comes at an important moment.

We had another good squad during my senior year at Bartram, with Chris Kefalos; John Lampe, a six-foot-four forward; Leaping John Anderson; Frank Kunze, a six three guard; my friend Smitty at point guard; and me playing center. I had a real good year and led the city in scoring, averaging 21.4 points a game. That's when people—you know, sportswriters, college coaches, and fans—really started to notice me. I think our record was 13 and 3, and we played for the Public School League championship against West Philadelphia, which we lost 76 to 73. That was another hard-fought, very close game.

I made All-City that year and that was cool. I appreciated the honor and all of that, but I had expected to make that team because I had earned it. Still, my Bartram team hadn't won the city championship during the two years I played on the varsity, so that was a downer, and perhaps tempered the honor of even having made the All-City team. Because in the end it's all about winning championships as a team, and that's always been my goal, even though individual honors are important, too.

There were some real good players who made the All-City team that year, too. Guys like Billy Oates, who went to Bishop Neumann and later became an NBA referee. Another guy named Matt Guokas made it, too, and he later played with the 76ers. He went on to coach the 76ers, was the first coach of the Orlando Magic, and later became a commentator for the NBA. Then there was George Mack, who played for Edison High School and went on to play guard for North Carolina A&T, where we went up against each other many times. There was also a guy named Tom Duff, who went to Saint Joseph's Prep and then on to LaSalle College, on that team; it was a pretty decent class.

There were other good high school players around then also, like

Cliff Anderson, who played with George Mack at Edison and went on to play at Saint Joseph's University and in the NBA with the Lakers for four years. Fred Carter (who later played pro ball with me with the Baltimore Bullets and is now an announcer for some NBA games) was at Franklin High School; Frank Card played for West Philadelphia and I think scored 24 points when we lost to them in the Public School League final. The All-City team from Philadelphia always went to Allentown, Pennsylvania, to play in the Allentown tournament, and I played pretty well up there, too.

After I graduated from high school I only had two scholarship offers, so I really didn't know what to do with myself. But this was the beginning of a kind of lost year, one where I hung around Philadelphia playing ball in the summertime, working some, and trying to get my feet up under me. It was kind of weird finding myself in this situation, but it was also kind of good because I started to do a lot of thinking about my life, you know, where I was going and whatnot, so in the end that was good for me going forward. I knew I had become a really good basketball player, that my skills had improved greatly. I was also beginning to marry the playground game to the more structured traditional one.

Part Two

STEPPING ON THE GAS:

RUNNING OVER POTHOLES

ON THE

ROAD TO GLORY

Chapter 4

BECOMING A STAR
IN SOUTH PHILLY:
THE TURNING POINT,
SUMMER 1962

AFTER I GRADUATED FROM HIGH SCHOOL IN 1962, I really didn't want to go to college at first. I thought instead that I was going to play pro ball with the Philadelphia Tapers of the ABL (American Basketball League), but the league folded that December, in the middle of its second season. That really disappointed me and forced me to start thinking about my future, you know, weighing my options. I had been thinking about going pro right away because in my head I thought I was ready. By this time I just had total confidence in myself, in my game, and in my ability to make the jump and play with the big boys. Looking back now with the knowledge I possess of the pro game, it's clear to me that I wasn't ready, as far as my talent was concerned. But that's what I wanted to do, what I had in my head at that time. So I stayed out of college for a year. Instead I went to a prep school affiliated with Temple University with the idea that I would then go on to Temple University,

New York University, or one of the other schools in the East that had shown interest in me.

Somehow I didn't receive as many scholarship offers as some of the other top players in Philadelphia. I knew I had two offers, one from Western Michigan, in Kalamazoo, and the other one from Montana State. But I didn't want to play at those schools because they were too far away and I didn't think either would prepare me to play professional basketball, which was my ultimate goal. But guys like Matt Guokas and Cliff Anderson, who both graduated the same year I did, received major scholarships.

Then, in 1963 I found out that my high school coach, Tony Coma, had kept a lot of college scholarship offers from me. He just didn't show them to me. I never did understand why he did this, because I thought I had a very good relationship with him. I don't know if it was racial or not, but I never went back to see him after I found out, until Bartram held a dinner in his honor in 1995, about a year before he died. I didn't talk to him much at that dinner, so I didn't get a chance to ask him why he did that to me. So until this day I don't really know the reason why he did it. We were cordial at that dinner but that was all. As I said earlier, I can be a vengeful person when someone does something I feel is wrong to me. I felt that Coach Coma had wronged me by not letting me know about those other scholarship offers, so I just kept my distance from him from then on.

After leading the city in scoring in 1962, I felt that my whole game was coming together. I had played center in high school, but I knew I would have to play guard at the next level. So I intensified practicing my floor-game skills, you know, my ball handling, passing, and shooting skills, with constant workouts. My guys Smitty, Wilkie, Clis, Leaping John, and me used to gather at Landreth schoolyard to play against the guys from across 25th Street, which was actually the dividing line between the territories of the Road gang, led by my cousins Jimmy and Joe, and the 24th Street gang, which was on the north side of South 25th Street. A train trestle ran straight down 25th Street and became a bridge about a block away from where I used to live and two blocks from Landreth schoolyard.

On a very hot July day, my guys and me went over to play rise and shine basketball at Landreth. We won all of our games that morning, and as we were walking off the court, the team we had just beaten started jawing at us—a player named Matt Jackson in particular. Matt had been the leading high school scorer in Philadelphia in my junior year, scoring about 23 points a game playing for Bok Technical. He had made All–Public League and All-City, and he was considered the top high school player in South Philly. Matt was about six foot five, with a sweet jump shot and a velvety touch around the basket. He had the body type of a pro forward. I was six three and about 170 pounds at the time, but what he didn't know—because he had been away attending South Carolina State College—was that I had some shit for his ass that wouldn't wait.

When all the jawing started we were right outside the schoolyard, so I just turned to Matt and said, "Hey, why don't we settle this one-on-one?"

He looked at me kind of shocked and then said, "You got it. Let's do it!"

When Matt and I went back into the playground to get it on, word went out like crazy on the community drum. Suddenly, while we were warming up to play, the entire schoolyard filled up, like a wildfire spreading. It seemed like everywhere I looked, even outside the fences, there were people, some I had never seen in my life! That was amazing. Everybody there was egging us on—my guys for me and his guys for him.

We agreed the game should be played to 22 points and that the first one there would be the winner. We didn't shake hands or nothing like that, but flipped a coin to determine who would get the ball first. Like I said, I bet five dollars on the game and when I said that Smitty looked at me in amazement, knowing I never bet on a game. I looked back at him and just winked. I figured I'd give Matt a little something else to think about, let him know I was confident. So he said, "Okay."

Matt won the coin toss, got the ball, and hit the first bucket on a nice jumper. Then he took me down low and hit another. Then he made another jumper. Before I knew it, the score was 6 to 0. We were playing "make it and take it," which meant that if you made the basket you kept the ball. My rooting section was silent, but I wasn't worried because I knew I could score bunches in a hurry. Then Matt missed a jumper. I grabbed the rebound and took the ball to the foul line, which is what you do in one-on-one if the ball touches the backboard or the rim.

I looked Matt in the eye and he looked me back in mine. He was bigger than me but wasn't quicker, so I faked a jump shot and when he jumped out at me I went around him for an easy layup. When I got the ball back, I looked him in the eye again and he didn't move, so I pulled up and hit a jumper from the free throw line. Now I had him on a string, because he didn't know what I was going to do. This made it easier for me to go to the rest of my stuff, my "la-la" moves going to the basket. I had options now. I could go up in the air and spin the ball off the backboard, or as I floated in I could switch hands and lay it in. Or I could ball fake and score. Either way, by the time I finally missed I'd run off 10 straight points to make the score 10 to 6 in my favor.

When I missed, Matt got the rebound, took the ball to the foul line, backed me down, and made a short jump hook. Ten to 8. Then he missed his next shot and I got the rebound. I took it to the foul line, faked a jump shot, and when he went for it I spun around him to the left and banked in the shot off the backboard with my left hand. The crowd started going wild and my juices were flowing. I proceeded to hit two more jumpers over Matt, which made the score 16 to 8. Three more baskets would end the game. At this point I thought I could do no wrong and, knowing that I had an audience out there that was going crazy, I started toying with Matt like a child plays with a yo-yo. I made another nice move to the basket and scored. Matt was looking worried now, but I was overconfident and on my next possession I tried a flukey-duke spin shot off the top of the backboard and missed.

Matt was a year or two older than me and had a big reputation to protect. He was angry by this point, and after grabbing the rebound off my missed shot he started to bull me with his stronger body, running off 6 straight points. Then he looked at me and said, "It's all over!"

The score was 18 to 14. He made another nifty move, a running bank shot off the board, to close to within two at 18 to 16. A hush fell over the crowd. I started recounting all the moves he had made in my mind and realized that he was always going to his right. If he went left he would pull up and shoot a jumper. So on his next possession I played up on his right hand, forced him left, and as he pulled up to shoot the jumper as I knew he would, I put my hand on the ball, stole it from him and went in and made a layup. Now the score was 20 to 16. Matt was shocked and pissed. I saw fear in his eyes. The crowd went crazy and my guys were slapping hands and cheering like mad.

In my mind there was no denying me now. My confidence was just soaring. He knew it and I knew it. I could already see defeat in his eyes. My next move was a double-fake. I started by faking a jumper, which drew Matt out. I put the ball down with my left hand, then pulled it back between my legs and as his momentum carried him toward me, I made a strong move to the basket, went by him, and as I soared (I felt like I could have dunked) I laid the ball over the rim and into the basket. Twenty-two to 16. Game over. The crowd went berserk. People ran onto the court and hugged me. I felt like a hero for the very first time on the basketball court. I had felt good making All-City, but this was a different feeling because I hadn't felt like a hero then.

When they carried me off the court up on their shoulders, I felt that I had done something heroic in my own community. As I went by him, Matt and I shook hands but he didn't say anything. There didn't seem to be any hard feelings, but I don't know. It was evident who was the best man on that day, you know, the best player. I was able to pull it off and beat him, beat him handily. He had his fans there, too, and they went away glum. My people went wild.

Like I said, Matt went on to play at South Carolina State, a black institution, and had an okay college basketball career. But I don't think he was ever the same after I beat him because he knew what had happened to him, knew that whatever reputation he had had now belonged to me. That game established my status and reputation as a basketball player in South Philadelphia, because it's out on the playgrounds where you earn your reputation as a basketball player. Word of what I had done to Matt Jackson spread quickly in the basketball community. It also opened up the eyes of some people who weren't in my tight little circle as to the depth of my game. Up until this point, most guys I played against only saw me making certain moves they knew I could make, like little shots around the basket, or making little moves from down in the post, because I had played center in high school. They never knew I could shoot great jump shots or dribble and execute spin moves out on the floor like they saw me do that day. So I surprised a lot of people with my new bag of basketball tricks that day.

Like I said, Matt didn't say anything to me, not even "Nice game." Nothing. My guess is that he was very disappointed in himself, and I could understand that. I had just gotten out of high school and I had proved a lot not only to myself, but to others as well. Everything had just changed hands. That win not only gave me a lot of satisfaction, it also gave me a reputation to protect, a crown, so to speak, that a lot of players in South Philly wanted to knock off my head. Now a lot of players wanted to be "like Earl," and in order to do that they had to challenge me. I knew it wasn't personal. They just wanted to be the best, too, and I could understand that. But it never happened.

That game against Matt Jackson was also the turning point in my basketball life, and on the way home I was so pumped up that I don't think my feet ever touched the ground. My reputation was growing by leaps and bounds, and things would never, ever be the same again. I never got the five dollars we played for, but I got everything else I wanted that day.

Later on that day I began reflecting back on how I had reached that point, a place in my life and basketball development where I could win a one-on-one game against a guy like Matt Jackson. This led me to recognize the fact that I had always practiced hard since I'd fallen in love with the game, since I decided that I wanted to be great at playing the game of basketball. After a certain point I was always playing ball, you know, shooting around, even in wintertime. If it had snowed, my guys and me would get shovels and shovel the snow off to the sides so we could shoot the ball on the court out there at Trotters Ground.

Basketball just consumed me at that time, and I had in my head the idea that if I wanted to be that "number one" player, I had to work at getting better and better, and that meant practicing hard every chance I got. That wasn't difficult because basketball had become such a huge part of my life, not only being able to play but also having guys around me that liked to play as much as I did. It was around this time that I started to really understand what I later called "the science of the game," which basically starts out as trial and error and was what the old heads had been teaching me out on the playgrounds. They told me we just had great basketball in Philadelphia back in the day, but that it was on the playgrounds where the *really* great basketball was played. And it was on the playgrounds where the science of the game was (and still is) passed down from generation to generation.

There were guys on the playground who had been playing basketball in Philly for a long time and had learned all the nuances of the game. Their knowledge of the game, which we called "30 years," was invaluable to me. These old heads had seen and played against them all, too, from John Chaney to Wilt Chamberlain and Guy Rodgers. Today, the old heads talk about my generation, on to guys like Gene Banks, then Rasheed Wallace and Kobe Bryant and Eddie Griffin. The old heads now are the sons of people I used to play against, which is a trip: guys like Kobe's father, Joe "Jellybean" Bryant, who made the NBA for a few years before playing out his career in Italy. In other words, "30 years" was being passed down to young players like me on Philadelphia's playgrounds, and that tradition continues to this day.

The old heads helped me realize that the Philadelphia game was a structured finesse game, full of finesse players. And there was always a teaching element to Philadelphia basketball. Even when I would be playing against a certain guy on the playground, he would come up to me after the game and say, "Earl, you could have done another move than the one you tried on me when I stole the ball." We shared that information with each other so we could all get better.

I would take that information with me for the next time I played. Philly players weren't great dunkers, like they were in North Carolina, and we didn't drive to the hoop like they did in New York City. We were just smooth players, and that's part of the makeup of people from Philadelphia; we try to be smooth in most things that we do. And all of this goes back to the way the city is: It's a finesse city. The music, the humor are also about finesse, you know, laid back, but at the same time on the mark. We're doing little runs in the music and in basketball games and we learned that just from playing against guys who taught us. (I would learn later that in New York City you have all these areas—

Staten Island, the Bronx, Brooklyn, Queens, and Manhattan—that each play separate styles. In Philadelphia you have different areas, too, but everyone—white and black—basically plays the same style, though mine was a little different, more creative, more original to me and my personality.)

There seems to be a coming together of talent and teaching in Philadelphia. When I got older, people were always asking me if I was influenced by the Harlem Globetrotters, and I wasn't, because I never got to see the Globetrotters play until one night when I was playing pro ball in Baltimore and they played the first half of a doubleheader before our game. That was the first time I ever saw them play in person, or even on television or film. But from the style I developed, many thought they had influenced me. But I never had any Globetrotter in my game. My game just came naturally, you know, through trial and error. And it came out of the Philly game; I just added some stuff to it that was my own. My foundation came from what the old players kept telling me and showing me out on the playgrounds and it all came rushing back to me that day when I was walking home after beating Matt Jackson.

You know, it's interesting how I saw all of this transpire by looking back, how I arrived at the place I found myself in at that moment. I realized it was almost like a movie, my life, and it was all up in my mind. The thing is that reflection is almost always good. You can't really appreciate good things that happen to you unless you've had a lot of problems in your life that you've been able to work through. I understood that some of my motivation to succeed was a desire to become good at something a lot of people thought I couldn't do, and that some of my drive came from being very dark skinned.

I knew I had to be twice as good as many of my counterparts in everything, especially Caucasians, but light- and brown-skinned black people, too. I knew this after my sister Ann hipped me to it and by the way people treated me, even in the black community, where the color thing can be even worse because you have that separation of class along skin-color lines there. So I had to deal with that problem, also. It was only then that I was able to appreciate what my talent laid out for me. And playing ball gave me the opportunity to understand this.

Beating Matt Jackson was the culmination of all the things I had gone through, and then, reflecting back on that journey, I was able to appreciate just how far I had come. I was thankful, spiritually speaking, and I felt blessed.

Chapter 5

A LOST YEAR:
1962 TO 1963

I DIDN'T KNOW IT AT THE TIME, but beating Matt Jackson in that grudge match etched my name onto the list of all the best basketball players in Philadelphia. But because I only had two scholarship offers that I knew of, and because my dream of going pro straight out of high school ended when the Tapers franchise (and the entire ABL) crashed and burned, I found myself at a crossroads of sorts.

After that huge disappointment, I decided in the fall of 1962 to enroll at Temple Prep, which I thought would prepare me academically to attend LaSalle College, Temple University, or New York University (my grades at Bartram hadn't been high enough to allow me to enroll at major universities). Then one day this guy named Leon Whitley came and interviewed me. I knew him from his having been around at some of the games I played. In those days, recruiters were guys who had played at their respective schools and looked for players who they thought would be good for their school teams. Leon was about 10 years older than me, and he had gone to a black college down in the South called Winston-Salem Teachers College (now Winston-Salem State University), in Winston-Salem, North Carolina. Leon asked me if I wanted to go to school.

I told him I was going to prep school to play basketball and pull my grades up so I could go to a major school.

"Okay," he said. "I'll check back with you later."

Smitty and I both had applied and gotten accepted into Temple Prep, so in the fall of 1962 we started attending classes there and practicing with their basketball team. Besides pulling my grades up, I had chosen Temple Prep because I wanted to see how I would measure up against the top-flight competition of the highly rated freshman teams of the Big Five, which consisted of LaSalle, the University of Pennsylvania, Saint Joseph's, Temple, and Villanova University. Back in those days freshmen couldn't play on the varsity level, so they had their own teams. That's who we would be playing against, as well as against some other squads.

I found out very quickly that I was out-and-out the best player on my Temple Prep team, and against all the freshmen I played against that season. No question. Smitty also played well. We beat up on all the freshman teams we played, whacking them all by wide margins. As for my own personal play, I was busting all those teams out, meaning that I played very well against all of them, scored a lot of points, dished out many assists, and just generally led my team to wins. I played for Temple Prep until I saw that I could dominate against highly rated competition. For me, it was all about competition whenever I played the game of basketball.

Around this time there was some talk of my possibly enrolling at Rider College (now Rider University) because someone told me they were considering offering me or another ballplayer a basketball scholarship. I always liked Rider and thought I might want to go there to study and play basketball. So Temple Prep and Bartram sent them my transcripts and a photograph, but we never heard back from them. Later, through the grapevine, I heard they selected the other guy, who happened to be white.

Maybe it was my grades, which weren't as good as they could have been. The funny thing about the Rider incident is that Digger Phelps, who went on to coach Notre Dame for 20 seasons, was a graduate assistant coach there at the time, having graduated the year before. Now, I don't know if Digger had any say in who they recruited, or if he had any power at all at that time, but I would have loved to have played on a team that Digger was coaching.

By the time I found out that Rider had chosen another player over me, I had already proved that I could be successful against the competition the freshman teams of the Big Five provided. So I dropped out of Temple Prep after the basketball season, in February 1963. I found myself a job and went to work at Tartan Knitting Mill to think things through and earn some needed money. But the negative effect of dropping out of Temple Prep was that it killed my chances of improving my grades to a level that would qualify me to enter elite universities. The job I took paid $1.15 an hour, which was about 30-some dollars a week (I got Wilkie a job there, too). It bought me a little time to try to figure out a game plan for my future, and that's what I focused on doing. No big thing. I just rolled with the punches, because, like I always say, "it is what it is."

Then, later on during the summer of 1963, Leon Whitley came back to see me and asked if I wanted to go to school at Winston-Salem. This time, after what had happened at Temple Prep, I said, "Yeah, why not?" But then I added, "I'll go if my man Smitty can go with me."

"Okay," Mr. Whitley said. "I'll pass that information on to Coach Gaines and I'll get back to you."

So Whitley spoke with Coach Gaines and Coach agreed to arrange work-study scholarships for Smitty and me for our first year down in Winston-Salem, provided we scored high enough on our SATs and he liked us as ballplayers. The work-study scholarships provided us with part-time jobs to help pay for our books, tuition, and food, and the

school paid for the rest, like room and board. This arrangement, according to Coach Gaines, would begin with the fall 1963 semester. After
that, the deal was if we played well then we would get full scholarships
the following year. Leon told me Coach Clarence Gaines, better known
as "Big House," would pick us up at the train station. Then, later in the
summer when we were ready to go, he came by and gave us money for
the train fare and a little extra money for meals. That was that. The day
Smitty and I were to travel on the train, I went to work wearing a suit.
When he saw me dressed like that, my boss knew something was up.

"Why are you wearing that suit?" he asked.

I told him I was going off to attend college later on that afternoon.
He looked at me and said, "You might as well go home now, because
there's no sense in you being here half the day."

So I left and that afternoon around three or four, my mother and
stepfather took Smitty and me down to the train station and put us on
a train bound for Winston-Salem. It was so cold on that train that we
huddled up together because we only had one trench coat between us.
Man, we spread that trench coat out across both of our bodies and still
froze our behinds off all the way down to Winston-Salem. Man, that
was the train ride from hell! I don't remember much about that ride
except how cold it was and that we had to move to the back of the train
with all the other black people once we passed Washington, DC. Me
and Smitty sat in the last seats of the train car on the left side and we
saw fields and farms and gardens passing by. Then, when another train
would pass us going north, there would be this big whooshing sound and
our train would shake like nobody's business.

This was my first time going south of Washington, DC, and when
we were somewhere in Virginia, I looked out the window and, because
the train was moving slow, I saw these huge fields of white balls on the
tops of vines. Black people were picking the balls with their hands and

stuffing them into sacks. Now, I'm a city guy and had seen collard greens, tomatoes, vegetables, and whatnot growing in my grandmother's garden and around the neighborhood. I had also seen peach trees and some other fruit that looks like grapes. But I had never seen anything like this.

"Look, Earl, people pickin' cotton!" Smitty said.

"Is that really cotton?" I said.

"Oh, yeah. That's cotton," he says.

"That's what the clothes we wear are made from?"

"Yeah," he says, "that's where they come from."

Smitty had obviously seen people picking cotton before, perhaps even picked some himself. But the only picking I had done was when I picked blueberries in New Jersey one summer when I was thirteen or fourteen. The owners of the fields would come and pick us up off street corners in South Philly and load us up in trucks early in the morning. Then, after we arrived on the farms, we'd pick blueberries all day at 10, 15 cents a bushel. After we finished picking we'd get back on the trucks and they'd drive us back to South Philly. I would get home around five or six o'clock in the evening with two dollars and 50 cents in my pocket. Man, that was hard work.

After we left the huge cotton fields in Virginia, and right before it got real dark, I saw all these expansive meadows with large-leafed plants growing everywhere. And an older black man, the Pullman porter, said, "Look at that, look at that. Look at all them tobacco fields."

Then he looked at us and asked us where we were going.

"We going to college," Smitty said, because I was too shy to speak.

Then the porter just laughed. But soon after that he got off the train and another Pullman porter got on. When we arrived in the Winston-Salem train station after a 12-hour trip, it was late at night, after midnight, maybe two or three in the morning. It was pitch black and nobody was there to greet us. Plus, we didn't have any numbers to call anyone. We knew the coach's name was Clarence E. "Big House" Gaines, but we didn't know what he looked like. When we got to Winston-Salem we were the only ones who got off at that stop and the platform was totally empty. It was just the hawk, you know, the cold wind cutting through us like a razor blade, and it was so cold!

So we stood there, shivering at one end of the platform, looking down to the other end as the train left the station and continued choo-chooing south. We stood there shivering, huddled up against a wall, looking down the platform. After a while we saw coming toward us this little figure that kept getting bigger and bigger and bigger until it got right up on us. It was Coach Gaines. He came up, introduced himself, and we shook hands.

"You boys from Philadelphia?" he asked.

"Yes, sir," I said, "Leon Whitley sent us down."

"Okay," he said. "Is this all your bags?"

We nodded our heads and said in unison, "Yes, sir."

"Okay," he said, "bring them on upstairs and I'll take you to the campus."

Then Coach Gaines turned around and walked away. We followed him upstairs, dragging our bags, and put them in his car, which was a brown Mercury station wagon. He drove off and took us to the campus, which was about three or four minutes away. By this time light was starting to come up. Coach Gaines took us to the downstairs part of the gym and we bunked down there, sleeping with the football team. That's where we stayed for a while. It was something. A real wake-up call, sleeping alongside a bunch of football players, who are much more physical guys, more aggressive then basketball players are. I think basketball players deal with things with a little more finesse than football players do. But that's how I started my college career in Winston-Salem. In the end it all turned out for the good.

School hadn't started yet and the football team was practicing in the gym and out on the football field, which was why they were staying there. There were a lot of rooms in the gym, and in the basement there was one large room. That's where Smitty and I stayed, both sleeping on small cots. I had brought down a bag with my clothes, toilet articles, and a .25-caliber automatic silver gun in it. The gun was so small I could put it in my pocket and nobody would know I had it.

I'd taken the gun from a young guy in Lawnside, New Jersey, that past summer when me and my guys had gone over there one Sunday to a liquor store to get some wine (you couldn't buy alcohol in Philadelphia on Sundays in those days). When we came out of the liquor store, this young black guy pulled a gun on us, asking for money. I just took it from him, pushed him aside, and told him to get on up out of there. He left, in a hurry. Now I'm not a gangster or nothing like that per se, but I was very apprehensive about going down south to Winston-Salem. Because first of all it wasn't someplace I knew anything about. I knew it was in the South and I had heard about the KKK, so I wasn't going to be down there without any protection, you know what I mean? I was going down there sight unseen, so I took my little gun with me just in case I might need it. I wasn't about to take any stupid stuff from racist white people if I could help it, you know what I mean? After all, I was black and this was North Carolina and I knew by then how a lot of whites down there really felt about black people. So I had my little gun in my bag when I got there and when I went to sleep at night, while I was staying in that big room in the gym, I always slept with my arm across the spot in the bag my where my little gun was. (Later, Coach Gaines heard about the gun and took it out of my drawer.)

There were two bathrooms down there that we all shared and where everyone showered. After being there a while we started getting to know the football guys a bit. So one day Smitty and me were throwing a football back and forth to each other and one of the football players said, "Oh, you guys are football players? I thought you were basketball players."

"No," I said, "we *are* basketball players."

"But y'all throwin' around a football."

"Yeah," I said, "we're just doing it for fun."

Then they all laughed and joined in throwing the football with us. And over time, because we stayed down there for a couple of weeks, we got to know certain guys on the football team very well. We hadn't enrolled in school yet, so we couldn't get a dormitory room, and they couldn't, either. We had a little money our parents had given us, but we ate with the football team. If we got hungry after that we could get a big sandwich, you know, baloney and cheese, for something like 10 cents. I didn't know what was going to happen because we were waiting on the results of our SAT tests. So we played a little basketball in the gym and off campus and waited. Coach Gaines would come by from time to time and watch us shoot around, or while we were scrimmaging with each other to see if in fact he liked our game and was going to keep us. But he never said anything.

One day after one of our shoot-arounds Coach Gaines, who did everything matter-of-factly, came by to see us.

"We got your SAT scores and they were good," he said. "I'm going to go see the admittance people in the office and from there, they are going to assign you dormitory rooms. Okay?"

"Cool, let's do it. Let's get on out of here," I said.

"Get your stuff together and I'll be back shortly," he said. Then he left.

Our SAT results made us really happy, so Smitty and I went upstairs to the gym and pretended to announce each other to the imaginary crowd as members of the Winston-Salem basketball team.

I would say, "And starting at guard, Number 7, Steve Smith!" Then, after we faked applause and screams, Smitty shouted, "And starting at the other guard, Number 5, Earl Monroe!" We gave ourselves another round of applause, then imitated the crowd screaming their approval. After this we trotted out to the middle of the court and took our bows, waving our arms in the air, with big grins on our faces. Nobody was in the stands, but we were overjoyed that we were not going home and that we were going to be enrolled in school.

When Coach Gaines came back, he took us to a large dormitory building called Bickett Hall, where we were assigned rooms. Coach had decided he liked what he saw in us as players and that he wasn't going to send us packing back to Philadelphia. I was assigned to room with a guy named George Weldon and Smitty got assigned to a room with a football player named John "Night Train" Lane. "Night Train" was his nickname because one of his relatives was the famous football player with the same last name. We had formed good relationships with some of the football players staying in the gym, so it was kind of sad to leave them behind. But we were also happy to go because we knew our future was ahead of us now and what we'd make of it was in our own hands. I know I was confident that I was going to do well, especially on the basketball court, and I also knew that Smitty felt the same way.

The only thing I was sad about now was that I had missed going up to Washington, DC, on August 28 for the March on Washington. More than 200,000 people had crowded into the National Mall to hear Dr. Martin Luther King Jr. give his famous "I Have a Dream" speech in front of the Lincoln Memorial. I had planned to go with some friends from Philly, but I got stuck in Winston-Salem getting ready for college and the upcoming basketball season. By this time Dr. King was a hero of mine and I really wanted to hear him speak in person. So I made a vow that if Dr. King was ever close by to where I was, I'd be there to hear him. Unfortunately that opportunity never came and it's haunted me all my life that I never heard him speak in person. Still, I embraced the spiritual essence of his message—love, peace, freedom, and justice for everyone—and wove those principles into the guiding philosophy of my life.

Smitty and I both had a great feeling about our futures that day and I, for certain, was ready to embrace with a passion whatever challenges came my way. I also felt in my heart that I would succeed on this next level. In my mind there was no doubt about it.

Chapter 6

LESSONS FROM MY FIRST YEAR AT WINSTON-SALEM: 1963 TO 1964

IN SEPTEMBER MY NEW WINSTON-SALEM TEAMMATES AND
I started having informal games against each other because according to
the rules we couldn't hold formal practices until late October. Coach
Gaines already had some good veteran players there, like Willie Curry,
who was from Indiana and a real nice pull-up jump shooter. Then there
was Mickey Smith, a real smooth player from Washington, DC. Richard
Glover, one of our forwards, was from Newark, New Jersey, and stood
about six four or six five. Richard couldn't shoot a lick from the outside,
but he was a good garbage man around the basket, always looking to get
the rebound and put the ball back up and score, which he did very well.
Then there was the real character of that team, Louis Parker, who was a
six-foot-five-inch left-handed center from New York City. Louis was
really thin—all arms and elbows—a good rebounder, and shot left-
handed hooks and little jumpers.

Louis was a good ballplayer, but he played with a closed barbershop
razor in his jockstrap. He used to say that if some stuff went down he'd
pull out the razor and do whatever he had to do. He said he started

carrying a razor in his jockstrap back when he was playing on the New York City playgrounds, where anything could happen. Louis was something else, but Coach Gaines never knew he had the razor. Luckily for us nothing happened the whole year, because I wouldn't have wanted to see if Louis was bluffing or not.

We had interchangeable guards and forwards on that squad, like Mickey Smith and Willie Curry, both of whom could really play out on the floor and who shot really good jump shots. But they could play close to the basket, too, whenever it was necessary.

The top player on the team was Teddy Blunt, who was a six-foot-one-inch point guard. Teddy had a nice little jumper and handled the ball really well. He was also a very heady player and was the quarterback of the team. Teddy was also from Philadelphia, and I had played against him on the playgrounds (though we didn't hang out together) and in my junior year at Bartram, when he played at Simon Gratz High School. (Leon Whitley was also responsible for recruiting Teddy and steering him down to Winston-Salem.) He was very good at Simon Gratz, and when I heard he was at Winston-Salem I really looked forward to playing with him.

The year before I came to Winston-Salem Teddy had led the team to the CIAA (Central Intercollegiate Athletic Association) championship and made the 1962–1963 All-CIAA team. In my first year we won 22 and lost 4 games, and we were 17 and 3 in CIAA conference play. But we were banned that year from postseason tournament play because of some rule infraction (which I never fully understood) that happened during the year before I came to Winston-Salem.

Teddy was a very good passer and a very good floor leader, but we used to tease him because he was light skinned. See, there was a joke going around amongst some of the players that Coach Gaines liked for all his point guards to be light skinned because he figured they were close to being white, and that would help them control the dark-skinned players.

Of course I didn't think it was true, but a lot of people felt Coach Gaines thought that way because of some of his idiosyncrasies, like when Coach went and got a white kid named Bob from Ridley Township, near Philadelphia, to play on the football team because, as athletic director, he wanted to integrate the team and the school. Bob would ride with us in the car when we'd go back and forth between Winston-Salem and Pennsylvania for visits. I remember one time he proved very handy for us, because the driver was speeding and we got caught. Anyway, the cop pulled us over to the side of the road, came out with his flashlight shining on us, and said, "Where you boys going?"

"We're just leaving school," I said.

"Well, you know you going over the speed limit," the cop said. "You know how you boys can be when you don't pay attention to street signs."

"Yes, sir," I said.

Then the cop shined his flashlight into the back of the car and saw the white kid sitting there in the backseat. He seemed shocked to see him there.

"What you doing in here?" the cop said.

"Oh, I go to school with them," Bob said, nodding his head to whoever was in the backseat with him. The cop really looked strange then, shook his head as if this whole scenario was confusing him now, kind of laughed under his breath, and said, "Well, all right, you boys go on now, but watch the speed limit. You hear me?!"

"Yes, sir," I said.

When the cop left, someone in the car said, looking at the white kid, "Man, we sho' glad we had you in here."

Bob broke out in a grin big as daybreak, and all of us riding in the car just started laughing so sidesplitting loud and long it made our bellies hurt real bad and we ached in pain all the way back to Pennsylvania. That was something.

Coach Gaines was six five, 300 pounds (that's why all his friends—but not his players—called him "Big House," or just "House," because he was so big!). And he was *real* big to us. We might have been slapped upside our heads if any one of us had ever stooped so low as to call him "Big House," or just plain "House," to his face. To us he was "Coach Gaines," or "Mr. Gaines," or just plain "Coach."

Staying with the football team for those first few weeks taught us what to say and what not to say to Coach Gaines. That was one of the good things we got from staying with them. Plus, we got to know them—got tight with all of them—which later on saved our asses from the hazing that freshmen had to go through. When all the other male freshmen got to school and had to do all that stupid initiation stuff, me and Smitty were cool because a lot of the football players were the ones dealing out the punishments. We didn't have to go through that stuff, like getting hit, as some of the other freshmen did. They would make a freshman sit in a chair and then someone would turn off the lights and they'd start smacking the freshman upside the head. Stupid stuff like` that. But me and Smitty didn't have to go through any of that.

After Smitty and I moved from the basement, got our dormitory rooms, enrolled in classes, and started practicing, we found some time to explore the town before the season really started. Winston-Salem was a small city compared to Philadelphia. About 70,000 people were living there at the time, while more than a million lived in Philly. We found out that Winston-Salem was where RJ Reynolds Tobacco Company was located, which was why we saw all those endless huge fields of tobacco when we were coming down on the train. RJ Reynolds made Salem, Winston, and Camel cigarettes. Man, a lot of people in Philly, including some—I think—in my own family, smoked Camel and Salem cigarettes. Now we knew where they were made. Hanes

Mill, the company that made Hanes underwear, was also located in Winston-Salem.

The city itself—and our college, too—was named after Winston and Salem cigarettes, I believe, and a white high school in town was named RJ Reynolds High School. There were four high schools for blacks in Winston-Salem: Anderson, Paisley, Atkins, and Carver, the last of which was named after the famous black scientist, botanist, inventor, and educator George Washington Carver. Winston-Salem was located in the Piedmont section of North Carolina, at the foot of the Blue Ridge Mountains, so it was a little hilly there, but mostly flat. Black people lived predominantly in the East Winston section of the city, which is where the college was (and is) located. But there was another area called Boston where black people lived, too. Both communities had upper-class, middle-class, and poor people living within their boundaries, and there was nowhere near the violence in either of the communities as there was in South Philly. That in itself was comforting to me and Smitty, because we had grown up around so much violence.

There were a couple of clubs located in East Winston where older black people used to go, like the Cosmopolitan and the Tree. Both clubs served food and had live music, and people would dance there. Winston-Salem segregated their movie houses, so there were two movie houses black people went to, the Lincoln on Church Street and the Lafayette on East Fourth Street. There were two bus companies in town, one for whites and the other for blacks. Safe Bus Company was owned by black people and picked up students from the college and bused them to the downtown section of Winston-Salem. (Later, Safe Bus Company took over all the transportation for Winston-Salem and became the Winston-Salem Transit Authority in an effort to expand integrated bus service.) There were also two black-owned taxicab companies, Harris and Camel City Cab, that black people used if they had a few dollars.

Black people used to go to Knox's Soda Shop and Grocery Store on

Cherry Street to shop for their food; Knox's also served lunch and dinner, and a few whites would eat there sometimes because their food was
really good. But mostly the students ate in the school cafeteria and went
to the canteen on campus to get hot dogs, baloney sandwiches, and hamburgers with soda pops. When we went off campus we frequented Miss
Lou's on Cleveland Avenue. That's where we mostly hung out off campus. Miss Lou's sold good hamburgers, hot dogs, and Nehi orange and
grape sodas, RC Cola, Pepsi Cola, and Coca-Cola.

Across the street from Miss Lou's there was a bar and restaurant
called the College Grill owned by Bobby Pearson, where middle-class
blacks—mostly professionals—used to hang out and eat and drink. A lot
of times students would go in there and pick up a little spending change
from those who were willing to give some money to a poor college student. Up the street from there, at the corner of Third Street and Cleveland Avenue, was a greasy spoon named Hucks', where they made really
delicious food. But the grease was so high in the air there and smelled
so strong, I would yell out my order from the street. Then, when my
order was ready, I would take a deep breath, hold it, run in there real
fast with exact change, put it down on the counter, pick up my baloney
sandwich, and then boogie back out quickly so I didn't have to smell all
that grease. But boy were those sandwiches good, and that made it all
worth my while.

One of the most prominent blacks in Winston-Salem was the president of the college, Dr. Kenneth R. Williams. Dr. Williams, who was
born in 1912 in Virginia, grew up in Winston-Salem, went to high
school there, and then traveled to Atlanta to attend Morehouse College. After graduating from there, he got his PhD from Boston University. Then he came back to Winston-Salem, entered politics, and was
elected a city alderman in 1947, having defeated a white opponent.
That marked the first time that this had happened in the South in the
20th century. After growing tired of politics, Dr. Williams became pas-

tor of the West End Baptist Church for a few years before leaving to teach at Winston-Salem Teachers College (which became Winston-Salem State College in 1963). In 1961 he was appointed president of the college and remained there until he retired in 1977. Dr. Williams was a distinguished-looking man and a great leader for the school, and he was very well respected throughout the entire Winston-Salem community, even though he acted a little stiff for me, you know what I mean? He was one of those really proper-acting Negroes who never seemed relaxed, even when he was smiling and laughing. But he and Coach Gaines were longtime friends, and I remember seeing him at many of our home games cheering for us. He would come up to me when he saw me on the campus and congratulate me and other members of our team when we won an important game.

I started out my first year at Winston-Salem sitting on the bench and stayed there the entire season. I learned later that Coach Gaines never started freshman ballplayers, hadn't even started the great Cleo Hill when he was a freshman at Winston-Salem (the rule prohibiting freshmen from playing on the varsity didn't apply to NAIA—National Association of Intercollegiate Athletics—schools), and Cleo was one of the greatest players to ever play the game of basketball, in my opinion. Hill, a six-foot-one guard, played for Coach Gaines from 1957 to 1961, scoring 2,530 points in his career and averaging about 28 points a game in his senior year. I later found out Hill had insisted on bringing his best friend, Arthur "Artie" Johnson, a five-foot-seven point guard, with him from Newark, New Jersey, where they both had grown up, and Coach Gaines accepted this arrangement because he wanted Cleo so bad. I guess when I insisted on bringing Smitty with me, Coach Gaines must have thought it was déjà vu.

Anyway, Cleo took Winston-Salem to the NAIA national championship game in March 1961, but they lost to the defending champions, Westminster College, an all-white team from Pennsylvania, 35 to 33 because Westminster just held the ball (this was in the days before the shot clock). Winston-Salem was accustomed to scoring a lot of points because of Cleo Hill. But Westminster just slowed the game down to a crawl and Winston-Salem lost by two points. After his college career Cleo Hill became a number-one draft pick in the 1961 pro draft, the first player from a small black college to ever be drafted that high. I didn't know that much about Cleo Hill at the time because he wasn't from Philadelphia, though I heard people speaking of him with awe when I got down to Winston-Salem. But even if I had known, it probably wouldn't have mattered much to me that Coach Gaines hadn't started Cleo Hill in his first year, either, because I just thought I should have started and been playing more and that was that. But when I later understood just how great Cleo Hill was, I did start looking at the situation a little differently, but not so much that it eased my anger.

Throughout my first year I would find myself sitting at the end of the bench with Smitty, waiting for my turn to go in and burning up with anger. When Coach Gaines did put me in I would light up the scoreboard, hitting shots and dazzling the crowd with my passes, dribbling, and ball handling. I quickly became a crowd-pleaser, a fan favorite who people loved to watch play. I had a great following down there from the first time they saw what I could do. But, you know, Coach Gaines wouldn't play me much. So when he would motion for me to go in the game, a buzz would run through the crowd like a bolt of electricity and, being a bit of a ham at the time, I just loved it, loved hearing my name called out as I walked slowly from the end of the bench to the scorers' table before going in to play.

"Earlllllllllllll!" they would be yelling every time he called my name, and I'd get up and unzip the top of my warm-up jacket. "Earlllllllllllll!" the crowd would explode. Then I would enter the game and shoot and score and get us back up when we were behind. Then Coach would sit me back down and the crowd would moan. After I saw he wasn't going to play me that much, I started messing with the crowd now and then. So, I'd be standing around in the team huddle during time-outs and then I'd just fake like I was unzipping my warm-up jacket and the crowd would scream, "Earlllllllllllllllllllllllllllll!" Then I'd sit back down with the rest of the subs after the time-out was over and the crowd would just let out a loud moan. I'd do that now and then for fun because I was upset that I wasn't playing, so I had to do something to settle my nerves down. I think, however, these antics of mine got on Coach Gaines's nerves, though he never said anything to me about it. But when he did put me into the game it made me very happy.

There was only one problem: Coach Gaines used to always call me "Chocolate" whenever he wanted me to go in the game, because of my dark complexion. I hated that name and finally I thought of a way to get around it: I decided I would just ignore him whenever Coach Gaines called me by that name.

One game, I was sitting in my regular spot at the end of the bench with Smitty when I heard Coach call out, "Hey, Chocolate, get into the game!"

I didn't move. I just looked like I didn't hear him. I looked up into the crowd, turned my head from side to side.

"You know he calling you, don't you?" Smitty said.

So I whispered back to Smitty, "Yeah, I hear him, but I ain't going to do shit. I'm going to stay right here until he doesn't call me by that name."

"Hey, Chocolate!" Coach Gaines yelled again, looking down my way.

So I told Smitty, "I'm going to get this motherfucker out of the habit of calling me by that name, calling me "Chocolate." That ain't my name. I'm going to get him out of that shit right now!"

I was still looking around like I didn't hear him calling out my name when he said, "Earl. Get down here!"

So I got up with a big smile on my face and went into the game. Now, I must admit that I let it go a couple of times because Coach was so big. He was also light skinned, with piercing brown eyes, and didn't take shit from anyone. But he stopped calling me "Chocolate" before long. I was still angry at him for not playing me, though, and we didn't really start to get along with each other until my sophomore year. My first year of basketball at Winston-Salem was filled with anger and disappointment, although I did learn a lot by watching the game from the bench. I just could never adjust to Coach Gaines's philosophy of never playing freshmen because he didn't think we were ready to play on the college level. He just felt our first year should be a learning experience and the best way to absorb the nuances of the game was to watch from the bench. But I didn't care about that, you know, about his philosophy, because I was young and thought I was better than the guys starting over me. All I wanted to do was play.

In my freshman year of college, one of the things that really affected me besides playing basketball and studying happened on the day after my 19th birthday, in November. I remember I was walking across campus and noticed that almost everyone I saw looked sad, and some were even crying. As I continued to walk I began thinking about what could have possibly happened that would make so many people so sad. When I got to the campus canteen, everyone was gathered around a radio.

"What's happening?" I asked someone.

Looking very sad, he said, "President Kennedy was shot and killed today."

"What?! Where?" I asked.

"In Dallas, Texas."

"Damn," I said, shocked beyond belief.

It was a bright blue, sun-filled day outside, but hearing that all of a sudden turned it into a very dark day. It was stunning for me to hear President Kennedy had been killed, because I remembered how excited all the black people had been in my neighborhood in South Philly the day he was elected, and I had followed him and his family after that day. For me, President Kennedy's death was like the passing of someone in my family, even though I had never met the man. But for some reason I felt close to him because of my perception then of what he meant to black people, how he cared about us and was willing to fight for our rights to become first-class citizens. November 22, 1963: That's a day I will never forget.

But, other than this day of sadness, I was starting to acclimate to college life, socializing a little bit, you know, going to parties. I dated a few girls during my freshman year at Winston-Salem. I can only remember a couple, though, including one named Louise, a senior from Philadelphia. Louise—I called her Lou—was a short, nice-looking girl with big bowlegs and a beautiful spirit. I remember after she graduated I went to visit her where she was teaching in Gretna, Virginia. Smitty loaned me his Buick and I drove. Lou had told me it would be about a three-hour drive, so I left in the late afternoon.

By the time I reached Danville, Virginia, just over the North Carolina border, the sky had grown dark. I looked in my rearview mirror and saw all these cars flashing their lights and a bunch of guys in white hoods. All of a sudden I realized I was in the middle of a Ku Klux Klan rally! I saw a street off to my left and I just turned the car down it to get out of that mess. A couple of cars followed me, though, but then they turned back around because I was pressing pedal to the metal, speeding to get away from there. Anyway, I drove around in the darkness for a little while until I finally found my way back to the highway, got back on it and drove until I saw the exit sign for Gretna. Fortunately, Lou's house was right there by the exit and we got together for the night, which was nice. We talked about my little run-in with the KKK and I decided I would be more careful, considering where I was living now, when I was in areas with a lot of racist white people.

In the morning I had to plot my way back to Winston-Salem, because there was no way I was going to go back the way I had come. I left Lou's house at first light because I didn't want to be out on the road driving in the dark. I got on US Route 29 headed toward Greensboro, North Carolina, then hooked up with Interstate 40, which shot me into Winston-Salem. Boy, was that an adventure.

Another time during my freshman year I had another girlfriend named Eula who was from a place called Haw River, North Carolina, which was close to a place called Mebane. She wasn't great looking, but Eula was sensuous. She was tall, brown skinned, about five eight or five nine, with nice, big legs (I guess I've got a thing for legs). She was just a very nice, sweet girl. No sparks flying, no lightning rods throwing off electricity or anything like that. I was still shy at the time and I was still seeing Louise, but she had gone home for Thanksgiving and I was seeing Eula a little bit, too. So when she invited me down to see her and have Thanksgiving dinner with her and her family, I accepted.

So I took a bus to Haw River, but I didn't have her address or a telephone number with me. I had forgotten them, left her address and telephone number in my room. So I figured that when got there I would ask someone if they knew her. When I arrived and started asking around, though, nobody knew her. I only saw white people, so I went to the police station to ask. Now, I had this nice suit on, so I walked into the station and approached the policeman sitting behind the little desk.

"I just got off the bus and I'm looking for a family," I said. "The daughter's name is Eula. I go to school with her up in Winston-Salem."

"I don't have any idea who that could be," the policeman said. Then the guy looks hard at me and says, "You sound like a Yankee. You a Yankee?"

I was puzzled because I didn't know what he meant. The only Yankees I knew were the New York Yankees baseball team. So I said, "Naw. I'm not a Yankee."

"Yeah, you are," he said. "You one of them slick Yankee niggers!".

So now I knew where I was and it wasn't anywhere on the beaten path I wanted to be. So I just sucked it up and said, "Well, sir, I think I'll just go back to the bus."

He just looked at me and said, "You do that, because we don't like your kind round here."

So I left and went to the bus stop and waited for the bus to come. I didn't need that kind of shit in my life. With my short temper, I just didn't want to be around that kind of stupid stuff, you know what I mean? I've always looked around for an escape route wherever I find myself, and there was none in Haw River except to catch the bus, which I did. Later, after Eula came back to school the next week, I told her what had happened. She was cool about it, but disappointed. I found out from her that Mebane, the town next to Haw River, is the place where all the slave owners had fathered their illegitimate kids. So Mebane was a town filled with light-skinned black people and some of them went to school up at Winston-Salem.

In February 1964, my heart was lifted sky-high when Cassius Clay knocked out big, bad Sonny Liston and lifted the World Heavyweight Championship crown off his head in Miami Beach, Florida. His victory thrilled a lot of people, even though some thought his brashness, cockiness, and confidence were over the top. I didn't because I loved his attitude and admired how he did what he said he was going to do. He was an inspiration to me, a fresh new face on the American scene. I loved his creative boxing skills, his audacity, from day one and I would feel that way throughout his entire career, especially when he later made his heroic stand against being inducted into the army to fight in the Vietnam War.

I averaged about 7 points a game that first year at Winston-Salem without ever starting a game. Coach Gaines would bring me off the bench when the team needed some instant offense. I would come in, score, bring our team back, and then he would take me out. I remember one incident when we played the Georgia Invitational in Atlanta. I forget the name of the team we were playing, but we were behind when Coach Gaines called my name and put me in the game. I went into the game and scored nearly 20 points in just eight or nine minutes, brought our team back, and then Coach Gaines took me out for the rest of the game. We won, but our opponent almost caught us.

Coach Gaines never said anything encouraging to me during that first year other than an occasional "You did good. We needed that." He only said those kinds of things when I scored a lot and brought the team back in close games. So after my freshman season, I had a beef with him. I felt strongly that I should have played a lot more than the 10 or 12 minutes a game that he was playing me, and that I had earned it by beating up on the guys playing ahead of me in practice. I thought I should have started, and I was pissed off about that. So after the season I went to his office and we had a talk.

"Coach," I said, "I thought I should've been starting. Every time I got into the game my scoring brought the team back, got you even. Then you take me out. I don't think that was good because I can play."

"Well, Earl," he said, "you know I don't play freshmen."

"Well, you played me enough sometimes to get you back in the game," I said. "So why wasn't I—"

"Well, maybe next year it'll be better," he said, cutting me off.

"Well, I don't think I'm going to come back next year," I said. "I've been talking to some people and I think I might transfer to Temple or someplace else this coming year."

Then Coach Gaines reared back in his chair, put his hands behind his head, leaned back, and rolled his eyes up in the air as if looking at the ceiling.

"Tell you what," he said. "Why don't you step out of the room for a little bit and I'll call you back in about 10 minutes."

"Okay," I said.

I stood up, left the room, and closed the door behind me. What I didn't know was that he called my mother. So after a short while I heard his voice calling me back in. After I went in and sat down, I saw the phone was off the hook and lying on his desk.

"What's up?" I said

"Pick up the phone," he said. "It's your mother."

I was shocked. So I picked up the phone.

"Earl," my mother said, "Coach Gaines told me you're getting ready to leave school. Boy, you better stay down there. I'm not going to say anything more. You better stay down there."

"Okay, Ma," I said, stunned. "I'll call you back later."

"No," she said. "Do you hear what I'm saying to you? Do you understand what I mean when I tell you you better stay down there?"

"Yes, Mama," I said. "I'll talk to you later. Okay?"

"Okay," she said.

So I gave the phone back to Coach Gaines, and as I did I heard my mother say to him, "He's high-strung, but he's a good boy."

After he hung up, he looked at me and said, with a little smile playing around his lips, "Now, your mother wants you to stay. What do you want to do?"

"I guess I'm staying," I said.

That was the end of that. That's when he flashed me a big smile and said, "Great decision. Everything's going to work out next season." I just nodded my head as I was getting up to leave.

"See you in the fall," Coach Gaines said as I was leaving. "Everything's going to work out just fine. Trust me on that."

And it did. Coach Gaines was smiling when I left his office to go pick up Smitty. We stayed in Winston-Salem for a while and went to summer school to make up for having both failed biology in the spring semester. The biology final exam looked like Chinese arithmetic to us when we first took the test because we hadn't studied hard enough for it. But this time we buckled down, read the material, and passed the test with flying colors because we didn't want to be ruled ineligible to play ball in the fall.

After they told us we had passed, Smitty and I went home to Philadelphia to play summer ball. It was now 1964, and I was 19 years old. I was determined that when I went back to Winston-Salem I was going to be ready to start and play up to my potential. So I worked hard on my new, upgraded game out on the floor that summer. I had really improved my jumper by then, my dribbling, ball handling, and passing, too. Everyone in Philly was stunned and surprised by how much I had improved the shooting range of my jump shot. Most of them only knew my game to be about making slick moves to the basket, or pulling up and shooting midrange jumpers. Now I was making my jumpers regularly from beyond the top of the key, though it was years before college basketball would introduce the 3-point shot.

The legendary Sonny Hill, who was the head of Philly's summer Baker League and would later become my mentor, was really starting to watch me closely now. But playing in those playground games and in a few leagues that summer, plus in some all-star games, honed my skills to razor sharpness. All of my constant practicing was beginning to pay off. My confidence was high and I was prepared mentally and physically for my sophomore year at Winston-Salem. And as the summer months drew to a close, I found myself eagerly looking forward to going back down to play in college and to show everyone, especially Coach Gaines, that I was ready to take my game and my team to a championship level. But before the summer of 1964 ended, I was presented with another unexpected surprise and a great gift. I finally met my father.

Chapter 7

REUNITING WITH MY FATHER: SUMMER 1964

I MET MY FATHER AGAIN IN 1964, when I was 19, right around June, after my first year at Winston-Salem State. My father had moved around a lot as a young man, singing and dancing with jazz-blues great Bessie Smith, or at least that's what he told me when I got to know him and what I later heard from other people who knew him. I found out he hustled pool up in Canada and down in the upper regions of the United States. He never had a legitimate job until he was 61 years old, when he started working as a night watchman at Philadelphia Community College. I guess that was one of the reasons he never came around, because of all his moving around.

I found out through talking with him that, in between all that, my father had always been a salesperson. My father told me a funny thing that happened to him one time when he was selling medicines to people. One day, he told me, he decided to try what he was selling to customers and found out that it was some kind of laxative, and it kept him going to the bathroom all day that day. But he told me he had a clean body for a long while after that because those laxatives cleaned out his body and a lot of his sicknesses went away. I guess why he told me that story was, because his body had been squeaky clean and cool after he took those laxatives, he was suggesting that maybe I do the same thing. That's when I started taking laxatives to clean out my body and I have been taking stuff like that since that day. No question, my father was a very wise man.

My father wasn't a big man; he was only about five foot 10 (I got my height from my mother's side of the family). He was very distinguished looking, though. Slender. He had gray hair and he spoke with a kind of accent, because he was from South Carolina, so I guess it was Geechee. I remember him always carrying himself with his head held high, with a lot of self-respect. Later, when I introduced him to people, they would say, "Yeah, I know that's your dad because he's very distinguished look-ing." When we got to know each other better I found out he was just a nice person. So I guess it hurt me when I finally met him—although I was overjoyed, too—because I would've liked to have had him around all my life.

Anyway, around the time that my father came back into my life, my sister Ann had already been seeing him on occasion in and around Phila-delphia. Now, my sisters and I are all from different fathers. Each of us had a different father. But it was my sister Ann who saw him in down-town Philadelphia one day. He talked to her and told her that he wanted to see me. So she came back and relayed the conversation to my mother. I overheard that conversation and agreed to go down and see him. Then I started having reservations about the whole thing, about seeing him altogether, because I had always told people over the years that he was dead. So I wasn't supposed to even have a father, you know what I mean? I told everybody that he had died in the service, in the Korean War.

At first when my mother told me I was going to meet my father, it was kind of strange for me to be talking about going to visit somebody who was supposed to be dead. But I got over that and finally decided to get together with him because I was curious about what would happen. When I got to where he was living, I was really surprised to see cutout newspaper photos of me playing basketball and clippings about me on top of his TV and mantelpiece. When I saw this it kind of made me feel good to know that even though he wasn't there in my everyday life, he was still thinking about me. He was living in North Philadelphia at the time, with a lady by the name of Hattie. He was living off of Girard Avenue. When I got there he was so warm it kind of broke down my defenses. He told me he'd always wondered if that was me in the newspapers. Hattie was just as happy as he was when I came by, and she had never met me or known me except through him. So, we kind of bonded that day. But it still wasn't the same as being with someone that you've grown up with all your life. Certainly, just knowing that I really did have a father was another little triumph in my life. To know that there was somebody out there for me was a great feeling.

There was this connection between us, and, being a young guy at the time, I didn't really understand what that was, though I knew it was something that could draw me closer to him in time. He seemed like such a good guy. Still, I didn't hug him that first day we met. I just shook his hand, even though he seemed like he wanted to hug me. But he respected the handshake. There was this warmth between us, especially when I shook his hand. I felt an electrical current that shot between us, you know what I mean? There was this connection, and I knew from the electricity that coursed through my hand to my body that this was my real father. It was a deep, deep feeling I felt from just touching his flesh, a current that was almost spiritual. I believed it, right then and there, that it was something I had been waiting for all my life to experience.

I am a pretty observant person, and whenever I walk into a room I basically scan it so I can see and feel things. I saw that day that he was very meticulous about the way he lived, with everything in place. I am like that also; I want everything in its correct place, you know, like a neat freak does. And, like I said, I saw all those clippings and pictures of me. Then, Hattie came up to me and said, "You know that he kept all these things not knowing if it was you or not, but he kept them anyway, because he thought you might be his son."

That really impressed me, and even though we had already begun to bond I started to like him as a person from that point on. I knew right then and there that he had been thinking about me all those years, that I had been in his heart and mind, even though we lived apart. When I really looked at him, I could see myself in him. I mean, I saw we were a lot alike, even looked alike, and both of us were very reserved kind of people, with the same mannerisms, things like that. So I knew he was really my father.

When my father and I first got back together I initially looked at him as a source of money, you know, to help me with expenses as I was going through college. Maybe that was because my last memory of him was of him pouring all those silver dollar coins into my cupped hands when I was four or five years old. But over time I learned to know and respect him for himself, for his having bought land, houses, different things he could leave me if I needed them. That's what he wanted to do for me, and I really liked that.

For the first time I really began to realize what life in general was all about, understood that here was somebody who loved me very much, even though he hadn't been around when I was growing up. I just recognized that he had his own life to live and maybe he wasn't the cause for things not working out between him and my mother. And as I grew to understand that, I realized I shouldn't hold him responsible for not being there because he had to do his own thing, had the right to live his own life in whatever way he chose. I feel that about a lot of things, because a lot of times people leave a relationship and then you fault them for leaving. Perhaps things might have gotten worse if they had stayed in the relationship, you know what I mean? The friction between them might have become unbearable, so it might have been best for him to just leave. When I understood this about my mother and father I got a different kind of respect for him. As I got to know him better and we became closer, I would call him on the telephone whenever I had a moment and we would talk about all kinds of things, and that was good.

My mother thought it was a good thing my father and I had met, had gotten back together and liked each other. Over time, especially after I turned pro and played with the Baltimore Bullets, I would occasionally drive up to Philadelphia, pick up my mother and then my father, and take them to a nice restaurant in downtown Philadelphia. I really enjoyed these times we had together, and so did they. We would eat and they would talk about what I did growing up, what I was doing now, but they would never discuss what had gone on when they were together, and that was okay with me because it was water under the bridge.

Still, like I said, I grew close to my father, his mother (who he introduced me to), and Hattie, even though I wasn't as close to them as I was to the rest of my family. I would stay close with him for the rest of his life.

Chapter 8

REACHING FOR STARDOM
IN MY SOPHOMORE YEAR:
1964 TO 1965

THE JOY AND HAPPINESS I FELT after my reunion with my father in June was offset the following month by the death of my Aunt Mary. She was only 47 years old. I went back to Philadelphia for her funeral after finishing up summer school. That was a very sad day for my entire family and for many people—black and white—in Philadelphia, especially in South Philly, where she had run her numbers business. I guess after a while it got to the point where she couldn't take being an invalid anymore and so her spirit just went downhill and she died in her sleep. Her wake was held at Chew Funeral Home and it was overflowing with mourners. It was a big affair because a lot of people knew, respected, and just loved her. I don't remember if the casket was open or closed, but I do remember feeling really sad about her passing. Still, I was anxious to get back to basketball because that was what I loved. But I also needed basketball to fill the hole in my heart that my aunt's passing had left in my life. Playing basketball was a joyous thing for me, and at the moment it helped me push back all this grief.

The biggest thing that happened for my game between my freshman and sophomore years at Winston-Salem was that my ball-handling skills improved considerably. I really got a lot better over the summer of 1964 playing in Philadelphia every day, nonstop, with the Trotters and other teams around the city. I practiced my dribbling a lot when I was home, and then I kept it up when I returned to Winston-Salem, doing three or four hours of drills a day. It was all starting to pay off. My outside shooting had improved also through constant practice, so I knew by then that if I could get to a certain spot on the floor, I could make that shot. But this required having a great handle—you know, dribbling skills— because by then I could make my jumper. So my dribbling got me wherever I wanted to go on the court and that improved my offensive game and scoring potential tremendously.

I remember hearing in-the-know basketball people saying to coaches when I was playing up in Philadelphia that summer, "You should see how this kid handles the ball! He's amazing!"

Hearing that made me feel good. So that's what turned my game around that summer. Plus, I was getting a lot of minutes in the games I played in on playgrounds all over the city, where the level of competition was top-notch. Playing against really good players can only make you better, and it did; it made me a lot better. Like I said, my ball-handling ability helped me get to those spots I had to get to in order to score. But the biggest thing that happened when I got back to Winston-Salem was that I was finally free enough to let my talent shine through, which is where Coach Gaines came in.

Coach Gaines had already had a lot of success at Winston-Salem before I arrived, winning four CIAA championships and three conference Coach of the Year awards, and he did it by playing to the strengths of his players. With my style, the freelancing mode I had developed playing the game, a lot of coaches might have just pulled me back and said, "I don't want you to do this and I don't want you to do that." But during the first scrimmages we had after we got back, Coach Gaines saw how much I had improved over the summer and he just let me go. He recognized how I could shoot the ball and score, how much my dribbling and my knowledge of the game had improved, and he believed in my talent. He allowed me to play my style of the game as long as it was effective, and it was. It was as if he was saying, "Why change it?"

That endorsement built my confidence up to a very high level, and I averaged 23 points a game in my sophomore season at Winston-Salem, scoring a total of 697 points. I remember playing in a tournament out in Kansas City that year and seeing Buddy Jeannette, the coach of the Baltimore Bullets, speaking to Coach Gaines about me. So I made up my mind right then and there that I wanted to play with the Bullets after I got out of college, and that's who drafted me when I graduated. (I had already wanted to play for them after seeing Gus Johnson dunk over the Boston Celtics' Bill Russell and said, "Wow, I'd like to play with him!" And voilà! I did.)

The big change on our team in my sophomore year was that Coach Gaines teamed me up with Teddy Blunt in the backcourt, and we worked together very well. Teddy was the point guard and I played off him at the shooting position. Now, Teddy was what I call a "nurtured" player, meaning that when he came to Winston-Salem he instantly ingratiated himself into Coach Gaines's basketball culture. Coach trusted Teddy to run the team. See, Teddy was very mature, and he might even have already been married—or close to it—when we started playing together. I accepted this and understood that my role was to play off Teddy, for him to set me up and feed me, so that I would be free to create and then score, which I did.

Teddy and I both understood and accepted our roles, and that's why we worked so very well together. Teddy was also a very good person, always had a smile on his face—*zing!*—whatever the case might be. And we played together really well for two years. But Teddy had bad feet— really bad arches—that eventually gave out, so he couldn't get around like he used to after a while. For instance, during my sophomore year he couldn't practice sometimes because his feet couldn't take the pressure. So Coach Gaines saved him for just playing in games. Everyone on the team was cool with that because we had so much respect for Teddy and, like I said, we all liked him so very much. But when he could play he saw the floor extremely well, was unselfish, passed the ball to players in the spot they needed to be in to get a great shot. Teddy just controlled the game with his intelligence and knowledge and I really loved playing with him.

Teddy was very smart, always had the upper hand when it came to using his brains, and we were a great combination together. Teddy did whatever he had to do to win games. Once, a reporter asked me about winning and what I thought Teddy brought to that concept.

"You can be on a team and be a star scorer," I said. "You can be the star point guard, you can be the star defensive player, you can be the star rebounder. But the name of the game, the main purpose, is bringing all the stars together so they can mesh and co-exist to become a winning squad. That's the real challenge and that's what Teddy did for our team; he brought us all together and taught us all how to become a winning squad. And I learned a lot from him when it came to knowing how to lead a team to victory, and to be able to win championships."

Now, Teddy got his points, too, because he was a scorer—not a great scorer, though—as well as a great passer and floor general. But he made us all better because he was there. Besides Teddy and me, our starting team that season consisted of Ted Ratchford, who was a six-foot-10-inch center; forward Sonny Ridgill (who seemed like he had been in school forever), who was six feet three; and Joe Cunningham, who was about six feet seven, at the other forward (Joe later played for the Harlem Globetrotters). Smitty was the first player off the bench.

I made All-Conference my sophomore year and didn't have any problems with Coach Gaines, because we were winning and I was playing very well. Things were obviously better than they had been during my freshman year. I think he and I had grown as people, not just as coach and player; I think we all grew together as a team. Coach Gaines became more of a father figure to me, as he was for everybody else. He also treated us all like men and we appreciated that. Letting me play my game was actually an outgrowth of Coach Gaines's philosophy, which involved a belief in the star system. Whoever Coach's star player was—and now it happened to be me—he let that guy, if he had a certain amount of talent, shine.

Coach Gaines ran a pro-style offense, which meant we got the ball up and down the floor quickly. If we didn't have a fast break possibility, then we'd match up with our opponent's defense and run our half-court offense, which revolved around Teddy, because he was the point guard. We'd switch up the offense according to who we were playing and tried to take advantage of whatever weakness our opponent had. If a team didn't have a good inside game, we'd play more of a two-three offense, in which we shot from the outside, because we had good shooters and that opened up a lot of stuff for our inside game. Against other teams we sometimes played a two-one-two offense. We'd bring our center out to the free throw line and then players would cut off him to create lanes for me to drive to the basket. We could also set up screens, pick and roll, or free up our shooters to take jump shots out of this alignment. It was a very creative system.

My thing was to free myself up and be able to create, or drive to the basket for a layup, maybe drive and dish to the free man. I could also drive and pull up and shoot my jumper, so our offense made us a lot different than we had been the year before because those guys didn't drive that much. Now I could do all my playground moves and Coach Gaines freed me up and allowed me to use them. I was doing my Thomas Edison creative moves to the basket and pulling up and shooting the long or midrange jump shots, too. See, I was never a catch-and-shoot kind of guy. I always wanted to be able to have the ball in my hand and then create, and Coach Gaines allowed me to do this in my sophomore year. We played good team man-to-man switching defense, too, though our forte was running, shooting, and scoring the ball.

I have always been a little cocky, especially after I reached a certain plateau as a player. I guess it started to show in the confident way I carried myself around this time, not so much to turn people off but to let them know I could really play this game. My confidence let my opponents know that I was there to turn up the heat on them every time I stepped on the court. It was interesting how some people liked to play with me and others liked to play against me. The ones I played against knew that if I got the chance I was going to embarrass them. I was going to shake and bake them, put my spin move on them, cross them over with my dribble, and leave them standing somewhere looking silly after I had nailed them with a creative move. Then, when they looked around, I would be gone to score the basket. I'd have a smile on my face after I had done this to one of my opponents. It wasn't arrogance—it was something more like supreme confidence and cockiness—but it was just my way of saying to them that I really could do this, so they'd better be prepared to deal with me every time they came up against me, because I wanted them to know I was always going to be bringing it to them, you know what I mean? I did this all in my own quiet way, because at the time I was still too shy to be talking trash to players I had embarrassed; all that would come later.

See, in my mind, it was all about competition, about competing with another player that's good. I always loved this aspect of playing basketball. It made me excited to just be out on the floor going up against the very best. It made my adrenaline flow. Like I said, for me it was all about competition and had nothing to do with arrogance, at least not in my mind, not in the way I saw it.

I really began to mature as a player during my sophomore year when I realized I had to step up and accept and embrace my role as a scorer and leader on the team if we were going to win games. I recognized that our team was going through a period of transition, while other teams in our conference, like North Carolina A&T and Norfolk State, for example, had stabilized and strengthened their rosters. The year before, I had been a benchwarmer, scoring only 7 points a game, while Teddy Blunt had been the absolute leader of our team. But now I had blossomed as a person, scorer, and team leader, and Teddy, though still the unquestioned leader and captain of our team, understood this totally. He knew that I had improved a lot as a player, because we practiced together every day and he saw with his own eyes how much better I had gotten. And because Teddy was a very mature, smart player, he knew he had to adjust his own role to complement my newly elevated status on our squad. He did so willingly, even sacrificing his own scoring, though he still averaged around 12 or 13 points a game.

Following Teddy's example, all the other players on the team—with the exception of maybe one, whose name I won't call out in this book—accepted my new role on the team. But Teddy had nagging little problems with the arches in both feet all season long and that affected our team negatively as well, you know what I mean? Sometimes when Teddy had to go out because of his feet, Smitty would replace him, or sometimes Coach would move me to the point and I would become the key, you know, creating and running the team from there, which I enjoyed. Then, my role would switch from just scoring the ball to getting everyone involved in the flow of the game.

We had been conference champions the two previous seasons, winning more than 20 games in both of those years, and those teams had been led by Teddy. But although we were predicted to win the conference again in 1964–1965, Teddy couldn't practice a lot, which impacted our team play because he was the leader. In part because Teddy couldn't play at his usual high level, we finished third in conference play, behind A&T and Norfolk State, with a record of 11 and 6 in the conference and 20 and 7 overall (not a bad record, but we had expected much better). Now, no one blamed Teddy for this because it was not his fault his arches gave out, but he was a key player for us and had he been healthy, I just didn't think anyone could have beaten us.

Despite our disappointing third-place finish in the regular season, in the CIAA the winner of the postseason tournament was crowned league champion, which meant we still had a chance to win the overall championship. In the first round we beat Livingston College 84–59, setting up a meeting with Norfolk State. In a truly thrilling game, we lost in overtime after blowing a big lead because of turnovers. I scored 30 points in that crucial game, but I was disappointed because I thought we should have won. Both Teddy and I made the All-CIAA All-Conference team, and the team received an invitation to play in the NAIA tournament in Kansas City for the fourth time in five years.

In March 1965, we left Winston-Salem to travel to Kansas City. I was excited about this opportunity to play in the tournament, as was everyone else on our team. But when we played our first game against Saint Norbert College, an all-white team from De Pere, Wisconsin, it was the first time our players from the South had ever gone up against white players. I think some of our players from the South froze up and were, in my opinion, hesitant in their play in this game, perhaps because they had been told for so long that white people were superior to blacks in all aspects of life, including basketball.

Now, I don't know if that was true or not, but that's how I felt after we played so badly in the first part of that game, trailing by as many as 9 points, and went into halftime behind, 32–27. But we pulled it together in the second half and won the game 87–69 when some of our players from the South, like Howard "Sonny" Ridgill (who scored 23 points) and Ted Ratchford (who scored 19), got it going; I also scored

23 points in that game. I think the same thing might have happened in the next game, against High Point College, which was 20 miles outside Winston-Salem. But in that game we turned up the heat on them near the end of the first half and coasted to victory, 78–62; I had 22 points in that game.

In the next game, however, against Oklahoma Baptist, we came out cold and stayed that way and lost 71–62. In that game, despite scoring 20 points, I couldn't hit a brick wall with my shots, and I think Sonny finished with just 2 points. That was the game Teddy fouled out, I think, because his feet were hurting badly, as they had been throughout the tournament. Coach Gaines thought that the referees were biased in that game—so did I—because we only shot 18 free throws and Oklahoma Baptist shot 31.

That was the way I finished my sophomore year at Winston-Salem, and though I was happy about how I had elevated my play that season, I was disappointed that we lost in the NAIA tournament and in my poor shooting performance in our last game.

Malcolm X, another of my heroes, had been assassinated about a month earlier by three members of the Nation of Islam at the Audubon Ballroom up in Harlem. I never liked thinking about death, or seeing it manifested in someone lying in a casket. That's just the way I am. I love celebrating life, and that's what I did when I was out playing on the basketball court. Basketball was always a way I could express myself, be creative, imaginative. It was a joy for me to be out there playing, and I could lose myself in the joy of playing the game. I just never felt any joy about death, even though I missed people being there, you know, alive and joyous in their living. Like I missed Malcolm X's presence in the world, even though I never met him, you know what I mean? I loved the words he gave us and the meaning behind them for both black people and all people all over the world. I loved that.

After the assassination of Malcolm X and our loss in the NAIA tournament, I felt it was necessary to do some reflecting back on my life, and attending an all-black college helped me in this regard. Because I was surrounded by black people, I didn't have to do as much explaining about the death of Malcolm as I would have had I been at an all-white school. So there was comfort for me in being at Winston-Salem, being around people who understood, you know what I mean?

In spite of the unfortunate events of early 1965, I continued to celebrate life and being alive, taking solace in the knowledge that I could go out on the basketball court and express myself and my creativity there in the world of the living. That's just the way I was, and the way I am. I truly love living in the world, doing what I do, and I don't make any bones about it. I'm always trying to be positive, looking into the future with my eyes wide open to embrace what's next. Malcolm's death, losing in the NAIA, it was all water under the bridge now. I just had to focus more on basketball, continue to improve. I was determined to come back mentally stronger and more efficient in my game going into my junior year.

Chapter 9
___

BECOMING "BLACK JESUS" IN MY JUNIOR YEAR: 1965 TO 1966

I WAS SURPRISED—but not shocked—when flames and riots erupted all over the United States in the summer of 1965, especially out in California, in Watts. I had never even heard of Watts, which was a poor black community in southern Los Angeles. It was a wild time. Malcolm X had already been killed, Martin Luther King Jr. was leading thousands of civil rights marchers in Selma, Alabama, after the Ku Klux Klan shot some black people down there, and there were riots happening all across the country.

The Watts riots were being talked about everywhere because so many people had been shot and killed by the police and a lot of property had been destroyed. All of this was making a lot of young people—black and white—more politically aware, and I know I was paying more attention to how black people were being treated in this country. I could feel the racial tension in the air in Philadelphia and when I returned to Winston-Salem. I could see and feel that tension in the way black and white people interacted with each other, with fear in their eyes. But I didn't know what I could do about any of it, so I just retreated into playing basketball, determined to get better in all aspects of my game.

There have been so many things that I dreamed about in my life that came true, like becoming a basketball star. I worked hard at it, sure, but I've also been very lucky. A lot of people work hard at stuff all their lives, you know, and never realize their dreams. That's why I admit to being lucky, because I know that nothing is guaranteed, even with hard work and focus. It just might not be in the cards for some people. A lot, of course, has to do with being willing to sacrifice. But a lot of it also has to do with being lucky, and I've been very lucky.

One of the things I was lucky about was the caliber of my Winston-Salem teammates after Teddy Blunt graduated in June of 1965. Losing Teddy hurt, but Eugene Smiley could really play. Eugene was a guard, about six feet one, from Newark, New Jersey. We became roommates and good friends, and he replaced Teddy at the point. Sonny Ridgill, a hometown favorite from Winston-Salem, was still around, as was Joe Cunningham, who became our new captain (we used to call him "Capt Spec" because he was always saying we never gave him the respect he deserved for being the captain). Willis "Spider" Bennett rounded out the starters.

Now we had some other really strong players who were ready to step in coming off the bench, like Smitty, who backed up the guard spots with Johnny Watkins, a really good defensive player from Badin, North Carolina. Jim English was a six-foot-six-inch high-scoring fresh-man forward from Virginia, and he worked well in tandem with six-foot-six-inch junior forward James Reid, another really good player from North Carolina who probably should have been starting. I had elevated my game again by playing against some top-notch competition on the Philadelphia playgrounds over the summer. I had also gone up to New York to play some games on the playgrounds up there in Mount Morris Park and did very well, even wowing some of those die-hard New York

City hoopsters. So by the time I returned to school in September, I was really focused on playing at the top of my ability and on winning a championship for Winston-Salem.

When Teddy graduated, I understood I had to become the leader of the team and I took that responsibility upon my shoulders, which was a lot different from how I used to be. For the most part, I had stood back and let things happen and just kind of gone with the flow and created off of that. But now I felt as though there was an opportunity for me to become more assertive, you know, to step up and lead, which I felt would make us a better team. And it did. At the same time, even though I was determined to increase my scoring, I was always cognizant of the other guys on the team. So it was important for me to make sure that they understood I was for them as much as they were for me. That's why I got along with my teammates so well, because they always understood this. They understood that a real quick metamorphosis was going on now, that I was going from one of the guys to "the guy," and they accepted it. I relished the idea and the role, felt that it fit and that I was going to be up to the task.

I knew I had to score more if we were going to win, which meant that I had to take more shots. By this time I could really shoot the ball, make a high percentage of my shots, and all my teammates knew it. They knew I could create on the spot, improvise within the structure of the game. See, Coach Gaines had a system that he tried out on his players. Aside from all the running up hills, the miles we had to run in under six minutes and whatnot, climbing 20 feet up ropes, he also wanted to find out and know what kind of heart a player had, what kind of player you were going to be for him. So he had all these tests, you know, like shooting from the top of the key, from the free throw line, layups. If you made shots from out on top of the key, from other places on the floor, then you were a shooter. If you missed those shots then you were a defensive player, and if you fell somewhere in the middle, then you were a ball handler. It was crazy but he kind of separated players like that. This is how he understood who his players were and what they were all about.

He knew I could really shoot the ball, so that's what I did in practice, just worked on my shooting from everywhere. And Coach Gaines set up the offense to free me up to do just that in games; shoot the ball, that was my contribution toward helping us win games, that was my role. So all my teammates understood that they had somebody—me—who wasn't afraid to take the important shot at crunch time and was willing to pay the price if I missed, which I did on occasion but not very often.

I averaged 29.9 points a game in my junior year at Winston-Salem (I always say I averaged 30 points a game that season because they took some points away from me for one thing or another) and scored 746 points. I would shoot my jumper, *bang, bang, bang,* every chance I got. I had the confidence now, and the green light from Coach Gaines, to shoot my jumper from even farther out on the floor, and even if I missed a few times it didn't bother me. Because now I knew I was going to make most of them, and I did. That helped us win games, which was the most important thing in this equation.

I also decided that year to join a social fellowship group by the name of Groove Phi Groove Social Fellowship Incorporated. I guess the idea was that there were other organizations, like the Alphas, the Kappas, all the other Greek-named sororities and fraternities on campus. So those of us who started this new chapter at Winston-Salem thought we would offer a kind of alternative to that. Groove Phi Groove had initially started up in 1962 at Morgan State in Baltimore. It was pretty synonymous with all the other chapters that started up at black schools, except we might have partied a little more. So my guys and me, Smitty and a bunch of others, mostly athletes, were the core of our group. I went over—was initiated—as a Swanksman, and our motto was "I think, therefore I am," which came from a guy named René Descartes, a famous French philosopher.

One of the main differences between our organization and a lot of others was that members only had to have a C average, rather than a high B or A, to be in Groove Phi Groove. Our shield was black and white with chains that went over the shield from top to bottom. Plus, we had textbooks on the image, which were to evoke the feeling that our members were enlightened, above and beyond our grade point averages. There was a beer mug on there, too, which was to represent that we were grooving, you know, having a great time, and we were. We also believed in helping the disadvantaged people get ahead. But most people thought of us as kind of a rowdy party group because we were always having parties and a lot of people came to those get-togethers.

It was a funny thing that people perceived some of us as total party guys, particularly me. Now, I'll admit that I was a rowdy guy in the organization from time to time, despite my shyness. But Smitty was too, especially when he had a drink or two. See, he was the guy who, when we came out of high school, never drank. He was always our cushion. We could do whatever, get drunk, whatever the situation, and Smitty would be the one who drove us home. He was always there. He was like Mr. Church. He was the guy who would always go to class in a tie, looking real studious, and he'd be bullshitting people all along. He changed once he got to college; that's when he started to drink and get drunk. Man, we would be drinking wagon wheels (we called them "wagon wheels" because after you drank a lot of them you would be rolling around the floor drunk), which were made out of grain alcohol and Hawaiian Punch. We'd throw in some lemon slices, sometimes some wine, because we could do it for about four or five dollars a gallon. We'd dip it out with scoopers, pour it in plastic cups, knock it on down, and have a ball. We were listening to Ben E. King, the Drifters, James Brown, "Function at the Junction" by Shorty Long, Gladys Knight and the Pips, Clyde McPhatter, Ray Charles, and Smokey Robinson's "Tracks of My Tears." We'd be waiting for the slow tunes to come on so we could grind our lady friends back into the corners.

As a part of our initiation, our fellow men took all of us in Groove Phi Groove out sometime that year. But, unfortunately one of the health problems I had developed over the years was hemorrhoids. And on the night they were to take us out to a place called Kernersville, about 15 miles outside of Winston-Salem, with everybody blindfolded, my hemorrhoid problem rose its ugly head up. See, you know, the challenge for us guys was that we had to find our way back to campus after they took the blindfolds off. But I couldn't go because my hemorrhoids were acting up. So to ease my discomfort I sat in a tub of warm water in my dormitory. Still, I wanted to go really bad, because that was the night I was supposed to go over, you know, pass my initiation test, so I could really become a Swanksman.

After spending some time cooling myself down I decided to drive out there in my car. Now, they had a lookout waiting for me, and when they spotted me they made me stop the car and get out. Then they made me give up my car keys, blindfolded me, and took me to where everyone else was waiting. Now, it was winter, near the end of the basketball season, and it was around midnight. Very dark. No lights anywhere. But fortunately for me, when I arrived I had missed all the hazing stuff. Only Smitty and about six other guys were left when I got there. They took the blindfolds off, but nobody gave me back the keys to my car. So we had to walk and find our way back to Winston-Salem. No one had any idea where we were. I knew how to get back from the spot where they had picked me up, but that was about five miles away and I didn't know how to get there from where we were. And though it was frightening not to know what direction to go, the scariest part of this equation was that we were out in Ku Klux Klan territory, you know what I mean?

So we started walking back on this dirt road to nowhere and we're talking back and forth with each other and all of a sudden lights start coming on in the farmhouses we pass. Now, none of us wanted to go up to any of these houses and ask for directions, because as we were passing this one house a white guy came out on his porch with a shotgun in his hands and hollered, "Who's out there?"

That scared the holy shit out of everyone! So everybody just shut up and ran off the road into some bushes and kept quiet. After that we didn't say another word. We just kept on trucking until we got to another dirt road, which led to a paved road cars and trucks would be traveling on. Soon we saw this pickup truck coming up and somebody flagged it down. The truck stopped and there were two white guys in the cab who let us know they had shotguns by showing them to us. So we told them we were trying to get back to Winston-Salem, that we were lost and were basketball players. They looked at each other and the driver said, "All right, boys. Y'all get in the back."

So we got in the back of the pickup truck and they drove off. I remember Smitty whispering as we were going along, "Man, I feel like cattle sitting back here."

"I know one thing," I said. "We'd better shut the fuck up before they hear us and shit."

And we did. They drove us and stopped at the Winston-Salem city line, where they dropped us off and kept on going. That was nice of them to do that. After they dropped us off we walked our way back to campus. But that was a real strange night that ended up on the positive side.

On the social side of things my main squeeze back then was a lady named Betty. We hooked up and were an item most of my years in college. She was from Winston-Salem. Betty was about five foot seven or eight and brown skinned with nice legs, eyeglasses, and an Afro. She reminded me of Angela Davis. Betty liked to wear tight jeans and I liked that, because I like to see a woman's body. I don't like real big behinds, but I do like nice shapes. Betty and I got along real well, but we had one instance where things went off the tracks. What happened was Betty had gone somewhere and left me in my dormitory room. So I'm laying on my bed in my room and there's a knock at the door, so Smiley, my roommate, goes and opens the door and I turn over and Betty's father is standing in the doorway with a double-barreled shotgun pointed at my face.

"Where's my daughter?" he said. "Where's Betty?"

Now, I'm in shock, so I said, "I don't know where no Betty is."

"What do you mean you don't know where she is?" he said. "I'll blow your motherfuckin' head off!"

So I looked at him real hard, thinking, *Go ahead, do it. If not, man, get the fuck out of here.* But I didn't say that. I just looked at Smiley just standing there with his eyes wide open. So I told the man again that I didn't know where she was. I hadn't seen her and he could see she wasn't with me. So he finally left but he never apologized to me for pointing that shotgun at me, or for threatening my life, and that really pissed me off. When Betty finally came by the next day after hanging out with her girlfriends, she had found out from her father what he had done. By then I had calmed down and she said she was sorry for what her father had done. I told her it wasn't her fault and that everything was cool, which it was. But I thought about that incident a lot after it occurred and I never came up with an explanation for why it happened. I never saw her father again, either.

I also went out with a woman named Dorothy, who was a little bit older than me and one of the most beautiful women I have ever known. She was about five feet eight, really sophisticated, brown skinned, and had a very nice body. I think she had been Miss Winston-Salem one year. She was married and had a daughter, but when I first saw her I just fell for her like a ton of bricks. Wow! Eventually we got together and started sneaking around, laying up in motel rooms. After a while, though, word got out and her husband came up to me and asked point-blank, "Are you seeing Dorothy?"

"Dorothy who?" I said.

"You know who I'm talking about," he said.

"No, I really don't know who you're talking about," I said.

So he just stood there looking hard at me. He was about five 10, thin, light brown skinned. So I looked back hard at him because if something jumped off I wasn't worried unless he had a gun or a knife or something like that. Because I was so adamant in my denial he just turned around and left. But Dorothy was a woman I just couldn't resist seeing, and the feeling was mutual. So we kept sneaking around with each other, though her husband never confronted me again. But when Coach Gaines caught wind of the situation he called me into his office and said, "You know, Earl, there's nothing more dangerous than a woman scorned."

So I looked at him puzzled and said, "Coach, what do you mean?"

He looked at me real hard with those eyes of his and said, "You know what I mean, son. You'd better watch yourself."

"Yes, sir," I told him, and then I left. But I kept on seeing Dorothy and I didn't stop until late in my senior year.

A warning was one thing, but there was another incident that occurred during that year that really pissed Coach Gaines off. That was the time I was late for a game because I was just not thinking in a serious way. What happened is I was supposed to drive up to Philly for the weekend with Smitty but he couldn't make it, so I asked his roommate, Ernie Brown, if he would go up with me and he agreed. The deal was that I would drop him off at the Philadelphia bus station and he would go on up to New York, come back to Philly, and then we would drive on back to Winston-Salem together so we could get back for the game that next Monday.

Well, I got to running around in Philly, seeing old friends and old girlfriends, and having a good time. Then Ernest called me on Sunday and said he was coming back to Philly, so when he arrived I picked him up at the bus station, took him to my mother's house, dropped him, and kept on running around. I came back and had to drive the whole way down to Winston-Salem myself, because Ernie, like many New Yorkers, couldn't drive. So we hit it and I think we got to Virginia around two o'clock Monday morning. I was tired as a dog, so I pulled over and told Ernie I was going to sleep for a little while. Well, I didn't wake up until three o'clock Monday afternoon! Our game against Saint Augustine's that day was to be played in Raleigh, North Carolina, so we had to drive there. When we finally arrived at the coliseum the teams were already warming up, so we went and put on our uniforms and walked out to the court. I looked up and saw Coach Gaines and he was angrier with me than I'd ever seen him. He looked at Ernie and me and said, "Hell, y'all ain't playing!" Then he turned around and walked away.

They played without me and won anyway, because Sonny Ridgill and Joe Cunningham picked up their scoring in that game. After that silly incident I decided I'd better get more serious about my involvement with the team, and I did from then on. Nothing like that ever happened again because I realized that if I was going to become a team leader I couldn't be making those kinds of immature mistakes.

My junior year was a stepping-stone for me and the team. That year our record was 17 and 4, but 3 of our losses were to Norfolk State, another CIAA team, and we finished second behind them in the regular season rankings. Still, we went to the CIAA tournament and I scored 32 points in a 96–86 first-round victory over Johnson C. Smith University. Sonny (who made All-CIAA that year, as did I) also stepped up in this game, and his scoring helped us get the win. We played Hampton University in the next round and won 85–84 in a really thrilling game. That put us in the final against Howard, and we beat them to win the tournament. I scored 42 points in that final game and was named the Most Valuable Player of the tournament.

After winning the CIAA tournament, we qualified to play in the NCAA Division II Championship in March 1966, in Durham, North Carolina. It was the first time our school had ever competed in that tournament. We played Oglethorpe College, a small white team from Atlanta, in the first round. We lost 69–66 in a low-scoring game because they slowed the game down and that unnerved us. We lost also because we played a very sloppy, error-filled game. But I had a horrible night, too, scoring only 14 points on 6 of 21 shooting. I think Sonny Ridgill, who was our second-leading scorer that year, averaging around 16 points a game, scored around 20 points in that game. That game was a downer for all of us, but especially for me because I felt I had let my team down. Overall that year, we finished with a 20-and-5 record after the 3 tournament wins and that 1 final loss.

But a weird thing happened to me and my guys that night after the game. After we lost we were walking to a party we had been invited to when out of the blue a bunch of black men rolled up on us in a car. Then they jumped out of the ride and one of them started pointing fingers at us, saying, "Those are the guys that beat up my cousin!"

So one of our guys said, "Beat up your cousin? What are you talking about?"

Then the guy who had been yelling at us pulls out a gun and so did the rest of them. We were shocked, because now they were talking about shooting us and they were dead serious. This goes on for about 15 minutes, with us trying to explain to them that we were all basketball players and not even from Durham and that we were just in town to play in a tournament. But they weren't having any of it and were just waving their guns around. So they made us sit down on the ground and just as I was really starting to get pissed off—and nervous—the guy we were supposed to have beaten up showed on the scene. So one of our guys says to these crazy people, "Man, we're from Winston-Salem. We play on the college team, and like I just told you, we were playing in a tournament."

Then the guy they said we beat up got out of the car that brought him, came up to us, looked at me, and said, "Man, that ain't the people who beat me up. Do y'all know who this is? That's Earl Monroe, the basketball player. This here is Black Jesus, man!"

The man with the gun looked closely at me and said, "Oh man, you're Earl Monroe? I just saw you play tonight. Hey, man, I'm sorry."

By now I was hotter than a lit firecracker. I was almost foaming at the mouth. Then one of the guys with a gun says, "That's Black Magic! Black Jesus, who can walk on water on the basketball floor."

So they let us go. But I wasn't in any mood to go to a party after that, so I just walked back to the hotel, got in my bed, and fell asleep, trying to forget about what had just happened.

A few days after this, on March 19, 1966, Texas Western beat Kentucky, 72–65, in the NCAA Division I Championship game. Before they met, Kentucky had been ranked number one in the country and Texas Western number three. What made this game special was that Texas Western, coached by Don Haskins, who was white, started an all-black team and Kentucky, coached by the legendary Adolph Rupp, started an all-white team that included Louie Dampier, Pat Conley, and Pat Riley. After Texas Western won that game, Southern universities started recruiting star black players to play both basketball and football, and this was the beginning of the end for many of the great black basketball players—and football players, too—attending historically black colleges. But I remember Coach Gaines was disappointed to hear that Coach Haskins received hate mail from racist white people for starting five black players. Coach Gaines had always believed you started whoever were the best players regardless of race, and eventually his point of view turned out to be the correct one.

That summer my teammate at Winston-Salem, Ernie Brown, who was from the Bronx, invited me to come to New York to play against some of the best players up there. So I accepted his invitation. I found out that I would be playing against three of the players from Texas Western's championship starting five: Nevil Shed, Willie Cager, and Willie Worsley. The idea of playing against those guys just lit a fuse to my competitive fire. Anyway, some other guys from South Philly also went up to New York to play in those games, and they got there before me. We were supposed to play at Mount Morris Park, which is an outdoor playground in Harlem, but it started raining. So they had to move the games up to Saint Mary's Gym in the Bronx. By the time Ernie and I arrived at the gym, the guys from Philadelphia were already there, and when I walked in they started chanting, "Black Jesus is here and you New York guys gonna see Jesus walk on water!"

That made me feel really good, because there were some other great New York players there besides the guys from Texas Western, like the legendary New York playground player Pee Wee Kirkland and Tony Jackson, who played for Saint John's. They were looking at my Philly guys like they were crazy when they started talking about me like that. But after I got the ball and spun some white kid so hard I almost broke both his ankles, they started paying attention to me. Then I came down, put my spin move on two other guys, and hit a jumper from the top of the key. The gym went crazy, with people shouting, "Oh, man, did you see that move and what he did with that shot? That was crazy!"

And the Philly guys were saying, "It's on now, man, Jesus is here and he gonna walk on water."

And I did. Time after time I just put on moves and made spectacular shots that sent the people in the gym into delirium. They were screaming after I put a move on one of those guys from Texas Western, who had a real confused look on his face after I busted that move on him. Anyway, I was floating on air after I made those guys up in New

York believers in my game. It boosted my confidence for the rest of the summer that I could play the game on an extremely high level, and I carried that energy into my senior year that fall. When I went back to Winston-Salem in September, I was determined to do my best to lead my team to an NCAA championship, like those guys from Texas Western had, and to make a national reputation for myself. Little did I know that it would be a historic season for me and my Ram teammates.

Chapter 10

BECOMING "EARL THE PEARL" IN MY SENIOR YEAR AND THE PAN AMERICAN GAMES DEBACLE: 1966 TO 1967

MY SENIOR YEAR STARTED OUT with us playing some important scrimmages against the Wake Forest University basketball team that had been arranged by the Demon Deacons' head coach Jack McCloskey and his assistant coach, Billy Packer. Coach McCloskey had coached at the University of Pennsylvania when I was going to high school in Philadelphia, so he knew about me. Billy Packer had played at Wake Forest and had gone back there as an assistant coach (later, he would become a famous basketball color analyst for CBS), and he loved Cleo Hill as a basketball player. Anyway, Billy set up these practice sessions and our team and Wake Forest had about six of them at their gym. I remember when we got there, Coach McCloskey, who was a friend of Coach Gaines, saw that our ankles weren't taped and he told Coach Gaines they weren't going to let us play until he had us tape our ankles, which he did.

Now, we weren't used to playing with our ankles taped—it was a cost factor at Winston-Salem because the administration didn't have the money—and it almost felt like we were wearing casts. It was that stiff at first. So in that first scrimmage they beat us because we couldn't hardly move. But then we got used to our ankles being taped and we beat them five straight games. I remember me and their star player, Paul Long, having some spirited sessions. I also remember Coach Packer asking me to show the Wake Forest players my spin move. I tried, but the move was too quick and new for them—they were all white guys and weren't used to trying nontraditional basketball moves—to absorb. So he asked me to slow it down some so they could get it and I tried to do that, but my move was too intuitive, improvised, and spontaneous for them to wrap their heads around it.

After I realized I couldn't explain it to them verbally—it's hard to explain improvisation to someone who has never had to do it—I just stopped. One of my favorite sayings around that time was that whoever was guarding me couldn't ever figure out what I was going to do with the ball because I didn't know myself until I did it. So teaching them the spin move was out of the question. They had to feel their way through to learning and doing it and maybe, you know, their culture got in the way a bit. Perhaps the way they had been brought up in the game prevented them from being able to execute an improvised move. I don't know, but it's something to think about when comparing black basketball culture to its white counterpart. Still, those early scrimmages pulled our team together and got us off and running. Knowing that we could beat a major college team like Wake Forest gave our squad a lot of confidence going into the season. It also injected more purpose into my game.

We had a great year as a team my senior season and I put up some really outstanding scoring numbers. Our starters at the beginning of that year were Eugene Smiley, Smitty, Bill English (who would break my single-game scoring record of 68 the next year by scoring 77), Jim Reid (who was drafted by the Philadelphia Warriors the same year I was by Baltimore), and myself. Reid was about six feet six, a monster rebounder, good jump shooter, and great dunker. English was six six, and Smitty was five 10. I was co-captain of the team, sharing the honor with my longtime friend Smitty, who started at the beginning of the year, was replaced by defensive specialist Johnny Watkins, and then became an important contributor coming off the bench.

That year I led the nation in scoring, averaging 41.5 points a game overall, 44 points a game in conference play, and a total of 1,329 points, which is still the second-most ever. I shot 60.7 percent from the floor that year, and many of my points came on long jump shots. My highest scoring game was a 68-point explosion against Fayetteville, but I had a string of about 10 or 12 games scoring in the high 40s or more that Luix Overbea, a black sportswriter for the *Winston-Salem Journal*, referred to as "Earl's pearls." That nickname soon morphed into "Earl the Pearl," and it stuck to me from then on.

By the time I graduated from Winston-Salem I had set a school scoring record of 2,935 points, breaking the mark set by the great Cleo Hill. Our record that year was 31 and 1. We actually dropped 2 games that season, but the other loss was wiped away because the team that defeated us early in the season, High Point—they beat us 89–84—had to forfeit the game because of playing an ineligible player. High Point had some good players on that team, including Gene Littles, who played pro ball in the ABA and later became an NBA coach, and Tubby Smith, who coached Kentucky to an NCAA Championship. The other game we lost was to North Carolina A&T at the end of the season, in the CIAA tournament championship game. In between those losses we cleaned up on everybody we played.

I remember playing in the Chicago Invitational Tournament in late December of my senior year. I had been scoring a lot of points during the first games of the season, and a Chicago sportswriter said that I wouldn't get 50 points when I came out there to play. So in the first game of the tournament I just stopped shooting with two or three minutes to go, after I had already scored 48 or 49 points and we had established a manageable lead. I just wouldn't shoot anymore because I didn't want to get 50, just to let them know I was in control. Later, in the championship game against Wilberforce University, we were down at the half and I had to shoot in order for us to win 101–100. I got 50 points on the nose, okay? Because I could get 50 points anytime I wanted to. So I'm standing with my guys when they announce the MVP award, which I just knew would go to me. But they gave the trophy to Melvin Clark, a guy on the team we had just beat. He was a black, classic-style player, a forward I think, and he scored maybe 30 points in the championship game. I scored 50, and we won! Their excuse was that they had voted on the award during halftime. Everybody was shocked, but the guy who won went up and picked up his trophy like he deserved it and didn't even acknowledge me. I never saw or heard from him again after that. I don't know what happened to him and I'd even forgotten his name until I looked it up for this book.

We were playing great as a team despite losing a couple of key players off the previous year's squad, like Gilbert Smith, who would have started but quit because he couldn't get along with Coach Gaines. They were always arguing about something or other, and, Gilbert being a really smart guy (he's a PhD today), he just up and quit the team one day. The other guy who didn't come back was Sonny Ridgill, our second-leading scorer from the year before. I think Coach Gaines didn't want him back because Sonny thought he should have been getting more shots than he got and was probably a little jealous of me, but I don't know this to be a fact. Anyway, he had been at Winston-Salem forever and Coach just didn't want a problem on his hands. At least that's the way I looked at it.

One of the most gratifying memories of my senior year was when we had to move our games from our home gym to the Winston-Salem Memorial Coliseum—the same place Wake Forest played—because the crowds were getting so big. We were beating everybody and I was scoring so many points that we were packing them in like sardines, with every seat sold for every home game. Black and white people, young and old. People were being turned away, couldn't even buy seats, or find tickets anywhere. Even when we went on the road to play it was like this, with all of our games having to be moved from the school gym to the largest facility in any given town. All our games were sold out. Everywhere. It was something. Blew my mind.

People just loved to see us play, especially in North Carolina, and some people started saying that our team, with me as its star, was beginning to integrate the state. That was something, but there were a lot of white people at our games. So many, in fact, that they would take up the section of seats reserved for our students close to the floor. They were white and thought of themselves as being privileged. So they would just come in and sit down in those seats because they were some of the best seats in the facility. And I remember one time Coach Gaines saw them doing this and made them move, telling the crowd that the seats they were sitting in were reserved for Winston-Salem students, so they had to get up and move, and they did.

But the fans, black and white, started asking me for my autograph after every game, because I had gotten so famous now in North Carolina. Coach Gaines put a stop to that and made the fans ask the entire team for their autographs, because he knew it might create some tension on our team if I was the only one signing. So everybody had to sign their names to souvenir programs after every game that year, and that was a good thing.

Coach Gaines was really great for all of us, keeping us zeroed in on the realities of our lives and our futures. I remember one time during my last year at Winston-Salem, he sat the entire team down in the dressing room and asked us, "How many of you guys think y'all going to play pro basketball?"

So every hand was raised, I think, except for Ernest Brown's and Smitty's. So then Coach looked at us real hard and said, "I'm going to ask this question again and I want y'all to think seriously about it. How many of you guys seriously think you have a chance of playing professional basketball in the NBA or the ABA?"

So I raised my hand and James Reid raised his and a few others I can't remember, but less raised their hands than had the first time. Coach looked at everybody real hard, kind of smiled, shook his head, and said, "Yeah, well some of you sons-of-bitches aren't using y'all brains because ain't but probably two of you guys going anywhere near professional basketball and we all know who one of them is and that's Earl. And the other guy might be James Reid."

Then he smiled and looked at us again and said, "Those of you who didn't raise your hands ain't as dumb as I thought you were."

And everybody laughed and looked at me and James Reid. Now I must admit it made me happy when Coach Gaines said that about me and I could tell it made James Reid happy, too, because he had a big old smile on his face. But it also made me self-conscious that he had laid it all out there like that, because I was still really shy, even though I knew by then that pro basketball was definitely in my future. I guess I kind of felt bad for the rest of my teammates who weren't picked, though I knew Coach Gaines was telling them the truth.

Although I was shy I still led the team in my own quiet way, and everybody on the squad was cool with that. I wasn't a rah-rah kind of guy, you know, exhorting, "Let's go." That just wasn't (and isn't) my way. I wanted everyone to do well and they all knew this. I led by setting an example for everyone else to follow, by playing hard each and every time I was out on the court. I dove for loose balls, played tough defense, and was a good teammate, encouraging and supporting all my guys. And even though I scored a lot of points—which is what they expected me to do—I still had a lot of assists. I think I was also second on the team in rebounds.

After we lost our opening game of the season to High Point and saw the result reversed due to forfeit, we won 22 straight games, which made us 23 and 0 and regular-season CIAA champions. Then I scored 53 points in a 92–84 victory over the University of Akron Zips on a neutral court, making us 24 and 0 going into the CIAA tournament, which we were expected to win hands down. We beat Hampton Institute in the first game of the tournament, 114–73, and I scored 42 points. We were 25 and 0 and headed to the CIAA tournament championship game, where we'd face North Carolina A&T. We had beaten them twice during the regular season, 87–85 and 104–93. But they kicked our asses real good in the championship game, 105–82. I had a terrible game, due in part to the defense from George Mack, my old Philadelphia high school nemesis, and because of my own poor shooting.

But because of our outstanding record over the entire season we were invited to play in the NCAA Division II national championship tournament, which we won. In the process I became the second player ever (after Clyde Lovellette) to both lead the nation in scoring and play on the team that won the national championship in the same year.

We played Baldwin Wallace College in the first game of the tournament, and on that day I was told I had been selected to the United Press International small-college All-American team (I think Phil Jackson was on that team, too); I had made the Associated Press Little All-American Team the week before, as had Walt Frazier. We beat Baldwin Wallace in that first game 91–76, and I scored 34 points. The next day the *Sporting News* also selected me for their All-American Team, joining me with Lew Alcindor (later Kareem Abdul-Jabbar) from UCLA, Jimmy Walker from Providence, Sonny Dove from Saint John's, and Elvin Hayes from the University of Houston. That was a great honor for me, to be mentioned with those big-college guys. I remember the citation said that I had "tremendous ability with the ball" and that I was "a great scorer with a remarkable percentage from the field." I was really happy when I read that news!

Our next game was against a team we had already beaten, the University of Akron, but this time we would play them on their own home court, where they had a 54-game winning streak. Their fans had hung a derogatory sign about me in the gym that read, "Earl Monroe is just a myth! He can't compare with SUMTHIN' SMITH."

The player they were talking about, "SUMTHIN' SMITH," was actually named Bob Smith, and he was a pretty good little guard (Akron also had another pretty good player named Bill Turner, a forward, who was picked 27th in the 1967 NBA draft; Bob Smith wasn't picked at all). In that rematch game I scored 49 points, SUMTHIN' got 17, and I shut up whoever had hung that sign. On top of that, we beat them for a second time that year, 88–80.

It was during that game that the Akron fans started calling me "the Pearl," putting a new twist on Luix Overbea's "Earl's pearls." Coach Gaines used to always wonder if it was some of the Winston-Salem fans who had come up to Akron for the game that were calling out that name. We will never know. But after that the Akron papers used to say the nickname first started there and later they would say it started in Baltimore, after I turned pro. All I know is that Luix Overbea used that term before anybody else and I will leave the rest to the historians.

After we defeated Akron we moved on to Evansville, Indiana, to play Long Island University, and we beat them 62–54. I scored 29 points in the game and broke the single-season small-college scoring record. Then we played defending champion Kentucky Wesleyan College and beat them in a very close game. Their defense double-teamed me, so I decided I was going to pass the ball to my open teammates and I did, feeding my roommate, Eugene Smiley, who finished with 27 points, and Bill English, who scored 22 points. I ended up with 24 points and was happy we got the win.

Now we were 30 and 1 and going to the national championship game against Southwest Missouri State. We beat them 77–74 in a hard-fought, really close game. I scored 40 points and hit two crucial free throws with 25 seconds remaining to help seal the deal. After they shot and missed, I got the ball, dribbled the clock down, and threw the ball up in the air (always the showman) like I had seen Sam Jones of the Boston Celtics do once in a big game. When the ball came down there were only two or three seconds left on the clock and that was that. We finished the season 31 and 1.

We were the first black college to win an NCAA Division II Championship (Tennessee State was the first to win an NAIA championship). I was named MVP of the tournament, as well as the NCAA Division II Player of the Year. I had finally led a team to a big, important championship, and I loved the feeling. When we got back to Winston-Salem there was a large crowd—black and white people—at the airport to greet us, and I felt great for days after that. There was no other mountain for me to climb on the college level, so I turned my eyes to the NBA draft and turning pro. But a nasty little thing happened to me at the end of the season. The problem I had with beautiful Dorothy came back to torture me for a while.

What happened was I started receiving telephone calls from somebody telling me I had to pay them some money or else they were going to go to the newspapers with pictures of Dorothy and me together, which they said would hurt my chances of going high in the upcoming pro draft. By now sportswriters were predicting how high I might go, and early indications were that I'd be one of the top picks. So I figured these calls were about getting money from me that I would make in the future playing pro ball, because I certainly didn't have a dime to give to anybody at the time.

At first I was shocked and scared because I couldn't figure out who it could possibly be. Then I got a letter telling me specifically what motels Dorothy and I had been rendezvousing and making love in. So I started thinking real hard about who it could possibly be.

One day he called me again and said, "I saw you coming out of the motel with Dorothy yesterday, and unless you give me money I'm going to tell everybody. I'll be back in touch with you." Then he hung up the phone, but not before I had listened real close to his voice to see if I could maybe recognize if I had heard it before. Then I started really getting angry and thought to myself, *This motherfucker is trying to blackmail me for money he thinks I'm going to get when I turn pro.*

So now I was racking my brain trying to remember where I had heard the voice before. Then it came to me that it sounded like a guy named Tobias who had kept statistics and been a scorekeeper for our team. Now, I wasn't married, but Dorothy was and she had a kid. So I thought to myself that I wasn't going to give this asshole a dime. I just waited for his next phone call or letter, and I got this note from him a few days later that said, "Give me $2,000 and I'll keep this to myself. If you don't, I'm going to spill the beans."

There was a number on the letter for me to call and I called it. Someone answered and I said in a lowered voice, "Who is this?"

"You don't know me," the guy said, "but I saw you and Dorothy coming out of the motel and unless you pay me, I'm going to tell her husband and everybody."

So I said, "Hey, I'm not married, man. Fuck it, then. Go tell anybody you want to tell."

"You want me to tell?" he says.

"Fuck it," I said. "You tell anybody you want to tell. Don't matter to me because I'll be out of here in another month. Plus I know who you are."

And he hung up the phone and I never heard from him again. Nor did he say anything to anybody. Case closed. But that incident taught me something valuable and I decided to break off my relationship with Dorothy. But then she got divorced from her husband and moved to Baltimore and started teaching school there. We had a little relationship there for a minute, but it fizzled out after a while because I started getting into other things. But she had become like a drug to me for a while, and this was one of the deepest relationships I had been involved in up until that time, especially from an emotional point of view. I promised I would never go out with a married woman again in life, but that was a promise I broke many times during the coming years.

At the end of March, after we won the championship, me and a few guys went barnstorming around the state just playing games for fun and to keep our skills up. Then I left them and went and played in a North-South All-Star game at the Coliseum in Charlotte, North Carolina. I played on the South team and our coach was the legendary Jerry Colangelo, but I only knew him as "Coach" or "Jerry" at the time. Anyway, I scored 40 points, we won the game, and I was named MVP.

In mid-April I was invited to the Pan American Games trials, which were held in Saint Cloud, Minnesota, a town of about 60,000 people. When I arrived at the airport I saw only one black man, and he was sweeping the floor. So I walked up and asked him how many black people lived in the town.

"About five," he told me without hesitation, "and they all work either out here at the airport or in town at the bus or train station, doing what you see me doing."

He smiled a knowing smile that told me the place wasn't too cool for black people. Then he winked and went back to sweeping the floor. I went out the door to a waiting bus, which took me to a hotel. It was really cold up there in Saint Cloud and there was nothing for me to do but eat, sleep, and play basketball. I played on the NAIA team with Charlie Paulk and with Al Tucker, who, like me, was later drafted in the first round. I also played with Henry Logan, a little guard out of Western Carolina, on that team. He was a really good player who went on to play with Rick Barry on the Oakland Oaks in the ABA. Another guy on that team was Bob Kauffman, who played with the Buffalo team in the NBA and later became the general manager of the Atlanta Hawks.

But the best players on that team were Al Tucker and Charlie Paulk. Both were six foot eight. Paulk, who was drafted by the Milwaukee Bucks and later was a teammate of mine on the New York Knicks, played in the NBA until around 1974, so he had a nice little pro career. Tucker played for a while in Seattle and was a teammate of mine with the Bullets. Anyway, it was Logan, Tucker, Paulk, Bob Kauffman (who later became the general manager of the Detroit Pistons), and me on the starting five. The tournament was between four teams: one made up from the NAIA (the team I was on), one from the NCAA, one from the Armed Forces, and one from the Amateur Athletic Union.

The team I played on wound up winning the tournament, and I led everyone in both scoring and assists. We beat a team that had Wes Unseld and Elvin Hayes on it. But for whatever reason, I didn't get picked for the Pan American team. The only player on my team who made the squad was Henry Logan. Someone told me later that the coach, a man named Jim Gudger, didn't like my style of playing and thought it was an embarrassment—too street, too playground, too black for him. Here he was a white guy passing judgment on my game even though I had already proven that I was a team player and a winner!

When I asked around about the reason I was left off the team, several people told me that Coach Gudger thought my game would insult the international competition we would be playing against. Now, Henry

Logan was a hell of a player, don't get me wrong. He could do everything well and deserved to be on the team. But there were other guys
that made that team that shouldn't have been there over me. I forget
who they were, but they were there and they knew I should have been
on that team. I know Wes Unseld, Jo Jo White, and Sonny Dove were
on that team, and they should have been there. But Elvin Hayes didn't
make that team, either. Why didn't he and I make that team?

In my opinion, it was a racist thing, no question about it in my
mind. That kind of stuff would plague me throughout my whole basketball career. Some of those incidents hurt me, but none of them were as
painful as what happened to me in the Pan American Trials. That rejec-
tion prevented me from representing and playing for my country abroad.
That hurt a lot, left a scar in my memory that has lasted even until this
day. I'll never forget it. It was also a two-pronged insult, because
Winston-Salem State was the only winner of the national championship
that didn't go overseas to represent the NCAA.

Those incidents gave me a kind of anti-American feeling, and it
made Black Power a lot more relevant and prevalent in my life from then
on. After that I got into the movement in my own sort of way; I started
wearing the red, green, and black colors of the movement in my little
kufi cap and in the sweatbands I wore during games. And I wore green
battle jackets and the little sunglasses as a fashion statement. The Pan
American Trials incident changed me fundamentally, and I started being
more aware of everything I did as a black man. It also made me look
closely at how my country—a country that I loved!—was treating black
people, and it turned me from a pacifist into an activist from then on.

But the NBA draft was coming up. All the experts predicted I'd be
selected very high and I was, higher than any of the players picked over
me for the Pan American Games squad. That was sweet revenge,
although I still would have loved to have been picked for that team.
Still, as I always said, it is what it is, and I moved on with my life because

there was nothing I could do about not being picked for Gudger's team
but prove him wrong, which I did.

It happened for me on May 3, 1967, in New York City, when the
Baltimore Bullets made me the number two overall pick in the NBA
draft (Providence's Jimmy Walker was chosen number one by Detroit).
This served as an affirmation of me amongst the owners, coaches, and
scouts of the greatest professional basketball league in the entire world.
What my high draft choice meant was that my talent counted, and that
an NBA franchise was willing to pay me to showcase my ability, you
know what I mean? For me, that was my vindication and it marked the
end of the Gudger story, though it didn't end my pain at not being
selected for the Pan American team.

On May 2, the day before the draft, I had come home to Philadelphia from Winston-Salem to hang out with some friends, and I got
home very early in morning, about 3:30 a.m. When I drove up to my
mother's house, I saw that lights were on in the kitchen and I thought
maybe something had happened because Ma never stayed up that late.
So I got out of the car and went into the house and into the kitchen and
who did I see there but Buddy Jeannette, who was the general manager
and then head coach of the Baltimore Bullets; Gene Shue, the assistant
coach (who would succeed Jeannette later that year as coach); somebody else I didn't recognize; and my mother. I had met Coaches Shue
and Jeannette previously because they had come to a few of my games
and Buddy had expressed an interest in my playing for the Bullets
before.

I must admit that I had a feeling the Bullets really wanted to draft
me because in the middle of April I had come home one day and found
a red convertible 1967 Mustang sitting outside our house. When I went
inside, my mother told me that the Bullets had sent the car up for me to
ride around in. I had a car, but it was an old Oldsmobile and this was a
shiny new machine! But the funny thing about this car was that I didn't

know how to raise the canvas top back up. So when it rained I had to find a place to sit under a bridge until it stopped raining—I was too shy and proud to ask anybody how to raise the roof. Then, after the rain stopped, I would drive the car back home and dry out the insides with some rags, and then it would happen again and I would have to do the same thing all over. Now, the car was fun while it wasn't raining, but I was kind of glad when I had to turn it back in—it was a rental that the Bullets had paid for.

When I walked in the house everybody was grinning like Cheshire cats. Then Buddy said they were going to draft me in the second spot the next day in New York City (they already knew who Detroit intended to select with the top pick) and they wanted me to drive up with them and be there when they made the announcement. So I said, "Cool. When do we leave?"

"Right now," Buddy said.

"Cool," I said. "Let's go."

So my mother gave me a big hug and we went out and got in their car and drove up to New York to the hotel where the draft was being held. They had gotten me a room there. They were staying in the hotel, too. So when we got to our rooms and settled in they came back and pulled out these papers and I just signed them without reading them over or realizing it was the contract—that hadn't even been negotiated—I was signing. Now, we didn't have agents back in those days and I thought in my head that Coach Gaines had negotiated the deal for me, but he hadn't.

Later, we would have a disagreement about this because I thought if anybody was going to be looking over the contract it would be Coach Gaines, who would have negotiated whatever I was signing. See, I knew I wasn't sophisticated enough back then to know anything about contracts. I just came to play basketball. That's all I knew, and especially coming from a small black school I wasn't used to signing anything as complex as a contract with all kinds of clauses dealing with money.

Coach Gaines came up a short time after I had signed the contract. The Bullets had invited him up and paid his expenses. Coach knocked on the door and they let him in, and I remember he was so big that day he filled up the entire door frame. After he came in and said hello to everyone, he looked down on the table, saw the contract, picked it up, and read over it. Then he turned to me with his eyes blazing and said, "Son, what have you done? You signed the fucking contract for $19,000 for one year!"

So now I was sitting there with my mouth open. Shocked. Coach Gaines told me to step out of the room because he wanted to speak with Jeannette and Shue in private. So I did, and about 20 minutes later they called me back into the room and I read over the contract. This time it was for $20,000 a year for two years. They had changed it a little, but it was still a bad contract. I realized it was my fault, but I had to live with it. I'd deal with the next contract in two years. It was what it was, you know what I mean? But I wouldn't make that same mistake again. Ever.

Soon it was time to go down to face the press and take part in the draft ceremony. Then I realized I hadn't brought a jacket to wear, so Buddy took his off, which was an unhip-looking plaid jacket, and gave it to me to put on. So we went down to meet the press and the announcer introduced me as the number two pick after Jimmy Walker had been announced as the number one selection. They presented me to the press and a reporter asked me, "How much did you sign for?"

"A substantial amount," I said.

That was all I could think of to say. I had had visions in my mind of making $100,000. But that wasn't what it was going to be, and it was my fault. I was never bitter about the deal I made, but I promised myself I would be a lot smarter the next time my contract came around. I didn't know—and still don't know—what everybody else who was in that draft received in their contracts, though I know it was probably a lot more than I got. But, like I said, it is what it is and I had to go on from there with a positive outlook.

The number three pick after Walker and myself was Clem Haskins, another really good guard from Western Kentucky, who was selected by the Chicago Bulls. Walt Frazier, from Southern Illinois University, was the fifth pick, selected by the New York Knicks. Hey, what can I say? It was a great year for guards coming out of college! Other notable players selected in that draft were Sonny Dove from Saint John's University (selected number four), Al Tucker from Oklahoma Baptist (number six), Pat Riley from Kentucky (number seven), and Phil Jackson (number 17). Other players selected who I knew or had played against were Cliff Anderson from Philadelphia (by the Los Angeles Lakers), my teammate James Reid (by the Philadelphia 76ers), Bill Turner of the Akron Zips, and Paul Long of Wake Forest.

Smitty and I graduated from Winston-Salem on time, on Thursday, May 30, with Dr. Harold W. Tribble, the president of Wake Forest University, giving the commencement address. Now, that was something. I remember being so happy to see my whole family there and how happy they were for me, especially my mother. Big Jimmy, my sister Ann's husband, was running around trying to take pictures but his camera wasn't working. So I was up on stage trying to pose for him and he was running around cursing because he never got his camera to work. Somebody else took pictures, though, and documented the entire ceremony for the school.

Some days I look at those pictures and still feel proud of myself. Graduating was very important to me because I remember when I first arrived at Winston-Salem, Coach Gaines took all the basketball players aside and said, "All you guys, you athletes, come here thinking you're somebody special, and you are in terms of playing basketball. But don't think you are some kind of Don Juan or Rudolph Valentino with the girls down here because you can shoot a basketball. King Kong could come in here and get some of these girls because there's so many. But what's going to happen to you after basketball, or sports? So you better watch yourselves the first semester, because you're going to see all these girls and they're going to get into your heads. You're going to be walking around, holding hands, and you're not going to study or do your work and the next semester you will be on probation. Then, at the end of the year you're going to be out of school because you're going to be thinking about basketball and girls and not your schoolwork. So y'all better check yourselves and stay straight because many of you won't graduate and you will be sorry down the road."

I never forgot what Coach Gaines said that day, and on my graduation day there were only four or five guys—you know, athletes—that graduated out of around 230 people. I think it was Smitty and me, a football player named Melvin Mayo, and I think James Reid. So Coach was right, and I have always thought about what he said that day during my freshman year, how right and on the mark he was. I will always be thankful to him for that, for those words of wisdom and for all the other things he taught me about basketball and life.

There were more riots in the country that summer, in Cleveland, Detroit, and Newark, New Jersey. Dr. King led an anti–Vietnam War march in New York City. Muhammad Ali was indicted in Houston for refusing to be inducted into the American Armed Forces to fight the war. It seemed like the country was falling apart racially. But then a good thing happened when Thurgood Marshall was appointed to be a justice on the US Supreme Court, the first black person ever to serve on the highest court, and that lifted my heart and my spirit.

Now my eyes and energy turned toward playing for the Baltimore Bullets. I would prepare myself again with constant practice over the summer, honing and sharpening my skills. I was also going to be playing in the legendary Baker League for the first time, and playing against top-shelf competition, many of them pros. I knew playing in the Baker League would prepare me to go down to my new city, my new home, to make my mark in pro basketball. I knew I had a lot to prove because a lot was expected of me. But I also felt my talent was there, that I was up to the task. I was very focused, absolutely convinced my game had grown by leaps and bounds and would carry me through to stardom, something I had long imagined for myself. And I was sure, almost to the point of arrogance, that I would claim a spot amongst the elite of the game, and that I would do this in my rookie season.

Part Three

MY HUNGER FOR

NBA RESPECT

AND A

CHAMPIONSHIP
RING

Chapter 11

A PARADIGM SHIFT IN
PRO BASKETBALL:
MY ROOKIE YEAR, 1967 TO 1968

IN THE SUMMER OF 1967, I finally got my opportunity to play basketball in the famed Charles Baker Memorial Summer League. According to the guidelines of the league, players were eligible to compete only if they weren't high school or college students. So since I had graduated from Winston-Salem, that wasn't a problem. The league was a quasi-pro league, though no one got paid for playing in games. The league was founded by William Randolph "Sonny" Hill—everybody called him "Sonny" and sometimes teased him about his full name—who was still a great basketball player at the time the league was formed. As a matter of fact, one of the reasons Sonny started the league was so he could compete against all the top-flight players he planned to invite. But running the league became a full-time job and before long he stopped playing and became the coach of his own team.

A five-foot-nine-inch guard, Sonny was born on July 22, 1936, in Philadelphia, where he was raised. He was a high-jumping scorer in his day, feared for his outstanding, extremely accurate jump shot from any spot on the floor. Sonny had played against and was a close friend of the great Wilt Chamberlain, who once scored 100 points in an NBA game and still holds more than 90 NBA records, when they were in high school. Guy Rodgers, the extraordinary ball-handling guard who twice led the NBA in assists, was Sonny's mentor and friend. So Sonny came from a longtime Philadelphia basketball legacy and was a student and historian of Philadelphia basketball.

Sonny had attended Central State College in Wilberforce, Ohio, for a minute—two years to be exact—and made All-Conference in his freshman year (another notable name on that team was Dick Barnett, also a freshman, from Tennessee State and later my teammate on the New York Knicks). But Sonny dropped out of school in order to play in the Eastern League, where he also excelled. Then, in the summer of 1960, Sonny started a four-team pro league on a concrete court outside of Moylan Recreation Center at 25th and Diamond Streets in North Philadelphia. During the mid-1960s, at the invitation of a local pastor, Reverend William Gray, Sonny moved his league to a basement gym annex of Dr. William H. Gray Jr.'s Bright Hope Baptist Church at North 12th and Oxford Streets.

The league was reconfigured and its first games in the new league were played there. City commissioner Charles Baker, the uncle of Temple University basketball great Hal Lear, helped Sonny get the permits he needed to start the league, and after Baker died Sonny named the league after him, calling it the Charles Baker Memorial Summer Pro League. Over the years some of the greatest basketball players in this country—black and white—have competed in the league, including Hal Greer, Cazzie Russell, Chet Walker, Clifford Ray, Darryl Dawkins, World B. Free, Bill Melchionni, Billy Cunningham, and, of course, Wilt Chamberlain and Guy Rodgers. Later, I played against and with Bill Bradley, Willis Reed, Walt Hazzard, Wali Jones, and Archie Clark.

I played on the Gaddie Real Estate team, coached by Herb Janey. Frank Card, who I had played against at West Philadelphia in high school, was on my team. Tom "Trooper" Washington, who played at Edison High in Philly (and who was a teammate of Connie "The Hawk" Hawkins with the Pittsburgh Pipers in the old ABA) was also on that team; Trooper was also one of my very good friends. Sonny coached the Jimmy Bates B-Bar team and had some great players like Ray "Chink" Scott (later my teammate with the Bullets), Jim Washington, Wali Jones, and George Lehmann. In later years Sonny had Cazzie Russell, Hawthorne Wingo, Bobby Hunter (who played for the Globetrotters), and Bill Bradley on his team. The Kent Taverneers were coached by John Chaney and had Hal Greer, Chet Walker, and Ben Warley as members of that squad. Then there was the Century Chevrolets, which had Billy Cunningham and Luke Jackson on its roster. So you can see they had some well-known players dueling against each other in that league, including a bunch of future Hall of Famers.

We played two games a week from late June to the end of August. The games were played on a gray concrete floor set against wooden, moon-shaped backboards in a gym with no windows or air conditioning. So it would be hot as hell inside there in the summer, with temperatures reaching more than 100 degrees, even with the doors open. I remember when I played my first game there that summer, all of us players went outside at halftime to wring out our sweat-soaked jerseys. Then, after wringing them almost dry, we went back inside and played the second half just as hard as we had the first half. In addition, all the fans who had been jammed into that sauna bath of a gym—about a thousand people in all—came outside with us at halftime to get some much needed relief from all that heat themselves.

It was something playing in all that heat, with all those fans screaming their heads off—black and white. But that great competition was why all those players were there and what all of us—the fans included—were there to see. (I don't think this kind of competition could happen these days because of the money players now make and the injury risk.)

At the end of the summer there would be a tournament to determine the champion. Then there would be a draft and each team would select its players according to a lottery. That's how I got to play with the Gaddies team. As I said, no one ever got paid to play in the Baker League, which was hard for many people—including a lot of players at first—to believe, or understand. But it was true.

One of the first things I picked up regarding playing in the Baker League came from Ben Warley, a six-foot-five shooting forward and guard from Washington, DC, who could really play. He was playing for the Anaheim Amigos in the ABA at the time—he was an All-Star in that league—and had once played for the Baltimore Bullets, the Phila-delphia 76ers, and as a member of Tennessee State's three-time NAIA championship team. Anyway, Ben had pulled me aside in my first year playing in the Baker League and said, "Good luck when you come here to play, Earl, but I'm going to give you a piece of advice."

"What's that?" I said.

"Don't take the ball out of bounds."

So I looked at him and said, "What do you mean, don't take the ball out of bounds?"

Ben looked at me with a big smile on his face. Then he laughed and said, "Because if you take the ball out of bounds, you'll never see it again!"

I thought that was strange until I was in my first exhibition game and the ball went through the hoop after the first shot, hit the floor and started bouncing. And it bounced and bounced and bounced until it stopped on the floor and everybody was standing around looking at the ball. Nobody picked it up until the referee did and he just gave it to the nearest player—which wasn't me—and told him to take it out, which the pissed-off player did, shaking his head in exasperation. And I remembered Ben's advice as I was running back up the floor and just burst out laughing. Man, that shit was funny and I never forgot it.

That first summer playing in the Baker League I did very well, scored a lot of points, about 32 or 33 a game. I also dished out a lot of assists and put on some great shows for the fans with my crowd-pleasing game. (After that summer, Sonny Hill and I formed a very close friendship and he became my basketball mentor. I could go to him with any basketball question or problem I had in my life and he was always there to counsel me. My relationship with Sonny remains a very special one to this day.)

After I finished playing in the Baker League late that summer, I stayed around Philadelphia for a few days before going down to Baltimore for my first pro training camp. When I arrived there in late August, I was ready to get down to the business of playing pro basketball and having a great year and career. But first I had to find myself a place to stay, to lay down my head at night, where I could sleep comfortably. I was without a car because I didn't have enough money to buy what I wanted, but I did find a nice little apartment on North Avenue, near Druid Lake, right off Monroe. The apartment was in the back of a real estate office, which was like a brownstone. I had three rooms and I roomed with a guy named Malkin Strong, who was a second-round pick of the Bullets out of Seattle, Washington.

Malkin was a big strong kid, about six seven or six eight and 230 pounds. But he couldn't play basketball at the time because he had injured his knee, an injury he never recovered from. He never played with the Bullets and eventually went back home to Seattle. But Malkin and I became fast friends while we were roommates, because we were together a lot doing community service work for the Bullets organization. Like we would go to different basketball courts and shoot around with the kids to promote the team. We stayed together in that apartment on and off until the season started.

Malkin was married to a white lady named Betty, who came down to be with him. Around this time I met a beautiful lady named Cookie

at a party, and I started going out with her. But the four of us never went
out to dinner or anything like that together, because when I did social-
ize I usually took Cookie to parties that my social fellowship, Groove
Phi Groove, threw. The fraternity had started at Morgan State, which
was in Baltimore, so there were a lot of my brothers around there. Then,
when the season started, I moved into a place on Garrison Boulevard, in
the Beacon Hill Apartments, near the Green Spring Apartments. It was
a medium-sized one-bedroom apartment, and it was easy to get downtown to our home arena, the Baltimore Civic Center, from there. I had
gotten a car by this time, a champagne-colored Pontiac Bonneville. I
didn't spend very much money—in fact, some people probably called
me cheap—but I didn't put myself on a budget. I just tried not to spend
a bunch of money.

The Bullets' regular training camp was out at Fort Meade, Maryland, on an army base, but the rookie camp was held downtown in Baltimore, and they put up all the new players in the Downtowner Motel
on Reisterstown Road. The star player on our team was Gus Johnson,
and I found out that there was always some rookie or new player coming
to the Bullets' camp with the specific intention of taking Gus's job.
Now, there were sportswriters who were always writing about some
new guy that was supposed to be special and whatnot, you know, better
maybe than Gus. That is until the new phenoms got to camp and went
up against him and Gus would crucify them. Gus Johnson was a hell of
a player, and after he got done with these new phenoms, the sportswriters would have to wait until the next year. And the embarrassed new
players would be reduced to licking their wounded egos in the corner
somewhere, after they were cut from the Bullets' roster.

We also had characters at those camps like Dexter Westbrook, who
was a six-eight forward from New York City and had played at Providence College with Jimmy Walker. He was a real smooth player who
could handle and shoot the ball well, and he understood how to play the

LEFT: My mother, Rose, and my father, Vernon

BELOW LEFT: My grandmother, Mom

BELOW RIGHT: My Aunt Mary

All photos courtesy of the Monroe family unless otherwise noted.

RIGHT: With Ma and a neighbor in front of our house on Alter Street

BELOW LEFT: All dressed up

BELOW RIGHT: With Mr. John in front of Mom's house

Vacation Bible school, 1955. This is where I shot my first baskets. That's me in the white T-shirt, directly under the rim.

John Bartram High School senior prom, 1962

It was during my college days at Winston-Salem State that I first became "the Pearl."

ABOVE LEFT: *Associated Press*
ABOVE RIGHT AND BELOW: *Photos courtesy of Winston-Salem State University office of Athletic Media Relations*

ABOVE: With Coach Gaines *(left)* and Leon Whitley *(right)*, the man who recruited me to Winston-Salem.

BELOW: With James Reid *(left)* and Steve Smith, accepting CIAA award.

ABOVE LEFT: A 1967 game against Long Island University. *(Associated Press)*
ABOVE RIGHT AND BELOW: Facing Akron in the 1967 NCAA Regional
Final. *(Photos courtesy of Winston-Salem State University office of Athletic Media Relations)*

ABOVE: College graduation, 1967. *Left to right:* Ma, me, my niece Tijuana, Mr. John, Theresa, Andrew, and Ann

LEFT: With Winston-Salem's chancellor, Dr. Kenneth Williams, on my graduation day

A 1969 matchup against the Bucks. *(Associated Press)*

Me and Jack Marin after a 1971 win against the Knicks. *(Associated Press)*

Thinking back on all of those battles with Clyde before we became teammates, that time is like a blur. *(From the lens of George Kalinsky)*

Shooting over Wilt Chamberlain at the 1969 NBA All-Star Game *(From the lens of George Kalinsky)*

ABOVE: Handling the ball against Cleveland *(From the lens of George Kalinsky)*

BELOW: Taking Wilt to the hole in Game 4 of the 1973 NBA Finals *(From the lens of George Kalinsky)*

Shaking hands with Dave DeBusschere after winning the 1973 NBA Championship
(From the lens of George Kalinsky)

LEFT: My father, Vernon, later in life

BELOW: Ma in the mink coat I bought her on her last Christmas

game. In the beginning of the rookie camp he was killing everybody with his basketball ability. But the longer the camp went on, the worse he got, until finally, after Gene Shue insisted he go for a checkup, he had to reveal to the coaches and to management that he had mononucleosis. Then they found out the reason he had mononucleosis was because he had a drug habit and was using heroin. Man, that was so weird! So he was forced to leave the camp and I haven't seen or heard from him since. Personally, I was sorry to see him go because I thought he had a great game and he and I would have meshed very well together.

Then there was Ed Manning from Jackson State College in Mississippi. Ed was the father of Danny Manning, who led Kansas to the NCAA Division I national championship in 1988, became the number one overall pick in that year's draft, and went on to play 17 seasons in the NBA. Anyway, Ed came to camp with this big old footlocker and he had everything he owned in there because he said he wasn't going back to Mississippi. We called him "Razor" because he could cut off screens so well. He could also jump very well and was strong as hell. He had a nice little jump shot, and man, could he dunk the ball. I mean real quick. He was six foot seven, 210 pounds. He lived out of his footlocker until he made the team, which he did after playing really well in camp.

Bobby Allen was another player in rookie camp. Bobby was from Arkansas, and man, could he really shoot the ball. He was about six eight, maybe six nine, really thin, and he had a pronounced Southern drawl. He would say stuff like "When is the honey coming to Kansas?" *What? What did that mean?* I used to ask myself. But Bobby lived around Baltimore. I remember seeing Bobby play, I think, in the Georgia Invitational Tournament. Come to think of it, Ed Manning played in that tournament, too. Bobby didn't make the team but he was a really interesting guy.

There was also a guy at that camp named Jimmy Hall, who went to

Morgan State. Anyway, he had a hustler thing going on, you know. He talked out the side of his mouth. He was a good guy—he wasn't a thug—but he talked real slick.

Funny story about Jimmy. I remember that there was some kind of convention going on around the motel we were staying at during rookie camp, and there were lots of prostitutes hanging around. Jimmy was trying to pimp the girls on to guys on the team, trying to negotiate the money aspect of it, you know what I mean? The guys on the team were just trying to get their nuts up out of the sand, you know, get with a woman so they wouldn't be so horny, because most of them were a long way from home. So Jimmy's trying to help out by getting girls for some of the guys on the team (not me, because I had Cookie) and so I guess he was able to be the pimp of the rookie camp, to make a few deals. He didn't make the team, though. I know he stayed in the Baltimore area because I would see him around. I think he became a schoolteacher.

But out of all those guys who came to rookie camp, the only ones who stuck besides me were Ed Manning, Stan McKenzie, Roland West, and Tom Workman—a total of five players. I think management carried 12 players on our squad that dressed for games, maybe a couple more to round out the entire team. At least 50 or 60 players came to camp trying to make the team, though, so a lot of good players didn't survive the cut. After the cuts were made, the five of us who survived moved on to start practicing with the veterans out at Fort Meade. But all of a sudden Roland West, a six-foot-four-inch guard from the University of Cincinnati, just disappeared, you know, vanished from camp. Nobody knew where he was. Well, we found out later that he had gone to Elkton, Maryland, to get married. It was really strange, and it didn't bode well for him, either, because he eventually was cut from the team after playing in only four games. And he never played in the NBA again.

Now, we rookies went out to Fort Meade to compete against the

veterans like Gus, Johnny Egan, LeRoy Ellis, Bob Ferry, Kevin Loughery, Jack Marin, Don Ohl, and Ray "Chink" Scott. These were names
we had all heard of, so we knew we were moving into the big time and
I, for one, was pumped. I had been waiting for this for a very long time
and I was ready for the challenge. But the first practices weren't anything special, you know, because we were just running through plays,
getting to know guys I had already seen play at Convention Hall, where
the 76ers played before moving to the Spectrum. I knew Chink Scott
because he was from Philadelphia, and I had seen LeRoy Ellis play when
he was at Saint John's. I had met Bob Ferry because he had come out to
scout me for the Bullets, but I didn't really know him and had never
played with him. Of course, I had watched Gus Johnson, and it was a
thrill to finally meet him. I had watched Jack Marin, Kevin Loughery,
Don Ohl, and Johnny Egan play, but I didn't know them, either. But out
of all those guys, I found that I gravitated to Gus most, because of his
energy and charisma. I was cool with all the rest of the guys, most of
whom were married. And because I was single that became like a natural social barrier.

Then, after a while, the level of play in the practices picked up and
the competition got intense. Now I could see how hard it was to succeed at the NBA level, because all the players could play. But I relished
competition and it just helped to raise the level of my own game. These
practices were where the rookies were trying to show what we could
do. If you were a rookie forward like Ed Manning, Stan McKenzie, or
Tom Workman, you had to go up against Gus Johnson, and he would
be out there beating you down every day. He'd come in and start flex-
ing on us, because he was a real strong man, a really powerful player.
He did that to Dexter Westbrook, too, before Dexter was forced to
leave camp. Gus beat him down so bad it was pitiful to watch, but
that's just the way Gus was. By the time Dexter left camp he was a
shadow of the player he had been when he first arrived. Much of that

was due to the mononucleosis, but a lot of his collapse and demise was because of Gus relentlessly beating him down. Gus tried to do the same thing to Razor Manning, but Razor was able to hold him off. Razor was tough and had vowed not to go back to Mississippi, so he fought back and Gus grew to respect him.

Gus was hip, too. He had a gold star in one of his front teeth, wore great clothes, had style, sported a Fu Manchu goatee—I think he was the first player in the league to wear one—so all of the black cats on the team gravitated to him. Although he walked with a slight limp, he even made his walk look cool. Gus had a 48-inch vertical jump and could leap so high he could pick a quarter off the top of the backboard. He was a street cat, known to knock guys out and shit. But he was lovable, too. Still, you didn't mess with him. Gus was very charismatic. He just drew people to him, and I liked that. He had a funny way of talking. When we went out to restaurants he had this thing about trying to speak all proper, like he would say in his real deep voice, "Give me one of them excellent steaks and cover it with some of that War Chester Shire sauce."

Man, we would almost fall off our chairs with laughter when we heard him talking like that. But one evil look from Gus would shut our mouths up real fast and all laughter would quickly disappear from the air. Then Gus would grin at us and start laughing himself and everybody would know things were all right.

Gus had his flaws, too. Like we found out he had borrowed a lot of money from the team. When it came time to renegotiate his contract he couldn't put his best foot forward because of all the money he owed management. So they kind of gave him what they wanted to pay him because they had him over a financial barrel. I know I learned from this example not to ask for any more money from the team than was in the contract, learned this early from watching how they treated Gus. Management would advance you the cash if they thought you were a valuable player, but the catch was you had to pay it back come contract time. So I just learned to live on the money I was being paid.

I also decided in my rookie year that I wasn't going to get married while I was playing professional basketball. After seeing how some of my married teammates acted up out on the road and how their wives reacted to them after hearing rumors of other women, I knew I didn't want to be a part of that. I already knew what was out there with women, so I didn't want to be a dog to my wife, you know what I mean, with all kinds of ladies calling up my house. So I just stayed single, because I knew how much I liked being with many women and I realized my involvement with them would be a no-no if I was married.

I liked Gene Shue as a person and as a coach. Gene liked Gus Johnson, was a real Gus fan. Gene had one of those Johnny Unitas crew cuts, and he and the legendary Colts quarterback were probably the last two white guys in Baltimore to get rid of that hairstyle. People on our team used to call Gene "Jim Shoe," like "gym shoe," because he was in the gymnasium so much. He had a great love for the game and a good sense of what needed to be done. Plus, he was funny, too, had a very good personality that I could relate to. He was a very soft-spoken guy, analytical, and he could explain what he wanted players to do come game time. He talked basketball constantly, and tried to teach players on the fly as the practices went along. One thing about Gene was you didn't really make the team until you played him one-on-one, because he was still playing ball regularly. Gene was about six foot two and was still in good shape, weighing around 175 pounds. He was born in Baltimore, played college ball at the University of Maryland, and was the third overall pick in the 1954 NBA draft. As a pro he made All-NBA and was a top scorer in the league, twice averaging better than 22 points in a season. Coach Shue had a pretty long NBA career—twelve years, I think—and played in five straight All-Star games from 1958 to 1962. So Gene wasn't a slouch as a player.

Gene had a spin move himself, but his was done with two hands. Still, he was very slick with the ball and in the way he played the game. A lot of guys didn't make the team because they couldn't beat him one-on-one. (The next year, when Fred Carter came to try out for the team, he proceeded to hack Gene to death when he was guarding him. That's how Fred got his nickname, "Mad Dog" Fred Carter. So he became a defensive specialist. Plus he scored on Gene, too, and that's why he made the team.) I beat Gene when we played one-on-one. I didn't hack him or nothing like that, but just shot the lights out on him when we played, you know, beat him handily, scored on him at will with my own slick spin moves and outside jumpers.

Gene was instrumental in helping me develop as a pro ballplayer because he let me play my game and then reined me in when he saw me doing stuff like making passes that many on the team—with the exceptions of Gus, Chink, and Kevin—couldn't handle. Gene knew what kind of player I could be, what I might contribute to the team in terms of winning and people coming to see us play, which meant money in the team's bank account. He knew and understood this, you know, the entertainment aspect of pro basketball. He knew that with my style I was going to put asses in the seats of the Civic Center once word got out. So he brought me along carefully, allowed me to play my game so that I would become an asset in the future. When I realized this, I understood that I was fortunate to have a coach like Gene, because if I had gone number one in the draft to Detroit, I would have been in a very different situation.

Earl Lloyd, the Pistons' top scout, was one of three blacks (along with Nat "Sweetwater" Clifton and Chuck Cooper) who broke the color barrier in the NBA in 1950. Lloyd really wanted to draft me number one, but Detroit's management overrode him and took Jimmy Walker, a more traditional player and a safer pick, instead. Jimmy fit into the vision they wanted for their future team better than I did. Plus, he was a player from a predominantly white university who people had seen around the country, so it was an easy sell. And he was National Player of the Year! So why pick a player who averaged 41.5 points a game at a small black college, a guy with a multitude of weird nicknames, like "Slick," "Black Magic," "Einstein," "Pearl," and "Black Jesus," over him? It was a sure shot. And they didn't pick me and I dropped to Baltimore, which was great for me.

The same thing might have happened had I gone to another college instead of Winston-Salem with Coach Gaines, you know, because other coaches might have wanted to change my game. But both Coach Gaines and Gene Shue embraced the way I played. If I had gone to another pro team and they refused to let me play like I played, you know, and tried to marry my playground style to an on-the-edge traditional approach, my pro career probably would have been very different. But Gene let me flourish in Baltimore, so I'm indebted to him for letting me be me.

I got along with everyone on the team while we were practicing and playing games. But I socialized only with the black players because that's just the way it was back in those days. Of the white guys on the team, I felt Jack Marin and I were the most different, because he was a right-wing guy from the jump. Now, Jack was really smart, and a very fine player. He was from Pennsylvania, too, but he was from a small town and I was from a big city. He went to Duke and had a certain arrogance about himself that might have turned some people off. Gus pretty much kept him in place, just by being Gus. But then again, Gus kept everybody on our team in check.

Gus was from Akron, Ohio, and had played on the same high school team with Nate Thurmond, who was six foot 11 and, like Gus, also had a Hall of Fame career. (I can't even imagine how great that high school's team must have been! To think about it now is even scary!) On the court and off the court, Gus was the go-to guy on our team. He could shoot the ball, had a nice little one-legged fadeaway shot, was a ferocious dunker, could rebound and really play defense: Gus always guarded the opposing team's best player.

After a month or so of practicing together and trimming the roster, we finally had a squad of about 12 guys. When the season got under way I was the first player coming off the bench because Don Ohl, a white guy with a great jump shot, was the starter, along with Gus, Jack Marin, Kevin Loughery, and Chink Scott. I was averaging about 14 points a game coming off the bench for the first month or so of the season. But sitting on the bench proved a good thing for me—as it had my first year at Winston-Salem—because it gave me a chance to watch and analyze the pro game up close. I learned a lot from this. I could see the flow of the game, what the guys were doing, what was working, and what wasn't working. When I did get into the game I had a feel for what we were doing as a team at that moment and how I fit into that in terms of setting up my teammates to shoot or picking spots to score myself. Like maybe I saw we had to speed the game up some, or slow it down, or maybe get the ball down into the hole—the pivot—a little bit more.

Our team was a run-and-shoot group of guys, and we didn't have a lot of patience as a group because we had a lot of shooters. Like I said, Don Ohl was a great shooter, but he never changed the way he shot his jumper. So he would get it blocked over and over and he'd still be shooting it the same way, all the time, from the top of his head. Kevin was another great shooter, with a lot of energy, as were Jack Marin and Gus.

Gus's nickname was "Honeycomb," or "Comb" for short, because one day when he was in college someone in the stands had yelled out, after he made a great shot, "Wow, he's sweet as a bee's honeycomb!" That was his name amongst his teammates after that. Gus had a lot of flair in the way he played the game, and he was a very good passer as well. Like, he would get a rebound and we would be running at full speed down the court and Gus would throw a perfect behind-the-back pass to whoever was free and that player would catch it in full stride and shoot a layup for the score. Gus was something else. Even his opponents liked him.

But then in October or November I got the sad news that Mom had died in her sleep in Philadelphia. Her death set me back emotionally, because I have never really handled death well, especially someone as close to me as Mom was, or anyone else in my immediate family. But despite it being difficult for me—I have never liked attending funerals—I went up to Philly to attend her funeral with my mother and sisters.

The services were held at Chew Funeral Home, where she lay in state, and it was packed with mourners because she had a lot of friends. I stood in the back of the mortuary and didn't go up to view her body in the open coffin they had Mom laid out in. I hate looking at dead bodies laying there all waxen looking and lifeless in a casket, so I never do it. I wanted to remember her like she was when she was alive, vibrant, full of humor and a great, loving spirit. People came up and told me she looked good in death, but I just didn't want to see her in that way. Now, I don't know if that's a good thing, but it's just the way I am.

After the funeral and all the crying and sadness, I had to pull myself together to go back down to Baltimore and focus on playing basketball again. That was hard to do for a week or two—Mom's face kept jumping into my mind for a while, even when I was with Cookie sometimes, or playing in games—but eventually I was able to refocus my mind on basketball and the little things I had to do to get better as a pro.

The first part of my rookie season was all about the process, you know, learning the pro game and where I fit in with my teammates. One day, after we got through practicing, Coach Shue came up and said he wanted to talk with me about my passing. Now, what had been happening was that my behind-the-back and no-look passes were catching my white teammates by surprise and they were either not catching the ball or my dishes were hitting them upside the head. See, they weren't used to playing like that, with a player like me who could pass the way I did. They were missing the passes even when they were wide open because they were used to traditional passes from their teammates, not these razzle-dazzle dishes that were coming from me.

Coach Shue pulled me aside and said, "Earl, now you're a great passer and those are great passes you're making. Creative and imaginative. But these guys are not catching your passes because they're not ready for them. So you got to kind of hone them down. That way they'll be able to see the passes coming and receive them. And in the end, when they can't see them coming, they are bad passes because they're turnovers and they hurt the team. What do you think?"

Now, I was shocked at first when he told me this, because I thought I was being a good teammate by making good passes to players who were wide open to make shots. I was even looking at them with my eyes to signal I was about to pass them the ball, but they couldn't decipher what my looks meant, so they would miss the passes. It was frustrating, because they were wide open, all by themselves, you know what I mean? But I understood what Coach was saying. My passes *were* creating turnovers. They *were* surprising my teammates and that's why they were dropping or not seeing the ball. This was now clear to me.

"I understand what you're saying," I told Coach Shue. "And I will try to make passes my teammates can handle from now on."

Coach smiled. "Just hone them down a little until they get used to your style," he said, "and when that happens you can go back to passing like you know how to do. I'm sure it's all going to work out in the end for the better."

We shook hands and everything did work out, just like Coach Shue said it would. But I did start harnessing my game a little more, shooting the ball in situations where my instinct was to look for a creative pass. Another thing that meeting with Coach Shue taught me was if I made a pass to a guy who couldn't catch the ball or make a shot when he was wide open, those were bad plays. So for me it was important to know who could and couldn't catch the ball and make the play, you know, get a good shot off and make it. Because there's a lot that goes into passing the ball. You not only have to know who can make a shot if you give them the ball, but also where on the floor to get them the ball. These are things a lot of people don't think of when they're making a pass, and with Coach Shue's help I was starting to implement them as a rookie.

After a while my white teammates did get used to handling my razzle-dazzle, behind-the-back, no-look passes. Eventually they were even looking out for me to make them, and I did a lot as the season progressed. I learned a lot from that brief conversation with Coach Shue and I began to really trust him as a very good coach for me after that, because he embraced and encouraged me in the way I played the game.

After we broke camp, Abe Pollin, who was one of the owners of the Bullets, invited everybody out to his country club somewhere in the Maryland countryside. Now, some of the white guys played golf, so they went their individual ways out on the course like they had some sense. But the black guys had never been anywhere near a golf course before. Some of us got into the golf carts, but I stayed in the clubhouse and just looked out the window at the beauty of the place because I never liked playing golf and didn't know anything about the game at the time. So these guys were riding in the golf carts and playing hide and go seek with each other out where there were trees. They were running carts across the putting greens and one of the old white guys sitting in the clubhouse across from me saw them and said out loud to the manager, "What the fuck are those black guys doing out there! Get their asses off those greens and take them off the course!"

So they sent security to bring them in and that ended our stay at that country club on a sour note. Abe never invited us back again. But I

liked Abe Pollin and his family, especially his wife, who was a very stylish woman.

Besides starting over me, Don Ohl also wore my old number 10 on his
jersey. I had to wear number 33, and this kind of bothered me because I
had worn number 10 for so long it had become almost spiritual for me
(athletes are very finicky, almost superstitious, regarding the numbers
they wear, and I was no different). But I took it in stride because I was a
rookie and Don was a veteran. Plus he was a good guy. Our first game
of the season was against the New York Knicks, on October 18, and we
beat them 121–98 in Baltimore. This was a promising start for us, and I
scored 22 points coming off the bench. Jack Marin had 24 and Don Ohl
had 13. I think Willis Reed and Dick Barnett scored 22 each for the
Knicks. I remember Walt Frazier didn't play in that game—I don't know
why. I had been looking forward to going up against him, but that would
have to wait for another day.

    Sometime in late September or early October, Frank Deford, the
well-known, very respected writer for *Sports Illustrated*, came down to
watch me play and interview me. This would be the second story Mr.
Deford had written about me for *Sports Illustrated*. The first one was a
short article published on March 6, 1967, after I had scored 53 points in
a game against Livingston College and reached the 1,000-point mark for
the season, becoming one of the few college players to ever accomplish
the feat. Now the Baltimore native wanted to write about how I was
faring as a rookie in the pros, so he wrote another very favorable piece
titled "It's Earl, Earl, Earl, the Pearl." It appeared in *Sports Illustrated* on
October 30.

    Then on October 21 we played the Boston Celtics, again in Balti-
more, and we lost to them 125–109. Now, I must admit that playing
against the Celtics was special for me. They were my favorite basketball

team when I was growing up in high school, because Bill Russell and Sam Jones were on that squad. So I was a little bit in awe of them in that first game. I always looked up to Sam Jones because he came from the same college conference, the CIAA, that I had played in. Sam had been a star at North Carolina Central University and could really shoot the ball—especially that famous jumper he banked off the backboard from either side of the court. So I was too busy watching him the first time I played against him. But that awe evaporated after he treated me so bad that night, just shot me out of the gym. (But I vowed that the next time I played against the Celtics it would be different, because I was going to be ready to compete against him properly.)

The first time I saw an opening to go to the hoop in that first Celtics game, I did, beating my defender, Larry Siegfried, cleanly. I drove the lane for what I thought was going be a beautiful right-handed layup on the left-hand side of the basket, but the legendary, great defensive player Bill Russell came from seemingly out of nowhere and swatted away my shot! I couldn't believe it! I hardly ever had any of my shots blocked because I got them off so quickly. A little later in the game I beat my man cleanly again and dashed to the basket and shot the same shot and *smack!* Russell did the same thing to me again. This time he looked at me, wagged his index finger, winked, and, with a little grin on his face, shook his head as he ran back up the court as if to say, "Welcome to the big time, kid."

Now, I was really pissed off. A little bit later I saw that same opening and I put another nice spin move on my defender, left him nailed to the floor, drove hell-bent to the basket again from the left side. This time I had my eye out for Russell, so when he came to block my shot I ducked my head under his outstretched arm, put my body between Bill and the ball, switched the ball to my left hand, used the hoop as a screen, hung in the air until I was on the other side of the goal, spun the ball off the backboard with my left hand and into the goal for a score.

Bill looked a little shocked by the move. I was elated, and as the crowd was cheering wildly, I turned to run back down the floor and hollered at Bill with a big grin on my face, "You can't get 'em all, big fella!"

He looked at me and cackled *ha ha ha* with a big grin on his face. Wagging his finger, he said, "Yeah, but two out of three ain't bad, rookie!"

Those were moments from my first season in the pros that I will always remember: my first game against two legends, Sam Jones and Bill Russell. Those moments let me know for sure that I was in the big time of basketball. They also taught me that with some seasoning I could be on the same level with these great players, and motivated me to demonstrate through my skills and my play that I belonged there with them. I was used to getting cheers, not jeers, after my career at Winston-Salem. So now I was going to bring that game to the NBA and make everyone take notice.

But a really annoying thing kept happening to me early in my rookie season, and that was the referees calling me for palming the ball when I made a spectacular spin move and scored (I later found out that they had never seen anything like it before—it was so quick—they just couldn't believe what they were seeing with their own eyes, that it could be done without me doing something illegal). So I complained to Coach Shue about it and he took the refs aside, gave them some films to watch of me making the move, and after looking at them they realized I wasn't palming the ball and stopped calling that rule infraction on me.

There were two other important early-season games that had a significant impact on my psyche and the way I would play the game in the future. The first game was when we played the Detroit Pistons on November 3 and lost at home 115–113. The other was the next night in Detroit, where we lost again, 127–118 (I think these marked the last two games of a six-game losing streak that had begun on October 27). Dave Bing, Terry Dischinger, Dave DeBusschere, John Tresvant, Happy

Hairston, Eddie Miles, one of the identical Van Arsdale twins, Dick—
his brother Tom played for the Cincinnati Royals—and of course Jimmy
Walker were some of the players on that Pistons team.

What happened was Eddie Miles, a guard known as "The Man with
the Golden Arm" because he could shoot so well, picked me up defensively at the half-court line when I brought the ball down. Back in those
days a defender could hand check his offensive opponent, you know—
this was outlawed in 1994—he could put his hands on the offensive
player's back, stomach, legs, arms, sides, and hips to try and stop him
from scoring. So Eddie did this to me. Now, I had played against this
style of defending a little on the playground but not in high school or
college, and in that second game it bothered me a lot. His tactic prevented me from getting into the normal flow of my game because he
played me so close—or "in my jockstrap," as we used to say—when I
came into the front court. Eddie got inside my head when he guarded
me like this and I didn't get a chance to do anything, to shake him, you
know, to put my spin moves on him and get free to score. In the first
game I think I scored 12 points, but in the second game I was shut out.
This really perturbed me, you know what I mean? It really did, because
this was the first time I had ever failed to score a single point. There was
a big fat zero by my name in the box score.

On the bus ride down to Cincinnati, where we were scheduled to
play our next game, I kept visualizing Oscar Robertson and the way he
played offensively. I remembered "The Big O" used to put his back up
against his opponent as he dribbled the ball in the front court. Then he
would back the defender down to get closer to the basket and shoot his
turnaround jump shot over him from 15 to 18 feet away from the hoop.
So I said to myself, *Okay, I'm going to try that.*

Fortunately for us, Robertson didn't play in that game, and his absence
from the Royals' lineup helped us beat them convincingly, 122–100. I
bounced back from getting shut out with a 22-point effort. When we

returned to Baltimore I asked Gus, who had hands of steel and was a great, hard-nosed defensive player, to guard me and put his hands on my back and on my hips. What I learned from those practices with Gus was that when he put his hands on my hips he was actually leading me around the court, wherever he wanted to guide me. So after a while I was able to fight off Gus's pressure and back him down, though it was hard because he was so strong. Once I learned this move I was able to back Gus down, get into position, turn around, use my pump fake, and shoot my fadeaway jumper over him.

The next time I played against Eddie Miles, on December 12 in Baltimore, I implemented my new move at the beginning of the game. I started at half-court, where he picked me up, turned my back on him, backed him down to the foul line (I got there quickly, too). Then I pump faked. He went up to try to block my shot, and when he was coming down I went up over the top, shot the ball, and scored. *Wow*, I said to myself, *this is something else!* As I was running back down the floor, I glanced over at Eddie and he looked a little confused. He had never seen this kind of game coming from me before, because previously I was either shooting long jump shots or slashing to the basket. This was a new Earl, and he wasn't prepared for a Big O–style game from me. So this was my whole hookup for the rest of the game. I got 32 that night and we won going away, 140–117. Eddie scored 18, I think. And as I was walking off the floor after the game, Eddie told me I had played great.

"Yeah, don't even think about it," I told him, "because in the last game I got zero points. So over the two games that means I'm only averaging 16 points against you now."

He laughed, but the last laugh would be coming from me because I scored a lot of points against him and Detroit for the rest of the season. I liked playing against the Pistons because it was fun going up against them, and it's possible that I might've drawn some extra motivation from their having bypassed me at the top of the draft. I don't really know if that's true, but I do know I have always believed in getting revenge. Anyway, in my first season against Detroit, after I had no points against them earlier, I scored 32, 13, 37, 35, 35, and 37 points before culminating with a 49-point outburst on February 24 in Baltimore. We always had really entertaining games against Detroit because they had really good guards, starting with Dave Bing (who is now the mayor of Detroit) and Jimmy Walker. And I always enjoyed playing against those two guys.

I spent the bulk of that first NBA season learning and steadily getting better as a player, and over time, Coach Shue gained more and more confidence in me when I was in the game because of the flow and chemistry I was bringing to the team. We were running and scoring more easily when I was in the game, and that made everyone happy even though we were still losing. I was adjusting to playing against great players every night as opposed to only a few times a season when I was in college. We were still in last place, but I could sense the team was coming together and jelling as a unit.

We played Philadelphia on Christmas Day in Baltimore and lost 108–105 in a close game. I scored 13 points and Kevin Loughery led us with 21. Hal Greer and Billy Cunningham each had 27 points and Wilt had 15 and a ton of rebounds and blocked shots. I was a little sad that I couldn't go up to Philly to be with my family and close friends that day, but I was seeing Cookie more regularly at this time and we were getting along very well. Still, playing professional basketball was taking up more and more of my time with the constant practicing, playing, and traveling. So I couldn't be with Cookie as much as I would have liked to, because I really enjoyed being with her. It was hard sometimes, though it was something that I had to adjust to as a professional.

Then one day in late January I woke up and was greeted by the news that Baltimore had traded Don Ohl to the Saint Louis Hawks. That was shocking. But I guess Coach Shue and management had seen enough growth in me as a player and had enough confidence in me to make that important decision; I liked Don, but I was overjoyed now that I knew I'd be starting. I was also happy to be getting my old number 10 back.

But then I had to endure some unwanted (and unwarranted) media attention because of a story that Charles Rayman of the *Baltimore Evening Sun* wrote about me. What had happened was that on January 17 we had played the New York Knicks in Baltimore and lost a very tight game, 111–109. I scored 26 points that night but missed a last-second layup that would have tied the game and sent it into overtime. After the game I was really down on myself for blowing what had been a makeable game-tying shot. So I was sitting in front of my stall in the locker room, about to go to the shower, when Rayman came up to me to ask some questions. But instead of talking to me about the game, he pulled out his pad and said, "So, I hear you got your draft papers today. Are you going into the service?"

"Naw, I'm not signing up for no draft," I said, shocked by his question. "I'm not going to no damn service!" Then I just brushed it off. And the next day the headline of a front-page story in the *Sun* read "Monroe Refuses the Draft," which was completely untrue.

The truth is that when I received my draft papers I went down to take my physical and was declared 4-F because I had bad knees. I had hurt my knees before in an accident when I was working at the Knitting Mill and drove up to New York City with Wilkie. I had borrowed the car and was driving through Harlem and was hit by another car when I ran a red light. My car jumped the curb, hit a light pole, and was totaled. My legs jammed up under the dashboard and my knees were injured as a result. That was a scary event, but I walked away relatively unscathed. After all the police reports were filed, we took a bus back to Philadelphia, where all the legal stuff was worked out.

After the newspaper story I began getting letters from retired servicepeople about how they were going to do this and that to me and make sure I joined the Army and whatnot. I was perplexed by this turn of events, you know. People talking about how privileged I was being a black man playing pro basketball and making money. A lot of people were pissed off at me for a while, and the way I figured it, it was all because of Muhammad Ali's refusal to go into the Army in April of 1967. A lot of people were trying to put Ali and me in the same boat and tar and feather two famous black men with one stroke. But I never liked war anyway, and to paraphrase Ali, I didn't know anybody in Vietnam who was trying to enslave or lynch me in my own beloved country over the years. So the whole thing just got on my nerves and didn't make sense to me.

Then Alan Goldstein, who also wrote for the *Sun*, came to interview me after a game toward the end of January and he really pissed me off, also. Now, I liked Al, we got along well. But when he started asking me about being inducted into the Army, I got so angry about the topic that after answering a couple of questions I got up and left the dressing room. Then Goldstein wrote a story for the *Evening Sun* that was published on February 1, in which he reported that I had passed my Army examination and was 1-A, which, again, wasn't true. I was angry about all of this, so I stopped speaking with most sportswriters after that.

Some writers are always trying to distort what is actually being said for whatever reason, you know, trying to write something sensational, because they might not like you. And sensationalism is known to sell newspapers. Whatever. Either way, I was beginning to see how the media could possibly work against me. So I just tried to be careful from then on about what I said to reporters.

My scoring had been really picking up after the first of the year, but following the trade of Don Ohl on January 20, my scoring soared. Over a span of 13 games from that date to February 13, I averaged 39.8 points a game. But on February 13 I hit the jackpot, scoring 56 points against the great Jerry West in a thrilling 119–116 overtime loss to the Los Angeles Lakers (West scored 47 points in that game and Elgin Baylor added 32, while Gus had 18). I remember being very relaxed before that game. Cookie came over to my apartment and made my usual pregame meal of spaghetti and meatballs. Then she came into the bedroom and we started messing around and we had some great sex, which made me a little bit late getting down to the Civic Center.

Whether it was the spaghetti or the sex or something else entirely, I was very much at ease with myself that night. I felt really good, like I could do almost anything, you know what I mean? I always looked forward to playing against Jerry—and his teammate, Archie Clark—because he was not only a great competitor, but also one of the greatest players of all time, both offensively and defensively. But I was on fire throughout that entire game, hitting on drives to the basket, long jump shots—which would have been 3-pointers had that game been played today—bank shots I spun in off the backboard, dipsy-doo layups down the lane, little fadeaway jumpers in the paint. I mean everything was clicking. And Jerry and Archie couldn't do anything about it but watch. It was something.

After I scored those 56 points on the Lakers, everyone in the league started to notice me and my game. I remember in that game, even before it started, when the two teams were saying hello and shaking hands before tip-off, Jerry said to me, "Hey, Ben."

Now, I didn't know who he was talking about. I thought maybe some psychological shit was going on, you know, Jerry playing games with my mind. So I just said, "Hey, what's up?" Then we shook hands. With both of us scoring like crazy once the game started, it seemed like a mutual admiration society as we complimented one another after making great shots. But every time I would come down and score, Jerry would say to me, "Nice shot, Ben." And he kept calling me this throughout the entire game.

I was getting puzzled now. And since I didn't know what or who he was talking about, I decided not to pay him any mind. (I found out later that he was calling me "Ben" after another black player, Ben Monroe, who had played for the University of New Mexico and was drafted by the Lakers!) Later, after the game, Jerry came up to me with this big smile on his face, shook my hand, and said, "Real great game, Earl."

"Thanks, man," I said. "You played a great game, too."

Then he trotted away, grinning like a Cheshire cat. And I thought to myself, *He knew my name all along!*

After I thought about it I came to the conclusion that he was just really trying to play games with my mind—get inside my head, you know—and maybe, because I was a rookie playing against an experienced player, make me lose my focus. I never thought it was racial, because Jerry wasn't that type of guy. But he was a competitor to the bone, and he would use any trick he could to get his opponent off his game.

Jerry West was one of the quickest players I ever played against—"quick as a hiccup," to borrow a phrase from Sonny Hill—and he was all that and more. Jerry could stop on a dime and give you 10 cents change back, and man could he shoot the ball! He was just a fabulously quick, deadly jump shooter. He always went to the left when he shot his jumper, but he preferred to drive to the basket from the right side so he could shoot with his right hand. On top of that, Jerry was a great clutch scorer, one of the best of all time when the game was on the line.

I have always believed that in order to be a great clutch shooter you have to do it all the time and not be afraid to take that shot in order to make it. Because if you just do it now and then, you're not going to be a clutch player. You have to be accustomed to taking that shot. So Jerry was that kind of guy who was always ready to take it. He could dribble, get to his spot, pull up, take the shot, and make it. He did it over and over again. He was special in that way. And Jerry could jump, too, and take you to the basket and score. No doubt about it, he was something, and a very nice guy, too. So I felt it was a pleasure and a privilege for me to compete against him anytime, but especially that time when I scored all those points on him (and Archie Clark and Gail Goodrich, who also tried to defend me that night), because that game marked a turning point in my NBA career.

After that 56-point game against the Lakers, a sportswriter in Baltimore picked up on Luix Overbea's "Earl's pearls" quote—what they had already been calling me in Winston-Salem and in that game in Akron, Ohio, when they were calling me "Earl the Pearl"—and started using the nickname in his columns. It quickly spread to the national media and stuck in a way that "Black Magic" and "Black Jesus" hadn't, except in the black community. I guess those nicknames were too race specific to be used in the national media. "Earl the Pearl" turned out to be perfect because it was race neutral.

Before I learned Oscar's back-them-down move, my game had relied mostly on my shooting accuracy on long jump shots and my skill employing the spin move to leave defenders nailed to the floor, watching me slash to the basket for crowd-pleasing layups. But I was slowly beginning to adapt my game to fit into my evolving sense of how I could be more effective playing in the NBA. My game was always one of process, of evolving to the changing dictates of the modern game, and it would be no different going into the future.

I remember a game right before the All-Star game break (which I wasn't selected to play in, though I thought I should have been), when Kevin Loughery ran up to me up during a close game where I had been passing up my shots and dishing the ball to teammates and said, "Come on, Earl, take over the game. Take over the fucking game!"

I was shocked to hear that coming from him, but I really appreciated it because that's what I did—take over games. It was exciting for me, whether I scored points myself or got the ball to an open teammate.

It made me feel good that I had the confidence of veteran players like Gus and Kevin, because they wanted to win games. And we were starting to win games with me doing what I did best—score the ball. But I didn't think Jack Marin liked that idea so much, though he never said anything to me directly. I just heard whispers from other teammates that he thought I was shooting and controlling the ball too much, even though I was setting him up to score points, too. But Coach Shue never reprimanded me for playing the way I was playing. At the end of the day, the player who is in control of his team—and that was me now— dictates the flow of the game and gets all of his teammates involved. That was my job now, and everybody had to start getting used to it, making adjustments in their own approaches for the overall benefit of the team.

Once I recognized what I was capable of doing on the court at this level and my confidence grew, I started to make the crowds go wild. What they liked were the moves I made to get myself open to take shots. The fans were beginning to really like the show I was putting on. So did my teammates. Like I said, our team was starting to jell: Kevin was hitting his jump shot and so was Jack, banking in his jumper from both sides of the floor. Gus was throwing down spectacular windmill dunks so hard he was shaking the rim and the backboard, hitting his one-legged push jump shot, playing in his opponent's jockstrap with airtight defense, and blocking shots like a crazy man. Chink Scott was hitting nothing but nets on his long, sweet jump shots from anywhere he chose to launch them; Razor Manning was coming off the bench with his manic energy, jumping and running and throwing the ball down into the basket. Man, we were running as a team up and down the floor like rabbits. It was something to behold, very exciting. The Baltimore fans loved it and the crowds started to increase at the arena, the Civic Center, where we played our home games. And soon, by word of mouth, people were coming out everywhere we played to see us. And, like I said, we started winning games, and people love it when you're winning, when you're delivering both results and product. That's when they started coming out, you know what I mean? We were starting to put asses in the seats and management loved it. There were big smiles all around.

I was also learning a lot from playing against the best players in the world night after night. The competition was on a really high level and that just got my competitive juices flowing. I especially enjoyed watching and playing against Elgin Baylor and Oscar Robertson, two of my favorite ballplayers. Man, that was a treat. I didn't have to guard Elgin because he was a forward and I was a guard, so we didn't go up against each other head-to-head very often. But when we did it was special— competitive, but always respectful. Elgin could do anything he wanted to do with the basketball—shoot and score any way he wanted to— whether it was with jump shots, little hooks, or layups. It didn't matter. Elgin could dunk the ball if he wanted to, but he seldom did that, preferring instead to just lay the ball in on the backboard. He was also an excellent rebounder and passer, a complete all-around great player.

Same thing with Oscar, who to me was the epitome of a player who understood how to play basketball. Oscar would come out in the beginning of the game and set the tone by passing the ball, getting his assists, rebounding the ball. Then in the latter part of the game he would get his points. He'd back his opponents down, shoot turnaround jumpers over them, score on layups, whatever. I mean, he scored points in bunches, just took over games. And he was a big, strong guy—but not as strong as Gus—at six foot five and 220 pounds. I always liked the way he played. He was something else, too.

Then there was Wilt "The Big Dipper" Chamberlain—everybody from Philly called him "Dip"—who was in another category all by himself. He was the greatest player that ever lived, in my opinion. No question. Though he stood seven foot two and weighed 275 pounds, in his prime Wilt could run and jump like nobody's business. He could pretty much score on whoever was guarding him anytime he wanted to and pass, get assists, block shots, and snatch any rebound that came close to where he was. But he also had a legendary personality, could talk trash with the best, stay out until all hours of the morning and still outplay anybody—even those who had gotten all their rest—the next day. He was scary good, but he was a good guy, too, with a great sense of humor. Man, his talent was totally out of this world. He would have been a dominant player in any era, no doubt.

The NBA's top team in my rookie year was the Celtics, who went on to become the NBA champions that season (and the next year, too). They had Bill Russell, Sam Jones, John Havlicek, Bailey Howell, Larry Siegfried, Tom "Satch" Sanders, Don Nelson, and Wayne Embry on their roster. But I think the Philadelphia 76ers had as much pure talent as they did, with Chamberlain, Billy Cunningham, Hal Greer, Luke Jackson, Chet Walker, Wali Jones, Larry Costello, and Matt Guokas; with a regular-season record of 62 and 20, the 76ers were 8 games better than the Celtics that season. The same thing with the Lakers, who, despite finishing 4 games behind Saint Louis in the West, lost to the Celtics that year in 6 games in the NBA finals. They had, besides Jerry West and Elgin Baylor, Archie Clark, Gail Goodrich, Tommy Hawkins, Mel Counts, Darrall Imhoff (both of them really tall centers), and Freddie Crawford.

But the constant traveling was wearying, especially when we had to travel on poorly maintained airplanes with windows so loose the airline had to cover them with boards. The Bullets mostly traveled on Piedmont Airlines in those days, and I used to joke that their motto should be "We never lose sight of the ground." I said this because the planes never flew up very high. I mean, I could always see the telephone poles from my window, so long as it wasn't boarded up. Sometimes we flew on North Central, which was another ragtag airline. It seemed like their planes were always encountering turbulence. Of course back in those days we carried our own bags and washed our own uniforms. I mean there were some cats who would forget to wash their uniforms and they would be a little sweaty, maybe a little dried out, crusty and funky. So the smell up in the air would be humming.

Then there were arenas like the Cincinnati Gardens, home of Oscar Robertson's Royals. It was so raggedy. In the locker room we had to step on boards going in and out of the shower. I never took my socks off when I showered in the Cincinnati Gardens. The gym floors were terrible there, too. When we went to Cincinnati to play, we always stayed in the Sheraton Hotel. So when we'd go down to eat or to have a drink there would be a bunch of white guys sitting around the piano bar, drinking and talking and singing loud. I remember one particular night when me and two other black guys on the team—Ed Manning and Stan McKenzie—went down to the bar, these white guys started drunkenly singing a rendition of "Ole Black Joe," looking at us and grinning. I was glad Gus wasn't there because he might have killed one of those stupid assholes, and then we would have all gone to jail. Anyway, we just looked at them disgustedly, shook our heads in amazement, then got up and left. Boston was terrible, too. Back then the court at Boston Garden had dead spots that, when you dribbled the ball over them, would cause the ball to bounce oddly or veer off weirdly in some unexpected way. But the Celtics players knew where those dead spots were and would avoid them. Their visitors' locker room could be suffocatingly hot or real cold, too. But the Celtics locker room was really nice. So between the dead spots and the conditions in the visitors' locker room, Boston Garden offered the Celtics a true home court advantage.

As bad as Cincinnati and Boston were, I always liked going to New York, because Madison Square Garden had real great facilities. They also had really loyal crowds who cheered loudly for their Knicks. The floors were great and so was the city, so I always loved playing there, even when we lost. I liked playing on the West Coast, too, in Seattle, Los Angeles, and San Francisco. They had great facilities, the cities and people were hip, and there were beautiful ladies everywhere. Detroit and Chicago were also cool. I learned a lot by traveling across America, seeing how people were in different parts of the country. And hanging with Gus was really special because he knew where and where not to go in every city, and he passed this valuable information on to me.

Our last two games of the 1967–1968 season were against the Boston Celtics and the Philadelphia 76ers. We beat the Celtics 147–139 on March 17 in Boston, and I scored 29 points in that game. LeRoy Ellis scored 32 for us, Jack Marin had 28, and Chink Scott added 26. I don't think Gus played in that game. For Boston, Sam Jones scored 26 and Don Nelson had 24, but John Havlicek led them with 29. That was a high-scoring game, and after that loss the Celtics went on to win the NBA championship, beating the Lakers in the finals. After the Celtics won the championship I felt really good about that win and about our prospects for the next season.

Three days later we closed out our season with a 137–119 loss to the 76ers in Baltimore. I scored 46 points in the game, but it wasn't enough. Seven different 76ers scored in the double figures that night, with Chamberlain and Wali Jones leading the way with 26 and 24 points, respectively. Wilt's fall-away jumper, with just a few seconds left on the clock, hit the backboard, then skimmed along the top of it and fell in the basket to score. That basket gave him 1 more point than I had for the season, making him the league's third-highest scorer behind Dave Bing and Elgin Baylor. After the game he commented to me that he couldn't let a rookie outscore him. That was typical Wilt.

The 1967–1968 NBA season was kind of a weird one in that the Philadelphia 76ers had by far the best record in the NBA—62 wins and

20 losses—while the Celtics' record was only 54 and 28. But the Celtics beat the 76ers in the 7-game Eastern Division finals, coming back from a 3-games-to-1 deficit. Saint Louis had the best record in the Western Division, with 56 wins and 26 losses, but they were upset in the first round by a Nate Thurmond and Rudy LaRusso–led San Francisco Warriors squad, 4 games to 2. Los Angeles, who would beat the Warriors to secure a spot in the finals, had a regular-season record of 52 wins and 30 losses. So the season was kind of unpredictable in that way. My Bullets teammates and I finished our season sixth (and last) in the Eastern Division, with a record of 36 wins and 46 losses, but we were encouraged by our performance after the All-Star game, as we went 19 and 16 over the final 35 games.

Even though the Celtics won the NBA championship, the Lakers' Jerry West was named the Finals MVP. As for other individual honors, Wilt Chamberlain was named MVP of the regular season, and the All-NBA First Team was comprised of Dave Bing, Oscar Robertson, Wilt Chamberlain, Jerry Lucas, and Elgin Baylor. Hal Greer (MVP of that season's All-Star Game, which was played in Madison Square Garden), John Havlicek, Willis Reed, Bill Russell, and Jerry West were named to the second team. Dave Bing led the league in scoring that year, with 2,142 points and a 27-points-per-game average. As for me, I was voted onto the All-Rookie team, with Walt Frazier and Phil Jackson from the New York Knicks and Bob Rule and Al Tucker from the Seattle SuperSonics. I was also named the league's Rookie of the Year and was awarded a gold basketball, though I didn't receive it until the next season started. I wasn't the unanimous choice for Rookie of the Year, but I received all the first-place votes except one. For the season, I scored 1,991 points, averaging 24.3 points a game and leading the Bullets in scoring. I also dished out 349 assists, which was the most on the squad, averaging 4.3 a game. I played in all 82 games and led the team in minutes with 3,012 for the season. So all in all it was a pretty good season for someone they used to call a play-ground, "hotdog" player.

Then, on April 3, our team received some great news when the coaches and management selected consensus All-American center Wes Unseld of the University of Louisville Cardinals as the second overall pick in the 1968 college draft. Elvin Hayes, the high-scoring forward from the University of Houston, had been picked number one. But getting Unseld, a six-foot-six-inch, 245-pound rebounding and defensive college legend, was just what the doctor ordered for our team. Unseld's addition enabled us to move Chink Scott and LeRoy Ellis to their more suitable positions at forward and pair Wes with Gus Johnson under the basket. Plus, with Wes's rebounding and outlet passing skills, he could really trigger our running game and I envisioned us running the floor and scoring all kinds of breakaway shots off our up-tempo, fast-break style. I was really looking forward to teaming up with Wes, and I knew everyone else on our team was also.

We also picked up another fine rookie, Barry Orms, a six-foot-one-inch guard, in the second round of that draft. So with the good rookie year I had just finished, I felt great going into the next season. My off-season goals in the competitive Baker League were to double down on my conditioning and to practice and fine-tune my new move of backing my opponents down. During that time I would also gain a little more weight so I could be stronger and more successful in implementing this maneuver.

On another note, the NBA had expanded again, with the Phoenix Suns and Milwaukee Bucks joining the Seattle SuperSonics and San Diego Rockets, who had entered the league together the year prior. On top of that, the Saint Louis Hawks relocated to Atlanta. So the league was growing, and rapidly.

Obviously, my rookie year in the NBA was as great as anything I had dreamed of regarding my growth as a player. But in my personal life and in the world swirling around me, there were some shocking and stunning developments. At first, after the season was all over, I really enjoyed resting my weary body, spending time with my lovely lady, Cookie, and going back and forth between Philadelphia and Baltimore to spend time with my family and friends. I was beginning to like Baltimore, was getting to know the city better with the help of Cookie, Gus, and Lenny Clay, my barber. So I was feeling good, charging my battery back up, and just enjoying having some time off.

With all that in mind and to gauge where my head was at on my contract, Coach Shue called me a couple of weeks after I had gotten back to Baltimore from New York, once the playoffs were over. He said he wanted to take me for a ride to discuss the upcoming season and my new contract. So I said okay and we picked a day to get together. Anyway, he came and picked me up and we were riding around talking about the year we had just finished and then he said to me, "Earl, the owners recognized that you had a real good season and they feel as though they want to do something for you. They want to tear up your remaining contract and give you a three-year deal for $25,000, $30,000, and $35,000 for each of the three years."

Now, I hadn't complained out loud or anything like that over my two-year rookie contract. But they all knew I wasn't appreciative of what I got. So I just looked at him and burst out laughing. Then I said to him, "Well, Coach, I think I'm just going to go ahead and play this year out because I made that commitment. That's what I said I would do when I signed for two years, so I'm just going to ride the commitment out and see what the deal is after that."

Coach Shue didn't say anything after I said that. We rode around some more, talking about our team and the game of basketball, and then he took me back home and dropped me off.

But then on April 4 one of my all-time heroes, Dr. Martin Luther King Jr., was assassinated while standing on the second-floor balcony of

a motel in Memphis, Tennessee. The authorities said a lone white gun-
man named James Earl Ray had shot Dr. King with a rifle, although
many people still don't believe he acted alone. I didn't know what to
think about who really had him killed, because there were a lot of
white people that wanted Dr. King dead, especially with all the important civil rights work he was doing at the time. He was in Memphis
at the time of his death to support a strike by that city's sanitation
workers and planning a Poor People's March on Washington for later
that year that I was secretly planning to participate in. This was all in
addition to his many speeches opposing the war in Vietnam, a stance I
also supported.

I'm not sure about that one-gunman theory, but it always seems that
when something terrible like that happens it's usually one lone, angry
killer full of hate who does it and not a collection of people, you know,
forces that are part of a conspiracy. Dr. King's death sparked riots all
across the United States. His assassination shocked millions of people in
this country and around the world. I know it made me really sad to
think about how a man of peace, who had received the Nobel Peace
Prize, could die like that. For me it was shameful and I felt his death
deeply because I loved what he stood for. I was also sad and disappointed
that I never got a chance to meet him or to participate in one of his
marches. His funeral, which I watched on TV, was very sad but digni-
fied, and I will never forget the pain and noble sadness his widow,
Coretta Scott King, displayed in every photo I saw of her at the time.
But the pain of Dr. King's death stayed with me and it was one of the
reasons I decided that from that time on, I would participate in my own
quiet way to give back something to the black community in America,
and that I would start this while I was playing ball in Baltimore.

In addition to Dr. King's death, my first child, Sandy, a daughter,
was born in Philadelphia in May of that year. Her mother was a girlfriend of mine who worked in our grocery store and lived up the street

from my mother's house. I got her pregnant when I came home once on a weekend from Baltimore in September 1967. I had met her when I was in college. Her name was Sheila and we would get together from time to time whenever I would come home from school. We were close. I was also seeing a lady named Gloria in Baltimore, and at the same time I was hanging with Cookie. Gloria and her sisters were these light-skinned young women with nice legs that always sat in the front row at Bullets games. They were all very pretty. I got Gloria pregnant in April 1968. Our baby, a boy named Rodney, would be born later in that year, in December.

Now, there were a couple of funny things about going out with Gloria. One was that we broke up shortly after she got pregnant and she never told me she was pregnant. I had also—now, I know this will sound crazy—been going out with *another* woman named Gloria. But I decided I couldn't handle seeing her any longer because it was just getting out of hand with her boyfriend threatening and stalking us all the time. So when Gloria would try to call me to tell me she was pregnant, I thought it was the *other* Gloria and I wouldn't answer her call. My refusal to talk to her led to some complications between us that I will address later. Suffice it to say that things on the home front were getting a little complicated, and this was just a sign of my immaturity at the time. I wasn't proud of my actions, getting two women pregnant, but I wasn't ashamed of it, either. In retrospect, I should have known better because I hadn't been raised by my real father and didn't get to know him until I was already much older. But this fact didn't register in my thinking at the time because I was just too immature and, yes, selfish about what I wanted to make a better decision. In the end, though, it was my responsibility because they were my kids and I was just going to have to figure out a way to handle it. I hoped I would grow from these mistakes and I did, but not before I impregnated another beautiful young lady named Linda around 1970. But more about that later.

During late April of that year, I was one of three players on the Bullets—Bob Ferry and Chink Scott were the other two players— selected to travel to Japan as part of a USO tour. This was my first time ever traveling out of the country and it was an interesting experience. We took a flight from Baltimore to San Francisco, then another plane from there to Tokyo. In all, with both flights we spent 12 to 13 hours in the air, which is no joke for real tall guys like Bob and Chink (who were both six foot nine or six foot ten) and me being almost six foot four. Fortunately they provided us with seats that had legroom on all of our flights but we were still tired as hell when we arrived in Tokyo. Anyway, after we arrived we got into one of these little cabs and we were trying to explain to the driver where we wanted to go, you know, the name of the hotel, but he didn't seem to understand what we were saying. So we're sitting there with our knees bunched up under chins, mad as hell, and it's looking like this driver is trying to take us on a slow ride into Tokyo. This pissed everybody off so Bob, not thinking the driver understood English, jokingly said, "If you don't get us to the hotel in a hurry we'll blow this motherfucker up again!"

Well, the cab driver immediately stopped the cab, pulled over, turned around to Bob, and said, "You don't talk about Japanese motherfucker! Japanese fuck you up!"

Man, that cat was mad as hell with Bob. He wasn't a big guy but he was ready to fight all three of us. You could see the anger in his eyes. He understood English real well, including everything Bob had been saying. We were shocked. Then he turned around and started driving again and we rode in silence to our hotel. So we got there and he drove off without even taking a tip. When we got to our little rooms we found out that we had to share bathrooms with everyone else on the floor. That, too, was different for us, though we got used to it.

We were brought over there to visit hospital wards and troops who had been wounded in Vietnam. Our visits were supposed to encourage them but many of the troops were wounded so badly—very young guys with arms and legs blown off, burned so badly their faces had no noses or lips—it was very difficult for us. But the most traumatic visits for me were the burn wards. After a couple of visits I just didn't want to do them anymore, though I continued to do the visits anyway. Now, I understood why we were there but I just couldn't fathom seeing young guys alive one day, then the next day, when you come back, they're dead. I had never been around anything like that before and it wasn't something I was comfortable doing. It was hard and tragic for me to see young guys my age blown up, burned to a crisp, blinded and crippled for life. It's not a pretty sight and I applaud people who can visit people in that kind of state because I know I don't have the stomach for it. Aside from those visits we visited Guam and Okinawa as well and continued to make visits to wounded troops there. All in all we were there for over a week.

During that time, obviously, we had an opportunity to go out and do some things. We visited a geisha house, which was an eye-opening experience for me, a guy who hadn't been out of the country before, going overseas and seeing all of this. Every night we went out to dance clubs and in the ones where they had the most beautiful looking women we found out that they were really men made up to look like ladies. Every night I had been dancing with transvestites. Man, I almost threw up when I found that out. It was very frustrating, you know what I mean, thinking these guys were women and they were all men. Then again, it just taught me how naïve I still was at the time. So I told Bob and Ray that I was going back home. But I had to get a special dispensation from the late Vice President Hubert Humphrey to come back home because the tour wasn't completed. So I got my dispensation and since I had a government rank of a GS-15 for the tour they put me on a transport plane that stopped in different places and it took me 26 hours to get back to Philadelphia. That trip showed me I wasn't cut out for the military. I applaud those guys who go into the armed services because I saw with my own eyes that they were doing a great service for the country, risking their lives and well-being by fighting wars to protect us over here.

That trip was a heck of a learning experience for me; seeing all those young men wounded like that affected me deeply, gave me a different perspective about war, that we shouldn't engage in them unless it's completely necessary. I have the same thoughts about war today.

Chapter 12

PRESSING PEDAL TO THE METAL, FULL SPEED AHEAD: 1968 TO 1969

BEING NAMED ROOKIE OF THE YEAR was something that I relished, because it was like a validation of Philly basketball, the Baker League philosophy, the "science of the game" approach, and Coach Gaines's Winston-Salem style of playing, you know, to get out and run and create and be imaginative. For me, that's what the Rookie of the Year Award affirmed, you know, a black approach to the way basketball should be played: with a whole lot of music up in the moves, a lot of rhythm like James Brown's music or Miles Davis's approach to jazz. Now that approach had gone national through me and my style of playing, had spread through the word-of-mouth drumbeat of real people— both black and white—who loved basketball and found my approach thrilling.

Why do I say this? Because they were starting to come in droves, from the East Coast to the West Coast and from the middle of the country, to watch me play. It was something for me to behold, and you have to remember there was no ESPN, no highlight shows, no famous sports media personalities to push who they liked on the fans. No, it was the fans themselves who were voting for who and what they liked by buying tickets to come watch their favorite players play, and I was high amongst those they most wanted to see. It was Oscar Robertson, Jerry West, Elgin Baylor, Wilt Chamberlain, Dave Bing, Bill Russell, and me. That was something. Because when I first came into the NBA people on the West Coast only saw me when I played out there. Same thing on the East Coast and in the Midwest. NBC was the only national network that showed basketball games on a regular basis at that time, and they only showed games on weekends. The NBA's relationship with television was just beginning back then. Really, it was in its infancy.

Now, I don't know exactly why the fans took to my style of playing, but I'm pretty certain it had something to do with the entertainment aspect of it. Like ordinary people and fans of basketball—and players— thought I was fun to watch because I was unpredictable in my approach. I think some of that unpredictability came from the way I kind of saw myself back then. There was a lot of trickery in my game. Like I would come down, spin left, then right, or I would fake like I was going to spin and then just keep on going straight. Or I might come down the floor and if I was juking or whatever the case might be, I would maybe fake my opponent with my dribble and by moving my body from side to side. Then the defender wouldn't know which way I was going and I didn't really know either, because with me it was all about improvisation. But if he leaned one way, that gave me the opportunity to go the other way. Then the defender wouldn't be able to get in front of me. And that was the premise for all the shaking and whatnot, to see which way my opponent was going to go and then determine which way I would go by him.

I don't like to admit this, but I do know for certain that I was consciously trying to embarrass the guys I was playing against. But in a good way, you know? Because I always smiled at guys to let them know that what I was doing to them was just in jest. But I always wanted to beat my man and score so I could help my team win games, which was the bottom line. And I think the kinds of stuff that I did were all really predicated on what the defense would allow me. Plus, it all had a lot to do, as I have said, with improvising in the moment, being spontaneous and creative. That's why I have always said that the way I played was like a musician plays an instrument in a freestyle-jazz-solo type of way. I always thought of myself as an artist when I was out on the basketball court. But what I wanted to do in the final analysis and after everything was said and done was to help my team win games. That was always my primary goal.

So I think the fans really loved the way I played, because they could see I was having fun out there, being entertaining. And they were drawn to it, like people are to all great entertainers. So I think the entertainment aspect of my game had a lot to do with my growing popularity. People would come up to me and say they had never seen a player like me before. Sportswriters were saying the same thing in the articles they wrote. I was quickly becoming like a cult hero, and that was thrilling. But it also carried within it the seeds of downfall, of destruction, of people getting jealous of my success, you know, being envious and whatnot. A lot of people like to put those they love up on pedestals and then knock them off and bring them crashing down. But that wasn't clear to me at first, you know, the responsibilities that a lot of quick fame brings with it. The pitfalls of that weren't truly clear to me then because I was still growing as a person; I was only 23 years old and still a bit naïve. At that time I thought I was Superman, that there wasn't anything I couldn't do in the game of basketball, and at this stage of my development I thought I would only get better. And I came out of my rookie season with the mind-set that my life couldn't get anything but better. Over time, though, I would begin to recognize I was wrong. But this wasn't the time for that kind of thinking and so I just pressed on, you know what I mean? I just kept moving to the music of my own drumbeat.

After lying around Baltimore with Cookie and partying for a minute, I had to refocus my energy, start conditioning myself to go up to Philadelphia to play in the Baker League. I had to keep my momentum going. Now, I have always thought that I felt the most freedom when I was playing in the Baker League, because in those games I could always be creative, imaginative, take risks not only with the shots I took but also with my ball handling, my razzle-dazzle passes, and the fans loved it. So I looked forward to going back home to try out new things there, and to seeing my family and friends and eating my mother's great home-cooked meals.

Then in early June, before I arrived in Philadelphia, Robert Kennedy was assassinated out in Los Angeles. I remember thinking, *What is happening in the United States with all these political killings?* First it was President Kennedy, then Malcolm X, then Dr. King, and now Senator Kennedy, who was running for president at the time. I started thinking that all these killings weren't just coincidental, that possibly some unknown, powerful forces were coordinating all or some of them. But I couldn't point any fingers at anyone because I was uninformed about these kinds of political things. But I did find it disheartening and interesting that all these murders seemed to target only left-leaning political leaders and not those who were more conservative in their beliefs. I did find that fact troubling, but hey, what could I do about it? I was only a young, naïve black basketball player, though I was really beginning to open my eyes to what was happening politically all around me and to the issues that would deepen my involvement with the progressive black movement in the coming years.

That summer, however, I focused my mind on becoming a better basketball player going into my second NBA season. My Rookie of the Year season was now behind me and it was a great accomplishment. But, being practical, I was looking forward now, not backwards, and towards helping to lead my team to an NBA championship, which is every NBA player's ultimate goal. So I felt that playing in the Baker League for the next couple of months would really help sharpen my game and focus my mental attitude toward the game in a very competitive way, and keep my game evolving. That was the way it was in the Baker League, with very skilled players putting on tremendous offensive shows, running up and down the floor scoring the ball in every conceivable way. The games were also very hard fought, with players trying to either gain or maintain their reputations. It was fantastic and I just loved playing there. Plus, I had great teammates like Trooper Washington, a six-foot-seven-inch forward who played on the 1968 Pittsburgh Pipers ABA championship team with the great Connie Hawkins, and Ty Britt, a six-foot-four-inch guard who played briefly in the NBA with San Diego. Both were from Philadelphia, and I had played with and against them on Philly playgrounds in the past.

Now, the nature of these games, in my opinion, was a lot like famous musicians sitting in with bands playing in clubs all over Philadelphia and New York City back in the 1940s, '50s, and '60s. They used to call those sit-in encounters "cutting sessions," which meant that a great musician would go up on stage and duel against some other great player, just to see who could play better. Well, that's exactly the way the Baker League was. You could lose your reputation in the blink of an eye to someone you didn't really know, who would come in and shoot you out of the gym and embarrass the hell out of you. So you had to watch out for that. But the play there was fan oriented, meaning the players catered to the people who came out to watch them perform. And because the games were entertainment based, players could work out their imaginative moves there and either win the approval of the crowd or their disapproval, if they fell flat on their faces trying to do something that failed. Then you would hear boos and that wasn't a good thing. But for me it was fun and highly competitive at the same time, and everyone had a sense of freedom playing there. Plus playing there always kept you alert to the possibility of failure, and helped you maintain your conditioning in the offseason.

But I learned a lot there, too, especially from Sonny Hill, who people in Philly round ball and political circles call "Mr. Philadelphia Basketball" because he has done so much for kids and basketball in that city. Sonny just knows so much about the history of the game as it's played in my city and all across the United States. I remember him giving me history lessons one summer about the Jewish influence on Philadelphia basketball, specifically regarding a particular team that called themselves the Philadelphia SPHAs—I had heard of them, but only in passing—which was an acronym for the South Philadelphia Hebrew Association. Now, the SPHAs were organized by a Jewish guy named Eddie Gottlieb, who could be considered the "father of the NBA." See, the team dates back to around 1918 and an amateur team that was put together by Mr. Gottlieb (I think he played on the team, also) and two other Jewish friends of his, Harry Passon and Hughie Black. Then, in the late 1920s, the SPHAs defeated two of the best teams around, the Original Celtics (no relation to the modern-day Boston Celtics) and the New York Renaissance, also known as the Rens (a fabled all-black team) in two best-of-three series. First they beat the Celtics in three games, then the Rens in two. These wins really put the SPHAs on the basketball map. So during the 1920s and '30s and into the mid-'40s, the Jewish players on the SPHAs, playing in the American Basketball League (ABL), dominated amateur and professional basketball with their skill and won 7 league championships out of 13, with players like Harry Litwack (who later coached Temple University for 21 seasons) and Moe Goldman leading the way.

By the 1940s Gottlieb, now a coach and part-owner of teams in the Eastern League, was looking to form another professional basketball league after the ABL folded, and in 1946 he founded the Basketball Association of America (BAA), which merged with the National

Basketball League to become the NBA in 1949. So it was eye-opening to learn that the first professional team formed in 1946 was the Philadelphia Warriors and that they won the inaugural BAA championship with players mostly drawn from the SPHAs' roster, with Gottlieb as their coach (and, later, owner). Also on the roster were two Philly guys, Matt Guokas Sr. and Jerry Rullo, who later ran the Thirtieth and Tasker playground.

The SPHAs continued playing in the Eastern League, eventually becoming a touring squad that played against the Harlem Globetrotters when the Trotters toured all over the world. (After Gottlieb sold the team in 1950, the SPHAs were renamed the Washington Generals.) It was fascinating to learn that a lot of Jewish players had a direct influence on the game of basketball back in those days, much like the influence of black players on basketball today. This information was very important for me to hear as a young player, especially since so many Jews, such as Abe Pollin, became owners of professional basketball teams. They just moved from the playing court to the boardroom, and that's something black players have to do more of in the future.

Also, Sonny had come up playing with Wilt Chamberlain, Guy Rodgers, and Hal Lear. Guy and Hal played together at Temple, where Lear was a great scorer, while Rodgers was a ball handler extraordinaire. Sonny was great friends with all three of these very important Philadelphia players, had balled against them all, so when he talked, people listened, especially me. He also was friends with and played against John Chaney, the important Philadelphia player and coach at Simon Gratz High School, Cheyney State, and Temple, as well as Chink Scott, who was my teammate in Baltimore. John and Sonny ran a basketball summer camp outside Philly for years.

Anyway, Sonny had heard about me when I was getting a rep playing on the playgrounds in South Philly. He knew about my unorthodox style, that I didn't have a traditional game, that I was always working on moves, on the angles of shots. But the first time he saw me play, he said, was in one of those New York–against–Philadelphia summer games, when he was the coach of our team. I must have been a sophomore in college. But anyway, the New York team we played against had Lew Alcindor (later Kareem Abdul-Jabbar) on it. So we went up to New York to play and I lit them up with about 40 points and when I walked out of their gym my name, not Lew's, was on everybody's lips, even though he scored 35 or 40 points. So after Sonny saw me play in that game, he always wanted me to play in the Baker League after I graduated from college. He told me later that he liked the showman part of my game and that it would be very popular in the Baker League, which it was. So our relationship really started with that game, although I didn't realize he was watching me so closely because he never said anything to me at that time.

So when I played in the Baker League the summer after my rookie season, people were flocking to the Bright Hope Baptist Church gym to see me. You couldn't get in because the place was so packed. So Sonny started calling me "Mr. Baker League," and I was truly flattered by that because Wilt, Guy Rodgers, Andy Johnson, Woody Sauldsberry, and a whole host of great players had played in that gym. So that summer I had gotten myself in great physical shape because I knew I was going to be playing against big-time players like Billy Cunningham, Luke Jackson, Chet Walker, and Bill Bradley, who had committed to playing in the league for the first time that summer. So I was stoked and ready to compete against all those guys.

Like I said, I played for the Gaddie Real Estate team, coached by Herb Janey. Sonny was coach of the Jimmy Bates B-Bar team. Sonny had Bill Bradley on his team that summer. (Bill had come back from attending Oxford University in 1967 and felt that his game was a little rusty. So he came to Philly to work on his ball handling skills with Sonny and to get ready to play the upcoming season with the New York

Knicks.) Chink Scott, Jim Washington, Wali Jones, Cazzie Russell, Bobby Hunter, Hawthorne Wingo, and Matt Jackson, my old Landreth playground opponent, were on that team (I remember that Matt played pretty well and that he made a few outside jump shots in that game). The Kent Taverneers, coached by John Chaney, had Hal Greer and Chet Walker. The Century Chevrolets had Billy Cunningham and Luke Jackson. I can't remember all the teams, but I do know that Fred Carter and Geoff Petrie played on teams because they were co–rookies of the year in the Baker League that summer.

I remember distinctly a game we played against Sonny's team where I scored 63 points and Bill Bradley had 54. The game went back and forth with all kinds of amazing plays and shots being made by both teams. So the game was nip and tuck, with the lead seesawing back and forth, and it all came down to Bill taking the last shot from deep in the left corner with a couple of seconds left on the clock. When he got the ball, all the fans were screaming. I mean, it was almost bedlam! I can remember seeing my father there and the great Tom Gola of LaSalle— who at one time was the leading all-time college scorer and was an outstanding pro player—standing against the wall near the exit with his mouth wide open. Plus, I can see my best friend, Sahib, who was sitting on top of a soda machine, screaming his head off every time I made a great play or scored on an incredible shot. Anyway, "Dollar Bill" got the ball, went up for the shot, and I think Trooper Washington got a fingertip on it and it hit the side of the backboard as time ran out. People went crazy. They were running around either screaming with joy or mad as hell, depending on which team they were rooting for. Now, Sonny will tell anybody willing to listen that Trooper fouled Bill on that shot, but I don't know about that because I didn't see any foul and the referees didn't call one. Today, it's just water under the bridge, you know what I mean? I always tell Sonny that it is what it is and we both just laugh. But man, that game was a classic, no doubt about it, a heart-stopper. And

I'm just sad that there isn't any film of that game to preserve for history, because it was something to remember and a lot of people who were there still talk about it today. This was a playoff game. I think it was in August and my team, Gaddie, went on to win the league championship that year.

What was also thrilling to me about playing in the Baker League was that my family and friends could see me play all the time. And I was really happy to see my father at a lot of those games. He was there when I scored those 63 points and later when we won the championship game against John Chaney's team. Anyway, it made me happy to see the joy and pride in my father's face. The two of us were getting closer and closer as time went on, and he was also getting close to Sonny Hill, which I thought was a good thing. My mother still never came to my games, and that was okay because I never expected her to be there. She just never wanted to see me get hurt. But I would be with her a lot whenever I was in Philadelphia and I could see her face light up with pride whenever my friends and relatives told her about the great games I was having in the Baker League. Seeing that always made me feel good.

Another inspiring thing I had factored into my upcoming season was a book I'd bought by Dr. Lerone Bennett, the prominent African-American historian, entitled *What Manner of Man: A Biography of Martin Luther King Jr.* Dr. Bennett's book contained many excerpts from Dr. King's speeches and I decided to read passages from these speeches before each and every game and during halftimes throughout the upcoming NBA season for motivation.

I was ready to set the NBA on fire when I went down to Baltimore to begin my second professional training camp. It's interesting, because I had decided that I needed to carry more weight coming into my second year because I saw how strong Oscar Robertson was, how no one could push him around down low. So I thought the added weight would improve my strength if I conditioned myself correctly, which I did over the summer. So being at home and eating my mother's great food helped me put on some extra pounds. But when I reported to training camp in the fall, Coach Shue thought at first that I was out of shape because I weighed about 210 pounds—instead of my usual 190—until he saw me running and sprinting up the floor. Then I told him *why* I had gained the weight and it was never a problem after that.

After reducing our squad to 12 players, including 4 new guys—guards John Barnhill and Barry Orms, forward/guard Bob Quick, and the much-heralded center/forward Wes Unseld—we broke camp and started our season at home in Baltimore on October 16 and won against the Detroit Pistons 124–116. We led at the half, but Detroit caught and passed us and led 85–82 at the end of three quarters. But then we pressed pedal to the metal in the last quarter and won going away. It was an exciting game. Gus led us with 29 points, I had 28, and Wes had 8 points but rebounded well in his first NBA game. Dave Bing picked up where he had left off the previous season and had 39 for Detroit. I think Kevin fouled out of that game trying to guard Dave Bing—which was almost an impossible task because Dave was so quick and good—and so did Barry Orms, who was playing in his first NBA game. But we were happy to get the win and I remember we had a pretty good crowd there on opening night.

When I woke up the next morning, October 17, I was greeted by a miraculous, beautiful image in the *Baltimore Sun* that overshadowed our opening night win against Detroit. It was the image of Tommie Smith and John Carlos standing on the victors' podium down at the Mexico City Olympics the day before, their black-gloved fists held ramrod straight in the air in Black Power salutes. Smith had won the 200-meter gold medal, and Carlos the bronze. Australian Peter Norman had won the silver by finishing second. So when the three were standing on the podium and "The Star-Spangled Banner" was being played to celebrate

Smith's victory, the two raised their fists to protest the poverty and treatment of black people in the United States. (Norman supported them in their protest but didn't raise his fist, though all three wore human rights badges on their warm-up jackets.)

That image was both stunningly beautiful and powerful for me and most black folks in this country, but it also made many white Americans angry, and some black people, too. I must admit to loving it because I was becoming more and more aware of the circumstances of blacks in this country, which was causing a profound change in my political attitudes. That day, their actions knocked our victory over the Pistons from the sports headlines because the image was so controversial and remains iconic even to this day. So I didn't mind so much that our victory had to play second fiddle to that image, because we would give the basketball fans of Baltimore—and basketball fans all across this country—a lot to talk about in the coming days and months.

We lost our next game to the 76ers in Baltimore, 124–121, in another close one. We led by 6 at the half and 9 after the third quarter, but the 76ers played extremely well in the last quarter, outscoring us 34 to 22, and beat us by 3 points. Again, Gus played well and led us with 31 points. I scored 30 and Wes got 13 but rebounded again like a demon. Archie Clark, my future backcourt partner that summer in the Baker League, scored 26 points for the Sixers and meshed well with Hal Greer, who also had 26, as did Billy Cunningham. Chet Walker had 20, so we could see that they had a lot of scoring weapons even though Wilt had been traded to Los Angeles. Again we had a good crowd and everybody felt good about our team despite the loss.

I bought my mother a house in Germantown, a neighborhood in northwestern Philadelphia, in October, though she couldn't move in until December when the sale closed. I purchased the house with the help of Gaddie Real Estate, which sponsored the team I played for in the

Baker League. It was a very nice, upscale integrated neighborhood, though there weren't many dark-skinned black people living out there. Mostly, the blacks were light skinned and kind of snooty, which was a little strange for us coming from South Philly. But what we liked about it was in fact its distance from all that violence, which was a welcome change for all of us. The house was next to the last house on the block and sat up on a little hill. It had a big backyard where we would have friends-and-family gatherings during the summer. Singer Chubby Checker (who was also a South Philly cat) lived up the street, and Leroy Kelly, a star running back for the Cleveland Browns who would later make the Hall of Fame, bought a house for his parents across the street from me. He would be over there a lot during the summers.

The three-bedroom house had hardwood floors. After Ma moved in I outfitted the basement with a bar, stocked it with hard alcohol, beer, wine, soda, snacks, and whatnot. I gutted the garage and made it into my bedroom. I set it up so I could enter it from the outside and not have to disturb anybody if I came in late. I created a lot of privacy for myself in there with a TV and whatever else I needed when I came to Philadelphia. I could bring my friends and my girlfriends over and we could be together in the basement, too, because I had also set up a separate entrance there. With my bedroom and the basement set up like this, I could get inside both areas without ever disturbing anybody else in the rest of the house. So we partied a lot in the basement whenever I came home. All kinds of gaiety with my guys (and players from the Baker League the next summer) happened down there, you know, drinking, dancing, chicks everywhere. Talk about partying, man, we had some great times down in that basement. If only the walls could talk! Cars parked up in the driveway, out on the street. In December Ma moved in with my stepfather and my sister Theresa, who transferred from the school she was attending to Germantown High, where she graduated from. It was a very stable, middle-class neighborhood and my family loved living there.

Our next game was in Phoenix, Arizona, on October 20, against the expansion Suns. We won 134–122. Kevin led us with 24 points, while Gus chipped in 22 and I had 20. What was significant about that game was that Wes's great rebounding and outlet passing triggered our fast-break running game, which got everyone their touches and shots. That was a very good thing, and I saw the future of our team getting better, and quickly. Phoenix had some good players, too, especially Gail Goodrich, Dick Van Arsdale, Dick Snyder, and George Wilson. But we were just too much for them that night.

Then we traveled west and played our next seven games on the road, first against Seattle in Vancouver (a city I really liked), then against the San Diego Rockets, where we got our first look at top pick Elvin Hayes, who didn't disappoint with 25 points. I got 35 in that game, though, and we won 119–115. We went 2-and-2 the rest of the trip, and our record during that exhausting seven-game, 10-day road trip was five wins and two losses.

But as tiring as that road trip was, it brought us together and let us know we could be good teammates on the road. I could also see it helped us jell as a team, and Wes Unseld, a rookie wise beyond his young age, had helped us do this with his great attitude, tough defense, and out-standing rebounding that helped to unleash our increasingly devastating running game. We returned to Baltimore and avenged our loss to San Francisco with an overtime victory over the Warriors. Gus led the way with 31 points, while Mullins led San Francisco with 27.

We took our 10-and-3 record into the Big O's lair in Cincinnati, where we split back-to-back games against the 9-and-2 Royals.

We were really starting to click as a team now and had some good victories to show for it, including one against Detroit, who we beat 128–127 in a real shoot-out. They were winning going into the last quarter, but we got it together and beat them at the wire.

The great thing was that we were winning a lot. Starting with our win over Detroit, we lost only 2 of our next 16 games, with those 2 losses being to San Diego in a doubleheader at Detroit and to Cincinnati at home when the Big O killed us by scoring 38 points, grabbing a bunch of rebounds, and dishing out all kinds of assists. But besides those two defeats we were on a roll, beating elite teams like the Lakers, the Celtics twice, the Knicks, and the Warriors. We started a 9-game winning streak by beating Seattle on Christmas Day in Baltimore, 118–112. We had won 27 and lost only 7 when, again, we traveled up to Philadelphia and they beat us for the third time that year, 127–120. It seemed like they just had our number and we couldn't get over the hump with them. Jack Marin played very well for us in that game, scoring 31 points, but it wasn't enough to offset Chet Walker and Billy Cunningham, who combined for 65.

There was a big crowd that night in Philadelphia, more than 15,000 people, and many of them had come to see me play. It was good to perform in front of the home crowd, even if we didn't get the win. I wanted badly to beat Philadelphia that night—my dad was there, as were Sonny Hill, friends, and family—but it just wasn't in the cards. Still, I got a chance to be with them after the game up at Ma's new house, and that was memorable. I went back to Baltimore the next day to play against Milwaukee and we beat them, 136–122. I scored 32 points and we had five other players reach double figures.

Things were definitely looking up for us, but we lost our next 2 games, the first to Atlanta on December 29 and then to the Knicks on New Year's Eve, 121–110. So we ended the first half of the season on a down note, as both losses were to teams that were on the rise, especially Atlanta. They had absorbed some very fine players from the Saint Louis

Hawks after that franchise had folded up its tent, including Zelmo Beatty, Bill Bridges, "Jumping Joe" Caldwell, Lou Hudson, Paul Silas, and my old friend Don Ohl. Plus, they had acquired Walt Hazzard from Seattle, so they had a very good squad. The night they beat us in Atlanta, they came into the game with a record of 21 and 15 and had won 9 straight. So they weren't playing around. Beatty led the Hawks in scoring that night with 23, while Hazzard had 17. Only three Bullets reached double figures that night, and one was me with 33 (I always got up when I played Walt Hazzard because he was from Philadelphia and always left everything out on the floor). As for New York, they had acquired power forward Dave DeBusschere from Detroit on December 19, and he was just what the doctor ordered for that team. So when we went into Madison Square Garden that night, with more than 15,000 people screaming their heads off, New York was also on a roll after having won 8 straight to lift their overall record to 25 and 17 after beating us. Willis Reed completely dominated Wes Unseld that night, scoring 39 points and grabbing every rebound in sight. We lost 121–100.

So we limped back down to Baltimore to lick our wounds and pull everything back together again. We had two days off until our game on January 3 against Cincinnati, so I spent my downtime hanging out with Cookie, who was my main girlfriend at the time, even though I was seeing other women, too. See, I wasn't married and neither was she. So we agreed that we could see other people, and both of us did. Cookie was a great lady and she and I had an interesting relationship. I had met her at a Groove Phi Groove party during my rookie year in Baltimore. She reminded me of Angela Davis, but was better looking. In fact, she got picked up once in New York City when the police thought she was Angela during the time when she was on the run and they were looking for her. But Cookie and I were tight, so much so we even started talking about getting married, you know. But then, like I said, she was a lot like me.

Cookie liked going out and doing things by herself. One time she went to some West Indian island with a guy and charged the whole thing to my credit card! But it just so happened that I was seeing the guy's wife, another really pretty woman, on the side. So maybe Cookie found out about that and was trying to get back at me. I don't know, because we never discussed it. The woman I went out with was named Delores, and she was hooked up with some big black gangster in town. I remember one time I took Delores down to a club in Washington, DC, and lo and behold this guy comes in. So he walks right up to her and says, "You got to get out of here with this guy." And we left.

Another time I was with a different woman (whose name escapes me) in DC. We were at her house when all of a sudden there was a knock at the door. Now, this lady was truly fine, too. So she yelled out, "Who is it?"

"You know who it is," the voice on the other side of the door said. "It's Jerry. Open the door!"

So I asked her who Jerry was and she said, whispering, "My old boyfriend."

So Jerry kept knocking for a while. Then he went around to the back door, broke in through a window, and came into the bedroom where we were. So she yelled at him, "I told you I don't want to see you no more!"

So he said, "I don't care. You *my* woman! I'll kill you in here."

So they went back and forth like this for a while, and as all of this was going on I put on my clothes and started easing out the door because I didn't want any part of this. Up until this time he'd been just yelling at her while she was screaming back at him. So then, finally, he looked at me and said, "Oh, hey, Pearl! How you doing, man?"

So I looked at him and said, "Hey, man, this is y'all problem. I ain't got no part of this. I gotta get up outta here."

So I eased on out the door, got in my car, and drove back to Baltimore, and that was the last time I saw her. I was always getting caught up in stuff like that back then. I just liked women. But the same thing happened with that woman named Gloria, only this guy came to my apartment to get her. And that was the reason I didn't want to see her anymore and stopped taking her calls and mixed her up with Gloria, who was the mother of my son, Rodney. I kept telling myself I had to stop getting into these weird situations with women, though at the time it kept happening. I guess I just liked living dangerously, on the edge, at the time. I always like to think that Cookie was my anchor at that time and she was, though I couldn't marry her. Maybe I was afraid.

Anyway, we started playing again on January 3 against the Royals in Cincinnati and we beat them that night, 130–125. That game was a shoot-out between me and Oscar, with him getting 42 points and me 35. Then, on January 4, we finally beat the 76ers back in Baltimore, 117–112. For the first time that year Wes led us in scoring, hitting for 29 points and a lot of rebounds.

The All-Star game was coming up on January 14 and it was going to be played in Baltimore. But before that game dropped on to LA and then we got back on the winning track, taking 3 straight games. We beat the San Diego Rockets twice, then added Phoenix to our list of victims. Then, after the All-Star game, we won 2 more, beating Boston and Chicago. Our record was 33 and 11 before the All-Star game and 35 and 11 counting the 2 wins after the game, so we were seemingly putting a championship season together.

As for the All-Star game, I was voted into the East's starting lineup along with Oscar Robertson, John Havlicek, Bill Russell, and Jerry Lucas. For the West, the starters were Elgin Baylor, Lenny Wilkins, Elvin Hayes, Jerry Sloan, and Don Kojis. The coaches were Gene Shue for the East and Richie Guerin for the West.

I was happy to be voted onto the All-Star team because it's a great honor to be selected as one of the top players in the NBA. It's something I had dreamed about since I first got serious about playing basketball. So yeah, it was a rush, and a very big one. I was stoked to play in that game, especially in front of more than 12,000 fans in my newly adopted hometown, fans who were screaming out my name every time I made a great play or hit a big shot. We—the East team—won that game 123–112. Oscar Robertson led us in scoring with 24 points, while I got 21. Elgin Baylor led the West squad with 21. Oscar was voted the MVP of that game, but the award usually goes to the hometown guy on the winning side if he plays great, and that player was me. I thought I should have received the award because I was instrumental in our side winning—other players thought so, too—but I didn't get it and I have no regrets about that. Oscar played a terrific game and he got the nod and that was that. But, you know, I hadn't even made the All-Star team the year before and I thought I should have, as did a lot of other players. So it was what it was and I just had to keep on rolling.

Anyway, after the All-Star game we won, as I said, two more games and then lost three straight—to Seattle, Atlanta, and Boston—before we righted ourselves by beating the Pistons on January 27. But then three days later we lost a close game to the Knicks, 109–106, at home. The Knicks led most of the way but we almost caught them in the final quarter. That game was notable because Walt Frazier and I went head-to-head against each other. I scored 33 points and he got 28. But Dave DeBusschere and Gus Johnson had a very big battle that night, too, with Dave getting 23 points and Gus 22. They were battling on the boards, as were Willis Reed and Wes. So in a way this game mirrored what was to happen in the future of this developing rivalry.

We had started out the season with a great sense of purpose, and despite whatever differences we had as individuals, we had become a very harmonious group of guys who understood that we could be a really good team. As for me, I was having an outstanding season, scoring more than 25 points per game. But everyone on the Bullets knew that the difference in our team from the previous year was the addition of Wes Unseld. Because Wes, with his wide body that enabled him to get position under the boards and grab 14, 15 rebounds a game, was a game changer. He was throwing incredible outlet passes that triggered our potent fast breaks, setting screens that allowed shooters like me, Kevin, Chink, and Jack Marin to launch our deadly jump shots, and playing all-around solid defense. See, Wes was very efficient with what he did, and that efficiency translated into wins. Those wins really helped us believe in ourselves as a unit and convinced us that we could beat anybody. I think it also helped a lot that Wes didn't necessarily need the ball in his hands all the time to pass or to score—but he could do both. That also helped our cohesion factor as well. Plus he was a great teammate, so everything was clicking.

After losing to the Knicks, we won five straight, starting with Philadelphia on January 31 and ending with Milwaukee on February 7. But the win over Boston—the game before Milwaukee—was important because Gus got hurt in that game and didn't play again for the rest of the season. That really hurt us as a team because Gus Johnson was very important to us, as important as Wes had become. Gus rebounded, played truly great, hard-nosed, in-your-face, intimidating defense, and always guarded the opponent's best player, no matter their size. He passed well and scored whenever he had to, averaging 18 to 20 points a game. He was our leader, team captain, the glue that held all the various parts of our squad together. So his loss tore a very big hole in our team and its impact could not be really measured because he did so many things. But as strong as Gus was, he was fragile, too, especially his knees, which is what grounded him in Boston: His knee went out and that was that.

After Gus went down in Boston we continued to play well for the rest of the season. We played the Knicks again on February 8 but lost 106–100, then won 4 straight before losing 117–112 to Cincinnati on February 17. Then we won 4 straight again before losing to Milwaukee 126–117 on February 27, which was our largest losing margin in a month. After that loss we were 49 and 18 for the season, which was one of the best records—if not the best—in the NBA that year. People in Baltimore were continuing to come out to see us play, and that was a very good thing. That's why I didn't understand the rumors that were starting to go around that the owners were considering moving the team out to Houston at some point (I think I might have demanded a trade if that had happened, because I liked the East Coast, and Baltimore as well). Then there were rumblings that they wanted to move the franchise down to Washington, because that was a bigger market. The word was getting out that we would play our home games at the Landover, Maryland, Field House.

The thing I liked most about Baltimore was that the guys on the team were tight and hung out and fraternized together. We went by each other's houses—it wasn't like in a big city like New York where the players' homes were spread around a wide area—because we all lived close to each other and everything was manageable. All the black guys used to hang out at Lenny Moore's club out near Gwynn Oak and downtown at the casinos. I mean Kevin Loughery would hang out sometimes, too, and I really liked him as a player and as a person, you know. Kevin used to smoke his big cigars and was a real cool guy. Baltimore was a nice city to see big acts like Stevie Wonder, who used to come through and perform at least once a year. It was also a good place to see and hear stand-up comedy, which was one of my favorite artforms from the time I was young.

Sometime in early March, a guy name Jimmy Phelan, who came to some of the Bullets games, found out that I enjoyed comedy. He was a New York comedian and when he went back home he sent me a stack of comedy albums like Pigmeat Markham, Moms Mabley, Redd Foxx,

Lawanda Page, Mantan Moreland, and a few others. One of the album covers had a picture of a black man sitting on a rock with a ring in his nose, holding a spear. The record's title was *That Nigger's Crazy* (that was the original cover and I think they have since changed it and toned it down). Anyway, this was the first album out of the stack he sent that I played and I was floored by it. I became an instant Richard Pryor fan. I started watching him a lot when he was on TV shows.

So I started working up a comedy act of my own and had the opportunity to perform it live at the Lyric Theater in Baltimore. Now, some of my Bullets teammates like Wes Unseld, Gus Johnson, and Chink Scott came to the show to support me. I remember there wasn't a large audience in the club that night. Anyway, the MC comes out and introduces me by saying, *And now, ladies and gentlemen, introducing our own, Earl the Pearl Monroe!* Then there's a round of applause and I come out on stage dressed in a white suit and white shoes. So I get out there and start telling jokes that I had written. And immediately all my teammates, led by Wes Unseld, start heckling me: "Boooo! You ain't doing it. Get off the stage!"

So I'm trying to get through it all but about halfway through my routine I said, "There's this guy named Peg Leg Bates. Can you hear him saying, 'Come on, feet, don't fail me now?'"

As soon as I said "now" the MC rushes out on stage and says, "Well, folks, that's him! That's Earl Monroe! Give him a big hand!"

So the crowd claps and my teammates crack up and I look at the MC stunned by this revolting development. Then I say, "I'm not finished yet!"

So he just looks at me smiling and without batting an eye turns back to the audience and with an even bigger smile and clapping his hands says, "Let's give him another big round of applause, folks, for the inimitable, the indubitable, the one and only, Earllllllll the Pearllllllll Monrooooooooooe, ladies and gentlemen!"

Then he turns to me, grabs my arm in a vise-like grip, and hustles me off the stage, grinning broadly as we go. Now, I was mad as hell but didn't show it, so I grin and wave at the audience, too. But that was my last bit of comedy I ever did. My teammates and I had a big laugh on the way home that night, even though I was furious inside.

March was the last month of the regular season and we started it with 2 wins followed by 4 straight losses. Then we reeled off 5 straight wins before losing 3 of our last 4 games going into the playoffs. Our record at the end of the regular season was 57 and 25, which was good enough for us to finish first in the Eastern Division of the NBA and a 21-game improvement over the previous season. Then we got swept by the Knicks, 4 games to none, in the Eastern Division semifinals.

The sweep was a letdown because we thought we matched up better against the Knicks than the Sixers. I sat out the final two games of the regular season, which all but assured us having to face the Knicks. We had played them very well during the regular season, so we were kind of baffled that they beat us the way that they did. We also wanted to play them because the Knicks were viewed as arrogant asses by many in the league. The Knicks' players lived and played in New York City, the media capital of the world, which provided them with worldwide coverage and made all their players more famous. They had way more paying fans than any other team in the NBA, and they played in Madison Square Garden, the mecca of basketball. As a result of all this they had the best facilities and made more money as a team and as players than any other ballers in the United States. So yes, at the time, they were arrogant asses to us, though you could say there was an element of jealousy in it. And yes, they were fast becoming our enemy—more than any other team. So we just wanted to go up against that team and beat them, because our games were fast becoming wars and everyone on our team just loved the competition.

Sometimes you get what you wish for and then it doesn't turn out so well for you, as it didn't in this case. But if it was to have been in the cards for us to win that series, we would have needed to have Gus playing at full strength to pull it off, and we didn't have him. Anyway, we played the last game in New York and boarded a plane and flew back to Baltimore. When I got off the plane I was met by a man who handed me an envelope. I opened it right there and saw that it was a paternity suit filed by Gloria.

Damn, I thought to myself. *How much bad luck can I have? I just lost four games in a row to my enemy and I'm coming home and get hit with a paternity suit coming off the plane!*

After I got home and got in touch with Gloria I found out that she had been calling me all along to tell me that she had given birth to my son, Rodney. But I told her that I had thought she was the other Gloria, who I didn't want to see or talk to, and that's why I kept hanging up the phone on her. So eventually we worked it out. Now I was getting hit up to pay child support for another child. *Wow*, I thought to myself. *What am I doing? How fertile am I?*

Back in those days I didn't think about wearing protection. Now I would have to rethink that way of doing things. But I accepted the responsibility of having to pay for child support. So that's how my second season ended, but not quite. For one thing I was named to the First Team All-NBA squad, with Elgin Baylor, Wes Unseld, Billy Cunningham, and Oscar Robertson. The second team was Dave DeBusschere, Hal Greer, John Havlicek, Willis Reed, and Jerry West. My teammate Wes Unseld was named both Rookie of the Year and the MVP of the league, becoming only the second player to win both awards (Wilt Chamberlain was the other). And our leader, Gene Shue, was voted Coach of the Year. We ended up with the best regular-season record in the NBA that year, with 57 wins and 25 losses. The Lakers had the second-best record, at 55 and 27.

Elvin Hayes was the leading scorer that year with 2,327 points and an average of 28.4 points per game. I finished second in scoring with 2,065 points and an average of 25.8 points per game. Plus I dished out a team-leading 4.9 assists a game. Again, though, the Boston Celtics were crowned NBA Champions for the second year in a row, beating the Lakers four games to three in the finals, with Jerry West being named MVP of that series.

So all in all and considering the fact that we had lost Gus at a crucial time, we had a pretty good season and had something positive to look forward to in the fall when our new season opened. Everyone was hoping Gus's knee would respond to treatment, and from what he had been telling me from the medical reports his doctors were giving him, he would be ready to play. That was great news for everyone on our team.

We drafted Fred Carter, who I knew from playing against him in high school, in the third round of that spring's draft. Fred had gone to Ben Franklin High School, which is a bad-ass school in North Philly where city officials sent the notorious students that liked to fight a lot. I remember that when we used to play there, I could hear bongo drums being played up in the bleachers when I walked into the gym. So, while the game was going on I would find myself looking up in the stands to see if somebody was getting ready to shoot at me or one of my teammates because their fans would really be furious about us always beating them. And then, after the game, we would hurry up and get to our bus so we could leave quickly and not get our asses beat by some mob, you know what I mean? Franklin was something else. Tough. So was Fred Carter, and that's why he earned the title of "Mad Dog" when he first played against Coach Shue and beat him down at the opening of the next season's training camp.

Now, that particular year we had elected Wes Unseld as our player rep for the union that we had started up and I told him about Coach coming to make me an offer that I turned down. Even though he was a rookie, Wes was good at this kind of thing. So shortly after I told him this he called and said, "Earl, Larry Fleischer, the head of the players' union, wants to get in touch with you. I told him about your conversation with Coach Shue and he wants to talk to you about it. Is it all right if I give him your telephone number?"

"That's cool," I said. "Give it to him."

So Larry called me right away and said, "You know, Earl, I've been watching what has been going on down there and I understand you don't have an agent?"

"That's right," I said.

"What do you think of me being your agent?" he asked.

"I hadn't really thought about anything like that yet," I said, "but give me your number and I'll get back to you."

So he said all right and that he would be waiting for my call. I got in my car and went for a ride, listening to music, which is what I used to do when I wanted to think things out. After a while I came to the conclusion that I didn't have an agent and hey, if this guy was someone who wanted to do this for me and he was in a position to be knowledgeable about it (as the head of the players' association), why not do it? Because nothing was going to get by him that I wouldn't know about if he was my agent. So I called my mother and told her about Larry and she told me that if I felt good about it then I should go ahead and do it. So I did. I called him and told him I was cool with him representing me as my agent.

Then we discussed and worked out the percentages over the phone, that he would receive 5 percent of the deal. Then, to get to know him, I went up to Chappaqua, New York, where he lived (and where Bill and Hillary Clinton live today), to meet him. I liked him right away. He was about 30 years old at the time and I was 24. He was a straightforward type of guy who liked basketball and had a great house. He introduced me to his wife, and I stayed overnight. (That summer, before we worked out the deal with Baltimore, Gabe Rubin, the owner of the Pittsburgh Pipers—the team Connie Hawkins played for—came to visit me. But I turned down his offer because I really didn't want to play in the ABA. Those contracts tied you down back in those days and you didn't see all of your money until way in the future. Plus, I wanted to stay in the NBA because I thought the competition was better there.)

After a week or so of back-and-forth trying to resolve whatever conflicts of interest his representation presented (and there definitely were some conflicts because of his position with the players' union; I don't know if I was the first guy he represented, but I was certainly one of the first), we signed our deal and I went back down to Baltimore and waited. Then, a little while after I got home, he called and told me he had worked out my contract with the Bullets for $140,000 a year for two seasons. I would get $100,000 per year and the other $40,000 per season would be deferred and that money would accrue with interest. Now, this was the kind of money I had dreamed of making before I signed that ridiculously bad first contract. So I was happy as hell because this would take care of a lot of my personal needs. I could get a new place to live, a new car, and take care of my children better. So I called my mother immediately after I signed the contract and she just about went through the roof with happiness.

Now I could look forward again to sharpening my game by going home to Philadelphia, to Germantown, and to playing in the Baker League. Then, after running and gunning there I would turn my attention back to helping the Bullets get better as a team so we could get revenge on our mortal basketball enemies, the arrogant-assed New York Knicks, by beating them in the Eastern Division and competing for an NBA championship. I was down for it and I knew my teammates were, too. And you could take that to the bank.

Chapter 13

REACHING FOR THE DREAM OF AN NBA CHAMPIONSHIP: 1969 ᴛᴏ 1970

I WAS FEELING GREAT IN THE SUMMER OF 1969, as good as I had felt at any point in my life. I was preparing myself to travel up to Philadelphia to play in the Baker League again and to spend a couple of months living in my mother's new home in Germantown, and I was looking forward to both. My new contract had lifted a lot of pressure off of me regarding my ability to take care of personal business, like providing child support for my kids. I also decided to get myself a different place to live in Baltimore and to buy myself a new car to tool around in. First I ditched my old car, a Pontiac, and bought myself a luxury car for the first time, a new dark silver-blue Cadillac Eldorado with fishtails. Man, that was a real nice ride—it was roomy, comfortable, and stylish— and I loved driving around Baltimore in it. Then I got a new place to stay, a townhouse in an area of West Baltimore called the Village of Purnell, which was a gated community right off Forest Park Avenue, with a golf course nearby. Had I wanted to play—and I would later on—I could have just walked up there and played a few rounds. Gus lived close by and it got to be a community where a lot of black sports guys—Wes Unseld moved there, along with Ray Scott—and white athletes lived.

My townhouse was furnished really nicely. You came in the entrance and went up some stairs to the first floor, where the living and dining rooms and kitchen were. Then, upstairs I had a couple of bedrooms with TVs, one of them a small set I had won when I was named MVP of the Portsmouth Invitational Tournament in my senior year and my teammates were Jimmy Walker, Mike Riordan, and Cliff Anderson. I had another small kitchen put in up there. So I hired a decorator to make it look hip but funky. He put carpet down in both bedrooms and introduced me to Mylar, a thin polyester substance that sort of works like a mirror because you can see your reflection in it. I had the decorator put a very large sheet of it with circles up over my bed. Man, I had fun up in that room.

Besides some of my teammates on the Bullets, a lot of football players lived around there, including four great Baltimore Colts players: offensive tackle/guard Jim Parker, running back Lenny Moore—a real classy, nice guy and a pillar of the community—and defensive tackle Eugene "Big Daddy" Lipscomb. Some baseball players from the Baltimore Orioles, like Frank Robinson and Paul Blair, also lived close by. It wasn't like we were all living right next door to each other, but we were all at least a short car ride away from each other, and some of us lived close enough to walk. Even though it was a somewhat segregated neighborhood, it was a tight-knit community, with some white people hanging out with us, too. Though whites and blacks played sports and lived together, there were still some areas in Baltimore where black people weren't welcome, no matter how much money they made. But we made the best of it and didn't think too much about it until some incident raised its ugly head, which hardly ever happened where we lived. We were just happy with what we were doing, playing professional sports. We were enjoying our success, the money we made, and just being with each other and having fun.

Lenny Moore had a great club out in the Gwynn Oak section of Baltimore called Lenny Moore's Sportsman's Lounge, where a lot of athletes and regular people in the community went to eat, drink, dance, and have fun. Lenny kept a well-stocked jukebox in the club and people would play the top hits of the day. So one night I remember going there and this young guy named Marvin Cooper put his dime in the jukebox and played songs by Sly and the Family Stone and started singing along with the tunes and dancing. He was a light-brown-skinned, medium-built guy, about six foot one, regularly dressed, nothing fancy. So everyone watched and kind of cheered him on and then went back to whatever it was they were doing before he started singing and dancing. I didn't think anything about him until later on that year. But that was the first time I remembered seeing him, at Lenny Moore's place.

One of my best new friends in Baltimore was a barber named Lenny Clay, who had a barbershop called House of Naturals. Lenny not only became my good friend and barber, but also a guy I could go to with any problem, like when Gloria had me served with paternity papers. Lenny turned me on to Billy Murphy, who was a very affluent, smart, well-connected lawyer (his father was a prominent judge and Billy became a judge later on). Billy was really flamboyant and theatrical, but he was a very good lawyer, and he represented boxing promoter Butch Lewis. It was Billy who worked out my paternity suit with Gloria (and my next one, with Linda). But a lot of black folks in Baltimore had their hair cut at Lenny's barbershop. He had pictures of H. Rap Brown, Malcolm X, Dr. Martin Luther King Jr., and Muhammad Ali on his walls (later he put a photo of me up, too). He was a very conscious guy and I grew to trust him with almost anything in my life.

After I settled into my new place, I drove up to Germantown, deposited my things, and got back in the swing of living in Philadelphia again. A lot had fallen into place for me in a positive way, which allowed me to concentrate fully on getting better at playing the game of basketball. I had intentionally put on some weight the previous offseason after observing Oscar Robertson, and I was still determined to get stronger a year later. Oscar was so much stronger than I was, especially when he played down low, when he backed opponents down and got into position to score over them. I had some success doing that against smaller guards, but I found I needed to gain more weight in order to do it on a regular basis against larger opponents.

When I arrived at my mother's house in Germantown, I started eating again. But I also conditioned myself by running what we called suicide drills. Suicide drills are when you run from one end of the floor to the other, then backpedal to where you started. You do this from baseline to baseline. Then you run from the baseline to the foul line and backpedal to where you started. Then you do the same from the baseline to half-court and back, and then to the far-end foul line and back. You do these suicides for perhaps a half hour and this really gets your juices flowing, your legs and thighs in shape. Plus it helps with expanding your lung capacity. So I coupled the exercise with eating my mother's food so I could still gain weight and stay in shape. See, we didn't lift weights or do any kind of iron work back in those days. Whenever I was in Philadelphia during the summer I ran suicides and hills to strengthen my legs, which Coach Gaines had us do to get in condition back at Winston-Salem. Then I played basketball all day, which was also about running and jumping, and that's the way I stayed in shape.

Playing in the Baker League games was different from playing in the famous Rucker Pro League in Harlem. One very important difference was that Baker League games were played indoors in a gym. Rucker's games were played outdoors on a concrete court, surrounded on two sides by wooden bleachers, a wire-mesh fence, and trees. So when it rained or the wind was high they either cancelled the games or the elements affected the way they played, mostly in a negative way. Long-range jump shooters like me had to adjust their shots on days when the wind was high because it affected their accuracy; wind gusts frequently blew well-aimed jump shots off course. So players at Rucker adjusted their game when the wind was up, opting for short jump shots and drives to the hole for layups or dunks. Baker League players didn't have to make those kinds of adjustments because the games were held inside a gym. Still, I enjoyed seeing games played at Rucker because the games were highly competitive and a lot of great players, like Lew Alcindor, Connie Hawkins, and Julius Erving, balled up there.

As usual, the games in the Baker League that summer were tremendous. Archie Clark joined our team late in the summer after the Lakers had traded him and Darrall Imhoff to the 76ers for Wilt Chamberlain. So after Archie joined us, we formed a hell of a backcourt, me with my spin move and Archie with his great, shake-and-bake crossover move. Plus, we had a lot of pro players from the NBA, ABA, and the Eastern League dipping in all the time to play a game or two. Like I said, I think I loved playing there more than I did in the NBA because of the freedom I felt playing there. I was not only hitting my long-range jumper, doing my spin moves, and slashing drives to the basket, but also practicing my low-post game—basically, 18 feet out from the basket or closer—rather than from outside the key.

I had found out through practice that if I bumped down my defender—I called it "bumping down"—I could, after I got the position I wanted, fake up as if I was about to shoot a jump shot to get his body moving toward me. In that instant I would extend my elbow with the ball in both hands, then put that elbow in his face to force him to move back a little. That way I got the space I needed to get my shot off. Then I would tippy-toe jump—I never was a great jumper—as I faded back and shot my jumper over his outstretched hand as he was falling backward. I rarely, if ever, got this shot blocked. It also was a great way to draw a foul by forcing the guy guarding you to hit your elbow as you went up for the shot. And if you made the shot it might become a 3-point play if you converted the free throw.

I perfected this move that summer in the Baker League games and added it to my long-range jump shooting repertoire. I teamed up again with Trooper Washington and Frank Card. As usual, good and great players played in the league that summer, such as Billy Cunningham, Matt Guokas, Hal Greer, Luke Jackson, Wali Jones, Connie Hawkins, Fred Carter, Chink Scott, Guy Rodgers, Freddie Crawford, Bernie Williams, Bill Bradley, Trooper Washington, and so many others. Sometimes Wilt would drop in and play a game with Sonny's team, and so would Hal Lear and others. So we had another great summer and we won the championship again.

Philadelphia has always been a great party town. The parties there were unbelievable because most parties are held in someone's house. And as I grew older the parties were usually held in the house of someone that I knew, so everyone there was happy to be together. That was the beauty—for me—about getting together with people I knew and having a great time. At first it was a lot different from Baltimore, or New York City, which is much bigger than Philadelphia. In New York City you have all these different areas, like the Bronx, Brooklyn, Harlem, other parts of Manhattan, Queens, and Staten Island. And the people living in these areas, for the most part, rarely party together. Philly is large, too, and diverse, but there were smaller communities there back in the day, and as we got older we were more close-knit. At least I thought so, especially back then. I was still learning my way around Baltimore, and even though it was half the size of Philadelphia, it reminded me of Philly in some ways—even the row house type of architecture. But I was beginning to like the city in certain ways and I would grow fonder of it as time went on.

Anyway, I had some really great parties out in Germantown, down in the basement, after many of those Baker League games. A lot of players would come out to those parties and hang with some of my friends from the neighborhood and from South Philly, too. So Ma's house would be jumping into the wee hours of the morning. That was a lot of fun, and my mother liked having all those famous athletes around. So did my sister Theresa. Cookie came up a few times over the summer and that was cool. I saw her sometimes when I drove down to Baltimore a few times to check on my new digs. But I had some lady friends coming over in Philadelphia also, especially Juanita, a fine-looking girl who was a friend of Theresa's, and we started hanging around. Then there was Sylvia, who was a nurse. So that was who I was seeing that summer. Whenever they were around Cookie stayed down in Baltimore. But soon enough it was time for me to go back to Baltimore to start getting ready for the upcoming season. So toward the end of August I packed up my stuff and drove back down there to begin training camp.

After getting swept by the Knicks in the Eastern Division playoffs the previous spring, we were looking for revenge coming into this new season. The Bullets had finished first in the Eastern Division and had posted the best record in the NBA, so to lose like that had been disheartening for us. In our minds we had a lot to prove to ourselves and the rest of the league entering the 1969–1970 season. We knew we had a very good team; we just had to prove it, and we were determined to do just that. We always had injured guys on our squad like Gus, who was always fighting through knee injuries, and Kevin, who had fought through that injury bug with his ribs, as well. Our nucleus of players was still relatively young, with Gus and Chink being the oldest guys at age 31. We had added a couple of good rookie guards to our roster after training camp, Fred Carter and Mike Davis, who had been our first-round pick that year. Fred was really a great addition to our squad because he brought a sense of true grit to our mix that meshed well with the toughness of Gus Johnson.

Like I said, we were an up-tempo team. Gus or Wes would get the ball off the boards and the rest of us would get out there and run. Gus and Wes used to bet each other who would get the most rebounds in a game, and Wes usually won, though Gus won sometimes, too. I loved being out in the open floor on a break. If someone was caught trying to guard me out there they were in a whole lot of trouble, because I was going to take them to the hole with a bunch of moves they couldn't deal with and score the ball. If I was running the floor with a couple of teammates on either wing, I could dish to one of them for the score. Or I could fake like I was going to dish it to one of them and then, when the defender went for the fake, I would just go right by him and score. So we had a very dangerous team, and we knew it.

We entered the new season with a sense of purpose, a renewed confidence in ourselves that we knew would be tested early, because our first five games were against tough opponents: the Bulls, Celtics, Lakers, Royals, and especially the Knicks, who we played in our fifth game of the season at Madison Square Garden. So we would get to see soon enough how we stacked up against some top teams, how our new sense of purpose withstood those early challenges.

We opened the season on October 15 with a 98–93 win over the Chicago Bulls in Baltimore. I had a good opening game, scoring 26 points in that victory, while five of my teammates scored in double figures. Jerry Sloan led the Bulls with 21 points. If my memory is correct (though it could have been later that year) I think this was the first time I saw Marvin Cooper outside of Lenny Moore's club. All of a sudden I see Marvin dressed in a big gray Applejack cap and a blue cape around his shoulders and he's not really dancing but he's putting a hex with his hands on the opposing team! And the music being played is Kool and the Gang. I was stunned to see this but the crowd was cheering and we won. So he comes back for our next game, does the same routine, and we win again against the Celtics three days later, 124–117, behind 34 points by me and 25 from Kevin Loughery. So that was the beginning of the Dancing Harry legend in Baltimore and it lasted throughout my entire career in that city and took on another life later on, which I will talk about later.

It looked like we were rolling, but we split the next two games, including a loss to the Lakers in which Jerry West went off for 39 points.

Then, on October 25, came the day we had been looking forward to all year, when we traveled up to New York to play the Knicks. The Garden was packed to the rafters, with more than 19,000 rabid Knicks fans jammed into that legendary basketball shrine. Everyone on our team was fired up in the dressing room before the game. But we came out flat and they damn near ran us out of the building with a 128–99 drubbing. I mean, we were never in that game, you know what I mean? We had six players reach double figures and I got 22 points, but my knees were still bothering me. Bill Bradley led the way for the Knicks with 23, Walt Frazier added 21, and almost everyone on their squad scored.

At this point in the season our starting five was me, Gus, Jack, Kevin, and Wes, with LeRoy Ellis and Chink Scott coming in for the big men and rookies Mike Davis and Fred Carter spelling Kevin and me. So we were basically playing nine guys. Then, in October, my knees started hurting real badly and Mike Davis had to spell me. This went on for a while until the pain eased up.

After we lost to the Knicks, which was a real downer, we went out to Detroit, beat the Pistons, then lost three in a row before winning three straight. It was weird. We lost our next game, on November 8, to the Royals when Oscar got 38 (I had 27, as my knees were starting to feel better), but then we got back on track and won nine straight. I averaged more than 26 points a game during our winning streak, which ended with a 121–106 loss to the Celtics on November 29.

After that loss to the Celtics we beat Cincinnati, then lost 3 straight again. One of those losses was to the Knicks in Baltimore, 116–107, before our largest crowd of the season (more than 12,000 people) on December 5. The next time we faced the Knicks, we were coming off a 4-game winning streak, only to go into Madison Square Garden and lose to the Knicks for the third straight time that season. Walt Frazier put on show with 29 points to my 13. They literally shot us out of the arena, beating us by 37 points to the delight of more than 19,000 rabid fans. That loss dropped our record for the season to 22 wins and 12 losses. New York was 29 and 6 and in control of the Eastern Division.

This was really turning out to be an up-and-down period of wins and losses for us, one we hadn't expected to have this early on, especially because of the record we had compiled the previous season. We just knew in our hearts and minds that our record should be much better at this point in the season. But it wasn't, so that fact triggered some soul searching. We also knew, however, that my injuries had hampered our team a lot during this period. They weren't season-ending injuries, but they were nagging and lingering in their nature in that I hadn't been completely free of them since they had started in November. At the time of our loss to the Knicks on December 20, I was still hurting. And by the time we played and defeated the 76ers in Baltimore on Christmas Day, I was finally starting to feel a little better, though not much. But Jack and Kevin picked up their scoring, combining for 60 points, and we won 121–113. We won our next game against San Francisco, too, then lost three in a row, ending the calendar year with a 122–111 New Year's Eve loss to the Hawks in Atlanta. After the game we received some more bad news when we learned that Mike Davis, our rookie guard who had been playing so well, was injured. He wouldn't return to the lineup for more than three weeks. So that was a downer, especially considering how I was still suffering from knee pain. Now Fred Carter would have to be the first guard off the bench, replacing Davis, and Bob Quick, our second-round pick that year, would have to play a more significant role.

We went back to Baltimore to get ready for our next game on January 2 against Cincinnati. We had two days off, so I spent that time relaxing in Baltimore and having dinner with Baltimore Colts star Bubba Smith at his apartment in the heart of downtown. I had gotten to know Bubba (his real name was Charles Aaron Smith) pretty well. We were about the same age—I was 24 and he was 23 but would be 24 early in 1970—and both of us had come to Baltimore around the same time. He had been a legendary college defensive end at Michigan State (he would have gone to the University of Texas had Darrell Royal, the Longhorns head coach, been permitted to offer him a scholarship, but the Southwest Conference didn't integrate until 1967 and Texas didn't integrate their squad until 1970) and was the first overall player selected in the 1967 NFL draft, the same year I was chosen number two in the NBA draft (surprisingly, he was chosen in the 11th round by the Bullets that year, too). He was six foot seven, weighed 265 pounds, and was extremely fast and quick for a man his size. Bubba was also very hip and wore a Fu Manchu moustache. He was one of the first cats I knew who had a place downtown, and it was a real big apartment. And Bubba was very funny, like he used to tell me with that deadpan look of his, "You do know, Earl, that I was a real good basketball player when I was in high school and I could have made the NBA if I had concentrated on playing that instead of football. You do know this, don't you?"

I would look at him, laugh, and say, "Sure I do, Bubba, I heard about your basketball game. But I don't know about you making a team in our league."

He would just shake his head and tell me he could have made it if he had tried. And we would go back and forth like that, with him being deadpan and me laughing. And then we both would burst out laughing. Bubba was really something. He would have great parties down at his place and after all the reveling was over it would be like freak city. It was a wonderful place to be.

I remember one time during the previous summer, before this season had started, when I got introduced to angel dust. Now, I was very reluctant because I didn't even smoke at the time, and still don't. But I was sipping on my Courvoisier cognac and starting to feel a buzz when some guy came up to me and handed me a cigarette-looking thing he had rolled and said, "Go on, try it. But don't take too much now."

So I looked at it and because I wasn't feeling any pain, I said, "Hell, why not?"

I took two long drags and the next thing I knew I felt like I was somewhere else looking back at myself. I couldn't move. My mind was running and my eyes were watering up but I couldn't move! Everything I saw was, like, jumping up and moving in slow motion. But I wasn't in control and I'm a control freak. So I started getting frustrated. Chicks were rolling around naked on the floor and then coming up to me and there was nothing I could do. I was just staring at them and it was like a psychedelic film I'd once seen about experimenting with marijuana. But everything was serene and it went on like this for, like, two hours. I wanted someone to throw water in my face to break the spell but I couldn't seem to speak. It was scary.

Finally, somehow I made it home. I still don't remember how I got there, but somebody must have driven me back to my townhouse in my car because it was there when I woke up. I remember staying in bed the entire day after that party. And I promised myself after that incident that I would never, never smoke anything like that again. And I didn't.

By the time of our January 2 game against the Big O and his Royals in Baltimore, the pain in my knees had subsided. We won that game 118–116 in a hard-fought, very tightly contested encounter. I led us in scoring that night with 25 points while Oscar led the Royals with 31 and a bushel-load of assists. I always felt good when I played well against Oscar, especially when we came away with a win, because he always taught me something. But then we lost our next two games, the first in another shoot-out with Cincinnati, 129–128. We led most of that game, but in the fourth quarter the Big O, Tom Van Arsdale, Johnny Green, and Fred Foster turned up the heat and they caught and edged us by 1 point. Van Arsdale and Oscar combined for 65 points, while I led the way for us with 28 in the losing effort.

Our next loss was again to our "enemy," the New York Knicks, on January 6 in Baltimore. The day before we played New York, management had traded Ed Manning—I really hated to see Razor go because we had become good friends—to the Chicago Bulls for Al Tucker, my old teammate from the Pan American Trials. Anyway, Al joined our squad in Baltimore, where we got killed by the Knicks again, 129–99, in front of a very disappointed crowd. My knee pain had flared up again, and I only scored 6 points in that game. I don't think anyone played well for us except Wes Unseld, who scored 27 points and grabbed a whole lot of rebounds. But Willis Reed played well that night too, scoring 25 points and snatching his share of rebounds. I think everyone on the Knicks team scored that night, with Dick Barnett and DeBusschere getting 21 apiece and Frazier adding 19.

Bouncing back from that defeat, we won our next four games, beginning with a 121–116 victory over Detroit in Baltimore on January 7. The pain in my knees had eased up a bit, enabling me to drop 28 in that game. It was my first real shoot-out with Jimmy Walker since we came into the league, with him going for 31 points to lead Detroit. Jimmy's scoring had begun to pick up, as I had expected it would. Now he seemed to be clicking well in his game and I was happy for him, because he was a very nice guy also. We played our last game before the All-Star extravaganza on January 18 and lost to the Phoenix Suns 134–133 despite Loughery and Marin combining for 67 points.

I wasn't chosen for the All-Star game, which took place in Philly, that season, and I was very disappointed I wasn't able to put on a show for my hometown fans. But hey, what could I do about it? The selection process was totally out of my hands. Oscar Robertson, Walt Frazier, Jimmy Walker, Hal Greer, and Flynn Robinson were the guards chosen to represent the Eastern Division, and Gus was the only Bullets player selected. The East squad won the game 142–135. Willis Reed scored 21 points, took down 11 rebounds, and was named MVP of the game, which drew more than 15,000 fans into the Spectrum. I know a lot of the fans loved the show the All-Stars put on, but a lot of them, especially my family and friends, also expressed disappointment that I didn't play.

Our next game after the All-Star game was in Philadelphia and we lost, 133–118. Mike Davis returned to the team that night and everybody knew Bob Quick's days as a Bullet were numbered (in fact, he was traded to the Detroit Pistons on February 1 for Eddie Miles, my old nemesis). Mike scored 6 points in his return and I got 23, but we never led in that game. We exacted some revenge the next night, however, by beating the Sixers in Baltimore 112–111 behind Gus's 27 points. Philadelphia still had a very good team, though they were not as good as they had been when they had had Wilt, Billy Cunningham, Hal Greer, and Chet Walker all together. When they traded Wilt and Chet, they started—in my opinion—a slow slide downhill, even though they got Archie Clark and Darrall Imhoff from the Lakers for "The Big Dipper." Now, don't get me wrong, they still had a good squad, but they weren't as dominant as they had been when I came into the league because their roster had changed so much.

Now, they still had Greer and Cunningham but, like I said, they weren't the force they had been. Cunningham was still a great player who could jump out of the gym and put the ball in the basket with that left-handed jump shot of his. Born in Brooklyn, Billy was a fierce competitor who just never quit. He was six foot six with brown-red hair and a pigeon-toed walk that made him look like he was falling down when he walked toward you off the court. But you couldn't let that fool you into thinking he couldn't play because he could, and he came to do it every night he set foot on the court.

Hal Greer, who was Cunningham's sidekick for many years, was another thing altogether. He could really play also, but he and Billy were complete opposites of each other. Billy was outgoing, with a large personality, an electrifying player. He always wore a big smile on his face and that was reflected in his approach to the game. Hal, on the other hand, was quiet but steady as a ballplayer. To look at him, you wouldn't have thought he was as good as he was. He was six foot two, 175 pounds. I know a lot of players—including me—who used to say to themselves when they first saw him, *What's he going to do out there on the floor?*

That was a mistake, because we soon found out exactly what he could do. Now, Hal wasn't a leaper. Nothing like that. And even after you knew who he was you would say to yourself, *Okay, I'm going to come here tonight and just roll over him and not let him shoot.*

But that wouldn't happen. The next thing you knew, Hal would have 25 or 30 points on you and you'd be wondering what he did to get all those points. Every night. Steady. Got them coming off screens. One-on-one. You knew he was going to pull up and shoot the jumper, but you were never ready for it. His ability to get into position to shoot that jumper is what made him great, because he knew when he was going to shoot it and the defender didn't. You just couldn't stop him from getting his shot off. That little jumper. And man, could he shoot the ball. I don't care what the deal was, Hal was going to shoot the jumper—not from way out, but from around the free throw line and in the corners from maybe 18 feet. That's where he got his shot and did his damage. He probably made more jump shots than anyone else in the history of the NBA. He even shot his free throws with a jump shot! Sometimes I used to wonder how he did it and I would find myself saying to someone, "How does he keep getting his shot off? Why doesn't anybody stop him? Because we know what he's going to do."

But that didn't matter, because he did it. He always got his shot off, no matter what you did to try to stop him. It was weird and a mystery. And that mystery is a part of all great players, because the thing that makes them great is the fact that they know when to do what they have to do and the defender doesn't. And boy, was he deadly. He had a real slight build, and he wasn't a great dribbler. Like I said, if you passed him on the street you wouldn't think he was a basketball player. He wasn't flamboyant. He had a quiet demeanor, was very soft-spoken. It's funny, because when you think about all the great players, you never think about Hal Greer. But he was truly great, one of the best shooting guards of all time, a pleasure to watch play, and a real gentleman. But he was tough as nails on the court. Old number 15. He was something else.

Our wins and losses after the victory over Philadelphia kept alternating—we would win one or two, then lose one or two. We were just inconsistent the rest of the season. But we finally got the Knicks monkey off our backs when we beat them on February 22—George Washington's birthday—110–104 at home in Baltimore in front of 9,000 appreciative fans. I really got off in that game, scoring 37 points. Walt Frazier—he was known as "Clyde"—had 30, and we both put on a show. But the really significant thing for me was that Gus outplayed Dave DeBusschere and Wes held his own against Willis on the boards.

Unfortunately, our team suffered a significant blow when, three days later, in a 115–113 loss to the Bucks, Kevin Loughery went down again with the same rib injury that had been plaguing him. Kevin would be out until the start of the playoffs, and Fred Carter would start in his place for the rest of the regular season. His injury was just another reminder of how our team—any team—had to stay healthy if we were going to be legitimate championship contenders. Already this season I had had lingering aches and pains in my knees. Mike Davis had gone down for almost a month, and now Kevin. All of this had taken a toll on our team and was one of the main reasons for our up-and-down play over the course of the season. Now we would just have to suck up Kevin's loss and pull it together with a different lineup—which meant a different team chemistry and identity—until he got back.

The next time we played the Knicks was in New York on the 28th, the last day of February, and they beat us by 14 points, 115–101, in front of almost 20,000 fans all screaming for revenge. Dave DeBusschere rebounded in that game, outscoring Gus 23 to 6 and winning a bruising battle on the boards. This was our fifth loss to the Knicks of the season against only one win. So heading into the postseason, our prospects against them didn't look as good as we'd thought they would at the beginning of the season. We still held out the hope that if we did meet them in the playoffs we could win, though, because we were a very confident team and crazy things are known to happen come playoff time.

Anyway, we went up to Philadelphia to play the 76ers there on March 1 and I came out of that game with only 1 point because of pain in my knees and because I had gotten sick to my stomach eating too many cheesesteak hoagies before the game. Now that was real embarrassing, especially because my poor performance was in front of my home folks, and we lost the game also, which was the most important thing. Philly beat us 104–99, with Hal Greer lighting us up for 38 points.

After going five and three over our next eight games—six of which were played on the road, including a double-overtime thriller in San Francisco—we won our last two games of the regular season, beating the Bulls and the Warriors. The team received a shock after the season ended, though, when Mike Davis went to the Buffalo Braves in the expansion draft.

We finished the regular season with a record of 50 wins and 32 losses, good enough for third in the Eastern Division (instead of first, which is where we'd thought we'd be when the season started). Those

50 wins earned us a playoff matchup with the Knicks, our hated enemy, in the Eastern Division Semifinals, starting on March 26 at the Garden.

We only had five days to prepare for the series, but we felt confident that we were ready. What we had to learn this time around in the playoffs was how to finish the Knicks off. What we'd come to understand when they'd swept us the year before was that they knew how to finish a series off and we didn't, even though our team was missing Gus Johnson. To finish another team off, your team has to have a certain attitude, you know what I mean? When you and your guys go into a game everyone has to leave it all out on the floor, all the time. You have to play hard all the time. Because a lot of times when a team gets a big lead they feel as though they've got the game in hand and then start coasting. Or they start playing more cautiously and stop executing the way they were doing earlier in the game. Then suddenly they find themselves in a dogfight. They not only have to do better, but also pick up the momentum that they lost from before. If they don't do this and the other team is coming on and gets over what I call "the hump," then it's very hard to beat that team. That's what had happened to us the season before when the Knicks swept us. And it's what happened to us again during the games we lost to the Knicks this season, too, regardless of our injury problems. We just weren't finishing games and New York was, except in that one game when we beat them. They had finishers, guys like Dick Barnett, Willis Reed, Walt Frazier, Dave DeBusschere, Bill Bradley, and Cazzie Russell. All of them knew how to throw the knockout blow on any team in the NBA. Even Dave Stallworth, who was coming off the bench, was a finisher. So, we had to become like that if we were to beat the Knicks, and we felt going in—having Kevin back at full strength would make this task easier—that we had finally arrived at this mindset as a team. We thought we were ready.

We started the series off, however, with two straight losses. They beat us up in New York on March 26 in double overtime, 120–117. I had 39 points in that game, outplaying Frazier, who had 16. Kevin came back to the squad in that game but still wasn't himself, scoring only 7 points. But his presence alone lifted our spirits. All five of the Knicks' starters reached double figures, with Willis Reed the high man with 30. It was an exciting game in front of a capacity crowd. Even though we lost, we felt good about our chances in the next game, because of how well we had met the challenge in Game One, with everyone playing very hard.

But, like I said, the next night we lost the game in Baltimore in front of more than 12,000 fans, 106–99. We were in this game up until the end, when they pulled away and won by 7. Gus led our team with 28 points, outplaying DeBusschere. Man, it was shaping up to be a war between those two great power forwards. Willis Reed again played a great game, scoring 27 to Wes Unseld's 10 points, though both men had a ton of rebounds. Again we felt good about our effort in this game, even though we lost. So we were eager to play the next game, which would be up in the Big Apple on March 29.

I must say we went up there with fire in our eyes and beat them decisively in front of a packed house again, 127–113. We started the game well and were behind by only 1 point at the half. Then, in the third quarter, we stepped it up and went ahead by 11 points and never looked back. Six of our players reached double figures in that game, and I led the team with 25 points. Wes Unseld and Fred Carter got 23 apiece and Jack Marin notched 20, while Kevin scored 17, the most he had put up in a very long time. For the Knicks, Frazier played very well and got 24 points, while DeBusschere scored 12 in his head-to-head with Gus. But the good thing was that Wes outplayed Willis in that game—Reed only had 12 points—and Jack outplayed Bill Bradley, who only had 12. Now everyone on our team was pumped and feeling it. We all felt we could pull off winning the series after this victory, and that was great.

We came back to Baltimore for our next game on March 31, and in front of a crowd of more than 12,000 rabid fans cheering us on after every bucket we made, we won to tie the series. Again, we started out in front and held the lead all the way, though the Knicks did come back some, and beat them 102–92. I scored 34 points to Clyde's 25 in our head-to-head matchup, while Gus outplayed DeBusschere, scoring 18 points to Dave's 12. Now we had beat the Knicks two in a row, one more than we had beat them during the entirety of the past regular season, and we really liked our chances to forge ahead of them back up at the Garden on April 2.

But New York had regrouped and they ran us out of the Garden in Game Five, routing us by 21 points, 101–80, in front of a packed house. Although both teams had multiple players in double figures—we had four and they had five—it was really Willis Reed who made the big difference in that game, dominating with 36 points to Wes's 10. I played okay, getting 18 points, while Clyde got 16, which I would call a draw. But, like I said, it was Willis Reed who dropped a hammer on our playoff chances in a game the Knicks led from start to finish. Now it was us who had to go back home and regroup, which we vowed we would do.

With our backs to the wall in Game Six we did just that, winning a thrilling back-and-forth game 96–87 in front of a boisterous, packed-to-the-rafters crowd. I played a very good game against Clyde that night, scoring 29 points to his 18 in our media-hyped one-on-one matchup. But Gus Johnson jumped all over Dave DeBusschere and won that celebrated duel 31 points to 4. It was Gus and me who made the difference in that game. We were thrilled as a team to be going back up to Madison Square Garden to play in the seventh and deciding game of the Eastern Division Semifinals.

But it wasn't in the cards as the more experienced Knicks jumped all over us after the opening tip-off went their way, outscoring us in the first two quarters to lead by 15 points at the half. We mounted a comeback in the third quarter and cut the deficit to 6 points going into the final period, but they stepped on the gas and ended up winning the game by 13, at 127–114. Still, even in defeat, we could hold our heads up high as a team because we had fought hard and pushed a great team to its limit. But still—again—no cigar for us. We would just have to try again the next year, and we would, because now we were all confident we could beat this team that had become both our enemy and our destiny.

That year the Knicks went on to win the NBA championship, beating the Lakers in the Finals in seven games. Willis Reed was voted both the Finals and league MVP (to go along with his All-Star game MVP earlier that year). So Willis had a once-in-a-lifetime season. As for other individual awards, Lew Alcindor was voted Rookie of the Year, the Knicks' Red Holzman was picked as Coach of the Year, and Jerry West led the league in scoring, averaging 31.2 points a game. Lenny Wilkins led in assists, getting 9.1 a game, while Elvin Hayes won the rebounding crown with 16.9 a game (Wes finished a close second, snatching 16.7 a game). As for the All-NBA, the First Team consisted of Billy Cunningham, Jerry West, Walt Frazier, Connie Hawkins, and Willis Reed. The Second Team was made up of Oscar Robertson, Gus Johnson, John Havlicek, Lou Hudson, and Lew Alcindor. As for the All-Defensive NBA team, Dave DeBusschere, Willis Reed, Jerry West, Gus Johnson, and Walt Frazier made up the first squad, while the Second Team consisted of Bill Bridges, Lew Alcindor, John Havlicek, Jerry Sloan, and Joe Caldwell. The All-Rookie team was Eldo "Dick" Garrett of the Lakers, Mike Davis of Baltimore, Jo Jo White from Boston, and Lew Alcindor and Bobby Dandridge from Milwaukee.

Despite my knee problems, I still led the Bullets in scoring with 1,922 points, an average of 23.4 points a game. Kevin Loughery finished second with 1,325 points and an average of 21.9 points a game. Like I said, we missed his scoring in the last month or so of the season, especially down the stretch and throughout the playoffs. I often found myself wondering what the outcome might have been for our team if Kevin and I had both been healthy—and Mike Davis, too—throughout the entire season. I also led our squad in scoring during the playoffs, averaging 28 points per game. In addition, I dished out 4.9 assists a game. So all in all I had a pretty good year, despite not making the All-Star team or the All-NBA team, both of which I had made the year before.

After the season was over I could rest my body for a while in Baltimore, party a little, spend some snuggling time, and just think a lot of things through regarding how the Bullets could get better as a team. I knew I had to get some medical attention for my sore knees, so I would have to take care of that over the summer at Kernan Hospital. Then, after the operation, I was going to go home to Germantown and spend some quality time with my family and my old close friends at my mother's house. Mostly, though, I would get myself some much-needed rest, then rehab my knees and get in tip-top shape to play another long NBA season with the hope that its conclusion would be more satisfying than the last two had been.

Chapter 14

THE PAIN OF GETTING CLOSE BUT NO CIGAR: 1970 TO 1971

AFTER ALL THE PROBLEMS I HAD HAD with my knees during the past season, I decided I had to do something to fix them, which meant I couldn't play in the Baker League that summer. So the first thing on my agenda that offseason was to have operations on both knees. This was the first time in my basketball career that I had been hampered by injury, and the problem went back to jamming my knees up in that car wreck I had in Harlem with my good friend Wilkie back in the day. That was when the problems with my knees first started. I knew I had little bumps on both knees after that accident, but the pain soon went away and I never really thought about it again because I didn't think it was serious. But when I first came to the Bullets I started having this pain in my knees and it kept getting worse, though it never prevented me from playing. So I went to the Bullets' trainer, a guy named Skip Feldman, to see if he could help me with the pain. After a couple of visits with him he came up with the idea for me to wear kneepads that had a contraption in them—a sort of mechanism—that ran across my knees and kept them warm during

259

practices and games. Skip's contraption was hooked up to batteries inside the kneepads and worked like one of those heating pads that people apply to their sore backs. That was Skip's idea, and it was ingenious. So that's why I started wearing kneepads and they worked for a while.

But in the 1969–1970 season the little knots had grown so serious that the pain hampered me to the point where sometimes I couldn't perform at my usual high level, and that was a problem. So I really had to have them looked at and taken care of during the off-season. So I went to see a team of doctors who were specialists in dealing with knees, especially those of athletes. They told me I had developed inflammation in these little knots below my kneecaps called "bursas," which are little fluid-filled sacs that help muscles and tendons slide over bones. I had it in both knees, though it was worse in the right one. The pain I was having was a lot like the discomfort of jumper's knee, which is what players that jump real high in basketball, like Gus Johnson, can suffer from. Bursas are really painful when they are inflamed, which can happen over the course of the 82-game NBA season. So the Bullets' doctors recommended that I have them surgically removed. With that in mind, I scheduled the operation for sometime in the middle of June at Kernan Hospital, which is located in Woodlawn, Maryland, near Baltimore, on an 85-acre wooded campus. Man, that place was beautiful! My only request was that they make the cuts sideways, you know, horizontal instead of vertical—up and down—so the scars would blend in with the lines on my knees, because I've always been vain about things like that. The surgeon thought that was crazy and started teasing me about having a procedure done in a certain way to satisfy my vanity. He thought the vertical cuts would be better, especially in terms of my rehab. But I was adamant about the way I wanted it done and so they satisfied my wishes and made the cuts horizontally, which they kept teasing me about by calling them "Earl's vanity cuts."

The operation went really well because the surgeons at Kernan were some of the best in the country. After the operation I had straight plaster casts fitted on both of my legs, from almost up to my hip to the tops of my ankles. I couldn't bend my legs or walk, so my guy Smitty came down on the train, picked me up from the hospital, and drove me to Germantown in the backseat of my El Dorado. That's where I stayed for the entire summer, in my basement apartment in my mother's house. Anyway, it was tough being at home all alone, even if I didn't have to go upstairs to get anything: I had everything I needed down there, including a refrigerator full of food, a bar with drinks, and a nice soft leather sofa to lie on to watch TV. But if I wanted to change channels on the TV I had to get up and do that manually on the set because this was before remotes. And getting up like that every time I wanted to change the channel was very tiring with these casts and whatnot. So I just left the channel wherever it was and watched a lot of stupid shows and that was it. From time to time, though, I had to get up to go to the bathroom. Luckily, I was young and didn't have to urinate all the time and was able to hold my bowel movements for hours. Still, it was a struggle just to get to the toilet and back to the sofa. By the time I had done all of this I'd be tired as hell. With everyone going about their business and nobody at home until the evening to help me, I was stuck. Then, when they did get home, I would whine and complain.

One day I remember giving some real thought to trying to drag myself up the stairs, which would have been extremely difficult with those heavy plaster casts on both of my legs. On that day my mother had gone off with my crutches and left them upstairs. So I thought I would go get them, but I had never tried to do that before because I was worried about falling down the stairs and lying at the bottom, unable to move. So I just stayed where I was in the basement and endured.

This made me realize how difficult life must be for people with handicaps. There are things that people who don't have disabilities just do automatically without ever even thinking about it. But those who are not able to do those things do think about them. So going through this period in my young life when I couldn't even do the simplest of things for myself gave me a deeper appreciation for what people with disabilities have to go through every day of their lives. I realized at that moment that it's a big thing to want to do stuff and not be physically able to do it. So that was a kind of wake-up call for me, because I knew in time I was going to heal. Eventually I would get back to my normal routine of playing basketball, something I truly loved and was getting paid handsomely to do. So what did I have to complain about compared to a person with a handicap? Nothing. So after that revelation I stopped whining and complaining about my condition and vowed to move on and make the most of the life I was blessed to have.

The casts stayed on my legs for six weeks. Then, one day in August, Smitty picked me up from Germantown and took me back to Kernan Hospital in the backseat of my Cadillac to have them removed. After they took the casts off I started going to rehab at Kernan, working with a therapist named Neil, who helped me get strength and motion back in both legs. When we first started therapy on my knees I was very reluctant. See, I had stitches going across my knees as opposed to up and down on the side, as the surgeons had advised. So I had to get used to bending my knees when I did squats because it felt like the stitches would just pop open when I bent down to do them. That's when I realized that the surgeons had been right when they advised me to do vertical cuts and I was wrong. I had let my vanity overrule their judgment, but that was water under the bridge now. I had to just make do now and suck up my fear that the wound would not open, which it didn't. Still, it took me a long time to get myself to the point where I actually felt comfortable doing squats and bending my knees. Maybe two weeks. In the meantime I was doing extension-type stuff to get my legs back up to normal movement, in addition to massage, whirlpool therapy, and heat treatment (Bill Neill really had great hands and I always went back to him). It was a process to work myself back into playing condition, and I was so serious about it I didn't even go out to parties during my rehab. I wanted to be as ready as possible when training camp started sometime in mid-September, and for our first game against the San Diego Rockets on October 14 in Baltimore.

It took me a while to get adjusted to playing after the operation and the rehab, and when training camp opened in mid-September I started slowly. I didn't want to mess things up, and Skip's kneepads helped me tremendously throughout this period, especially with the right knee, which was worse off than the left. So I wore Skip's kneepad on my right knee regularly. This was the first time I had really been seriously hurt like this, so I took everything slowly during those early practices because I didn't want to risk having any setbacks. But at the same time I wanted to be up to speed as quickly as I could. That's just my mind-set as a player. I basically wanted to do whatever was best for me to get back. I never even thought about the operation in terms of it possibly being a career-ending thing, like I wasn't going to be able to do this or that move. No. I just thought of the operation as a corrective, elective procedure, and I knew that as soon as my knees felt better I would be back right where I was before the bursitis. I never was traumatized by the surgery. It was just a matter of having to do it so I could get back to being the player I was before. That was my mind-set then and it is the same today. I just didn't want to take a risk and go backward, and that was why I took things slowly at first, especially since I hadn't had surgery before.

The NBA was expanding to 17 teams for this season, having added 3 new franchises: the Buffalo Braves, the Cleveland Cavaliers, and the Portland Trail Blazers. The league was also divided into two conferences, East and West, with four divisions: Atlantic, Central, Midwest, and Pacific. The Bullets landed in the Central Division along with the Atlanta Hawks, Cincinnati Royals, and the expansion Cleveland Cavaliers. Some of the placements didn't make a whole lot of geographic sense to me. Like why were Cleveland and Cincinnati placed in the Central Division instead of the Midwest? And why was Phoenix in the Midwest instead of the Pacific? Was it because Phoenix isn't on the coast? And finally, why did they place the Bullets in the Central Division instead of in the Atlantic when Baltimore is so much closer to the Atlantic than Buffalo is? It was a little confusing at first, but hey, I got used to it because what could I do about it? All I had to do was play basketball wherever the Bullets landed, so it really wasn't a big thing to me.

After training camp broke I didn't play in our first game against San Diego because Coach Shue felt I wasn't quite ready to play mentally or physically. We won that first game anyway, 123–105, with Jack Marin's 28 points leading the way. But the story of that game was that Gus Johnson played fabulous defense against Elvin Hayes, one of the great scorers in the game, holding him to just 12 points. Now that was something.

Three days later, when we hosted the Lakers, I did feel ready, because nothing got me up like playing against Jerry West, and with Oscar Robertson, Dave Bing, Hal Greer, Archie Clark, and Walt Frazier all looming on the schedule, I knew that it was now or never. Anyway, we beat the Lakers in overtime, 118–116. I only scored 8 points in that game, but six of my teammates scored in double figures, again led by Jack Marin, who had 25. Jerry went off on us that night, scoring 34 points even though Fred Carter and Eddie Miles were dogging him all over the court. Wilt chipped in with 23, but it was not enough to save them from defeat.

After dropping our third game to San Francisco 125–105 at home and beating the Royals in Cincinnati, we were set to face our "enemy," the New York Knicks, in Baltimore on October 23. We had been pointing toward this game as a team since we'd lost to them in the playoffs the previous spring, when they were on their way to becoming NBA champions for the first time. So mentally I thought the team was ready, and we were. We beat them that night 98–92, upping our record to four and one while the Knicks fell to four and two. Fred Carter and I led the way with 21 points apiece, and four other Bullets reached double figures. Willis Reed led the Knicks with 25 points, while DeBusschere chipped in with 18. Fred Carter's fierce defense against Walt Frazier held Clyde to only 10 points. There was a large crowd in the Civic Center that night and everyone went away feeling good, except the Knicks.

The next day we flew into Milwaukee to play against the much-improved Bucks, who had acquired Lucius Allen, Bob Boozer, and Oscar Robertson in major trades. We fell in double overtime, 122–120. Lew Alcindor dropped 39 points that night, scoring on an array of eye-popping sky hooks, dunks, and turnaround jumpers. Man, he was awesome that night, and he totally dominated Wes in the paint because of his six-inch height advantage. My knees were starting to feel stronger and I had 25 points that night, though Wes Unseld led us with 27 gritty points against the much taller Alcindor. Up next was a surprising Detroit Pistons team that had come out of the gate with an eight and zero record. They beat us in a hard-fought, close game, 109–103. Detroit had much improved its team by drafting Bob Lanier, the six-foot-11-inch All-American center from St. Bonaventure, and Terry Driscoll, a six-foot-seven sharpshooting forward from Boston College. Jimmy Walker led the Pistons with 20 points that night and was starting to look like he was going to be a star in the league.

On October 30 we went up to Philadelphia to play the 76ers. I got a couple of days' rest in Baltimore and received some massage treatments on my knees, and they felt a lot better by the time we rolled into the Spectrum to play in front of my hometown crowd. I didn't want to disappoint my family and old friends, and I didn't. That night I won my duel against my old Baker League sidekick, Archie Clark, outscoring him 30 to 24, and we beat the 76ers 123–110. We followed that up the next

night back in Baltimore with a 106–103 win over Phoenix, but my knees
started acting up again. The doctors had told me this would happen, that
it would be up and down and the pain would go away and come back
until it stopped for good, which was the day I was looking forward to. I
only scored 12 points in that game, but the most important thing was
that we won, finishing six and three for the month of October. Not bad
considering I wasn't at full strength yet, so I was optimistic about our
team winning in the days ahead, after I got back at the top of my game.

November was an up-and-down month for us, but even steven in
terms of winning and losing games: We won eight but also lost eight. We
beat the Knicks for the second time that season on November 12 in the
Garden, 110–108. Beating the NBA Champion Knicks was good for us.
Despite our .500 record, the press was talking about the spirited rivalry
that had developed between our two teams, which was real. Every time
we played the Knicks now, it was a hard-fought game with a lot of team
and personal intensity on display.

What I was beginning to realize was that I was going to have to
learn to play through my discomfort, to block out the twinges of pain
and trust in the surgery and in my rehab. I had to play as I had in the
past and just believe that my knees would hold up and that everything
would be all right, even when I took risks, which I had to do if I was
going to be the old Earl the Pearl, or Black Jesus, who would walk on
water. I was getting closer every night I played, though sometimes I
found that I was having trouble taking some of the risks I had taken
before because I was afraid my knees would give out. That had to stop,
and the only way it would was if I trusted more in my belief that the
surgery and rehab had been effective and that my knees had healed. So
it was just a matter of time before I believed in it totally and my game
returned to the way it had been before and I could play freely, take
risks, and execute all my moves. Now, though, I had up and down
nights (as both my surgeon and my trainer told me I would). I realized

that healing from injury is a process, and that it involves a psychological barrier the mind has to jump over. And my mind-set had to be that I would push through all of this adversity and come out of this struggle as good as or better than I ever was.

So that's where my head was at going into December, which we opened with a 97–93 loss to the Lakers in Baltimore. Jerry West and I had a real shoot-out that night, with him getting 37 points and me notching 33. I felt good physically that night even though we lost, but I knew now that there would be other games when I would struggle with the pain. After the loss to Los Angeles we won four in a row, then lost two, then won another, and our wins and losses seesawed back and forth like that over the next four games. One of our wins during that stretch came on Christmas Day in Baltimore, when we defeated the Chicago Bulls 128–112, overcoming 41 points from Bob Love, who seemed to be scoring from everywhere. We followed that up two days later in New York with a disappointing 110–105 loss to the rival Knicks in what was another fiercely fought game.

After that loss we bounced back by winning 6 in a row, ending the year with a 21 and 16 record. In our rematch against Atlanta, we avenged our earlier loss to them with a 110–102 win. That game was very satisfying for me personally because I got the upper hand on Pete Maravich, outscoring him 32 points to 23. Then we went back to Baltimore and defeated them again, 125–104, with Gus Johnson exploding for 31 points in his physical war with Bill Bridges. In the game before, in Atlanta, they had fought each other to a draw, with Gus tallying 14 and Bill notching 11. It was always interesting to hear these two exceptionally physical men grunting and bumping each other under the basket when they collided. It was unbelievable. The same kind of physical battle could be expected whenever Gus played against Dave DeBusschere, too, you know. Because DeBusschere, Gus, and Bill Bridges were hard-nosed, blue-collar players who never, ever backed down from a challenge.

So it was a pleasure and a wonder to watch Gus go up against those two guys.

For our next game, on January 10, we traveled out to Milwaukee to play a rapidly improving Bucks team led by their increasingly dominant young center Lew Alcindor, who was already making an indelible mark on the NBA game. Seven feet two inches tall, agile, and gifted with an indefensible array of shots (including his patented Sky Hook), he was fast becoming the dominant player in the game. Now he had been teamed with the great Oscar Robertson, Bob Boozer, and another emerging star, Bob Dandridge, who I had played against my final two years in college. Anyway, the Bucks were a very good team that year, and when we arrived in Milwaukee to play them their record was 35 and 7, while ours was 26 and 16.

That night they destroyed us 151–99—our worst loss of the season—with Bob Dandridge (who I feel belongs in the Hall of Fame) exploding for 34 points while Alcindor put up 30, totally dominating the smaller Wes Unseld. Yet, despite the whipping the Bucks laid on us, Gus Johnson made the most memorable play in the game. What happened was, with about two minutes left in the game and the Bucks ahead by 46 points, Gus came down the floor and went up with one of those windmill dunks of his and threw it down so hard everyone heard the wire that held the backboard up snap, *pow!* and the backboard shattered and the entire contraption came down, *boom, splat,* onto the floor! Everybody was amazed, including Alcindor! Gus bruised his forearm on the play and was sent to the hospital for precautionary x-rays, which turned out to be negative. They also had to stop the game for a while. I thought it was for an hour, but a local sportswriter said it was for "33 minutes." Another writer said that Gus was "on a search-and-destroy mission" when he made that dunk. He might have been right saying it was a "search-and-destroy mission," but I don't know about the 33-minutes report because I was there and they didn't have a replacement backboard

in Milwaukee Arena. So they had to go out and find a backboard somewhere to finish that game, and I think that would have taken longer than
33 minutes. I don't know. Maybe my memory is playing tricks on me.

Anyway, all the players were really pissed that they went to find a
backboard to finish the final 2 minutes of a game that was already
decided by nearly 50 points. What was the point in doing that? But they
did and we finished the game. But by the time it was over there were
only a handful of the 10,000-plus people who had filled the seats at the
opening tip-off. After watching that dunk, Lew Alcindor said he
thought it was one of "the most memorable shots" he'd ever seen. I also
read in *Sports Illustrated* or somewhere else that Alcindor said, "Wes
Unseld was a real physical player, but Gus Johnson could get a job as a
hockey puck he was so tough." And he was.

What was funny about Gus's dunk is that when we got back to the
dressing room he was gone. We didn't know that he had already caught
a plane to the West Coast because we were scheduled to start a four-
game swing out there in Seattle after the All-Star Game on January 12.
So when me and the guys got to Seattle, Gus was already there, in the
hotel, kicking back and acting as if nothing had happened. We were
surprised to find him there because no one had known where he disappeared to. Man, that shit was funny, because he was acting like nothing
had happened. Anyway me, Gus, and Wes were named to the East
squad for the All-Star Game, so we had to leave and travel to San Diego,
where the game was being played.

After playing in San Diego, Gus, Wes, and I flew up to rejoin our
teammates in Seattle, where we promptly lost a close game, 114–110.
This was the beginning of a four-game, four-night West Coast swing
that would take us from Seattle to Phoenix, then to San Diego and
back up to Seattle. We split the four games, continuing our up-and-
down season. But I was finally getting back in the swing of things with
regard to my recovery from knee surgery. For a couple of months in the

early part of the season, I wasn't able to do different cuts to the basket, or to plant my foot and push off without feeling a twinge of pain in one or both of my knees. So I was reluctant to do those types of moves on the court. And I certainly knew I couldn't be twisting my body like I used to when I was executing my spin moves. It scared me to death to even try to make those moves for fear of blowing out my knee. So I played conservatively. I also wasn't backing anybody down into the paint with my copycat Big O back-down move, because I didn't have the strength in my knees to be able to plant, lean back, and shoot. Plus I didn't know if my knees would go out making this intricate move. So that maneuver was out at the moment, also. What I was left with in my arsenal of shots was the long jumper, and that's what I did—shoot long jump shots. I would come down, fake a spin move, and then, when the guy guarding me committed to trying to defend against it, I would have the space I needed to fire my jumper. See, because the spin move was instinctive for me, when I stopped doing it I ceased being instinctive, too, you know what I mean?

Then one time in a game in January I came down the floor and was feeling good in my legs and this player jumped out at me—I can't remember who he was—and, without thinking about it, I instinctively spun on him and took the ball to the hole and scored the basket. That's when I knew I was back. And I remember saying to myself as I was run-ning back down the floor, *Hey, I can do this. I'm back.* And my game started to elevate a little more after that, and game by game everything started to fall back into place for me. Because, see, I was a scorer, no ifs, ands, or buts about it. When I was scoring, my game flourished. And it was important for me and my team to get back to that. Even though I didn't *have to* score—because I knew I could get my points anytime I wanted to when I was healthy—just knowing that I *could* score again made my game that much better. And I knew this sometime in January of that season. And it felt good to be back on my game.

But I could also see that there was a problem with my returning to form with one of my teammates, Jack Marin, who had stepped into the scoring breach left by my absence. He had elevated his game to the point where he was leading us in scoring at the time. Without me there at full strength, our offense had acquired another rhythm and chemistry with Jack in the scoring leadership role. We played a more traditional game rather than the up-tempo showtime, run-and-shoot one we had become popular for with me at the helm. That was okay, because we needed a little more of that. Even Coach Shue had begun to push this philosophy on us, that we should become more like the Knicks offensively and choose our shots more carefully. What he wanted was for us to blend run-and-gun basketball with the more traditional pass-and-screen, pick-and-roll style the Knicks played. Now I could understand this, too, because I also had been thinking we needed to marry both styles after we'd lost to them in the playoffs at the end of last season.

But with my return to the team and as my knees felt better, it changed the cadence of our offense, which impacted the chemistry of the team. So everybody had to adjust back to the way we had played before I went down with my injury. Everyone had to adjust themselves to my return, mentally. And this, in my opinion, specifically affected Jack, who seemed to struggle with it a little bit, since his game had flourished in my absence. This, I felt, damaged the chemistry of our team. Because Kevin Loughery never had a problem with me coming back balling the way I had always played. Hell, Kevin was just going to play his game whether I was there or not. Same thing with Gus and Wes. Plus Fred Carter was going to play the same way—hard—every night, if I was there or not, whether I scored a lot or not. Fred was going to leave everything out on the floor. At least that's my opinion. I'm sure if someone asked Jack about that period with the Bullets he would have a different take on the whole scenario. And that's cool.

Anyway, I felt this had a lot to do with our up-and-down record during that season. Because jealousy and envy can be dangerous, cancerous things in a group of guys from different social, cultural, political, racial, and ethnic backgrounds who are trying to play together. It is sometimes very difficult to get a quality mix so the chemistry can work seamlessly—or close to that—you know what I mean? So we were going through some rough patches during the first months of 1971, not to mention all the injuries that were impacting the team.

But Coach Shue always believed in us as a team, that we would get over our differences and tensions and pull it all together. Having been a very good pro player, he knew all about jealousy and envy amongst a talented group of players like we had. He had picked most of us to play on this team and he let us know that he believed in our abilities—individually and as a team—and that we would eventually pull it all together for the good of the squad. So during this problematic period he was always there to support us. He would listen to what we had to say and tell each and every one of us what he thought. But he was always pointing us toward winning a championship because he knew we had the talent to do it and because, in the final analysis, he was also sure each and every one of us wanted to win one badly.

Then I had an unexpected setback when I was arrested after a riot at a high school basketball game between Dunbar, an all black public high school, and Mount Saint Joseph, an all white Catholic league team. See, I was invited by some of the Dunbar players to watch the game, which was being played in their gym. At the end of the game—which was a championship game which Dunbar lost—a fight broke out on the floor that escalated up into the stands where I was sitting. All of the cops were white and as they were hitting the black kids with their night sticks I started trying to protect the kids from getting beaten by these policemen. They were just swinging at anybody, including me. Anyway, I was wearing an army battle jacket and jeans, little round wire-framed sunglasses, and a black and green kufi. So when I tried to stop them from hitting the kids, the police arrested and handcuffed me and took me to jail. I don't know if any of the cops recognized me or not at the time. But I remember how badly the handcuffs hurt my wrists because they cuffed me so tight. When they got me down to the station I called my lawyer, Billy Murphy, who was a well-known lawyer in Baltimore at the time. He came down to the station and got me released. And the charges were dropped. But I always remembered that incident and was never pro-cop after that.

On February 20 and 21 we played a home-and-home series against the Hawks, the first game in Baltimore and the second in Atlanta. What's important about these two games other than the fact that we split them is that Pete Maravich and I almost got into a fistfight during the first game after he elbowed me in my ribs. We had been involved in a shoot-out—I finished with 33 points to his 31—and it pissed me off because Pete and I had established a friendship with each other that grew out of respect for the way both of us played the game. Plus I knew him to be a nice guy and a clean player, so when he hit me in my chest and ribs with those sharp elbows of his (he was a very skinny guy) and hurt me, it shocked the hell out of me. And with my temper I just wanted to punch him out because I don't believe in playing the game like that. So people had to separate us. Anyway, the next night my ribs hurt badly and it bothered me to lift my arm to shoot my jumper. Still, we won the game 121–119 in another close game. I scored 24 points despite the pain (Skip Feldman, our trainer, had wrapped my chest with bandages) and Pete got 28 points. But this rib injury would bother me until the end of the season, just as my knees had come around.

Still, throughout the month of February we continued to struggle with marrying our two conflicting, opposite identities as a team. Then in early March, Wes Unseld, our rebounding rock, went down with a severe ankle sprain that took him out of the lineup until the end of the regular season. Now we really did resemble, as the *Sports Illustrated* writer Peter Carry wrote in an article as the playoffs approached, a bunch of "players with their casts and their crutches . . . Coach Gene Shue's cripples." Now, with Unseld out and without his rebounding and outlet passes triggering our fast breaks, it finally dawned on everyone— including me—that we would all have to change for the good of the team if we were to advance through the playoffs and compete for the NBA championship. And so we did. We finally brought our two oppos- ing styles together for a run at the end of the regular season, and with this change in our offensive thinking we became a better, more danger- ous team, especially after Wes came back and Gus's sore knees and Kevin's and my sore ribs got better. Now we were truly ready to make that championship run.

But we lost 4 straight games before the end of the regular season and won only 4 of our last 14 games. At the time we looked like the walking wounded. We split our last 2 games on March 20 and 21, losing to the 76ers in the final game of the regular season. A significant thing happened when, in either the first or second game with Philadelphia, someone hit me hard in my injured ribs and the pain came back with a vengeance.

Philadelphia would be our first opponent in the Eastern Conference Semifinals, beginning on March 24. We won that series four games to three, with some very exciting games, including Game One, which we lost 126–112. Despite the loss, the game was significant for us as a team because Wes Unseld returned from his ankle sprain and played like him- self, controlling the boards. Someone on the 76ers also hit me in my ribs—which were already sore—in Game One, and they hurt so bad I could hardly lift my arms to shoot. So I ended up only scoring 6 points in that game, and that definitely hurt our offensive production. But Skip rubbed analgesic stuff all over my ribs—I smelled like an old man when

I came out to play in the next game—and wrapped my chest up real well. This treatment loosened me up, and with my warm-up top on I was able to keep the injured area warm. Consequently, I played much better after that, averaging 25.5 points over the next six games, and we took the series in Baltimore on April 4 by winning the decisive Game Seven, 128–120. Jack led us in scoring that night with 33, while I dropped 20 and four of our teammates reached double figures. Now we were moving on to play the Knicks in the Eastern Conference Finals, beginning in New York on April 6.

In a very close first game, in front of a capacity crowd as usual, the Knicks beat us 112–111. The game came down to the wire and they pulled it out in the last minute or so. I led us in scoring that night with 29 points. In Game Two, which we lost 107–88, John stepped up and led us in scoring with 20 points (with my ribs hurting me I only managed to score 10 points that night). Willis Reed, who was hurting that game, scored only 10 points, but it was enough to give the Knicks a two-game lead as the series shifted to Baltimore for Game Three.

We bounced back in that game—even with Gus still out—and beat them 114–88. My ribs, having gotten a couple of days of treatment, felt good and I was clicking on all cylinders. My 31 points led the team, though we had four other players in double figures that night. We followed that up by beating them again and evening the series three days later in Baltimore with a 101–80 win. Gus missed his fourth straight game that night, but Kevin, who had missed Game Three, came back. Though he was held scoreless, his mere presence on the bench picked up our spirits. Now the series switched back to Madison Square Garden for a crucial Game Five.

The Knicks beat us in a close game that night, 89–84, with Gus still out and Kevin not playing at full speed. Still, we made it a tight game with our grit and our talent. We were proud that we stayed with such a great team and played them so close. So now the Knicks held a three-to-two series lead, with a chance to close it out in Game Six in Baltimore on April 18.

Gus Johnson came back for that game, driving to the game in his new charcoal-gray Lincoln Continental Mark IV. He walked into our dressing room at the Baltimore Civic Center dressed in a gray leather suit to match his new gray car. I came in dressed all in black, including my hat, which had a red hatband on it. So when one of my teammates saw me and Gus dressed like this and looking real serious—I forgot who that player was—he asked me, "Damn, Earl, what's up with this all-black look?"

And I told him without even a smile, "I came to do my work tonight. This is my sinister outfit!"

I felt we all had to have a mind-set going into this important game, and we had to come out and play like it was the last game of the series. And for us it was, because we had to win that night or it was all over. Now we felt we had to play harder, that we had missed too many opportunities to win games—like we had last year—and we didn't want to make those same mistakes again. Clyde and I were battling each other, and I could see in Gus's eyes that he had come to play DeBusschere that night like they were fighting each other in a war. And they were. And Wes, he was our rock, quiet and steady but a warrior nonetheless. I could feel it coming from his energy that he was ready and really wanted to win this game. So we went out there that night to do battle and we beat the Knicks 113–96 to tie the series and force Game Seven. We had six players reach double figures, with me, Jack, and John Tresvant combining for 69 points. Wes put in 10, grabbed every rebound within his reach, and outplayed Willis Reed badly. Willis finished with only 3 points and hardly any rebounds because he spent most of the night away from the basket, setting screens for his teammates. DeBusschere led the Knicks with 24 points (but Gus battled him all the way when he came in for John Tresvant), with Clyde scoring 22. The game was never close. Now we were going back to the Big Apple to finish this war off, but unlike the previous year we were confident that we'd emerge victorious.

We went out and partied that night after that Game Six win, went down to Lenny Moore's Sportsman's Lounge in the Gwynn Oaks section of Baltimore. Everybody wanted to buy us drinks A lot of people were betting on the games and wanted to know how we felt we would do in Game Seven. I just told them we thought we would win. So we kind of chilled that night with all these people at Lenny's bar. I went home after that and went to sleep because I had to get up the next morning and go to New York. A lot of people thought we didn't stand a chance against the Knicks, but we had another idea: We thought we were going to finally beat this team, and we were hell-bent on proving it.

When we walked out onto the floor at the Garden for Game Seven, the atmosphere was electric. As expected, another rabid, capacity crowd was on hand. Celebrities were walking by, beautiful women dressed to the nines. Hecklers hissed their catcalls, while others were hurling all kinds of trash talk our way, like, "All you gonna get here is the same thing you got before. An ass whipping!" Then they laughed. Then someone else said, "This is for you bums because you're not going to get out of here alive!" Then they made a nasty face and laughed and stuck their middle finger in the air and jabbed it up like they were ramming it up our asses. But with all the odds against us, we turned the tables on the defending NBA champions—our enemies—defeating them 93–91 in another barn burner of a game.

Damn, that was a great game, with the two teams going back and forth like in a championship heavyweight boxing match between two great fighters like Joe Frazier and Muhammad Ali. With a minute or so left in the game, Dick Barnett went down the court for a layup and Fred Carter came from nowhere and banged his shot up against the backboard. *Bam!* Everybody in the stands and on the Knicks team and their bench started hollering, "Goal tending!" But the referees didn't call it and that was surprising to fans in the Garden. The score was 93–91 in our favor when Bill Bradley had this open shot in the corner in the last seconds of the game—like that time in the Baker League—and I said to myself, *Oh, shit, I know this is going in!* But it didn't because Gus got a finger on Bill's shot and it fell short and Wes got the rebound and that was that.

We won that night with our grit and our talent, with me leading the way with 26 points, while Marin dropped 20, Wes got 17 and a lot of rebounds, and Fred Carter notched 14 points. Gus scored 8 points and battled DeBusschere to a draw. Willis came back in that game like the true champion he was, scoring 24 points, while Dick Barnett led them with 26 and Clyde dropped 13 points. Finally, we had gotten off our backs the Knicks monkey that had weighed all of my Bullets teammates down for two years running now, and man, did it feel good. Great, even. Everyone on our team was exhilarated. Champagne was drunk and poured over everyone's head in the locker room. I remember the Garden was strangely silent that night after we won. They couldn't believe the Knicks had lost. It was one of the best feelings I have ever had because it was like finally climbing a mountain and getting to the top. But I also saw how the Knicks took the loss: They were cool. Came over to congratulate us. Shook our hands and wished us good luck in the championship series against Milwaukee. I saw that night that they were a veteran, professional team because they had beaten teams before and lost important games before. So they just took defeat in stride and I learned something from that. Still, it really felt great that we as a team had finally gotten over the hump by winning that series against the Knicks that night and we traveled back to Baltimore in a state of exhilaration.

When we got back to Baltimore I partied a little with Cookie and some of my friends. Not too much, though, because I had to stay ready to play the Bucks and Lew Alcindor in Game One of the NBA Finals on

April 21 out in Milwaukee. The Bucks had the best record in the NBA that year, with 66 wins and 16 losses. They had a really good squad with Oscar, Bobby Dandridge, Jon McGlocklin, Greg Smith, Bob Boozer, and Lew's old teammate and friend from UCLA, Lucius Allen. But the wind was taken out of us after that series against the Knicks. Actually, we felt that that was the real championship for us because we had fought so hard to beat that team, and we didn't have much left in the tank. The other thing that happened during the Knicks series is that I had developed bone spurs on the top of my foot, so I was going to have to look into this during the offseason because they were beginning to hinder me.

Milwaukee beat us in the first game by 10 points, 98–88, and we were never even in that game, though I think it was the best game we played against them in the whole series. Gus was down again and I led us with 26 points, with Marin getting 18 while Wes had 16 points. Lew scored 31 points for the Bucks, Robertson added 22, and Dandridge dropped in 15. On April 23 we played them again in Baltimore and they beat us this time by 19 points, 102–83. Jack led us that night with 22 and I had a subpar game, scoring only 11. Gus played in that game but wasn't really himself, though he did manage to get 10 points. Lew again led the Bucks with 27, while Oscar had 22 again, Dandridge 16, and McGlocklin 14.

We went back to Milwaukee and they beat us a third time, 107–99 in a game that looked in the box score like it was closer than it was. Again Jack led us with 21 points, Wes had 20 and did yeoman work going up against Alcindor, Kevin finally got into the swing of things and got 19, while I scored 16. Gus didn't play in that game. For the Bucks, again Lew scored 23 points, Dandridge led them by dropping in 29, while Oscar scored 20 and Greg Smith hit for 15. Now we went back to Baltimore for the fourth game, which was going to be played on April 30. But the night before Game Four, Lew came over to my place and he and I were sitting around with two other people I had invited over, talking and telling stories. So Lew came out and said, "I'm going to go up to New York after we win tomorrow and see some of my people up there."

So I looked at him in shock. I had known Lew for a while and he had always been a quiet, modest type of guy, so I was surprised that he said something like that. So I said to him, "Whoa, wait, big fella. What do you mean when you win tomorrow?"

So he stuttered a little, like he forgot what he had said. Then I said to him, "Well, shit, we're going to have something to say about that! Whether you go up to New York. Because you still have to play and beat us first!"

So everybody laughed, and the next day when I got to the game I told everyone on our team what Lew had said and they got pissed off. So we started the game off hot, but then reality kicked in when they just started stomping our asses and that was that, you know what I mean? We lost to them 118–106, and Fred Carter—who I initially told about Lew's comment and it really pissed him off—led us with 28 points in this final game, while Kevin scored 18, Marin and me scored 12 apiece, and Gus—who had come back—scored 11 points, the same as Wes. For the Bucks, Robertson led them with 30 points, with Lew right behind him with 27 and three Milwaukee players in double figures. So that was that. The Bucks were the new NBA champions and we had finished second, our highest in franchise history.

Lew's prophecy of going to New York the next day proved accurate. He not only went up to New York to visit his family and friends, he also chose this occasion to announce that he had changed his name to a Muslim one and would now be called Kareem Abdul-Jabbar. Everyone was stunned and some didn't like it, including some players. But I have always felt it is up to individuals to choose the names they want to be called by. I love my name and wasn't going to change it, so I felt that Kareem had the right to call himself whatever he wanted to, and that was my take on him changing his name.

As for individual honors for the season, Kareem was named the MVP for both the playoffs and the entire season. He also led the league in scoring, averaging 31.7 points a game. The assist crown went to Norm Van Lier of Cincinnati, who handed out 10.1 a game. Wilt Chamberlain was the rebound leader with 18.2 a game (Wes Unseld finished second with 16.0 a game). The All-NBA First Team listed Dave Bing, Jerry West, Billy Cunningham, Kareem Abdul-Jabbar, and John Havlicek. The Second Team consisted of Willis Reed, Walt Frazier, Bob Love, Gus Johnson, and Oscar Robertson. The All-Defensive First Team listed Jerry West, Dave DeBusschere, Walt Frazier, Nate Thurmond, and Gus Johnson (the last two had been high school teammates). The Second Team listed John Havlicek, Norm Van Lier, Kareem Abdul-Jabbar, and Jerry Sloan. Dave Cowens and Geoff Petrie were picked co–Rookies of the Year, with the All-Rookie Team consisting of Bob Lanier, Calvin Murphy, Pete Maravich, and of course Dave Cowens and Geoff Petrie. The Cleveland Cavaliers made Austin Carr the first player chosen in the NBA draft, while the Bullets chose Stan Love with the ninth pick. (Stan is the father of Kevin Love, the current star of the Minnesota Timberwolves.)

As for me, I scored 21.4 points a game in 81 games, the lowest average I had had since coming into the NBA. I handed out 4.4 assists a game, and my minutes were down because of my surgery and injuries. Still, after all was said and done, our team ended up having a pretty successful season (despite our 42 and 40 regular-season record). We had defeated the 76ers in the Division Semifinals, beat the Knicks in the Division Finals, and finally lost to the Bucks in the NBA Finals. In the final analysis, we could chalk up a great many of our losses to key player injuries. So the team would have to heal itself over the summer and come back stronger in the fall.

I was looking forward to resting my weary body before going up to Philadelphia to do a clinic at Sonny Hill's camp for kids and playing in the Baker League, which was relocating its games to McGonigle Hall at

Temple University. I was looking forward to playing there. But for now I would just kick back and think about my future in basketball—and in life—because this had been a trying season for me, but one that proved almost rewarding in the end. What I wanted badly as a basketball player was to win an NBA championship, and I could definitely see that in my future. Now that I had been to the Finals I could taste the sweetness of winning one, which I knew was up ahead.

Chapter 15

LEAVING BALTIMORE AND GOING TO PLAY FOR THE "ENEMY": 1971 TO 1972

IN THE SUMMER OF 1971, after returning to Philly, I bought a two-toned dark- and light-gray 1967 Rolls-Royce Silver Shadow for $30,000. It had a red leather interior and a dark mahogany dashboard. What happened was that I was driving on Route 309 out in the countryside outside of Philadelphia and came into this small town called Flourtown, where I saw a car dealership with exotic cars on the showroom floor. So I parked my El Dorado, walked in, looked around and saw the Rolls, and it said, "Earl."

I didn't know it was a Rolls-Royce at first. All I knew was that it looked good to me and that the lines on the car were slick and classic. But I bought the car right there on the spot because it spoke to me. But the dealership had to clean it up and make sure everything was okay, which would take a couple of days. So I drove back to Germantown and a couple of days later, after they called and said everything was cool, I called Smitty, picked him up, and we drove out and picked up my new Rolls. I drove it back to my mother's house while Smitty drove the El

283

Dorado. So I parked both cars there for a minute and then drove the Cadillac down to Baltimore, where I left it with my barber friend, Lenny Clay (later, I gave Lenny that car). Then I caught the train back up to Philadelphia. Smitty picked me up at the train station in his car and drove me back out to Germantown.

So buying the Rolls was the beginning of my summer up in Philly. I had promised Sonny Hill I would make a guest appearance at his basketball camp for kids that summer, which I did. His camp, which was called the Sonny Hill Basketball Camp (Sonny had officially named it the John Chaney–Sonny Hill Basketball Camp, though, because John helped run it), was held on the campus of Cheyney State College, which is located about 30 miles west of Philadelphia. In order to entice kids to come out to the camp, Sonny convinced famous players like Bill Bradley, Wali Jones, me, and other well-known players to make guest appearances. So I came out one weekday in July in a limousine, and when I got out of the limo and the kids saw and recognized me they started yelling, "It's Earl the Pearl . . . Black Jesus . . . You gonna walk on water?"

Man, that shit was funny, seeing all those kids jumping up and down, smiling and calling out my name like that. Then, after things settled down, some of the kids started asking me, "Let me see some of those moves that you do in the NBA?"

Now, I just can't do those moves at the drop of a hat because they are instinctive, creative, and imaginative. I don't even know what I'm going to do until a defender jumps in front of me. Then I just do the spin move or whatever it is that I do out of instinct. I also can't explain, step-by-step, how to execute those moves when someone asks me to. I have to show them in a way that's natural for me. So I took a ball, went out past the top of the key, and asked them to try and guard me. I started by faking a jump shot. Then, when one of the kids jumped out at me with his arms up to stop it, I took a dribble to my left. And when he moved to try to block me, I spun with the ball to my right and took it to the basket and scored. The kids on the sideline went crazy, screaming and jumping up and down. The one who had been guarding me looked shocked. He just shook his head and smiled. What else could he do?

I then called three or four kids out to try and take the ball from me while I dribbled the ball. They tried their best, but it was all in vain. We ran all over the court, but they couldn't get the ball. Then I called three or four more and they couldn't get it away from me, either. But they loved it.

Then the kids asked how much was I getting paid to come out there and I said, "The same thing Sonny paid Bill Bradley and Wali Jones. Nothing. I do it for free. I do it because I want to do it. Because I want to give something back to you kids."

Now, that really surprised them. No question. But I was really happy to do it, and it made me feel happy to see the smiling faces on all those kids when I left.

That summer, the Baker League games were moved from the Bright Hope Baptist Church gym to the bigger and brighter McGonigle Hall gym at Temple University, on Broad Street at Montgomery Avenue. It held about 4,000 people and was not only brighter, but also had clear, Plexiglas backboards. I was a big believer in playing against great competition on a regular basis to keep the juices flowing, the momentum so to speak, and playing in the Baker League games every summer always provided that for me. In fact, as I've said many times, competition in the Baker League was so fantastic that games in the NBA were a letdown by comparison. Absolutely. See, once I got into the NBA everything was so scripted. Now, playing for the Bullets and Coach Shue I was able to deviate from the script somewhat, but for the most part I was still locked into a certain style of play, you know what I mean? On the playground and at Baker, I felt loose, though. There I was free to do all kinds of creative things that I would never do or even try in an NBA game. That's why I enjoyed playing there in the summertime, because it freed me up to release all that pent-up tension from playing in the NBA.

For some reason, I had a habit of being late for games. So being the entertainer I was, I thought up a novel way to make my entrance into games that summer. See, the idea came from this one time when I had arrived at a game late, and when I came into the gym all of a sudden people started chanting my name. They even did it when I went out of the game and when I came back in. It was a big surprise to me to hear "Jesus! Black Jesus! Earl the Pearl!"

They repeated this stuff over and over again, and you know what? I liked it! So I thought I'd do it again. I would arrive late and create the buzz. Because most fans would drive their automobiles to the games, there would be no parking spaces if I came late except for in the middle of the street, so that's what I'd do, right in the middle of Broad Street—one of the busiest streets in Philadelphia!

So I drove my Rolls to the game, parked it in the middle of Broad Street, and, because I was already dressed to play, I got out and went straight to the side entrance of McGonigle Hall. Now, there were always a bunch of people standing outside that entrance, because that was where the players entered and exited the gym. So standing there gave fans the rare chance to see their favorite players up close. When they saw me coming up, people started whispering my name, like "Here comes the Pearl," and "Hey, Jesus, you gon' walk on water today?" And I said, "Absolutely." So the bantering went back and forth like that as I approached the side entrance. Now, the people standing just inside the door heard this and started saying, "Earl's here," and "Oh, Earl's coming in the building," and "The Pearl is here," and "Black Jesus is here." Then that buzz spread inside. So by the time I walked in the door and entered the gym people had already picked up those whispers and then the buzz turned into "He's here, Earl's here!" Then that turned into "Whooooo! Whooooo! Whoooo! Black Magic's here! The Pearl is in the building! Black Jesus is here!"

Now, the game had already started, was maybe in the second

quarter, you know what I mean? Everybody was excited. And I never took any warm-up shots. I just walked to the bench, took off my warm-up, and Coach Janey sent me into the game at the next whistle. Game on. The crowd just exploded. Man, that was something else. *Now, don't let me come right in and hit three or four straight shots* (which happened a lot), I'd always think, because then we'd have bedlam in that gym.

This happened throughout my Baker League experience. I always had a love affair with the fans. That summer we won the championship again, with me and Archie Clark taking turns putting on a show. Sometimes I'd get 40 points in a half and he would get 30 or 35. Or it would be the other way around. Whatever. It didn't matter because we had big fun playing together. We formed a bond and even wanted to play together in the pros. (It just so happened, in the fall, that he was traded to Baltimore.) I also threw some monster parties in my mother's house in Germantown after the Baker League games that summer, with cars parked everywhere.

But on a trip down to Baltimore sometime in August I impregnated another woman, by the name of Linda. I first met Linda back in 1970 when I was messing around in Baltimore. Linda was 18 when I met her. She was nice looking, sweet, and very affectionate. So when I went back to Baltimore in the summer of 1971 we hooked up again and that's when she got pregnant. (Our daughter, Danielle, would be born the next year, in April.) Still, Cookie was my number one lady and had been for a while now. We had begun to discuss marriage, but I was still wary of committing to it because I was still playing basketball and seeing other women at the time, which was the way I wanted it. But I didn't factor having babies into that equation. Now, after my third child, I vowed I would be more careful in the future, and I was.

After the Baker League wrapped up that summer I returned to Baltimore for training camp. We had drafted Stan Love in the first round that year, and Phil Chenier with the fourth pick in the league's first supplemental (or hardship) draft, which for the first time allowed underclassmen to enter the NBA before graduating (a result of Spencer Haywood's successful antitrust suit). Another rookie, Rich Rinaldi, a six-three shooting guard, also made the team that year.

Gus wasn't around at that point because he was still rehabbing his knee, and it was a different team without him—he was our captain and the soul of the team. Kevin Loughery was still there and so was Fred Carter, but the Bullets waived George Johnson, our former first-round pick, in October. We had also just claimed Terry Driscoll off waivers from the Detroit Pistons. Jack Marin, Wes Unseld, and John Tresvant were all still around, but the energy of the team had changed dramatically and the league was expanding.

For this upcoming season, San Francisco would change its name and be called the Golden State Warriors. They would also move across the Bay and play their home games in Oakland. The San Diego Rockets became the Houston Rockets when they relocated to Texas. Another change occurred when the league debuted its new logo, patterned after the silhouette of Jerry West (that same logo is still in use today). We opened our season on October 15 in Chicago with a 106–82 drubbing at the hands of the Bulls, with Bob Love dropping 31 points on us. We bounced back in our home opener the following night, beating the Warriors 108–93, with me leading all scorers with 27 points. Three days later we traveled to Boston and got trounced again, 134–114. I scored 28 points that night in what would prove to be my last game in a Bullets uniform, though I didn't know it at the time. As things turned out, I would not play in another NBA game until November 11, when I suited up in the uniform of my "enemy," the New York Knicks.

On October 18, the day before the Celtics game, I was surprised to learn that the Bullets had traded Kevin Loughery and Fred Carter to Philadelphia in exchange for Archie Clark. So we were a bit short-handed against Boston. Our next game was scheduled for October 22 in

Baltimore against the Knicks. Larry Fleischer had opened up negotia-
tions with the Bullets for my next contract back in the spring, after the
finals. When the Bullets dug in, he let them know that I wanted to be
traded and provided them with a list of teams I'd be willing to play for.
But now it was several months later and it still didn't seem like they
were going to pull the trigger on anything just yet. Instead, management
traded to get Archie Clark. The Bullets said they were going to have the
best backcourt in the NBA, just like Archie and I had talked about up
at Baker. But without a new contract or a trade imminent, Larry advised
me to sit out the game with the Knicks and not to let anyone know
where I was. He told me he would talk to me later and I decided to follow his instructions. So I sat out the Knicks game to see what was happening. Archie Clark didn't show up either, and New York kicked the
Bullets' ass real good in that one, 110–87.

I just stayed in my apartment while the phone rang off the hook. I
didn't answer it. After a day of that it got too hot for me in Baltimore,
so I drove up to Philly and stayed at my mother's house. But I was talking with Larry constantly (our calls were prearranged) during this time
and I remember him saying, "Well, Earl, there's no trade on the table
yet, but some other teams are interested in you."

So I asked him, "Who?"

"The Indiana Pacers in the ABA have been calling. They definitely
want to try and work out something with you. Why don't you take a
flight out there to Indianapolis and just talk to them? Don't say anything definite. Just listen to what they have to say. See what's it's like,
see if you like it."

So I agreed to do that and the next day I flew out to Indianapolis.
Bobby "Slick" Leonard, who was the coach out there, met me at the
airport, took me to the hotel, and dropped me off. Then someone from
the team came back a while later and picked me up and took me to the
game. The Pacers had some very good players on their team, like George

McGinnis, Roger Brown, Freddie Lewis, and a few others. So I surmised
that this was a team I could play on. The only negative thing about the
situation was that I didn't want to play in the ABA, because I thought
the competition was better in the NBA. But I thought to myself, *If push
comes to shove I can do this. But I don't think it's going to happen.* The most
significant thing was that I didn't like the arena where the Pacers played
their games in Indianapolis. It wasn't like the Baltimore Civic Center or
Madison Square Garden. But I did like the team and the fact that they
were a winning franchise.

So I went to the game and the Pacers won. Then, after the game, I
went back to meet the Pacers' players in the locker room. I liked them,
too. But then, after they had showered and dressed, all the black players
reached up over their lockers and starting bringing guns down. I was
shocked to see this and asked, "Why do you guys have guns?"

"They got Ku Klux Klan everywhere around here outside Indianapolis and in the city, too," one of the players said. "So we got guns to
protect ourselves."

That did it, just took me and that situation to another level. That's
when I knew for certain that Indianapolis wasn't the place for me. Obviously I hadn't thought about the KKK being such a presence out in
Indianapolis, and now that I knew they were, it was a deal breaker. I had
already been through that scenario down in Virginia and in North Carolina when I was at Winston-Salem, and I wasn't about to put myself in
that situation again. The next day I thanked everybody. Slick said management was trying to work out a deal with Larry because they wanted
to sign me, and I said I would speak to Larry and he would get back to
them. Then they took me to the airport and I flew back to Philadelphia
and went home.

By this point it had been almost two weeks since I'd spoken with
anyone with the Bullets, and it was clear that I had played my last game
there. Archie Clark, after working out a new contract, had reported to

the team and was playing well for them in a starting role. But the team was losing and I was getting itchy because at the time I really didn't want to leave Baltimore. I had grown to like the city and had great friends there, not to mention Cookie. So I was starting to think to myself, *Hey, my future is at stake here. What's going to happen to me? Where am I going to wind up?* I had given Larry a short list of places I wanted to play in if I had to leave Baltimore. The list included only three cities: Philadelphia, Los Angeles, and Chicago. But none of those teams, that I know of, had been in touch with Larry, so I was really antsy when Larry called me around November 7 and said, "I've got a deal on the table for you."

"Really," I said. "Where? What's up?"

"New York," he said.

"New York? Shit! Are you kidding me?"

"No," he said. "It's legitimate. What do you think?"

After a few seconds of thinking about it, I said, "I don't think I can go play there. We've been playing against those guys for so long and so hard, plus they're our mortal enemies."

Then I heard myself talking, saying, "They're *our* mortal enemies," not *my* mortal enemies. I was still thinking like a Bullet! When I realized that, it kind of stopped me in my tracks and allowed me to listen objectively to what Larry was saying.

"I'm going to be honest with you," he said. "I'm prejudiced. I want to see you playing day in and day out. And I want to see you playing in New York City."

"Well, shit," I said. "I'm going to have to think about that, Larry."

And we left it like that. I told him I'd get back to him in a day or so. He agreed with this and we hung up. I immediately had a talk with my mother and she said, "Whatever my baby wants is cool with me. Just be sure you know what you're doing."

Then I called up Sonny Hill to talk it over with him and he said,

"Earl, all those individual things that you told me you wanted to accomplish in the NBA—all the goals you set for yourself—like scoring 20,000
points over your career, making so many All-NBA teams, All-Star
teams—that's not going to happen if you go to the Knicks. Because in
Baltimore you are the man, you are the franchise player, everything
revolves around you. With the Knicks it will be very different. They
play a different style and their team will not revolve around you, or how
you play. You will have to adapt yourself to their system and fit in with
their more conservative, traditional approach to the game. Five guys
moving the ball, moving without the ball. Setting screens for each other.
It's pick-and-roll basketball, not the kind of game you've been playing
with the Bullets, running and gunning. Fast-breaking all the time. Now
can you do that and still be 'Earl the Pearl'?"

What Sonny said stunned me for a moment and I thought hard
about it. Then I told him, "Sonny, I'm a basketball player. I'm from
Philadelphia and I believe in the 'science of the game' approach." When
I said that it made Sonny happy, and he gave me his blessing to make
whatever deal I thought was best for my future. Then we got together in
person and Sonny told me he thought it would be difficult for me to fit
in with the Knicks and that Baltimore was also a winning team. When
we talked about changing my style I told him, "Sonny, I can do this,
because in Philly we can play any style. I can adapt to their style. I'm
willing to sacrifice and not score points. But I'm going to think it
through and call Larry in an hour or so."

As I left to get in my Rolls to drive around Philly for a while, I
thought to myself, *I've alienated Baltimore and I haven't even thought
about going back there for a while.* I also knew that Bullets management
was pissed at me because Abe Pollin, who I had grown to like very
much, was telling people that he had given me money for the down payment on my house in Germantown. Now, they were underpaying me in
the first place anyway, and as far as the "down payment" Abe was

talking about goes, I looked at that as a bonus, something between him
and me. Now he had gone public with that shit and I felt betrayed. So
that's when I made up my mind to go with the Knicks' offer. I decided
right then and there I wasn't going back to Baltimore. It was the princi-
ple of it all. I was still young and rather naïve, but I knew I didn't have
to take that kind of shit. Then I thought about being arrested by the
cops back there at Dunbar High School and being falsely accused.
Thinking about that just pissed me off even more. So I went back home,
made a quick call to Larry, and told him I would accept the offer from
the Knicks. I knew I had to change myself completely and become a new
person, so to speak, if I was going to be successful in New York City. So
from that moment on, that's what I set out to do, only I didn't know
what kind of person I would become. I'd find out through trial and
error, a kind of instinctive shift.

Larry called me the next morning to tell me everything was cool
and to come on up to New York. He told me I would be staying at the
New Yorker Hotel and that he would come and pick me up from there.
I think this was November 9, 1971. I woke up the next morning, ate
breakfast, and kissed my mother. She wished me good luck and told me
everything would be okay, which was reassuring coming from her. Then
I got in my Rolls and went and saw Wilkie and Smitty. Later that day I
hit the road for the drive up to the Big Apple. Even though I had
decided to become a Knick, it still didn't set well with me, you know,
the prospect of becoming one of the enemy. But I had committed to it
and just had to suck it up. I crossed the Benjamin Franklin Bridge to
take the turnpike through New Jersey and just moved on north, thinking all the way. The reason I like to drive, especially when I'm driving
alone, is that it allows me to think a lot of difficult things through. So
that's what I was doing while I was driving up the turnpike. I thought
about all the recent things that had happened to me in Baltimore, like
getting arrested trying to help blacks at Dunbar. I thought about the fact

that I had just stopped playing like I did and forced the trade. Things like that. I knew I had to prove myself all over again as I had at Bartram, on the playgrounds of Philadelphia, at Winston-Salem, at the Pan American trials, and as a rookie in Baltimore. Up to that point I had been very confident in my decision, enjoying listening to my music, you know what I mean? But then doubts started to creep into my mind.

Although Sonny and I had talked about all the changes I had to make in my game—different sacrifices and whatnot—I was still adamant that those were things I could do. However, as I got closer to New York I started to have apprehensions about what I was actually getting myself into. A lot of times when I'm by myself my thoughts start to form themselves a little differently than they do when I'm around other people. Things began to enter my mind, like wondering how I would react to something or other, or if things went wrong. I really didn't know what to expect from Coach Holzman, since he hadn't played me as much as I had expected in the All-Star game the year before, even though I was a starter. All that stuff kept eating at me and as I approached New York City I suddenly pulled off the turnpike at the Jersey City exit and rode around there for quite a long time. After a while I calmed down and convinced myself that I had made the right decision. Then I said to myself, *Well, I got to go.* So I made my way into New York City through the Lincoln Tunnel, went to the hotel, and chilled. As I was making my way to the hotel, I got turned around and found myself on West Street. I made a right turn on 40th Street going east, back toward the tunnel, and then stopped for the light at the corner of 11th Avenue. There was a police car sitting on the corner with two policemen in the front seat. I just happened to look toward the backseat of the police car, and saw a pair of legs sticking straight up in the air. I was kind of puzzled but I played it off as if I didn't see anything at all (later I was told that the area was where the hookers worked). I just drove on and said to myself, *I think I'm gonna like it here. Earl, welcome to New York.*

EARL MONROE

The next day I went to see Coach Holzman and to sign my contract with the Knicks, a two-year deal worth $300,000. Believe it or not, I hadn't even known how much I was signing for until the contract was put in front of me. I just trusted Larry to make the best deal he could for me, and he did.

I told Red that I didn't want to start, but instead wanted to earn my way into the lineup. Besides, Dick Barnett was the starter and was a very good player, even at this part of his career. Coach told me that was okay with him, that he just wanted me to feel comfortable. Then he asked me what number I wanted to wear, but I knew I couldn't wear my old number 10 because Clyde was wearing that. So I asked him what was available and he told me a bunch of numbers. I think I wore number 33 at first, before settling on number 15, which was the number I wore for the rest of my career.

Then I said to Red, "I think I need an operation to fix bone spurs because they've been hurting real bad. They're on the top of my left foot, so when I run or jump the spurs hit each other and it's very painful."

So Red said, "We've just made this trade for you because we need and want you with us. Willis is out and we need to have you on the floor. Plus, we don't want to have any letdown at the guard position. That's why we brought you in. So you might have to just play through the pain this season."

That's when I told him, "Well, Coach, I'm cool with that. Let me go slowly at first."

He looked at me and nodded his head. I could see he had respect for me for saying that. I didn't want any controversy coming in here. I knew I had to accept being a reserve. And even when I got into the game, my intention was to be passing the ball. I wouldn't be looking to score at first, because my mind-set was to get the ball to the established scorers on the team, guys like Clyde Frazier and Jerry Lucas, Dave DeBusschere, Willis

Reed, and Bill Bradley. I knew my scoring would be down until I had surgery on my left foot anyway, and that even then it would be a slow process. I couldn't make hard cuts because of the pain, couldn't do the things I was used to doing out on the floor. I knew going in that it wouldn't be a very productive year for me, offensively speaking, because of my foot. I had learned from my experience playing through all that knee pain two seasons before that there would be ups and downs, that there would be times when I could bear the pain because it might not be as inflamed as on some other nights. So I would just have to take it one game at a time. But at the same time I knew this season was going to be a learning process for me and, as a player who hadn't yet turned 27, I knew there was a lot I could learn from playing with a veteran ball club like the Knicks. This kind of thinking helped to calm me down and made me feel better about my chances of playing and meshing well with my new teammates. I'd be learning new lessons about "the science of the game."

So then we went down to the press conference, where I was introduced to the media. I remember there was a lot of press there. The first question someone asked was "Since you were the superstar of the Bullets, why did they trade you?"

I knew why they had to trade me (because I had forced them to), but I didn't want to open up a bag of worms, so I just said, "I don't know why, they just traded me. You might want to ask them that question." (I always used to quip to reporters that the Bullets got Dave Stallworth and Mike Riordan and $450,000 in cash from the Knicks in that trade for me, but they could've just given me that money and I would've stayed in Baltimore.)

The next question was "Can you play with Clyde?"

"I can play with anybody," I said, "especially someone as good as Clyde."

"How many balls will the Knicks need to keep you two satisfied?"

"One," I said and smiled. "I don't think we play the game with two."

"Who's going to start?"

"The same five players that have been starting," I said. "I'll be coming off the bench."

That first day in New York was like a whirlwind, you know, between signing the contract and meeting with Coach, then the press conference, then taking pictures in my new uniform before, finally, doing a bunch of one-on-one interviews with the local beat reporters. That was painstaking stuff. I felt really strange at that moment because I knew I had to learn how to be another type of player, even another person in New York, since I had been used to starting for a long time. Plus I would have to *learn* to play coming off the bench, you know, the nuances of what to do, how to move with the pace of the game when I went in to play. Now, I could intellectually feel I could do this, but I had to emotionally go through it every day I didn't play. So I had to deal with that, too.

In Baltimore the game for me was in a rhythm and I knew that when I came into a game with the Knicks it wouldn't be the same rhythm. So I had to learn what the Knicks' rhythm was. In the past, the rhythm was determined by how I played and what I did, and things just flowed naturally from there. But here in New York I had to really think about the game in another way and I could see that the cadence of it wasn't the same. Here it was determined by Clyde's cadence and rhythm and I had to learn how to fit myself into that cadence—which I wasn't used to—and adapt to it. It was like trying to play to Miles Davis's cadence, or a trumpet's rhythm, when I was used to being the lead trumpet myself. I had to learn how to play inside a different rhythm. And coming off the bench and trying to implement my own rhythm, my own cadence, within the structure of a completely different style of play, that was hard, harder than I imagined it would be. But it also gave me the opportunity to become a student of the game once again. Because all the things I had been able to do as a Bullet, and as a Ram at Winston-Salem, I now had to learn to do as a Knick. It was different and it was frustrating. It would keep me up nights trying to figure out why I couldn't do this or that.

But as the year went on I started catching on and up and that was rewarding, exhilarating even. I had to kind of put myself in the backseat of a car and try to learn to drive from back there, where the view was so different. Sitting on the bench, though very frustrating and hard, taught me how to look at the game in another way; it also taught me humility. It made me cognizant of what all the other players who had been sitting on the bench behind me had gone through, what had been running through their minds. Sitting there on the bench and observing made me focus even more on the intricacies and nuances of pro basketball, and doing that made me an even better student of the game. It helped me adapt to a whole different style.

I knew that after a while I'd be able to play the up-tempo game I was used to. But first I had to learn how to play the more controlled type of game, which was Clyde's game, his rhythm and cadence. So I learned to really bob and weave my way into that tempo and make myself successful over time. A lot of the players on the Knicks empathized with me because they saw the struggles I was going through every day. They understood what it was, said to themselves, *Now here's a star player coming in here, humbling himself to sit on the bench and be a part of this team, as opposed to coming and trying to impose his own style and influence on the team and the game itself.* They really appreciated me for the attitude I took coming in, because it was a team-first attitude.

In the first meeting in the locker room the night of my first game as a Knick, November 11 (I used to always say that I came to the Knicks two days before Felix Unger, from *The Odd Couple*, was thrown out of his house by his wife, on November 13th), all the players came up to greet and welcome me to the team, one by one. It was great the way they made me feel right at home. DeBusschere was the first who came up to me. He hugged me and said, "Welcome to the team. It's going to be great!"

Then Bill Bradley, whom I had had a history with at the Baker League, came up and welcomed me with a hug. Then Willis came up, the captain, you know, and he expressed his happiness that I was there. I guess I was waiting for Clyde to come up, because we had always been fierce competitors with each other. I felt as though it was imperative that we hit it off in a way that would let him know I wasn't coming in to threaten his position or leadership or anything like that. I wanted him to know I was here to win and to try and make things better for everybody. But despite his stylish wardrobe, Clyde was kind of a shy person, a lot like me off the court, and a lot like me on it. But he came up and hugged me and I could tell everything was cool. Then Dick Barnett came up and I was relieved that he was cool, because he was the guy who could have been most threatened by my joining the team. When he came up and greeted me warmly, that made everything much easier for me. Then Jerry Lucas and Phil Jackson approached with the same kind of welcome. And, finally, Dean Meminger came up and we hit it off right away. So I felt relaxed going into that first game. Still, it would take a while for all the tension that been built up over the past few seasons of playing so fiercely against each other to fully melt away, and I understood that. But Dean and I became very close because he was new to the team also and we sat next to each other during that first game on the bench. (After that night we *always* sat by each other, watching the action from there and growing closer with every passing game until he became my best friend on the team.)

The Garden was buzzing that first night. We were playing the Warriors and the fans were screaming my name, even during warm-ups, but not in a nasty way like when I was with the Bullets. Even some of the Warriors players came over before the game started and wished me luck. So when Coach Holzman called my name to go into the game in the second quarter, you know, the crowd gave me a rousing standing ovation. That was really something. Now, I had been used to ovations, but this was one that I will always savor because I could see that the people appreciated the fact that I was in New York, you know what I mean? And that was special! See, I thought the fans here would always view me as a Bullet because of the kind of hard-fought games we always played against the Knicks and the series we had just had the season before where we finally beat them in the Eastern Conference Finals. So I just never expected that the fans would embrace me like that. But they did, and that was truly satisfying. I realized that night that the majority of the fans were there to embrace me and were happy for me, and that helped erase some of the doubts I was wrestling with initially.

We lost the first game I played with the Knicks 112–103, in front of 19,500 fans. I scored only 9 points that evening, but the fans cheered and screamed for every one of the four shots I made from the floor and even for one of the two free throws I made. But mostly I passed the ball that night. I threw behind the back, no-look passes that led to scores, and the crowd just loved it. Clyde scored 30 points that night to lead the Knicks, but Jeff Mullins scored 31 for the Warriors. After the game was over everyone went back to the locker room and looked at stat sheets (they had even looked at them at halftime, which was something they didn't do in Baltimore). The Knicks' locker room was very relaxed, but professional. And after Coach Holzman discussed the game, everyone mostly went their separate ways. We only hooked again at practices, which were very organized.

Being in the Knicks' locker room and understanding how these guys operated—understanding the importance of winning and how to win from their perspective—was a lot different from how we did things in Baltimore. See, the Knicks were just a more disciplined type of team than the Bullets were, even though we had a great team while I was down there. I felt the Bullets had great team chemistry, which really helped us move ahead. And we had a good core of veterans. But many of them had been on teams that lost a lot and when that happens you kind of settle for losing. So in order to move ahead as a team we had to embrace the culture of learning to win together, and that could really turn us around and make us into a different type of team.

Conversely, though, the Knicks had already learned to have a winning culture earlier than we had in Baltimore and were more calculated in their approach to winning games. I mean, I had already noticed when I was with the Bullets that when you looked at the Knicks' box scores you always saw certain guys with the same amount of points all the time. Other players had a certain number of assists all the time, and it seemed like it was all coordinated in a way to keep everything structured. Like, there was hardly ever any player scoring a lot of points all the time, you know, like 30 points a game, then the next guy having 15. No. Most times the scoring was spread out more evenly, with one guy scoring like 20 points and the next players chipping in 19 and 18, you know, a nice balance. So the Knicks' balance in scoring and assists and everything else was much different from what we'd had in Baltimore, even though we'd had a balance, too. Like, I would be getting 25 points a game—sometimes scoring 40—and the next guy might have 20 or 25 and on down the scale like that.

With the Knicks it was more about spreading the scoring across everyone in the starting lineup and on down through the reserves. This had something to do with Red Holzman's philosophy and approach to the game, which stressed ball movement and finding the open man, whereas Gene Shue, a great coach, just kind of cut us loose to play in a run-and-gun style that he loved to see played. When Gene thought we needed to be reeled in, he'd just call a time-out, settle us down, and draw up plays for us to run. But I found out that Red had everyone's statistics in his head, knew how many shots a player had taken, how many assists he had had, how many rebounds he'd grabbed, and how many turnovers he had committed. And if you took too many shots, or turned the ball over too many times, he would pull you out of the game.

So he kept everyone pretty much in tow (he also had Frankie Blaus-child, the team's publicity director, keeping personal stats for him). Like I said, we were given stat sheets at halftime with the Knicks, and they only gave those to us at the end of the game in Baltimore.

So guys with the Knicks always understood where they were and what they were doing. Red Holzman was a general while Gene was less militaristic in his approach, probably because he was an ex-player who had just retired from playing in 1964. It was a protocol with the Knicks, going from General Holzman down to Captain Willis Reed, then in his seventh NBA season. So that was the difference that I noticed immediately when I got there. I mean, hey, Gene was still practicing and playing against the players a lot of the time. He coached from a player's perspective, and that style influenced the Bullets' teams. Red Holzman, on the other hand, had been a player also, but that had been a long time ago. Now he was a general running things, so his approach was different from Gene Shue's.

I spent my first few weeks in New York living at the New Yorker Hotel, and then the Knicks' front-office people asked me where I wanted to stay. So I thought about it for a minute and told them maybe Greenwich Village, in downtown Manhattan, because I always thought I would like to live down there. So they arranged for me to visit some places. The first place I visited was a nice loft down on Grove Street in the West Village. So I asked them if it was available and they said it was. Then I asked how much the loft was going to cost and if I could make a down payment and whatnot. But then, in the end, somehow the place wasn't available and it just seemed the people—who were white—didn't want me living down there. See, the Knicks had arranged the visit, so they'd known I was coming. That's why the place was available until it wasn't when they saw I was black. The Knicks hadn't told them that. Now this was late November 1971. Racial attitudes were different back then, even in New York. So when this tall black man showed up they probably freaked out, even though they were smiling the whole time.

Then I found an apartment on 64th and Broadway, in a brand-new building across from Lincoln Center called 1 Lincoln Plaza, or The Ascap Building. It was a spacious, three-bedroom apartment on the 23rd floor. Nina Simone, the great singer, lived next door but I was afraid to speak to her. She had a no-nonsense, "don't bother me" attitude, so I just kept my distance, though I really loved her music. She was a very private person but she had a lot of guests dropping in, especially some beautiful women who I tried to get to come to my apartment. Nina's husband, Andy Stroud, had been in the music business for a long time and we used to talk about that. But I never had any conversations with Nina because I respected her privacy. I think I told her one time while we were waiting at the elevator how much I loved her music and she just nodded and that was that. I was very humbled by the fact that I was living next door to her. Her song "Young, Gifted and Black" was a song we all related to.

Reverend Ike, the most famous black minister and evangelist of his day, also lived in the building and had two apartments next to each other. He had broken down the walls and converted the two units into one very large apartment. He had *two* Rolls-Royces at the time. A flamboyant type of guy, Ike was always dressed to the nines. Hair done up. Big smile. He wore a lot of diamonds because he said he wanted to show people he was successful, so he lived that type of lifestyle, you know, and he had a chauffeur. After he saw I had a Rolls of my own parked in the garage, we used to talk about our cars, about his churches, what was going on in the world, and how to make money.

One of the most revealing things Reverend Ike said to me was his take on poor people and how to help them. "Earl," he said to me one day right before he got into one of his Rolls-Royces, "the best way you can help poor people is not to be one of them." Reverend Ike was something else.

Like I said, my apartment overlooked Lincoln Center and out west into New Jersey. It was cool. So I decorated it with floor-to-ceiling blackout drapes that spanned from wall to wall in each room, so if need be it could always be dark in there—I always slept better when the room was dark. Then I brought some of my stuff up from Baltimore, like my Mylar ceiling decoration—my mirrors over my bed—with the circles in it. But I sold off a lot of my Baltimore furniture and bought new stuff up here. Like, I had an orange sectional sofa in the living room and whatnot, a tan carpet, and dark-orange blackout drapes. I had green, blue, and red rooms because I wanted all of the areas to be different, you know what I mean? And there was a 24-hour doorman downstairs. There were restaurants and shops all around the area. People everywhere in the daytime and at night. I really liked the area.

But I started hanging out in the Village also, going to clubs and whatnot, and I found this little hideaway place on Little West 12th Street called the Needle's Eye. It was a real funky kind of bar, small, always crowded, upbeat, people not dressed up, long-haired guys and women, mostly white, with that Village look and cool feel. I felt good just being there. Anyway, I'd drive my Silver Shadow down there, and this one time I found a parking space right in front of the big window of the club. So I parked and went inside but forgot to turn off my lights, and they were shining in through that front window. So everybody was looking out and whispering, "Who's that in that Rolls-Royce?" When I heard that, I realized my lights were on and went out and turned them off. And when I came back in I saw this beautiful black lady bartending in the back. She had honey-brown, smooth skin and a gap between her front teeth that made her look even more sexy. She had a beautiful smile and short brush hair, just like I like it. She was about five seven maybe, with an air of elegance about her. So I was just looking at her, turned on by her beauty and style. So this guy I knew down there named Vernon, my namesake, saw me looking at her and said, "Hey, Earl, you want to meet her?"

"Yeah," I said.

So he introduced us. She was a hard sell, though, proper in her speech and attitude, and she kind of brushed me off at first. But I was persistent. I came back and tried to get her to go out with me almost every night for a week, but she kept putting me off. Finally, I saw her one night at the club again and asked for her telephone number. She finally gave it to me after hemming and hawing. So I called her from my apartment one night and told her I'd really like to take her out. But she didn't say anything. So I said, "Tina, when can we do this? You know, go out for dinner or something like that?"

"Maybe sometime next week," she said.

"Next week? Wow, that's a long time!"

So she was silent again and when she did speak, she changed the subject. So after we hung up I thought to myself, *Maybe I'll go down there tonight and see if I can talk her into going out with me in person.* So I got in my car and drove down to the Needle's Eye and lo and behold, there was that same parking space out in front. Now I was real nervous about seeing her and asking her to go out with me. So when I got out of my car I forgot to turn my lights off again and they were shining in through the front window again. But this time I didn't even notice, because I was so preoccupied with seeing her and asking if she'd go out with me. Man, I must have been a wreck. Anyway, I finally noticed my lights were on and I rushed out and turned them off. Then I came back in and I said to her, "Mind if I take you home tonight?"

Now, I could see she was reluctant by the way she was looking all around the club at all the people, because she didn't want them to see her getting in the car with me. Finally she relented and said, "Well, you can take me home, but that's it."

So I said, "Cool."

Tina got off early that night and when she did I took her out to my Silver Shadow with people in the club watching. Because by then many of them knew who I was, including her. So I opened the door for her like a gentleman and she gave me a sweet, beautiful smile. So I rushed around the car and got in, put my key in the ignition to start it up, but nothing happened; the engine didn't turn over. I turned the key again—nothing. I turned it once again—still nothing. I didn't know what the hell was happening because I'd just driven the car here! So after 15 or so minutes of trying to get the car to start (now, I'd turned on my big-ass lights and they were shining in the window of the club and people were looking out, pointing their fingers at me and snickering and shit), I looked at her and she was cool as a cucumber. So I told her that she should go back in the club until I could fix this problem. So she opened the door before I could get out of the car and open it for her, got out, closed the door, and went back inside the club without looking back. Now I was furious. So I went inside the club and called AAA. They told me they'd be there shortly, so I went back out to the car to wait for them and after a while their tow truck drove up and the driver asked, "What's the problem?"

"The car don't turn on," I told him. "I came here and I parked it, went into the club, and now the car won't start."

So he got in the car, put the gearshift in park, turned the key, and it started! Now, as dark as I am, I turned bright red! I was embarrassed like a motherfucker! I had left the car in the wrong gear when I'd parked because I was so anxious to see Tina. I was so embarrassed that I just paid the guy and drove away and left Tina in the club. I called her back the next week and explained to her what had happened and she just laughed and laughed. Then we got together and I really liked being with her.

A few weeks after I moved in at 1 Lincoln Plaza, for days or so I had been noticing out my window all these people with movie cameras running around down on 64th Street and Broadway. I thought that was interesting, so I asked my doorman what was going on and he told me they were filming a movie called *Taxi Driver* with Cybill Shepherd and Robert De Niro. Now, I would never have thought they were making a movie. I had just been watching all these people running around with cameras and shit for weeks and wondered what was going on. That was the first movie I ever saw being filmed, though it wasn't the last one since New York is one of the filmmaking capitals of the world.

I lived on Manhattan's West Side, and further uptown there were great clubs like Mikell's up on 97th and Columbus Avenue (today the spot is a new apartment complex, with a Whole Foods market where Mikell's used to be), which was right across from Park West Village, where a lot of middle-class blacks lived. Russ Brown's was on 96th Street near Amsterdam, the Cellar was on 95th and Columbus, and Under the Stairs was on Columbus between 94th and 93rd Streets. I used to see Miles Davis in all those clubs, and he used to sit in and play at Mikell's. So did the singer Al Jarreau and the South African trumpet player and singer Hugh Masekela. So that area was really jumping with a lot of stylish people and many beautiful women. I used to hang out there a lot and up in Harlem, also, at Big Wilt's Smalls Paradise and Jocks on Seventh Avenue (now called Adam Clayton Powell Boulevard) and Wells, which was famous for its chicken and waffles.

One night I met Miles Davis at Mikell's. He was a big sports fan and he recognized me and started talking to me. I used to see him from a distance in all of the clubs, but I was shy. I respected his genius as a musician, but also his privacy. Plus, I had heard you didn't just walk up to Miles Davis and start a conversation with him because he just might bite your head off. So I kept my distance until that night when he came up and started talking to me, just like that. Anyway, he was talking but I couldn't understand what he was saying because of that deep, scratchy, gravelly voice of his. So I was standing there smiling, wondering, *What the fuck is he talking about?* So he went on saying whatever it was that came into his mind and I said, "Yeah, Miles, I hear you," even though I didn't. Then one night Miles was in Mikell's with Freddie Hubbard, another great trumpet player, and we were just standing there talking. They were drinking shots of scotch whiskey and chasing them with bottles of Pabst Blue Ribbon. I never liked beer so I was drinking Courvoisier. Then Miles saw what I was drinking and ordered me a shot of scotch with a beer chaser. I guess I made a face when I downed that concoction and Miles and Freddie looked at me, shook their heads, grinned, and said, "Athletes." I have never drunk another beer since that day. I also hung out downtown at a club my friend from Philly, Kendall Flowers, had, called the Raspberry Freeze. It was jumping.

Anyway, I began to love being in New York City, meeting all the different kinds of people. Going to music concerts and eating in all those great restaurants, and of course, meeting all the ladies. But I was there primarily to play basketball, and that's what occupied most of my time while I was getting to know the city.

The season was up and down for both the Knicks and me. Willis Reed only played in 11 games that season because of his knee problem, and my play suffered somewhat as I adjusted to my new team, different players, and a new style of playing the game. I was also affected by the bone spurs on my left foot, which caused me considerable pain. I think I scored more than 20 points maybe two or three times during that season, though I began to feel more comfortable playing with guys on the team as we approached the playoffs. Statistically, I was having my worst year since I came into the league. And if that bothered me—I would be lying if I said it didn't, because I had always been a scorer—it never bothered my teammates or Coach Holzman. So I just accepted the mind-set that I was there to help the Knicks win a championship, not to compete for a scoring title.

Sometime in December, before the end of the year, I went down to the Needle's Eye to pick up Tina to drive her out to her place in Brooklyn. While I was waiting for her to get off work one of the regulars who I talked to sometimes—I forget his name but he was a nice white guy—came up to me and said, "Earl, you remember the white girl who used to work behind the bar with your girlfriend, Tina?"

"Yeah," I said, "I kind of remember her, but vaguely. Because I was too busy looking at Tina to see anybody else."

He kind of laughed at that and said, "Yeah, I know what you mean. But that girl was Linda Lovelace and she's the star of this new porno movie, *Deep Throat!*"

"Oh, yeah?" I said, "I've kind of heard about that. I guess I'll have to check it out."

"You do that," he said, "because in this movie Linda is something else!"

I told myself to remember the film but it soon slipped to the back of my mind because I was in the middle of playing basketball and after a while I just forgot about it. I don't even remember asking Tina about Linda Lovelace and I don't even know today if they were close, though I don't think so, especially after I came into the picture. Anyway, that night after she got off we drove to her place on Beverly Road somewhere out in Brooklyn. It was late and she said, "You can come up and stay but you'll have to sleep on the couch."

So I didn't know what to say to that, because if that's what it was that's what it was. So I parked the car and followed her up the stairs to her apartment, you know, thinking something else might happen, but it didn't. So I find myself sleeping on the couch. At one point in the night

I had this feeling like I couldn't tell if I was awake or dreaming. And all of a sudden I felt like something jumped on me, but I couldn't see what it was because it was dark. I couldn't move. Whatever it was prevented me from moving. I felt defenseless. So I started hollering, "Get off me, you motherfucker. Get the fuck off me, you asshole!"

But hollering didn't work either. This thing, whatever it was, was just pinning me down and it really was getting uncomfortable. I didn't know what it was. Maybe it was a ghost. Because I didn't know what it was I started saying my mother's favorite passage from the 23rd Psalm: *The Lord is my shepherd; I shall not want. He maketh me to lie down in green pastures; he leadeth me beside the still waters. . . .*

But that didn't work, so I started saying the Lord's Prayer to myself which didn't work either. But I still couldn't see anything and I'm really hollering now, what I don't know. Then the lights came on and Tina is standing there saying, "What's wrong? What is wrong?"

Then I was suddenly released. It was weird. So I said, "I don't know. Something jumped on me. Something's in here!"

I was sleeping in my clothes because it was cold outside, so I said, "I got to go. I got to go." And I just put on my coat and left. It was really strange. I felt like something or somebody was in there protecting Tina from me. That's how I felt as I was leaving. I was frightened that night and I got my ass out of there real quick. I know she thought I was crazy because she later told me so. But it was one of the scariest things that have ever happened to me. That was the first and last time I went out to her apartment.

Tina was part of the reason I changed, though. She kind of set the tone for the way I wanted to be in New York, you know, more urban, sophisticated, hip. I knew I had to be a different person and when people saw us together I was looked at as a very responsible person. Being with her helped give me that cachet. We stayed together for a long time and we went everywhere together, you know, to Mikell's, Wells chicken and waffles up in Harlem, all over the village. Like I said, Tina didn't take shit from anybody. But after she warmed up to me she was soft, just a warm individual. She laughed easy and our relationship just got better and better.

Two of the times I managed to score 20 or more points that season were against my old team, once on December 30 at the Garden in New York, when Baltimore beat us 110–102, ending an eight-game winning streak. I scored 21 points that night, as did Clyde. But Jack Marin was hot that night and scored 33 points (maybe just seeing me in a Knicks uniform fired him up!), while Archie Clark dropped 24. Still, my old teammates greeted me warmly before and after the game and I wished them well for the rest of the season. They were disappointed and sad that I was gone—especially to the Knicks—but they were professional about it and understood. I went over to Gene and we shook hands. I could see he was also very sad that things hadn't worked out for me with the Bullets. But it was what it was and nobody could do anything about it.

The Bullets were transitioning, with Phil Chenier and Archie Clark starting at the guard positions for them now instead of me and Kevin Loughery or Fred Carter, both of whom had been traded to the 76ers. So they had a new look and were getting used to playing with each other. The next two times we played them was in back-to-back games on February 26 and 27. In the first game, the Bullets beat us in the Garden 104–97, with Archie Clark scoring 30 points and Jack Marin getting 26. Wes Unseld ruled the boards that night because Willis was still out. I scored 17 points, but Clyde led us with 22. Then we traveled down to College Park, Maryland (where the Bullets were increasingly playing more of their home games), to play them again the next night. I think that was the game where some of the fans hung down banners that read "Benedict Arnold Earl" or something like that, insinuating that I was a traitor for leaving the Bullets. That just motivated me, though, and we beat them in a very close game that night, 97–95. I was the leading scorer for the Knicks with 21 points, which felt real good after seeing those banners. It was good to see Gus and we hugged each other for a long time, because we both knew we would probably never play together on the same team and that was a sad realization for the both of us.

One night I went to the game in Madison Square Garden (I have forgotten who was playing that night) and when the game was under way, during a time-out, I heard this wild cheering from the stands behind the opposing team's bench and I looked over to see what was happening and lo and behold there's Dancing Harry putting a hex on our opponent, doing his Baltimore act, only now it was more choreographed. I was astonished! He had followed me up to New York City to do his act and I just cracked up. Over time I heard officials in the Garden tried to stop him but somehow he just kept on coming, getting into the games. Now, I don't know how he did it because he never reached out to me to help him. But there he was, in a new, colorful outfit made by some company that I heard sponsored him. The next thing I knew he was doing shows up in the Catskills. Then he would appear at some of our games on the road. So he made a name for himself for a while. I never really knew him other than to say hello sometimes, but the fans loved him and the last I heard of him he was working at the airport in Baltimore.

Anyway, the great thing about playing with the Knicks was that we flew to games in first class, which meant we had a lot of legroom. Now, it's very important to tall guys like basketball players to be able to stretch out their long legs. So the first-class travel was a real plus. We also stayed in better hotels. The Knicks were the highest-grossing team in terms of revenue in the entire NBA, drawing almost 800,000 paying fans to their games every year, as opposed to 231,000 fans for Baltimore. I think the Lakers were second, with about 650,000 paying fans. So that made a huge difference in terms of the salaries the players made (this was way before the salary cap era) and all the rest of the amenities a top-tier team could provide its players. And I began to think that this was one of the reasons the Knicks players carried themselves in the confident way they did, because of the privileged culture surrounding them and the benefits that were provided by their owners. This was a revelation for me, because I had always viewed the Knicks as just being arrogant for the sake of arrogance. But it wasn't like that.

We ended the season with a 48 and 34 record, good enough to finish second to the Celtics in the Atlantic Division. But we won the Eastern Conference Semifinals against my old club, the Bullets, four games to two, after losing the first game on March 31 in Baltimore in overtime, 108–105. My bone spurs had really been acting up and I didn't play that much in that game, only scoring 5 points. Willis was still out and so was Gus. The second game, on April 2, was played in the Garden and we won that one 110–88. I had 12 points in that game, starting in place of Dick Barnett. We lost Game Three down in Baltimore in another barn burner, 104–103.

Now the Bullets were leading the series two games to one. But that would be the last game they'd win, as we swept the next three to take the series. Then it was on to play Boston in the Eastern Conference Finals.

The series started on April 13 in Boston, where we beat the Celtics convincingly, 116–94. Clyde had a monster game, scoring 36 points. Boston had four players reach double figures, but the team really was never in the game. Then, back in New York for Game Two, we won a close one, 106–105, to take a commanding series lead. We had five players in double figures that night. My bone spurs were acting up again and Dean Meminger played very well that night in my stead, scoring 12 points. We went back to Boston for Game Three on April 19 and the Celtics won that one, 115–109.

The series shifted back to New York for Game Four, which we won 116–98. I felt better in that game and led the team with 26 points. Then, we closed out the series by beating the Celtics up in Boston, 111–103. My bone spurs acted up that night, so Dean Meminger played some significant minutes. We had six players reach double figures that night.

I was happy—as were my teammates—to get this win, because for me it would be my second straight year of going to the NBA Finals, and for the Knicks, who had won the championship two seasons before, it would be an opportunity to win another crown. So it was all good. The Finals would be played against the mighty Los Angeles Lakers, who had the best record in the NBA that year at an impressive 69 and 13. The Lakers had also set a single-season record of 33 straight wins (which still stands; no other team has ever won more than 22 in a row), which started on November 5, when they beat the Bullets 110–106. Their incredible winning streak had ended on January 9 with a 120–104 loss to Kareem and the Bucks out in Milwaukee. So the Lakers were a very formidable team to say the least, one of the best of all time in the NBA. They had lost Elgin Baylor, who had chosen to suddenly retire from the game on November 5—the same day the streak began—which came as a surprise to everyone in the league. But his retirement didn't stop anything because the Lakers still had a very good starting lineup, beginning with Wilt Chamberlain (who was having a great year), Happy Hairston, Jim McMillian, Jerry West, and Gail Goodrich, who led them in scoring that year. They also had great backup players like Flynn Robinson, my old Bullet teammate Leroy Ellis, Pat Riley, and Jim Cleamons coming off the bench. So they were scary good that year. We had beaten them once that season but had lost four times, so our odds didn't look promising, especially with Willis gone for the season and my bone spur problem. Still, the Knicks were a very professional and confident team. We weren't conceding anything going into that series, and I was happy to see that.

My bone spurs had kept me from playing my usual slashing-to-the-basket kind of game, because the pain prevented me from pushing off or cutting when they were inflamed, as they had been for most of the season. I couldn't implement my back-down move, either. So I was reduced to my long-range jump shooting game, or coming off a screen and shooting. There was less pain in my foot when I played like that.

The Finals started on April 26 out in Los Angeles and we won that game, to the shock of all the media and critics, 114–92. Even the Lakers seemed stunned, and their fans were rendered silent. Bill Bradley played an inspired game that night, scoring 29 points, with Jerry Lucas getting 26 with his patented jump push shot from anywhere on the floor over the outstretched hand of Wilt, who had to come out from the basket to try to defend Jerry's accurate shot. The Lakers seemed off that night for some reason, because Jerry West scored only 12 points, the same as Wilt and Happy Hairston. Gail Goodrich scored 20 points to lead the team. The next game was in LA and the Lakers rebounded and won going away, 106–92. They had five players in double figures, led by Goodrich with 31 points, while Wilt dunked in 23.

The Lakers swept the next three games, winning Game Three in New York 107–96 and Game Four, also at the Garden, 116–111. We played pretty well in both of those games, but not well enough to win them. I scored 4 points in Game Three and only 1 point in the fourth game. Then we flew out to Los Angeles and they beat us again, 114–100, to take the championship. Clyde led us with 31 points in that game and I played my best game of the series in a losing cause, scoring 16. The Lakers had all five of their starters in double figures, led by Goodrich with 25, Wilt with 24, and Jerry West with 23 points. Now they had claimed their first NBA championship in Los Angeles after relocating there from Minneapolis in 1960. The Lakers had gone to the Finals a few times since arriving in the City of Angels, but hadn't won it all until now. It was particularly sweet for Jerry West because this was his first NBA title, and it was the second for Wilt. (He had won a title several years back in Philadelphia.) So they celebrated hard out in Los Angeles and we flew back to New York casting our eyes toward the next year.

As for me, I had had my worst NBA season to date. I scored only 11.4 points a game for the season and dished out only 2.2 assists per game. I promised myself I would eclipse those totals in the coming season by staying healthy.

This was the second straight year I had been a member of a team that had lost in the NBA Finals. And playing in the Finals only whetted my appetite to win a championship. Because for the second straight season, I had seen the absolute thrill and joy of winning the title in all the players and coaches (and fans, when the title was won at home) of the team that won. I wanted very badly to experience that feeling that I had once at Winston-Salem, when we won that national championship in 1967. Now I wanted to have that same joy in the NBA. I needed it for my spirit and, yes, my ego as a player. It was also the second straight year I had played with a debilitating injury. I promised myself that this had to stop. I would undergo surgery again this coming summer to remove my bone spurs. But I would have it as soon as possible so I could report to the Knicks training camp and bond with my new team from the very beginning of the season. All of us vowed after that game that we would be back the next year, and stronger. We hoped to have Willis back and I, for one, was looking forward to winning the NBA championship, and I felt we had the personnel to make that dream come true.

Chapter 16

THE DEATH OF MY MOTHER AND THE NBA HOLY GRAIL: 1972 TO 1973

THE FIRST THING I DID when I returned to New York after the finals was to schedule surgery to have the bone spurs on my left foot and ankle (it was true that I had two spurs) removed. I knew it would take about two months to rehab after the surgery, so I was determined to have it done as soon as possible so I could be ready for the Knicks' training camp in September. This meant I had to have the surgery done in time for my rehab to be completed by the beginning of August. That would give me a month to rest my ankle and relax before training camp started. Having this surgery and doing the rehab also meant I couldn't play in the Baker League for the second time over the last three summers, and that was disappointing. So I called Sonny Hill and told him my decision. He understood my situation, but I knew he was disappointed as well, because my presence in those games was very important to him and to the fans. I knew that, but I had to take care of my health first so I could play again at a high level in the NBA. So that was that.

I called the Knicks' trainer, Danny Whelan, who I had gotten close to over the past season, and asked him to recommend a surgeon. He put me in contact with the Knicks' team doctor, Andrew Patterson, who agreed to operate on my foot and ankle on June 20, 1972. Danny Whelan had helped me a lot with my bone-spur problem over the past season by expertly taping my ankle to ease my pain, so I trusted him. Anyway, I had the surgery and everything went well and I decided to return to Kernan Hospital rehab center to work with Bill Neill again. So I drove down to the Baltimore area in my Rolls. And since I had gotten rid of my townhouse and liked staying by myself, I got a room at a Holiday Inn on the Parkway near Woodlawn, Maryland, where Kernan's rehab center is located. I stayed there for almost three weeks. I had a cast on my foot for 10 days, so I went back to my apartment in New York and then commuted back and forth down to Kernan until midway through August, seeing friends—and, for a minute, Cookie—while I was there.

Now, things had changed since I left Baltimore, because I had met and started dating Tina, though Cookie didn't know it. Now, like I said, I was still seeing Cookie. As a matter of fact, we had gotten engaged to be married that summer, in June 1972. She had come up to New York and gone to Bergdorf Goodman to pick out her wedding dress. She had ordered all the bridal paraphernalia like bridesmaid dresses and engraved invitations and had booked a photographer, a caterer, and a venue for the wedding. But since I'd met Tina I had changed my thoughts about getting married to Cookie, because a lot had happened between us over the years. Like all of her indiscretions with men and also mine, with an array of different women. So I just wasn't feeling her like I used to, especially after Tina came into the picture. Tina was a one-man type of woman and I appreciated that. There was no drama with her. She was very independent, never wanted anything from me because she always wanted to make her own way. That was the way she was. She used to always like to say, "I don't want to owe anybody anything!" And she meant it. I was very impressed. I've always liked strong, independent women. That's always been very important to me. She wasn't like a wham, bam, thank you ma'am type. But what she was like was *I don't need to have you, my brother, you know what I mean? So chill*. She was from North Carolina and had been doing a little modeling in New York. In fact I remember seeing her in a poster with the actor Richard Roundtree. So it took a long while for us to really got to know each other.

So after Cookie came up to Bergdorf's and made all those arrangements and then went back to Baltimore, I called her one day in early June and said, "Hey, as much as I'd like to do this, I can't do it now. I just can't see myself doing this because I'm up here in New York now and things are different, you know? And I don't think this is something that's going to be good for us *right now*."

I had to put the emphasis on "right now" just in case she thought I wasn't serious. She was so pissed off she hung up on me. And her family was pissed off as well. See, Cookie was a very beautiful woman and she wasn't used to not getting her way. But I wasn't used to it either; we were both spoiled in terms of being used to getting whatever we wanted. And her family probably thought, *Here's this black bastard leaving our daughter at the altar.* You know what I mean? I liked her family, especially her father, who everybody called "Sarge" because he had made a career out of the army before retiring. I liked her mother, too. She drank a lot and I know she was calling me every nasty curse word under the sun. So I called my mother and told her my decision, and although she really liked Cookie—so did my sister Theresa—Ma said, "Okay, if that's the case, cool. If that's what you want to do, you just make sure you're making the right decision." I told her I thought I was, even if I did feel a little bad about treating Cookie the way I did. But I knew our relationship wasn't going to work out good for either of us and so I thought it was best to just end it before we got into a marriage that I know I would have been sorry to be in. So that's why I broke off the wedding the way I did. Quickly and cleanly.

I told Cookie that I would pay for all of the expenses incurred for the wedding, which I did. I just thought it was the right thing to do. So from that day Cookie was out of the picture for me and my main squeeze became Tina. And during my rehab period, when I was going back and forth from New York down to Kernan and the Baltimore area, I saw a lot of people I knew while I was living there. I had a good time for the most part, even though I couldn't walk too well. Things were a bit different now that I wasn't playing for the Bullets anymore, but for the New York Knicks—the Bullets' enemy—instead. From some people, though, I felt an ambivalence, you know, almost like I was still a Bullet. But at the same time, everybody knew I wasn't. Still, the feeling around Baltimore was definitely different toward me now. When I was playing for the Bullets it was like, "Oh, Earl, what do you want, man?" La-di-da-di-da. Now people were more reserved. And from some of the guys I actually sensed that they felt I had betrayed them, that I was a traitor for forcing my way out of Baltimore the way I did. But I couldn't do anything about that now because that's what had happened, you know. I couldn't take it back. So in my mind I'd just moved on, though some of them hadn't.

Still, some of my guys, like Lenny Clay, my barber, were always there for me. That's why I gave him my Eldorado after I got my Rolls, because Lenny always had my back. And Gus Johnson was still there, too. Even though he had been traded to the Phoenix Suns in April of 1972, he still had a place in Baltimore. It hurt both of us that he had been traded, because he had been a Bullet for so long and had been the captain and the soul of the team. The reality of it was hard for us to swallow, but it was what it was. So while I was there we'd shoot the shit and whatnot, see some girls, and it was all good. But at the same time it was sad as well, because we had once been so close. I saw Linda and my daughter Danielle while I was down there, and saw Gloria and my son Rodney, too. I just saw different people periodically while I was rehabbing there and enjoyed being with my friends and spending some time alone as well. I would sit in my hotel room, order room service, watch TV, and I was good. But I made sure I ordered everything early enough—before 8:30 p.m.—because you couldn't get any food after that.

So, all in all it was a great stay for me. It kind of cleared my head and helped me to realize exactly what I had gotten myself into in New York City, what kinds of things would be available to me now besides just playing basketball when I went back. It just brought into view the whole entertainment thing that I wanted to get involved in after my playing career was over. Because the Big Apple was a center of the entertainment industry at that time, you know, way more so than Baltimore. So by the time I left the Baltimore area and came back to New York to prepare myself for training camp, my mind was in a great place and I was ready for it.

I had experienced the city somewhat in my first season with the Knicks, but I wasn't really ready for all the different things it had going on. Now I was going back with a different perspective and I'd have a chance to see where everything really was, the places where I could fit in. So I had a renewed spirit when I came back and I was ready mentally and spiritually to deal with whatever presented itself to me, both in basketball and in my life outside of the game. So the first non-basketball thing I did when I got back to the city was to renew my relationship with Tina. Everything with her was as great as I had remembered and that just fueled me, you know what I mean, lifted my spirits up and prepared me to face each and every challenge, each and every day. That's the way Tina was. She was special and being with her made me look at my life positively every day.

But even though I really had a great feeling for Tina old habits die hard. I still was single and though I really liked Tina I wasn't even thinking about marrying anyone. So in July, on a Friday night, quite by accident, I went to a party up in Harlem with some old friends from Winston-Salem and met a lovely young woman named Marita there. We struck up a conversation and she intrigued me with her attitude, her intelligence, and the way she looked. Marita had a nice Afro and a great body. So I asked her about herself and she told me. Then she asked me about myself and I told her I was a basketball player.

"Oh, you're a basketball player?" she said. "My favorite player is Elgin Baylor!"

That intrigued me because Elgin was one of my favorite players, too. So, I asked her to dance—I could only dance slowly because of the surgery on my foot—and man could she move. I found out she had been born in the Central American country of Honduras, but had come up to the United States at a young age, first living in San Antonio, Texas, with her mother, who was a registered nurse, before moving to Brooklyn where she grew up. Her mother and father were divorced, so her mother was raising Marita and her two older brothers, Richard and Raymond.

Anyway, after a while I left with my friends to go to another party over in New Jersey and I spent the night and most of the next day hanging out with my friends over there. Then we came back into the city and for some reason went to another party over on East 88th Street in Manhattan at Flo Anthony's townhouse. Anyway I hadn't changed clothes, so when I walked in lo and behold there was Marita, looking fresh as a daisy. So she looked at me and said, "Are you homeless? I see you got on the same clothes you had on last night."

I thought that was cold-blooded but I just laughed it off because she was right; I hadn't changed my clothes. So we talked again and I found out she was going to school at Manhattanville College, majoring in political science, and that she was going to be going to law school at Antioch in Washington, DC, the next year. So I got her number and we sort of stayed in touch periodically after that until she graduated from Antioch in 1976.

After having a great summer of fun I started focusing my mind back on basketball and preparing my mind for going to training camp. When it came time to go to training camp in September I was in a great state of mind. My left foot and ankle were still a little tender, though they were much better than before. Now I could cut better and do my spin move with little pain and implement my back-down maneuvers. So I was feeling pretty good and hoping to get into a groove offensively speaking, you know what I mean? Anyway, I had been thinking back to how the Lakers had routed us in the finals the season before and how Gail Goodrich just kind of ran by me and had his way scoring because I had been limited by my foot. I had been starting in place of Dick Barnett by the playoffs, but I just wasn't effective at all in that series. So I was in a very redemptive mood going into the 1972–1973 season because I had a lot of shit on my plate from the last season that I wanted to rectify in the one coming up. I knew the system, but I thought training camp would be a great place to really get Red Holzman's philosophy down pat like the guys who had been with the team awhile had. Plus, since I knew I would be starting, I wanted to really jell with the other starters on the squad, like Clyde, Dave, Bill, and Jerry Lucas, since Willis wasn't going to be ready until later in the year.

In September, during training camp, I received a letter from a Knicks fan. It was addressed to Earl Monroe in care of the New York Knickerbockers, Monmouth College, Long Branch, New Jersey. I thought it was odd to receive mail at training camp, but nevertheless, I opened it after practice one day when I was alone in the dorm where we stayed. It was a letter from a fan wishing me luck and hoping that I had a great season coming up because he (and all his friends) thought I was the most exciting athlete in professional sports.

It went on to say that some people are born soloists, and if it turned out that there was a problem adjusting to the team play of the Knicks, he hoped it wouldn't worry me because my style and natural gifts were far more thrilling than anything else around. The truth is, the letter said, that the Knicks should bend over backward to adjust to me.

This threw me for a bit of a loop, but it gave me hope and faith that someone believed in me and that everything would be all right. At the end of the letter the fan wished me and the Knicks a great year and said that no matter what happens, to the real basketball fans, I was the greatest. Then it was signed, "Woody Allen." I was really floored. And flattered. Woody Allen, writing to me? My God! I relished the thought of Woody Allen thinking about me, and then all his friends as well—wow. Shit, I slept very well that night and continued training camp with new hope and vigor. I even thought of one of my family names, Allen. Could he be a distant relative? Hell no.

Red's approach to the game revolved around hitting the open man. That was his philosophy of the game. So it wasn't hard for me to buy into that philosophy because I had been doing it for my whole career. It was just that after I became a big-time scorer in college and then in the NBA, I had gotten used to my teammates passing the ball to me to take whatever shot I thought was appropriate because I was the main man, you know, the go-to shot maker and principal scorer. So I had to change my mind-set here a bit, though I hadn't had to during the past season because I wasn't healthy. Now, basically I was. So that's what I worked on in camp, creating a new mind-set for myself to distribute the ball to the open man and dropping my old one-on-one habits. See, we were still getting used to playing with each other, especially me, because I had been injured so much during the past season and couldn't really practice as much as I would have liked. So I had to get my chemistry together with this team, had to fit the cadence of my music into the concept of their more team-oriented game.

While I worked on fitting myself into the Knicks' system, I also used training camp as an opportunity to really get to know the guys on the team beyond Dean Meminger. Like I said, Dean had become my best friend on the team while we sat at the end of the bench together. We would just talk a lot down there when we weren't in the game and over time we grew very close. Dean was a very confident guy—some called him cocky, even brash—but I liked that about him because it reminded me of myself in that regard. Everybody on the team called him "the coach" because he always had an answer for every basketball question. "The Dream," as he was also called, could talk trash with the best of them, and he also liked a good party, like I did. He was from New York and knew his way around, and with both of us being single, we had some great times together. We're still close friends to this day.

I had good relationships with all the guys on the team. We related well to each other. Many of the guys on the team were married and I wasn't, so I didn't hang out with those players much because after practice, playing games, and traveling, they spent most of their time with their families when they got back to New York. We had a very good professional relationship, though, and on the road we got along very well, which is one of the reasons why I think we had a good team— because we were not only good players, but we mixed together very well when we were traveling, talking about politics, music, and culture. We were a bunch of guys who cared about things going on in the world and that bonded us closer, even though there were some differences between us, just as there are with everyone else in the world. And that closeness remains even today. That's one of the great things I have taken from that experience of being on that team is the fact that I played with great guys I feel would go to bat with me back then and would do the same today. Now, that's rare.

Willis Reed was our captain. He was always concerned about everything and everybody and he was our enforcer, too. So if anything went wrong anywhere, but especially out on the floor, Willis would be there to take care of it. He was also a very caring guy who was a role model for a lot of guys throughout the league. He was a blue-collar type of guy, hard working, and he and Dave DeBusschere represented working class people in New York. They were both great warriors who came to play every night.

Dave was a tremendous individual all the way around. Very steady. One of the things I admired about Dave is that he always said what was on his mind so you didn't have to think about it; it was always right in front of you. Bill Bradley, despite coming from an upper class family in Crystal City, Missouri, where his father owned a bank, and then going on to school at Princeton before becoming a Rhodes Scholar at Oxford, was a guy with a lot of heart. And he could really play basketball. But the real reason I gravitated towards Bill was because I always saw him as a person who really cared and who was a lot like me in that regard (I have always had a certain reverence toward Bill Bradley, and think after leaving basketball and becoming a United States Senator, he would have been an even better president of this country than he was a senator).

Phil Jackson roomed with Eddie Mast (I roomed with Dean) and they both held counter-cultural ideas. They hung out in the Village, liked to go up to Woodstock, where Phil had a place, and were almost a perfect match for each other, at least in my opinion. But I used to talk with Phil and thought even back then that he had a good grasp of the game. I think he could sit there on the bench and analyze what he saw happening on the court and put his own spin on what he thought should have happened in a given situation. Now I'm not saying I knew back then that he would become one of the greatest basketball coaches of all time—that was the farthest thing from my mind back then—but at the same time, I'm quite sure that sitting there watching Red coach made an impression on him as to what he was going to do when he retired as a player.

Jerry Lucas was another person who I really liked back then and am still in touch with a lot today. I mean, Jerry was a mathematical genius, who also was a Rhodes Scholar, like Bill Bradley. I remember one time he went on a television show (I think it was the Johnny Carson show) because Jerry had a penchant for memorizing things. Jerry had decided he was going to memorize the first 500 pages of the Manhattan White Pages. So they tested him and Jerry came up with all the right answers. He was—and still is—a wonderful guy to talk to. Another thing that astonished me about Jerry was that when we flew from city to city for games guys would play cards on the plane and make small bets, and Jerry kept track of all the bets people made in his head. So at the end of the season one time Dick Barnett had made all these bets and Jerry recalled from memory exactly what he owed and it turned out Dick owed his entire playoff check. Now I don't know if Dick paid the bill but Jerry surely told him exactly what he owed, down to the penny. He did this with every player on the team. Man, Jerry was unbelievable with that shit. And he was a hell of a player, too. He had game. He was a great rebounder and could really throw the outlet pass. He wasn't a great leaper but he understood the angles, where the ball would bounce off the rim or backboard and drop and he would be there to grab it. He also had a great shot from outside, could shoot a nice little hook, you know?

Now Dick Barnett was another hell of a basketball player, and had already been so for a long time by the time I got to the Knicks. Man, Dick could play. He had nice, slick moves, could really shoot the ball and hit that famous fall-back baby jump shot of his. He was, especially when he was younger, a great, great scorer. But when he came to the Knicks, besides getting his points, he made adjustments just like me and became the Knicks defensive guy who guarded our opponents' toughest players. And because he was also from Tennessee State, an all black school coached by the great John McLendon, I wanted to make sure when I came to the Knicks to let him know I wasn't coming there to take his job. I really liked Dick as a person. Before Clyde was known as a great dresser, Dick dressed to the nines and it was rumored by a lot of people that it was Dick who taught Walt how to dress. Dick was always dapper and whatnot, was a philosopher even back in those days, and man could he tell funny stories with a deadpan face that had everyone in the room cracking up. He would crack stories funny as shit, but he would never smile, even though he was a very funny guy (he's smart as hell, too—got a PhD from Fordham and taught for many years at St. John's University).

Now the toughest guy for me to talk about on the Knicks during this period is Walt Frazier, even though I love him like a brother today. Because back then, when I first came to the Knicks, we were still rivals, you know what I mean? Despite the respect Clyde and I had for each other it was difficult at first to suspend our rivalry because we had gone so hard against each other so many times over the years. I mean I couldn't be like Clyde when I came to New York because I had to become the anti-Clyde, so to speak. That meant I couldn't be flamboyant like he was off the court, couldn't dress in a certain way, or wear flashy clothes. So I had to wear things that made another statement.

I did think Clyde and I could have become (if we worked at it) a kind of Larry Csonka and Jim Kiick duo of New York City, as they had been in Miami with the Dolphins. (Csonka and Kiick had been portrayed as Butch Cassidy and the Sundance Kid in a cover story in *Sports Illustrated* in August 1972.) Nothing ever came of that idea, though I thought it could have worked and we could have taken over the marketing image of the Big Apple. Clyde thought I was kidding, but I was serious because I understood the importance of being here and making something like that happen. After all, New York was the media capital of the world at that time. Anyway nobody was ready for that idea back then, you know what I mean? So we didn't hang out too much when I first got to New York because Clyde had his own friends and a different agenda. I understood that and never held it against him. So Dean

Meminger and I hung out. But over time Clyde and I became close friends and we still are today.

As for the Knicks' chemistry we were a more methodical team than the Bullets, who were more of a fast-break, open-court, run-and-shoot type of team. That kind of play was more exciting to watch and more compatible with my natural style of playing the game. Here, I not only had to adapt myself to Red's philosophy of playing, but also make adjustments to playing with Clyde and the rest of the Knicks players. With Clyde that meant not having the ball in my hands as I had in Baltimore. I had to take a backseat to Clyde, watching what he did and reacting to that, while it had been the other way around with the Bullets. Again I had to underplay my game because I didn't want Clyde to think I was trying to take his spot. So I acquiesced a lot, you know, to make sure that didn't happen. And I think after Clyde saw that, he grew to respect me, because of what I had sacrificed for the good of the team. And, of course, I respected him a lot as well.

It took a little while for Clyde and I to click as a tandem, but the more we played together the more we knew what to expect from each other over the course of a game. And it was great for me to be able to work one side of the court—the left side mostly—and watch Clyde working on the other side and not have to worry, because I knew what he was going to do from playing with him. The same went for him when I had the ball on the left side of the floor. We were both very good one-on-one players—the best on the team—and we both knew that. So either one of us would just stand back on the other side of the court and watch the other one work magic on an opposing player. That was fun and gratifying, and over time we became fans of each other, would slap hands when the other did something real special.

Now, we also had other really great players on our team. Dave DeBusschere could really shoot the long jump shot as well as bang really effectively down deep under the basket. He was truly a blue-collar player who came to play hard every night. Then there were Bill Bradley and Jerry Lucas, who could both just shoot the lights out whenever they had an open shot. Also, they were both so damn smart, both Rhodes Scholars who had studied at Oxford in England. Then we had Phil Jackson and Dean Meminger and Dick Barnett coming off the bench and inflicting real damage on whoever they played against. Red could also throw Luther Rackley in there, too, sometimes, if he needed him. Then there were the rookies, Henry Bibby, John Gianelli, Tom Riker, and Harthorne Wingo. We had a big squad that season, but we had just the right mix of players. Everyone worked so well with everybody that we were like a well-run engine in a car being driven by a terrific coach, Red Holzman.

We started out like gangbusters that season, winning 8 in a row early on, and by the 10th of November we were 13 and 2, including a 25-point win over the Lakers, routing them at the Garden 125–100. We also beat the Bullets twice in back-to-back games, 92–88 and 94–90, during this stretch. I had averaged only 14.2 points a game up to this time, but we usually had five or six (or as many as seven) players in double figures in these games. Willis Reed made his first game appearance of the season against the 76ers on October 21 in the Garden and received a long standing ovation, with big cheers going up every time he scored, though he managed only 6 points in that game. Man, that really showed me how deeply Knicks fans loved their captain, and it was very moving to experience that kind of devotion.

The team that ended our eight-game winning streak was the Golden State Warriors, who stomped us out in Oakland 127–104. Rick Barry, the great player from the ABA, had left that league to compete in the NBA and was now playing for the Warriors. He dropped 26 points on us that night, and I saw what the folks who had watched him play in the ABA had been raving about. I could see now that all of those kudos were well deserved, just as they had been for Connie Hawkins when he played in the ABA. The Hawk was now tearing up the NBA at Phoenix, and there would be a lot of other great players, like Julius "Dr. J" Erving, George "Iceman" Gervin, Charlie Scott, Artis Gilmore, Dan Issel, Moses Malone, and Maurice Lucas, who would all also jump from the ABA to star for NBA teams in the future.

Golden State played its games in the Oakland–Alameda County Coliseum (now the Oracle Arena), and it was packed the night they beat us. I could see how Oakland could be a very dangerous team in the future, because besides Rick Barry they had Jeff Mullins, a great shooter; Nate Thurmond, a fantastic big man and defensive force; Cazzie Russell, the really fine former Knicks star; and Jim Barnett, another deadly shooter. The Warriors played together and had good team chemistry. So that night I could see them being a problem for many a team down the road. And they proved it when they came to the Garden and beat us again on November 11, this time in overtime, 103–102 in a very hard-fought, extremely close game. Again Rick Barry led them, scoring 27 points with an array of dazzling shots—long jumpers, wicked drives to the hole, hook shots—you name it.

I had a good game on November 16, when I scored 24 points in a 119–100 win over the Houston Rockets at the Garden. We had beaten them once that season already, in the fourth game of the year, 103–95, in New York. What was notable for me in both games against Houston that season was that I played against my old teammate Jack Marin, who had been traded to Houston for Elvin Hayes in June of that year. And also new to the Houston roster was Jimmy Walker, who had been traded to the Rockets by Detroit for Stu Lantz. They both seemed relaxed with their new team, and I was happy to see that they were.

We played the Celtics in back-to-back games on November 24 and 25, which was Thanksgiving Day. We lost the first game 114–97 in Boston despite 28 points from Bill Bradley. On Thanksgiving at the Garden, we won 97–94, pulling ahead in the final minutes. Boston had a really fine team that year and would go on to post the best record in the NBA, with 68 wins against just 14 losses. They had two blossoming young superstars, Jo Jo White and Dave Cowens, along with veterans John Havlicek, Don Nelson, Paul Silas, and Don Chaney. That Celtics team played hard every night and proved to be a handful for anybody in the NBA to beat that year.

Our performance in the first three weeks of December was up and down. Christmas was approaching, and ever since I had been in the NBA I had changed the way I looked at celebrating that holiday. I used to always try to find ways to go home to celebrate Christmas with my family regardless of how short my stay would be, because it always seemed like I had to play a game on that day. I would try, however, to drive up there when I was in Baltimore, because it was a shorter trip than coming from New York. I loved bringing gifts for everyone and just being there. I always remembered how much I loved being with my mother, feeling her presence, seeing how proud she was of me.

I remember this one Christmas when I was playing in Baltimore I bought her a mink coat and had it wrapped in a big beautiful box with a ribbon tied around it. I will never forget the love in her eyes, that radiant, great smile she flashed when she opened the box and saw the coat. She looked at it, then looked up at me, and started to cry. Then she came and hugged me and said, "Earl, this is wonderful. Thank you so very, very much!" Then she put on the coat and just danced around the room with it on. I mean, it just made me feel great that I could do that for her and make her so happy, you know what I mean? Seeing her smile like that, with tears running down her high cheekbones, was what I missed seeing each and every day, and especially at Christmastime. And it always made me feel good going to see my mother, because a lot of times I took things for granted.

That day I realized I had been taking things for granted for quite a while now since I had come to the NBA. And remembering that moment, seeing the smile on her face that Christmas when I was in New

York playing a game and couldn't be there to see it, brought this home to me. But I had left home for good in 1963 when I went to Winston-Salem and had unfortunately missed a lot of Christmas celebrations. Over time, holidays lost their relevance for me and really didn't mean that much because I was always playing somewhere, and that was especially true once I came into the NBA. I felt the same about Easter, Thanksgiving, and New Year's Eve, too, and I felt it would be the same problem even after I finished playing. But now that I had kids, I would have to figure out a way to address my problem of not celebrating holidays.

By Christmas Day, after beating the Pistons in New York, we had a record of 28 wins and 9 losses, which was pretty good considering everything hadn't fallen into place for us as a team yet. But I felt we were getting there in terms of team chemistry, and we closed out 1972 by beating my old team, the Bullets, for the third straight time on December 30 at the Garden, 100–98. We had been behind going into the final quarter, but we caught them and nipped them at the wire. I played my best game of the season to that point, scoring 26 points. That was a satisfying game for me because I played almost pain free throughout the game, and I was happy to have played so well against my old team. But the win was also gratifying because Willis played so well against Wes, outscoring him 20 to 6. It also sent a signal to the rest of the league that we were going to be a contending team throughout the balance of the season if Willis was healthy and continued to play the way he played that night.

The win over Baltimore was our third straight, and we followed that up by winning our next 8 as well, not losing again until January 19, when we fell to the Lakers in Los Angeles 95–88. That string of wins upped our record to 39 and 10, and during that stretch we were really starting to click as a team. But tragedy struck for me on January 3, four games into that streak, when my beloved mother suffered a brain aneurysm while trying to push my sister Theresa's car in the driveway of her home in Germantown and was rushed to the hospital.

What happened was Theresa's canary-yellow Volkswagen Karmann Ghia with a black convertible top had stalled in the driveway of the house, and Ma had gone out in the cold to help push it so the car would start. Theresa was trying to pop the clutch, but Ma couldn't hear what Theresa was saying to her because she had collapsed. So Theresa got scared, called a taxi, and took her to Germantown Hospital to see what was going on. That's when the doctors discovered she had developed an aneurysm. Now, my mother had high blood pressure and Theresa told me that Ma hadn't been taking her medicine because she had run out of the pills. Ma had exerted so much energy straining herself in trying to push the car that she collapsed. After they admitted her she was in there for more than two weeks before I was finally able to get there because of our schedule, though I had been calling her every day from wherever I was to get updates on her condition. The prognosis was that she was stable, but the doctors said they had to watch her carefully and that they would let me know if her condition worsened. If my memory is correct, I think my mother took a turn for the worse when I was playing in Houston on January 21, because I think that's the day my sister called and told me. I remember playing in that game and only scoring 3 points. My mind was not in that game and we lost 107–103.

When we got back to New York from Houston the team flew up to Buffalo and I went through the motions of playing in that game as we beat Buffalo 99–92. I scored 16 points in that game, and all the opposing players, having heard through the grapevine how sick my mother was, came up and gave me their best wishes for her survival. On the flight back to New York I told Red that I thought I was going to have to take some time off because of Ma's condition and to try and pull my mind back into playing mode. He said I could take as much time as I needed. When I got back to my apartment in New York, Theresa called and told me things had gotten worse. This was January 26. So after I took care of a couple of things I picked up my car on January 28 and drove down to Philly, arriving that evening. I went by the house, got myself together, and the next day I went to the hospital alone. By the time I got there visiting hours were over and I had to tell them I was visiting from New York. So they finally let me go to my mother's room. By this time it was almost night. When I got there I saw Ma lying in the bed and when she saw me her face lit up. I went over to hug her and could feel the warmth of all her love. We talked for about 45 minutes. I told her how good she looked and that she seemed to have a glow about her. When I got up to leave she walked me to the door and hugged me. Then she said to me, "Earl, if anything happens to me you and Ann take care of everything, including Theresa, because she's your younger sister."

I told her that I would and then I left. But she still looked radiant, as if she had a smile on her face, and it seemed to me she had a halo around her head. So I went home and they called me shortly after I left and told me she had passed away. She was only 56 years old. I was glad that I was able to see her one last time before she died.

My older sister, Ann; arranged for Chew Funeral Home to pick up my mother's body and made the arrangements for her service, which would be held a week later. I decided I would stick around in Philly until the funeral and the burial. I told Theresa that she should come up to live with me in New York for a while after the funeral, and she agreed to do that. We had the funeral and a lot of people came. All of our Philly friends, Sonny Hill, my kids' mothers. Thank goodness Ann was there, because she was a comforting presence for me. I sat in the front row of the Canaan Baptist Church that day. I never took my eyes off the casket throughout the service. Our pastor, Reverend Gus Roman, and Theresa,

Ann, and I were hugging each other and wiping each other's eyes of all those tears. I have never cried that much in my life before or since.

Anyway, after the service and the burial I hung out for about a week or so at the house in Germantown, trying to put everything into perspective. Sometimes you need to be away from whatever you do to see things in a new light. No one from the Knicks bugged me with telephone calls asking when I was coming back, and that was good. After a while I began to feel a little antsy, so I called Red and told him I would be coming back in a couple of days and he was cool with that. I also called Tina and let her know.

So a day or two later I packed my things, got in my Silver Shadow, and got on the turnpike up to New York City. On the way up my mind was swirling with all kinds of thoughts, you know, grief, loss, joy at getting there before she passed, thinking of all the great times we had together, the deep love we had for each other, and the wisdom she always gave me. So I focused in on that and remembered something she had told me the year before, when I was having all those problems with my knees. I was complaining to her one day when she was in New York to visit me for a few days, and after hearing me whining and complaining she reminded me of the time when she had given me that blue notebook to jot down all the names of the guys who were beating me and then cross them out after I had gotten better than them. Then she told me that it was all a matter of confidence. After a while, maybe to let that sink in, she turned and looked at me real hard and said, "Earl, you know you can do it, because you've been doing it for a very long time. So stop all this whining and complaining and get your butt out of here and get it done!"

That had just stopped me in my tracks and I stopped whining and complaining about my knees after that. That's what my mother always did for me. She brought clear thinking into my life, and I was going to deeply miss having her do that. I didn't know anyone else who could do that for me. Now, I was going to miss her love, too, but that clarity she had brought was irreplaceable. So on that drive I decided I was going to dedicate the rest of that season to the memory of my mother, though I didn't tell anybody this—I just kept it to myself. I also decided that I had to become more like "Earl the Pearl" again, when my knees and bone spurs allowed it. I wasn't in New York because I was Earl Monroe, but because I was "Earl the Pearl," or "Black Jesus." So I had to become "the Pearl" again. As a matter of fact, Red Holzman had already spoken to me about this.

"Hey, Earl," he said to me one day, "it's all well what you're doing, but you seem to have lost your ego."

"What do you mean?" I said to him.

"Well, you know, in order to be good, you have to want to be great, and if you want greatness you got to have an ego. And you don't seem to have the same ego you had before. So I think you have to go back to playing with more ego."

He told me this at the beginning of January that year. And it was only then that I realized that Red actually liked me, you know what I mean? I had always felt, ever since he hadn't played me a lot in that All-Star Game when I was a starter and he was the coach, that he didn't like me. But for him to come up and talk to me this way kind of freed me up to be me, you know, to be "Earl the Pearl" again. That was much appreciated on my part and it made our relationship a little bit different, less personal, you know. So I kind of relaxed in my approach to my game after that and it showed immediately in my scoring production. After we had that talk my average jumped up to 19.2 points a game over a nine-game stretch.

When I got back to New York everyone came up and gave me hugs and their condolences, which I really appreciated. But after losing my mother I couldn't really hear anything, because my mind, heart, and soul were just gone. There was this huge hole in my spirit and in my life.

Even the sweet, loving affection and tenderness of Tina couldn't fill it up, although it was comforting having her around. There was nobody who could make this anything but what it was, not even me. My sweet mother was dead, gone forever, and there was nothing I or anyone else could do about that fact.

I played my first game after my mother's death on February 3 at the Garden against Cleveland. The fans gave me a rousing round of applause to welcome me back and I was happy to hear all those people clapping, calling out my name, and wishing me well. The Cleveland players also came over and welcomed me back. Then we went out and beat them 95–90 in a close game that was ultimately decided at the free throw line, where we went 25 of 29. I scored 20 points in my return. As we were running off the court I looked over and saw Woody Allen sitting in his normal seat. I said to myself, *Everything is going to be all right.*

We essentially split the remaining 24 games of the season, winning 13 and losing 11. I began to feel pain in my foot down the stretch, too, which affected my scoring production. We lost twice during that span of games to our eventual Eastern Conference Semifinal opponent, my old team, the Baltimore Bullets. If we got by them—and we were all confident we would—our next opponent would most likely be the Boston Celtics, unless they got upset by the emerging Atlanta Braves, who had finished with the fourth-best record in the conference. Our record against Boston was 4 and 3 that year, which was pretty good considering that the Celtics had lost only 14 games that whole season. Two of those 3 losses had come in the last 7 games of the season, however.

Besides the Lakers (who we really wanted to play and beat to exact a measure of revenge for the previous season's Finals loss), the three most dangerous teams out West were the Milwaukee Bucks, Golden State Warriors, and Chicago Bulls. So we would have to see how all of this shook itself out. We had split 2 games against the Lakers over those last 24 games, and were 2 and 2 against them overall. We had the same record with both Milwaukee and Golden State.

The way we saw it, we had a pretty good chance against any team we'd have to face in the playoffs. If Baltimore was our first-round opponent, we were confident we could beat them without too much trouble. If it was Atlanta, we thought we could take them out, too—no sweat— even though they had a very good squad with Pistol Pete, sweet-shooting Lou Hudson, and Walt Bellamy. With Boston, we knew we'd be in for a dogfight to the very end, but we believed we were the better team despite their superior record. If we survived in the East, our only thoughts were on Milwaukee with Kareem, Oscar, and Bobby Dandridge, though we felt we could defeat them in a seven-game playoff series. We didn't give much thought to Golden State, although they were a very good and dangerous team with Rick Barry, Jeff Mullins, and the ageless defensive wonder, the great, much-underrated center, Nate Thurmond. But in the end, like I said, we definitely wanted to play the Los Angeles Lakers.

So that's what we all set out to do as a team: to get to the Finals and defeat the Los Angeles Lakers and lift the championship crown off their collective head. For all of us—and especially for me, because I hadn't won an NBA championship and because I had dedicated the season to the memory of my mother—the Lakers had become our "enemy," just as the team I was playing for now had been when I was a Bullet. The Celtics had also become an "enemy" of sorts, and we had a feeling we'd have to get past them if we were going to reach the Finals and win the NBA title, which is what I wanted now more than anything else in the world. Over those last 24 games I averaged just more than 15 points per game, though I was slowed down in 5 or 6 of those games with bone-spur pain in my left foot. But I wasn't going to let that stop me if we got to that final game and the championship was on the line. I knew I had to and would rise to the occasion and compete at the highest level for the championship, no matter the pain.

We ended the season with two straight losses. Then, just as we'd figured, we drew the Bullets in the Eastern Conference Semifinals, with the first game scheduled for March 30 in Madison Square Garden. Although we had lost our last two games to them, we were pumped to beat them in this initial outing. They jumped on us right from jump street and led us by 6 at the end of the first quarter, but we battled back and were behind by only 2 points at the half, 45–43. We caught and passed them in the third quarter and led by 4, going into the final quarter 69–65. Clyde and I were dueling with Archie Clark and Phil Chenier in a furious guard battle. But Clyde and I pressed pedal to metal and scorched them in the final quarter and we won going away, 95–83, with Clyde leading the way with 25 points and me dropping 23. Wes and Willis fought to almost a draw, though Unseld outscored the Captain 14 to 8. Chalk up Game One in the Knicks' win column. One and zero, our favor.

Game Two was played on April Fools' Day in the Garden. We jumped all over them from the opening tip-off, never trailed, and won by 20, at 123–103. I led the way with 32 points in one of my best performances of the season. For the Bullets, Phil Chenier came out hitting jump shots from all over and netted 27, while Elvin Hayes added 23. So now it was two games to zero in our favor as the series shifted to Baltimore. We came out fast against them again in Game Three and won 103–96, in a closer game than the last. We had five players score in double digits, with Bill Bradley the high man with 23. Elvin Hayes led the Bullets with 36 points, but Willis badly outplayed Wes, holding him to only 3 points. Now the Bullets' backs were up against the wall, down three games to zip. So we all felt they would be desperate for a win the next night, on April 6 in Baltimore, and they were, fighting their way to a 97–89 victory behind 34 points from Hayes.

Throughout the games in Baltimore I suffered again through catcalls and nasty names, as the fans there had dished out whenever I played down there since I'd left the Bullets. At first it was a little off-putting and caught me by surprise, but now it only fueled my competitive juices. Game Five was back at the Garden, but we came out sluggish and dropped behind by 5 points in the first quarter. Then we got serious and led them 54–45 at the half. Desperate to stave off elimination, the Bullets came back strong in the third quarter and trailed by only 1 going into the final period. But then we just came out and laid the hammer down on them, pulling away in the final quarter to win by 10, at 109–99. I shut up all the hecklers and catcallers by dropping 26 points—mostly on long jumpers—on my ex-teammates that night, leading the club in scoring. Archie put up 30 for the Bullets and Chenier and Hayes combined for 40, but it wasn't enough. We walked away with an Eastern Conference Semifinal series victory four games to one and were on our way to play the formidable Celtics in the Eastern Conference Finals, with the series set to open in Boston on April 15.

We had about five days to rest and practice to get ready for the Celtics, who had been taken to a sixth game by Atlanta. I decided to use that time to get some cortisone shots for my foot, have the fluid drained from my knees, and just lay around my apartment with Tina. I read somewhere that Nate "Tiny" Archibald, the great little guard from the Kansas City–Omaha Kings, had led the NBA that season in both scoring and assists, averaging 34.0 points a game and 11.4 assists. Those were some incredible statistics. But then again, Tiny was an incredible player, really lightning quick, smart, and man, could he shoot the ball and take it to the basket. He was on the All-NBA First Team that year along with John Havlicek, Kareem Abdul-Jabbar, Spencer Haywood, and Jerry West. Bob McAdoo of Buffalo (who would become a teammate of mine with the Knicks) was voted Rookie of the Year and Tom Heinsohn was selected Coach of the Year.

As I became better acclimated to life in New York City, I was getting into music more and more. Man, there was music everywhere—you know? Salsa, pop, jazz. Miles's albums—*A Tribute to Jack Johnson*, *Bitches Brew*, and *On the Corner*—with those weird-ass psychedelic drawings on the covers and that thumping music inside, really moved me. So did the music of Gladys Knight and the Pips, Roberta Flack, Donny Hathaway, Marvin Gaye, the O'Jays, Stevie Wonder, the Temptations, James Brown, Sly and the Family Stone, Aretha Franklin, Earth, Wind and Fire, and the Persuaders, whose song "Thin Line between Love and Hate" was a favorite of mine. Those were the artists whose songs we listened to at parties during this period. And in addition to all of that great music, I had also been influenced from a young age by the "Philly Sound," you know, artists like Gamble and Huff, the Delfonics, the Stylistics, Harold Melvin and the Blue Notes, Patti LaBelle, Teddy Pendergrass, Grover Washington Jr., Solomon Burke, and all the other great musicians from my hometown.

Also, the 1970s blaxploitation films had a big influence on black people and our culture, films like *Shaft*, *Sweet Sweetback's Baadasssss Song*, *Cotton Comes to Harlem*, *Hit Man*, *Blacula*, *Trouble Man*, *The Mack*, *Trick Baby*, *The Spook Who Sat by the Door*, *Gordon's War*, *Coffy*, *Cleopatra Jones*, *Black Caesar*, and especially *Super Fly*, which hit movie theaters in August 1972. This film had a huge cultural impact on many black Americans, especially in New York City. Everywhere you looked in the Big Apple, from 1972 until the beginning of the '80s—on the streets of Brooklyn, the Bronx, Harlem, and Midtown Manhattan—you saw black men and women wearing platform shoes (or, as some people called them, "ankle breakers"), long mink coats (in the winter), wide-brimmed hats, and bell-bottom pants, and women in real short miniskirts. Men and women both wore big, Afro-style hairdos, while other, more street-oriented men wore their hair in long, pimp-style processed hairdos à la the late Ron O'Neal's *Super Fly* character, Youngblood Priest. And Curtis Mayfield's hit soundtrack to *Super Fly* and Isaac

Hayes's to *Shaft* could be heard blaring all over Harlem and the black neighborhoods of Brooklyn.

It was *Super Fly*—directed by the late, great photographer Gordon Parks—Mr. O'Neal's character, and the film's soundtrack that defined a certain black urban style in that period. I know for sure that it influenced the personal styles of Walt Frazier and myself, as we adopted Youngblood Priest's look of wide-brimmed Borsalino hats, long mink coats, stylish suits with bell-bottom trousers, and platform shoes. But Clyde didn't wear his hair in the long pimp style Ron O'Neal wore in *Super Fly*. Instead, he wore a moustache, long sideburns, and a goatee. Clyde lived in the penthouse of a building on East 52nd Street, had a round bed covered with a mink spread, and tooled around in a two-toned burgundy Rolls-Royce with an array of beautiful women. On the other hand, I had come to town with a Rolls-Royce Silver Shadow myself, had a moustache and a tiny goatee, and wore long, stylish coats and platform shoes, too. But I lived on the Upper West Side and not in a penthouse. We both were influenced by the style of *Super Fly* and its classic soundtrack, which could have served as our theme music during this period. But neither of us was influenced by drug dealers, or street life, or any of the other stuff depicted in the film. For me it was the power of Curtis Mayfield's music that swept me away. But as I have said, both of us were shy, in fact quiet and private, off the court.

But because we also had flamboyant public personas on the basketball court and off and drove Rolls-Royces, and because the media dubbed us the "Rolls-Royce backcourt," we were wrongly thought of as loud, boisterous, and all kinds of other adjectives. Many didn't think we would survive playing together because they assumed our personalities and games would clash. But that never happened because we had great respect for one another—and deep affection, too—from competing against each other for so long. Now, we had discovered that our games could mesh and we were complementary parts of a well-oiled, efficient team of stars who never let their individual egos get in the way of play-ing and winning together as a team. Clyde and I remain close friends to this day.

By playoff time we were firing on all cylinders as a team, and after disposing of the Bullets we went to Boston with a lot of confidence. But we were thrashed by Boston in Game One, 134–108, one of our worst losses of the season. The Celtics had six players reach double figures, led by Jo Jo White with 30 and Havlicek with 26. Clyde led us with 24 points, but we were never really in the game. So we came back to New York and had two days' rest before Game Two. This time we came out swinging and thumped Boston 129–96, handing them one of *their* worst defeats of the season. Even steven. Eight Knicks reached double figures that night and 11 of our 12 players scored, which was a testament to Coach Holzman's philosophy of hitting the open man and playing team ball. Again, Clyde was the high man with 24. Series on.

We went back up to Boston for Game Three. We beat them 98–91 behind 23 points from Clyde. Havlicek, Cowens, and Jo Jo White combined for 80 of Boston's 91 points that night. It was a hard-fought game in which only 31 total points were scored in the final quarter, but we found a way to win. We now led the series two to one going back to the Garden, where we beat them again, this time in a double-overtime thriller, 117–110. I didn't play in that game because my bone spurs acted up. Danny Whelan, our trainer, advised me not to play because if Red saw me hobbling around he was going to take me out. So why bother suiting up? But Clyde hit some big shots in that game, and so did DeBusschere. Clyde led us in scoring that night with 37, while Dave dropped 22. Jo Jo White and Dave Cowens led the Celtics with 34 and 33 points apiece, but again it wasn't enough. So now we were up three to one, with a chance to close out the series and earn a return trip to the Finals.

But the Celtics played like the champions they were in Game Five and eked out a win against us, 98–97. I played in this game, but my foot was still sore and I only managed to score 11 points. Clyde led us for the fifth straight game, scoring 21, while DeBusschere added 19. Cowens led Boston with 32 points and played like the MVP he was. With our series lead trimmed to one, we headed back to New York for Game Six and got beaten again, 110–100, with Cowens and White combining for 51 points. Clyde led us again, this time dropping 29, and I got 22, mostly on long-range jump shots. Now the series was tied, three games apiece.

Game Seven was scheduled for Boston Garden on April 29, and we expected a war. The Celtics had never lost a seventh game at home in their franchise's history, and they seemed to have all the momentum. My bone spurs were really killing me, even though I had scored 22 points in Game Six, but I just played through the pain. So before Game Seven, Danny and Red came over and asked me how I felt. I told them I was hurting but that I would try to give it a go. I also told them that if I couldn't go, Dean Meminger could step right in and replace me. They already knew that, but they were happy to hear it from me, because it showed that I was a true team player. So I started the game but could tell right away that I was not going to be effective. Now, I wanted to win a championship probably more than anyone on the team because I hadn't won one yet, though I had been to the Finals two years in a row. So I told Red and he put in Dean, who held his own against Jo Jo in that game, scoring 13 points and causing White to foul out. More importantly, we won the game 94–74, taking the series. Havlicek was heartbroken after that loss, as were his teammates. But for us, it was on to Los Angeles for a Finals rematch with the Lakers. As a team, we were ready for the Lakers and had revenge on our minds.

Because the first game was scheduled for Tuesday, May 1, we had to travel back to New York Sunday night after Game Seven and then turn around and fly to Los Angeles the next day. So I got back to New York, had some dinner with Tina and Theresa—who was staying with me at the time—and went to bed. We caught an early flight to LA the next morning, got there around midday, and went straight from the airport to a practice session at the Forum, the Lakers' home arena. I remember when we came out on the court Wilt was there, just getting ready to leave. He greeted me warmly, but then Dean said something smart-alecky to Wilt and the Dip turned his attention to "the Dream" (that was Dean's nickname from his New York City high school ball team because he had been so good) and said, "Hey, how you doing, Dream? I know one damn thing. You betta not bring your little ass down here close to where I'm playing because I'll make you eat any and every shot you take. And that goes for you too, Pearl!"

Then Wilt smiled at us and left. Well, that first game was a really close, good game and Wilt was true to his word, patrolling the lane and cutting down on our shots in there. Gail Goodrich had a hot shooting hand and burned us for 30 points, while Jim McMillian got 27 and Jerry West scored 24. The Lakers won 115–112, though we almost caught them in the fourth quarter. Walt had an off night and scored only 12, but DeBusschere and Bradley combined for 49. I was able to get 18 points, mostly on long jump shots again. Wilt and Willis battled each other to a draw, essentially, with Dip getting 12 points while the Captain got 10. Even though we lost that first game, it wasn't like we all got that "Aw shit, here we go again" feeling. We were an experienced, veteran team and we sucked it up because we felt we should have (and could have) won that game. We just let it get away from us and we were confident that, having taken the Lakers' best shot, we'd bounce back and win the series. Nobody was down. It's kind of an eerie feeling when you lose and you're not really down in a championship series. But we weren't. Instead, we were like, "Okay, okay, so what's next?" That's kind of how we all felt about it going into the next game.

At least I know that's how *I* felt about it. So the next game we came out strong and ready to play and beat them 99–95. Bill Bradley played an inspired game and dropped 26 points, with Clyde getting 21 and Phil Jackson hooking his way to 17 points. I scored 14 in that game, but thought I played a good floor game. Jerry West dropped 32 that night for the Lakers while Jim McMillian added 26. Gail Goodrich and I neutralized each other, as he matched my 14. Now the series was even steven. We were headed back to New York for two games, and we really liked our chances.

We opened a two-game stand at the Garden on May 6 and beat the Lakers both times, 87–83 and 103–98. I was feeling good in the second game and scored 21 points, mostly on long-range jump shots again. I felt particularly good that night because I outplayed Gail Goodrich, holding him to just 14 points for the second straight game. My bone spurs started acting up again in Game Four, limiting me to just 4 points, but I passed the ball very well, drawing Wilt away from the basket and setting up Willis for a number of uncontested layups (while I talked shit to Wilt). Now we led three games to one going back to Los Angeles and everyone was feeling good.

Our next game was scheduled for the 10th of May, but Red decided that we should fly to Los Angeles that very night so we could be rested and get some practices in. Now, I always liked to drive to the airport and leave my car there, but this time Tina was going to drop me at the airport, drive my car back into the city, and then pick me up when I came back. So Tina and I were walking to my car on 34th or 33rd and Seventh Avenue—somewhere around there—when we ran into three big, nasty-looking, heavyset white cats coming down the street from the game. I could tell they had been at the game because they had on Knicks caps and shirts and they were talking loudly about being at the game; they were drunk. So when Tina and I walked by they looked at us and then one of the guys pushed me, punched me in the jaw, and called me a nigger.

I was shocked. In Manhattan? I mean, I didn't even know these mother-fuckers, so I was mad as hell. So Tina was pulling me back from them and they saw how enraged I was and ran off. Now, I had a gun in the glove compartment of my Rolls-Royce. So I was thinking I'd go get it and ride around the area looking for these racist, stupid bastards. We had a charter flight leaving from the airport and Tina was pleading with me while I was riding around looking for them to forget about this and make my flight. After a while she convinced me and we drove to the airport and I got there a little late. Fortunately, they were waiting for me. After I explained to a shocked Red Holzman what had happened, he shook his head and put his arm around me and told me that, as much as it hurts, I had to forget about it. But I couldn't forget about it and all the way to LA I was mum—I guess Red told everyone about the incident, so everyone left me alone—just burning up inside.

By the time we touched down in Los Angeles I was channeling that anger into my competitive spirit to play in this decisive game against a team that was now my enemy, the basketball embodiment of those white guys who had jumped me. I thought about Dr. King's speeches, about the incident I had had with the police at Dunbar High School in Philly, about Malcolm X, and Muhammad Ali getting shafted by the army over his draft. So when I got off that plane I was fired up, and I stayed that way until we got on the court to play. I wanted badly to win this game, to become an NBA champion. So on game night I felt ready to get out on that court and do whatever it took to help my team win this game. But I also wanted to have fun doing it, like the old "Earl the Pearl" or "Black Jesus" walking on water. Because once I was on the court and feeling good, everything else disappeared from my mind. I threw everything else away and focused in on what I had to do to win. That's what it's all about. When all else fails, I can always find refuge out on the basketball court. And that's what hap-pened to me in Game Five against the Lakers. When I got out there, everything else disappeared and I just started playing. There was no denying me or my team that night, because we were a team of destiny. We won the game 102–93 and I led the way, scoring 23 points. But what made me really proud that night was that I put on my old "Earl the Pearl," "Black Jesus" act in the fourth quarter when I torched the Lakers for 8 points. And as happy as I was, the Dream, sitting on the bench, was thrilled for me, too; I could tell by the grin on his face and the way he was just shaking his head in wonder every time I made another great shot. Bradley dropped 20 points in that game and Clyde scored 18, same as the Captain. Gail Goodrich put up 28 in a very good game, though it was not good enough. Jerry West only got 12 that night because he was hurting.

I remember coming down the court a few times and talking to Wilt as I was driving in off a spin move. As he would come out to stop me I would say to him, "You can't get this one, big fella! You can't get it!"

And he'd say, as he came out to challenge me, "Yeah, Pearl, you bring that little shit in here and I'm gonna stuff yo' ass!"

Then I'd go right at him and when he'd leave Willis to come block my shot I'd dish it off to the Captain and as Willis dunked it I'd say, "I told you, big fella. You couldn't get this one. I told you that. Now look at yo' ass out here stuck and Willis dunkin'!"

Now, Wilt didn't like that kind of talk directed at him one bit because we were friends, both Philly cats who had played against each other a lot in the pros and in the Baker League. Still, I could see where Dip sometimes was showing his age because his reflexes had slipped and he wasn't the same dominant player he used to be. That's what age does to all great athletes over time; it just robs them of the edge they used to have when they were younger. I could see that in Dip, in Willis sometimes, in Jerry West, in the Big O, and I would see it in myself the longer I played. I just hoped I would have the good sense to recognize it before some young buck embarrassed me. But on this night, even down the final stretch of the game, whenever I took the ball in on Dip he would just grin and shake his finger as if telling me, "I'm gonna get yo' ass, little man, the next time you come in here!" Man, he was cocky to the end and it was fun, that game, one that I will never forget because I became an NBA champion and got my ring, which is why we all played this game.

All in all, 13 players and coaches who competed in the 1973 NBA Finals were elected to the Basketball Hall of Fame, which is crazy when you really think about it. Even though it only went five games it was a historic series—the best against the best—and I was grateful to have played with and against such tremendous players, because it meant that we had truly earned the title of "champion."

When the buzzer went off I was with Dean, and we hugged, but nothing overly exuberant. I just said to him, "Whew, this shit is finally over. Now we gonna get us a ring! Let's go get us some room service."

Dean looked at me with love and respect in his eyes and said, "Earl, you were a bad motherfucker tonight! You were your old self and you took it to their asses!"

That made me happy and I hugged him again. Then we started walking off the floor. But first I went up and congratulated the Lakers—Jerry, Wilt, Gail, all of them. I gave them hugs, but I could tell they were disappointed, as they should have been. But I was happy it was them and not us. Dip asked if I wanted to come out to his place afterward and I said no because we had to leave in the morning, but that I would take a rain check on it. But what I really wanted to tell Dip that night was that I had finally come full circle, because I had finally beat him for an NBA championship. Mentally, I didn't have to wear his hunter socks anymore because I was a champion in my own right now. But I thought better of saying that, so I kept it to myself because I didn't want to sound arrogant and say something to one of my idols that might sound inappropriate.

I remember looking at Wilt when we hugged, and for the first time since I had known him, he looked a little vulnerable to me. Now, I don't know if this was true, but that's the way I saw him that night. See, what a lot of people didn't know about Wilt was that underneath all his bravado he was a very nice, sensitive guy. Very generous, understood a lot about life. So I felt for him in that moment. But like I said, better him than me because Dip already had two championship rings and this was my first, as it was for Jerry Lucas and the Dream. During the game, Red had taken me out for a while, I guess to rest my bone spurs for a final run, and replaced me with Dean. But after a while, after the Lakers started to come back on us, Red put me back in the game and we finished them off. So when we got back in the locker room and were celebrating, pouring champagne over everybody's heads, DeBusschere came up to me with a big smile on his face and said, "Goddamn, Earl, I was wondering when you were going to get back in the game, man. We needed you out there."

So that in itself let me know how Dave felt about me, and I was quite sure after that night and that win that the other guys felt the same way as well. It gave me a rush to know I had really been accepted by this team, by my teammates. Dave reminded me of Gus Johnson in his leadership values, how he related to the guys and whatnot. He wasn't the enforcer Gus could be at times, but they were similar in terms of how they related to guys and how guys felt about them.

Because we won in Los Angeles there were no parties to go out to, and we had a flight to catch the next morning anyway. We would do our celebrating in New York, you know, go to City Hall, get a key to the city from the mayor, John Lindsay, all that stuff. Then we'd walk around the city and soak up all the love from New York fans. Because basketball is a city game, and the NBA championship had just been won by a big city team, the New York Knicks! The only thing I regret about the way we won that championship is that we didn't win it in New York City, in Madison Square Garden. I would have loved to win my ring that way. At

home, in front of the New York fans who loved their team so passion-
ately. But that wasn't to be.

So I went back to my room with my roommate, Dean, and we
ordered room service and a bottle of champagne. I thought about how
much I would have loved to share this moment with my beloved mother
by talking with her over the telephone, but I couldn't do that. Still, I felt
her great spirit there with me that night. So I got undressed, got in bed,
and turned the television on. I watched the local news recapping our
win over the Lakers, and that made me feel good all over again. I called
Tina and let her know the good news and we both sent kisses to each
other over the telephone wires. Then I hung up, just about the time
when the champagne and food arrived. I ate the steak, fries, and salad I
had ordered, drank some champagne, then snuggled into the bed and
fell asleep and slept deeply, savoring those sweet moments of winning
my first NBA championship. That night I slept as peacefully as a baby,
without a worry or care in the world. It was a beautiful ending to a long
journey. And though I wished my mother could have shared it with me
over the phone, she was there with me in spirit, and I wouldn't have had
it any other way.

Epilogue

MY TAKE ON NBA BASKETBALL
AND THE FUTURE OF THE GAME

ON OCTOBER 29, 1996, at the Grand Hyatt Hotel in New York City,
I was voted one of the 50 Greatest Basketball Players in NBA History.
This was the crowning achievement of my basketball career and an
affirmation of my approach to playing the game. The people that voted
for me were coaches, media people, and fellow players. The players on
the selection committee who I had competed against included Kareem
Abdul-Jabbar, Al Attles, Elgin Baylor, Dave Bing, Bill Bradley, Wilt
Chamberlain, Billy Cunningham, Wayne Embry, John Havlicek, Willis
Reed, Oscar Robertson, Bill Russell, and Jerry West. Three players on
the committee, Bill Bradley, Willis Reed, and Wes Unseld, had been
teammates of mine. Amongst the coaches on the committee who I had
either played for or competed against were Al Attles, Red Auerbach,
Gene Shue, and Red Holzman.

Of the 50 players who made the list, I had competed against or
played with Kareem, Nate "Tiny" Archibald, Rick Barry, Elgin, Dave
Bing, Larry Bird, Wilt, Bob Cousy, Dave Cowens, Billy Cunningham,
Dave DeBusschere, Julius Erving, Walt Frazier, George Gervin, Hal

Greer, John Havlicek, Elvin Hayes, Sam Jones, Jerry Lucas, Moses Malone, "Pistol Pete" Maravich, and Kevin McHale. Twenty-two players in all. In my 13-year pro career with the Baltimore Bullets and the New York Knicks, I was on one NBA championship team (the 1973 New York Knicks), went to the NBA Finals two other times (once with Baltimore and the other time with the Knicks), was named Rookie of the Year in 1968, was voted into the All-Star game four times (five if you count the coin flip in 1970 between me and Flynn Robinson, which I lost), and was named to the All-NBA First Team in 1969. My number 15 was retired by the New York Knicks and hangs from the rafters high above in Madison Square Garden. In addition, my number 10 Bullets jersey was retired by the Washington Wizards (the Baltimore franchise was moved to the Washington, DC, area in 1973 and renamed the Wizards in 1995) and hangs from the rafters of the Verizon Center in the nation's capital. I scored 17,454 points in my career, for an average of 18.8 points per game, and handed out 3,594 assists, an average of 3.9 a game. And recently I produced a critically acclaimed documentary film entitled *Black Magic*, which documents the early involvement of black small colleges and their coaches and star players in the evolution of basketball in this country during the civil rights era.

It is from the vantage point of a former college and pro basketball player that I can analyze the pros and cons of today's game. I believe my placement amongst the 50 greatest NBA players of all time validates my views about the game of basketball. I would like to start from a very personal, specific point of view regarding one of my contributions to the sport. Looking back on what I was most proud of and satisfied with about my election into this august group of players was that I had been able to bring my playground style of play to the NBA and succeed by making people love it.

Some time ago I had dinner with an old teammate from the Baker League, John Edgar Wideman, who had also played for the University of Pennsylvania's basketball team. Today, he is a professor at Brown University and an eminent American writer (he was also a Rhodes Scholar, like Bill Bradley and Jerry Lucas) who has published more than a dozen critically acclaimed novels, short story collections, and works of nonfiction. One of John's books, *Hoop Roots*, is about basketball. (He has also written essays and articles on Michael Jordan for *Esquire*, Dennis Rodman for the *New Yorker*, and a number of articles for *Sports Illustrated* on basketball and other sports.)

That evening, when we were talking over dinner, I remember him saying that my style of playing the game—you know, the playground style—was "a paradigm shift in the pro game of basketball." He told me that I had "brought that style to the NBA before anyone else", made the players, the powers that be, you know, the management, bosses, and coaches, love it. Why? Because that style infused excitement into the game and brought crowds into the arenas. It put fans in the seats, so to speak, which meant money in everyone's pockets—the owners, coaches, players, agents, and referees, not to mention corporate media owners, on-air sports analysts, and play-by-play announcers. Everybody attached to the international commercialization of professional basketball, from the selling of merchandise—shoes, jerseys, jackets, basketballs, trading cards, you name it—has profited immensely from the game becoming more exciting to fans all over the globe.

So it was great to hear John describe my playground style as "a paradigm shift" in the NBA game. Now, looking back, I believe what he said was true. Why? Because I see my style of playing the game all around in the NBA today: you know the fadeaway jumper, the up fake, the stepback jump shot, the three-point jump shot, the shake and bake, and, most importantly, the spin move. All of those moves are on display every day in today's game, and it was my game back in the day, though it wasn't as popular then as it is today because now it's considered entertainment. If you go and look at films of the way I played in my rookie year, in my first two or three seasons in the league, you can see my influence on the modern game in the styles of the late "Pistol Pete" Maravich, Magic Johnson, Isiah Thomas, Allen Iverson, Kobe Bryant, LeBron James, Dwyane Wade, Chris Paul, and Kyrie Irving.

The reason I am listing all these facts about myself is because I want to establish my bona fides with folks who might not know who I am, especially younger readers. I think it's important to lay out my credentials because some of the observations I will be airing regarding the game itself are aimed at its players, coaches, owners, and referees and might be considered controversial by some, or mean-spirited by others. However, this is not my intention. I also hope my views on which past and present-day players I think are great and which I feel are overrated will be received with a spirit of fair open-mindedness, honesty, and truth seeking. Ultimately, I hope these observations will be greeted as an ex-player's thoughtful ruminations on what is good and bad for the game itself—a game that this ex-player truly loves. I will also address areas where I feel the greatness of pro basketball shines, but also other areas where I notice shortcomings, like the deleterious impact the vast amounts of money have had on the game itself and on the players who compete in this beautiful game. Finally, I will address the pros and cons of the NBA's internationalization of pro basketball, how this affects the future of the game, and what types of players will succeed in the sport in the future.

I want to begin by looking at one aspect of the culture of basketball that I think is one of the negative characteristics of today's game, but one that is masked by the popularity of the sport: the fact that so many young guys are coming into the league. Before you know it, the NBA is going to be comprised of a majority of players who are no older than 25 years old. When that happens, I think the quality of the game will suffer, because young guys still need time to become acclimated to being and playing in the pros. You'll still have some really good young players—a few—who become Rookie of the Year, but even those fine players make a lot of mistakes because of their lack of experience. They're shooting 3-pointers, but there's no real knowledge being imparted to these youngsters. If you can run, if you can jump, you can get into the league. And that's one of the things that's much different than what it used to be. You would look at a #1 draft pick to come in and help your team right away. But today it's more or less drafting on potential; when they can help your team in the future. Unfortunately, what happens is that these guys don't make an impact right away and by the time they start playing well it's now time for their max contract. So now you have to make a decision: Am I going to give this guy a max deal or am I going to let him walk? So, it's a lot of differences in how the game is viewed today and what the players are about—what they think about in terms of, when you go into "I'm a pro now, but I've been pampered since I was eleven years old when I started in AAU." Guys just expect, when they start out in AAU, that they're going to go into the NBA.

I always thought players needed to stay in school three, four years before coming out and going into the pros. That college experience will help the great majority of them become more adept at playing the game and able to understand it more fully, and make the game itself better than if they enter the league at 18 or 19 years old and sit on the bench, not really playing for their first two or three years.

When you think in terms of the newly formed G-League, you have kids missing the type of experience that they would get by staying in school. School is a learning experience. In high school or AAU, you're there because you have potential. In college, you kind of learn to hone that talent. But now if you don't go to college and you go to the G-League then, for the most part, they're going to be sitting on the bench. So the experience that they get is in practices and not the game, which they would get as a collegiate player. And the further you go in college, obviously the more adept you are in facing challenges and knowing how to resolve those challenges. As a younger player if you hit a wall, what do you do?

See, back in the day, when you were young and coming up and the older players thought you were good enough to play with them, your job was just to pass the ball instead of running up and down the floor jacking up shots. No, you didn't shoot until one of the older guys told you it was okay. That way you learned the basics of the game.

I came out of college my first year. In college you play only 30 games or so, but at the 40-50 game in the pros you're kind of sucking it up until you get your second wind. What do you do then? Is your talent gone? These are the things that go through your head. I'm not doing what I did earlier. These are the things that you need to work through as a collegiate player and going into the pros as supposed to someone who hasn't experienced any of that before.

There are a lot of guys who stay in college because they're not the hot-shot prospect. But when they get out of college, they're more prepared than the guy who comes in with only one year of experience. Coaching is different for them because they've experienced it over the course of years as opposed to coming into the league from one situation—as a G-Leaguer—and now going into another situation—as a professional whose coach is going to be expecting a lot more of them. And they're making money, so all those things can weigh on you. "Am I really worth it?" Most players think they are regardless of what their talent is, but most players are worth it—I'm here—but they don't know where it came from, why they're getting this money, who sacrificed before them to make sure they got this money. They have no sense of history, which is one of the reasons why I kind of thought well of LeBron when he came into the league—he had a sense of history.

One reason a lot of these kids are doing the one-and-done or plan on jumping right to the G-League (or overseas) is money. Everyone seems to be making money in college but them. Schools make billions of dollars.

The NCAA is one of the biggest money-making organizations in the world. I personally think they are opposed to so much change that they need to loosen up their ties a little bit and figure out a way to financially compensate these athletes. A lot of these players come from disadvantaged families and why shouldn't they be compensated for bringing money to the school? The college coaches are getting millions of dollars, endorsements, and things of that nature. Why shouldn't some of that trickle down? Furthermore, not only do they need to go into the league early for financial reasons, but they see who's making money out there. They see it's the leagues. They see it's the coaches and everybody else. So why can't they hurry up and get themselves out there so they can make the money as well? It's very hard to disagree with that way of thinking.

If you tried to get the game to go back to the way it was, the players' agents would be all up in arms and so would the National Basketball Players Association, which seems to me like a conflict of interest. The players association represents the players who pay it dues, so it doesn't need to be fighting for the guys who are coming out of school early and aren't part of the association yet. That being said, I'm pleased with the fact that the association has started to help the retired players, the fact that we're now getting some health benefits, depending on length of service. If the players association is fighting for these players who are not members, then the guys the association is supposed to be representing are the ones who are going to lose their jobs when these young guys come into the league. So it behooves the association to stand pat, so to speak, on this issue and let these younger players go to school for three, four years, which will enable the veteran guys to stay in the league and make their money and then kind of intermingle with the younger players as they are making their exits from the league. That's how I think it should be, because I think it's a conflict of interest for the players association to be so much into representing guys coming into the league as

opposed to being more forthright with the players who are already paying their dues and are already part of the league, you know. It's the
young players learning from the veterans that will make for a stronger
league, one where a squad's a mix of good veterans who are teaching the
younger players coming in how to conduct themselves as professionals.

That's what happened with a player like Kobe Bryant, for example.
He didn't come right in out of high school and start and become the star
he is today. No, it took a minute and a lot of hard work for him to put
everything together, and he became a great player because of it. LeBron
James is another example of a great high school player coming into the
league with phenomenal ability and having extraordinary expectations
heaped upon him. But although he came in right away and put some big
numbers up on the board, it took some years before he became the
player he is today, and he made a lot of youthful mistakes along the way
to winning his first NBA championship in 2012. A physically gifted
young phenom can't win an NBA championship all by himself, no matter how talented he is ("taking his talents to South Beach" and bringing
Kevin Love to Cleveland). Kobe and LeBron (and now Kevin Durant)
benefited from having outstanding veteran teammates surrounding
them when they won their first championships. After all, a phenom
cannot win just by himself.

Let me put it another way: When most people think about the modern game of basketball in terms of how super it is, they think of guys
flying through the air dunking the ball. That's what makes it exciting for
the average fan. I like it, too, because basketball has progressed in terms
of what the players are now able to demonstrate, visually speaking, in
terms of their physicality, you know, flying through space and dunking
acrobatically. But for me the game itself has regressed because so many
of the young guys playing the game can *only* do these high-flying acro-
batics, and that's unfortunate. There are not a lot of guys like LeBron
and Kobe.

When I think of players who laid the foundation for this modern game, we have to go back to the '50s, '60s, maybe the '70s, to guys like Elgin Baylor, Oscar Robertson, and Jerry West. Here I'm talking about guards and small forwards. I mean, I'm talking about players who came into the league after four years of college and made an immediate impact on the pro game. Even centers like Wilt Chamberlain, Bill Russell, and Wes Unseld. These players entered the league NBA-ready.

Now I have already talked about how Kobe didn't make an immediate impact and how LeBron did come in scoring but didn't win a championship until his ninth year. But these two guys were the ones that really opened up the floodgates of young players coming into the league straight out of high school with high-flying, exciting games (though Kevin Garnett made the jump before either of them). Derrick Rose and Kyrie Irving came out after one year of college. Before them there were Carmelo Anthony and Durant. But how many other young players have had a great and lasting impact on the NBA after coming out early? Not too many.

In my mind, this is all about money, about making the almighty dollar, for agents, needy young players, the NBA, and the media. But at the same time, I'm talking about the legacy and integrity of the game. It's just not being played at the same high level it used to be. Physically, like I said, it's played on a higher plane: above the rim. But mentally it's not being played on the same level it was back in the day. Thank goodness we do have players that play the game with their minds as well as their physical beings. That's where you find the winning teams: with guys like LeBron, Steph Curry, Durant, Kawhi Leonard, Joel Embiid, and others. (Don't be upset if your favorite player's name didn't make this list—there simply isn't enough space to include everyone.)

Because you've got so many younger guys in the league now, there are a ton of mistakes being made in games, you know, like silly turnovers.

And many of those turnovers are a direct result of how these really young, inexperienced players play the game mentally. And you don't have to have turnovers to have players making stupid, bad plays, you know what I mean? It can be just bad decision making, a bad shot selection, or a pass to a spot where a teammate can't do anything with the ball once he catches it because he's out of position. That kind of thing.

But just stop for a moment and think of the heights the NBA would reach in terms of its mental aspect if they pushed back on a lot of these mistake-prone, high-flying theatrics. It's entertainment, and I for one understand the value of that, because that's what I introduced into the NBA. But the entertainment aspect of basketball has to be informed by players first understanding the fundamentals of the game in the way a lot of young European players do—and like I did—but many young American players don't. In fact, today's game is, with each passing day, starting to resemble the European style of basketball more and more. The biggest difference from the style of the past is with regard to players being able to spread the floor. Instead of shooting the wide-open layup, they are kicking the ball out to guys standing on the three-point line. A lot of these shots are unconventional, because nobody is guarding them, since they haven't had a chance to get down there yet on defense.

If you ask me, the greatest of all time will be Wilt Chamberlain. For all the things that have happened in this game as we know it today, he started most of it. The widening of the lanes, staying behind the free throw line, shooting free throws because he used to leap from the free throw line and dunk. He still has 80 or something records on the books, so he's the prototype of what the game eventually became. However, he's a big man. So now the game is moving away from big men, per se. You have your 7-footers, and their main role used to be rim protection. But now those rim protectors are shooting 3-pointers—and this is not the American game, this is the European game. So the NBA started to venture out to get more European players they also adopted a lot of the

European style. The 3-pointer, the euro step, all these things...it becomes USA basketball. And the movement away from the big man is really tough. You only have a couple big men in the NBA right now—guys who play with their back to the basket. You got Rudy Gobert in Utah, Anthony Davis in New Orleans, Karl-Anthony Towns in Minnesota, Nikola Jokic in Denver, Joel Embiid in Philly.

In my opinion, Embiid is the prototypical big man of today. Now, I had a big beef with Sonny Hill because he previously said that Embiid was like Wilt Chamberlain. Well, Wilt used to shoot out there in practice but never in a game. Embiid shoots out there, he plays with his back to the basket, he can handle the ball—so it's a big difference in terms of his style, but he can be a dominant player. He rebounds, block shots, takes up position, and if you would ask me, he's probably the best big man in the game today—and he hasn't even played 100 games.

The other top-tier big man, I would say, is Anthony Davis. Another great talent, probably because he's shot up like he did—he started off as a guard at 6-foot-3 and the next summer he's 6-foot-10, so he still has a nice jump shot and can handle and pass the ball, as well as block shots because he's so long. These are the guys who make it exciting for me to look at the game because I see what they do. These are the guys that are franchise players.

But with the talent of these big men, there are just not a lot of rim protectors.

I used to do stuff that I knew the coaches weren't going to be crazy about, but because it would excite the crowd. Your superstar players do things that excite teammates and makes them want to play better. Play more with you. For you. Demarcus Cousins is not in that bag yet. Hopefully, I would think, going to Golden State, he would get the rep of how to play within the system and take that (to the future).

American announcers and analysts have changed the way the modern game is played by emphasizing particular things when they call games. The game itself is about the entertainment as opposed to being objective. And it's not just the in-game announcers but the talk show hosts. They all have the same motive, so to speak, in terms of promoting the game.

I don't underestimate the influence of announcers and analysts on the game itself and on young players coming into the league. ESPN has had a huge impact on all sports and specifically basketball. I mean, the game was played one way, fundamentally speaking, for a very long time. Then ESPN came along and showed nothing but dunks on their highlights reels. That in itself changed the way the game was played. Now it's moved over to the 3-point shot but for so long it was all about what kind of dunk someone was doing. Never mind that they're all by themselves when they're doing so. It's not like going through the lane and dunking on guys. I mean, how many dunks can you do that people haven't seen before? After watching all those highlights clips, that's all the young kids who saw them wanted to see and do; it was just so exciting looking at players doing them that after a while, all the youngsters wanted to emulate what they saw in those highlights.

Sometimes I'll hear an announcer say, "There's a good pick and roll." But to learn the essence of the pick and roll, the basics of that part of the game, you have to look at guys like John Stockton and Karl Malone, because they based their styles of play on fundamentals. Now, Karl Malone could shoot the ball, could go to the basketball and score. And John Stockton could also score the ball. But the way those guys executed the pick and roll was textbook stuff, masterful, just like Steve Nash in his prime, and now with such talented point guards as Chris Paul, Russell Westbrook, and Kyrie Irving.

And that's what I'm talking about here: understanding the game, the way it has been played for years. I mean, the Golden State Warriors, which is a very young team, seems to understand this. But as tremendous as Steph Curry and Klay Thompson are as players, they still looked for veteran leadership. That's when they brought in Kevin Durant, and before him Andre Iguodala and Shaun Livingston.

Mark Jackson also needs to be mentioned pursuant to this conversation. Being a premiere point guard himself, understanding the nuances of the game, Jackson was able to communicate with those players that he had and probably was the greatest influence on how they became the players they are today. I think that's the most important thing—being able to communicate your thought process about what you should do and how you should be—what kind of coach you should be. Mark had a very unique way of being able to have the players rally around him. Players feel as though coaches should be for them as much as they're for him. It's a give-and-take type of situation.

In the case of Steve Kerr, Kerr had been a general manager. So, he had been around a long time, and had played a long time. He had been with championship teams. Kerr had the aura of being around winning, and I'm quite sure that was one of the reasons that he has been able to do what he has done at Golden State.

I want to move on to talk about how referees back in my day exerted their own influence on the way the game was played (I can't talk too much about the referees today because I'm not playing now and I am not familiar with them). Back in the day, everybody cursed at each other—players, coaches, referees, and fans. I mean it used to be like an orchestra of cursing. If the referee called something on a player, the player cursed him out, whatever the call was. Cursing was almost considered normal, like you'd hear a player underneath the basket telling another player, if he was pushing and shoving him too hard, "Motherfucker, get off me."

As for me, I had a habit of going almost crazy if a call went against me, you know, after I had established myself in the league. Especially if the call resulted in my fouling out of a game, which didn't happen very often. That just made me go crazier because I knew I was out of the game—the call had been made and there was no going back on that. So my thinking was I might as well get my money's worth by calling the ref an asshole or a son of a bitch! Things like that.

But there was one incident with referee Earl Strom in the latter part of my rookie season that stands out in my mind in terms of my confrontations with NBA officials. Now, Earl Strom was what I would call a confrontational referee; there were several of them. Richie Powers was another one, though Strom was the worst. Anyway, these guys were always exerting their authority in ways that weren't really necessary. Like they were always in your face, almost enticing players to hit them, their fists balled up, their faces red as beets, daring players to do or say something so they could bust you. That kind of shit. Usually, I would just let it slide. But this time, Strom called an offensive foul on me that I totally disagreed with. Now, I had the ball up under my arm and Strom asked for it. So I held the ball out and he thought I was handing it to him. But instead, as he reached for it, I pulled the old Harlem Globetrotter trick of throwing the ball toward him and then spinning it back on the back my hand. And as the ball was spinning on the back of my hand, it was spinning in his face. Well, this pissed Strom off so bad he threw me out of the game for embarrassing him. He jumped up in the air with his arms and hands over his head and screamed, "Get out of here, Monroe! Get out of here!"

Then there was Sid Borgia, whose thing was calling traveling all the time. He was a little short guy who would, with his arms all spread out, make his call on someone with a high-pitched scream, "Na, na, na, na, na, na, na! Gimme the ball! Gimme the ball!"

Man, Sid was a character. But Mendy Rudolph was cool. He was a real slick dresser, smooth, suave, and he was a great referee on top of all of those other attributes. I liked him a lot, on and off the court. But Earl Strom? Man, he would antagonize entire teams and cost us games with his calls. If he favored a certain team, then the fouls would go their way, and many times it would cost the opposing team the game. So teams had to know who was refereeing each night so we all knew what kinds of calls were going to be made for or against us.

But referees definitely influenced the game back then because some of them were consistently making bad calls that cost teams games and championships, in my opinion. That's not cool, but no one ever talks about this in any meaningful way. And yes there was a lot of prejudice against black players. That's normal because there's racial bias in American society, especially back then. But all of this was definitely swept under the rug. Plus, there weren't many black referees back then, and of course no women. (Jackie White became the league's first black referee during the 1967–1968 season, followed by Ken Hudson, James Capers Sr., Hugh Evans, and Hue Hollins in the early '70s).

Today the league has tried to impose consistency on referees, and it's a good thing. But there are going to be bad calls, because referees are human and they still don't like certain guys. That's always been the case. It used to be that if a team was playing at home, that was worth at least a few points, but I don't know if that's true today. Still, there are always hard-asses, you know, refs that players can't talk to because they just want to fight with you for whatever reason. I don't really know. But what I do know is that the game needs more guys like Mendy Rudolph if we're talking seriously about making the game better and fairer.

Recently I have been thinking about changes to some of the rules that might make the game more interesting. Now, I know some of these ideas might be controversial, but here goes. First off, I think it might prove interesting if the baskets were raised some, maybe another six inches, because today you've got a lot of guys who are so tall they can just stand under the basket and dunk the ball without even jumping. So I think if the basket was raised, those players would have to jump a little bit to keep their advantage. It would also make the smaller guys have to get up higher to dunk. Now, obviously, guys that shoot jumpers and whatnot would have to change their shots and shoot them a little differently, too.

I also think perhaps they should drop the rim about six inches lower in the women's game. Because then you'd have young girls and women dunking more and that would make their games more exciting. I've seen games where the basket was at nine feet six inches, and the girls were dunking and the game was more exciting. It's only the purists, so to speak, who don't want changes. The fact is that the game has been changing gradually since its invention in the late 19th century, like with the introduction of the shot clock and the three-point line. Like anything else, the game has to evolve to meet the changing needs of the athletes and the fans. If it never changed, we'd still all be shooting at peach baskets.

Then there's that extra step players take when they tuck the ball and hop between guys, then take that step and go to the basket and score. This has become part of the game. It's another way to give players a little more leeway to score. There was a time when players weren't scoring the way they are now, and the NBA put some sanctions in to help increase scoring. It makes the game fun to watch.

Back in the day they allowed hand-checking, and today they don't. Players who scored a lot of points back then got them despite being hand-checked all over the floor. They also did it without the benefit of a three-point shot, and that definitely would have helped players like myself and others who could shoot the long-range jump shot. I played for one year, 1979–1980, after the NBA first initiated the three-point rule, which it borrowed from the old ABA, and I didn't take one, just for kicks. I like the three-point shot, though. It adds excitement to the game. But the problem with it is that teams can shoot themselves out of a game just as easily as they can benefit from the shot. Like, a team is making three-point shots and is in the game, but then they start missing them and the other team comes back. So it becomes a seesawing affair, with the team that was ahead now being behind because they missed too many threes and because they relied so much on those shots falling that they're now playing catch-up. So, it can be both a good and a bad thing. But on the whole, I like the three-point rule. As far as the no-hand-checking rule, today the referee will blow the whistle if you so much as touch a player, so it's much easier to score today than it was back in my day.

Back in the 1950s, when the NBA finally let black players into the league, the powers that be didn't want there to be any black stars. So the great black players who came into the league as offensive threats—guys like Woody Sauldsberry, Sweetwater Clifton, Andy Johnson, Chuck Cooper, and Earl Lloyd, the first black man to play in the NBA—were told to become defensive players. When Cleo Hill was drafted by the Saint Louis Hawks in 1961, he was a great scorer, and he scored a lot of points in Saint Louis during the preseason. But the white star players on the Hawks at the time—Bob Pettit, Clyde Lovellette, and Cliff Hagan—didn't like that Cleo was scoring even though the coach, Paul Seymour, loved Cleo's game. So the players started boycotting Cleo by not passing him the ball, and when Coach Seymour threatened to fine them for doing this, management fired him, and the new coach, Andrew Levane, reduced Cleo's playing time so drastically that his scoring average dropped from 10.8 points a game to 5.5. Eventually he was cut from the team and blackballed, never to play in the NBA again. (Speaking of which, on a more personal note, Gene Shue was under the same kind of scrutiny as Seymour had been, and Coach Shue let me play my game. By comparison to the situation with Cleo, at this point the league was starting to change with regard to the quota issue, so it was a turning point of sorts.)

And this was the case all the way down to when Bill Russell came into the league, though they didn't have to try and limit Russell's offensive production because he was mainly a defensive force from day one. But Sam Jones was a great scorer, totaling more than 20,000 points in his career. He's a Hall of Famer, but we don't hear that much about him today when the critics discuss those great Celtics teams that won 11 NBA championships. Sam was a clutch shooter and one of the main reasons Boston won all those championships, along with K.C. Jones—another defensive specialist—and Satch Sanders. These were black players who were integral to Boston's success back in the day, even though the Celtics kept their black quota intact for years (the old line amongst NBA coaches was to play "two [black players] at home, three on the road, and four when you're behind").

Broadcasters and sportswriters also like to employ coded language with regard to the black players they cover, such as when they refer to black players as "beasts" or as "athletic." Conversely, they are always calling white guys "thinking players" or "heady players," which reduces the game and its participants to a bunch of absurd stereotypes.

That's one of the main reasons I was one of the producers of the documentary *Black Magic*—to bring an African American perspective to the early great black coaches and outstanding black small-college players from back in the day. I mean, hardly anybody ever discusses the enormous contributions of my college coach, Big House Gaines, or John McLendon, who won three consecutive NAIA championships at Tennessee State. Why? Because they were black coaches, that's why, and because they both coached at small black schools. A lot of people don't want to hear this kind of talk. They'd much rather sweep it under the rug, because there aren't too many films around that document the greatness of these early great black coaches and players. Mostly the information is passed down by word of mouth. The same thing is true of early great black football and baseball players, because no one was filming them. There isn't any film of Wilt Chamberlain's NBA record-setting 100-point game in Hershey, Pennsylvania; there's only a radio tape of an announcer calling the game and the eyewitness accounts of the 1,000 or so people and players who were at the game, and most of those people are dying off now.

Speaking of great films, I'm proud of the fact that more recently I participated in *Basketball: A Love Story*, a Dan Klores documentary that needs to be seen as a film though. It's a wonderful tribute that puts in perspective different elements of basketball that make it the game it is today.

Before I turn my attention to some of the players I think are amongst the greatest to ever play the game, including a few of the young stars who are competing today, I want to tell a little-known story about Magic Johnson and I possibly playing together toward the end of my career. Back in late 1978 or early 1979, I was on a flight from Portland back to New York when this white guy sitting next to me said, "You're Earl Monroe, aren't you?"

"Yeah, that's me, every day of the year."

So we both laughed and then he said, "Do you know about this player named Magic Johnson who plays in Michigan at some college out there?"

"No," I told him. "Who is he?"

"Well, he's about six feet eight and he plays just like you. He's going to be something else!"

"Really?" I said to him, because I wasn't a big follower of college basketball at the time. "I'm going to have to check him out."

That conversation stayed with me, first because he said this player played like me and second because he said his name was "Magic," which was one of my old nicknames back in Philadelphia. So I made it a point to check out who this new "Magic" was. When I first saw him play, I could see the similarities in style because of the great way he handled the ball, his attitude toward the game, and the way he ran his team. I mean, he was in control of everything! And I thought to myself, *Shit, this brother is something else!* So I started following him just to see how far he would go. Then he and his team, Michigan State, beat Indiana State and their star, Larry Bird, in the NCAA finals that year. So, although I didn't know him, I just liked his personality. He seemed like such a nice guy with that big, bright smile of his. Then he came into the league that fall and I had an opportunity to play against him, in what turned out to be my last year in the pros. Now, there were rumors circulating at the time about me being traded to the Lakers. So the Lakers had my good friend from Philly, Walt Hazzard, come and visit me in the locker room. He wanted to know what I thought about being traded to LA to become a caddie of sorts, you know, a guide to walk Magic Johnson through the pros and cons of pro basketball.

I could see it was getting close to being over in New York for me, so I said, "Yeah, Walt, I'd welcome that."

I thought that going to LA, you know, La-La Land, would be a different kind of scenario for me, because I was interested in getting involved with music and film after I got through with playing basketball. So the next time the Knicks went out to LA, Walt came and asked me the same thing. So I told him again that I was interested and after that I thought it was going to happen. Then someone told me that Jerry West, who had been coach of the Lakers and now was serving as a scout for them, had nixed the deal.

Now, I don't know why it didn't happen. Jerry and I have always gotten along and as far as I know everything was good between us. I've never had a conversation with Jerry about this, and I guess that's my fault. Sometimes people might hear things that are somewhat negative about someone somewhere along the line, and maybe Jerry heard something about me. But I have no way of knowing what it was that killed that deal. I'm very sorry that it didn't. I would have loved to have played with Magic Johnson and to have capped my career with another championship.

Now, I want to turn my attention to listing some of the greatest players—in my opinion—to play the game of basketball in my time. My list dates from 1960 until the present day, and I will first list the best big men and then move on to forwards and guards. I said in an earlier chapter that I think Wilt Chamberlain is the greatest player I ever saw. Wilt was from my hometown, Philadelphia, though that's not the reason why I think he was the best. The reason is that he still holds more than 90 NBA records. In his prime he could do everything: run, jump—some say he had a 50-inch vertical leap—rebound, score, play defense, block shots, pass. He just was a great, great player. He was big—seven feet one inch—strong—he weighed 275 pounds—agile, and quick. In 1962 he averaged 50.4 points and 24.7 rebounds a game. He even led the league in assists one year. He changed the game with his presence when he was young. They widened the lanes from 12 to 16 feet because of Wilt; players shooting free throws had to stand behind the line until the ball hit the basket, because Wilt used to jump from the free throw line and dunk the ball. A standing jump! But beyond all that, Dip was the reason basketball players today are making big money in the NBA, because he was the first cat to demand that the owners pay him. He knew that he was the primary reason people were filling up arenas, because they wanted to see him play. And Wilt felt that if the owners made money, then he should, too. So they paid him. I think it was called "the Wilt Chamberlain Argument."

Today, "great" players are measured by how many championships they win. This is one of the arguments they make for Bill Russell,

Michael Jordan, and Magic Johnson. That's cool. But here, my judgment of "great" is rooted in a player's individual ability, and on that
basis Wilt, for me, is the most dominant player who ever played the
game. Case closed. I mean, he has records that will probably never be
broken, and he won two NBA championships. Plus he was an incredible
athlete, a high jumper who also ran the 400-meter dash. He was intel-
ligent and a very generous person who left a lot of money to charities
without being public about it. He also had a very large personality—
witness his claim of having had sex with more than 20,000 women—he
was very outspoken and proud, and he didn't suffer fools lightly. So he
probably pissed off a lot of people with his opinions regarding certain
things. But there isn't any doubt that he had truly transcendent, unsur-
passed talent as a basketball player, and that's why he tops my list.

After Wilt, the most dominant big man for me was Kareem Abdul-
Jabbar. From the time he was Lew Alcindor, he had big-time game, and
aside from Wilt, he was the one, though I thought he was actually
afraid of Dip when he first came into the pros. I think Wilt kind of
intimidated him early on—though Wilt did that to everyone, so Kareem
wasn't alone in that regard—because of Dip's weight and strength
advantage. Dip was seven one and Kareem was seven two, but Wilt outweighed Kareem by 50 pounds. I don't know exactly *why* Kareem was
intimidated, because he had that great sky hook, and that was definitely
an equalizer for Wilt's strength—a truly lethal offensive weapon. And
with the sky hook, Kareem didn't have to be physical or play underneath
the basket with Wilt; all he had to do was shoot that sky hook, and that
was a game changer. See, the sky hook revolutionized the game, and it's
interesting to me that no big man of today has mastered that shot,
because if they did they would be unstoppable. Kareem also had a nice
little soft jumper, he could shoot free throws well, and he could really
dunk the ball. He revolutionized the game, especially the college game.
I mean, because of him they even banned dunking on the college level

until a few years after he graduated. And then he changed his name to a Muslim one. Some other black NBA players did too, like Walt Hazzard, Don Smith, and Charlie Scott, who once famously said, "But you can call me Charlie Scott in the league, though."

A lot of those players that changed their names who weren't as famous as Kareem ran into some problems, though. A lot of them didn't last that long in the league because of the bias against Muslims amongst the powers that controlled the NBA. I remember once a group of black players was invited to a meeting in a hotel room in New York that had been rented by a Muslim faction out of Washington, DC. I think it was in 1972. And during the course of the conversation we were having, I recall one of the guys who was considering changing his name said the reason was that the names we all had were "slave names, given to us by our masters." So his solution was that we all needed "to go back to our African roots and adopt names that were synonymous with where we came from." A lot of guys were shocked by this turn of events, and a lot of questions and answers went back and forth. Then I remember someone saying, "Well, I know this much. Unless your name is Kareem Abdul-Jabbar, you ain't going to fare well in this league if you change your name to an Arabic one. So if you want to stay in the league, you better keep your American name."

And I think that held true for a long, long time. As for me, I never considered changing mine because of my father and my mother, plus I really like my name. But I never held it against Kareem for changing his name, because that was his right. As a matter of fact, he changed it a short time after he left my house in Baltimore, right after the 1971 Finals. All I know is that he was a helluva player, a dominant one, the NBA's all-time leading scorer and one of the three or four greatest players to ever lace up their sneakers.

There were two big men, centers, who could have been really great players if injuries hadn't brought them down: Ralph Sampson and Bill

Walton. Both of those players were really dominant before they suffered knee injuries, so I don't really know how they would have turned out if they hadn't gotten injured. But both of those players were really talented, could score, play defense, pass, run the floor, and rebound. Sampson was the taller of the two at seven feet four. He could shoot the jumper, put the ball on the floor and drive to the hoop. He also had a little hook and could play defense. Ralph could have been something else, a truly dominant player in my opinion, if he hadn't gotten hurt. He was just that talented. He and Hakeem Olajuwon formed what they called the "twin towers" in Houston. I think he could have been an amazing player, but that's something we'll never know. Same thing with Bill Walton, who was an amazing player at UCLA and at Portland, where he teamed with "the Enforcer," Maurice Lucas, and won an NBA championship. Walton was six feet 11 inches and could really run the floor until he hurt his knees. He had a nice little turn-around jumper and a ferocious dunk shot. Walton could really get off the floor, was an outstanding rebounder and passer and a helluva defensive player. But again, we will never know just how good he could have been. Now, most people are left with the memory of him playing for the Celtics, with Larry Bird, when he was a shadow of the player he had once been.

On the other hand, Hakeem Olajuwon was the real deal when he came into prominence in the mid-1980s. He was a Muslim like Kareem, but he came into the league from Nigeria with his name already in place. He was always a very classy guy to me, on and off the court. But he was a player who honed his game down to what he knew he could do and just did it. Olajuwon was seven feet tall, an elegant player with real nice moves around the basket, and he could rebound. He had great footwork around the basket for a big man, I think because he had been a soccer player, and he was a quick jumper in the paint. Hakeem had a nice little jump shot, had a lot of great ball fakes, and made the game look easy when he played. One reason he was so effective was he knew what his strengths were—his quickness, footwork, quick jumping ability, fakes, his little jumper around the basket, and dunks—and he didn't try anything he couldn't do. So his consistency was also very important in terms of his development. And he was so quick.

I remember when he had that great series against Patrick Ewing in the 1994 NBA Finals, which Houston won in seven games. Hakeem was named Finals MVP. Then the next year he did the same thing to David Robinson and the San Antonio Spurs in the conference finals. Then he badly outplayed Shaquille O'Neal and Houston beat the Orlando Magic in the 1995 NBA Finals to repeat as NBA champions, with Olajuwon being voted the Finals MVP for the second year in a row. Those two championship runs cemented Hakeem's place amongst the elite of the game.

Other really fine big men were Dave Cowens, who was a monster, a hard-nosed player that a lot of people didn't want to go up against. He was a nice cat off the floor, but a madman on it. He was a wonderful player, though, the kind you wanted to play with. He had a nice jump shot, could go to the basket, and had a little hook when he came across the middle. But man, was he tough and a force to be dealt with every time he stepped on the court, because he was utterly fearless. Bob Lanier was a prototypical center, a big guy who took up a lot of space. He could rebound, block shots, had a nice little hook shot and fadeaway jumper, and could go to the hole and throw down dunks as well. For a big guy—he was six feet 11 inches and 250 pounds—I thought he was very, very agile, even though he wore size 22 sneakers. Moses Malone was a player who banged the boards, got a lot of his own—and everybody else's—rebounds, then would put the ball back up, miss, get it right back—because he was a real quick jumper—and put it up again until he scored. He was relentless, had a lot of energy. Mo was another great competitor—he and Dave Cowens were cut from the same cloth.

He had great hands, and since he wasn't a great shooter all his points came from down deep, close to the basket.

Another gifted big man was Patrick Ewing, a powerful seven-footer, a warrior who came to play every single night. Patrick was a great rebounder, defensive force, shot blocker, and scorer in his prime. He had a good jumper, could take it to the hole, had a nice little hook, and could dunk the ball, and he was a fierce competitor. The same is true of David Robinson, only he wasn't as fierce as Ewing, but instead was more of a finesse player. Robinson had a lot of offensive skills, like he could take it to the basket and either lay it up or dunk the ball, and he had a nice little left-handed jumper and hook shot. And he could block shots, rebound, and pass the ball. No doubt about it, David was a very skilled player.

Then there's Shaquille O'Neal, aka Shaq. He was *the* dominant big man of his day. I would love to have seen Shaq in his prime go against Wilt in his, because both of them are seven feet one. Shaq outweighed Dip by about 50 pounds, but they both were very strong. So it would have been an epic battle down in the paint to see who could get in position to rebound or score. Wilt was a little bit quicker than Shaq and could have matched him in strength. But that would have been a battle of dunks and will and strength. Shaq, when he was in his prime, was the dominant big man of the last decade and a half. I think Dwight Howard is a good player but not a dominant one. He's a much better player when the team revolves around him and the ball is going to him all the time.

When you talk about the great guards and forwards in the NBA, especially from my time in the league, I've already discussed Jerry West, Hal Greer, Pete Maravich, Rick Barry, Oscar Robertson, Elgin Baylor, and a few others. But I didn't discuss one of the great guards from my time in depth. That player is Dave Bing, who was an exceptional talent. Dave was a high-jumping player who had finesse to his game. He wasn't an overpowering player, but because he could jump so high and because of the way he moved so gracefully with the ball, he was an exciting player to watch and to play against. And man, could he shoot the ball. He could shoot it from anywhere and he could also get to the basket really well and score. No question. He led the league in points scored in my rookie season, and he could handle and pass the ball as well. He was the kind of guy—a good, solid person—that I wouldn't have minded being in the trenches with. He was a pleasant person off the court, was always soft-spoken, but you know he didn't take no stupid stuff because he always had something else besides basketball on his mind. Today he is the mayor of Detroit.

Connie Hawkins was another player that could do anything he wanted with the ball. "Hawk," as everyone used to call him, had very big hands. He could hold a basketball like someone with normal hands held a baseball, which came in handy when he made those swooping, graceful moves to the basket that he was famous for. He was a finesse player who everyone said could jump out of the gym, but I didn't see him when he was young. His career was cut short because he was allegedly involved in a point-shaving scandal and was blackballed from playing in the NBA, so he became a star in the ABA. Later it was proven that he wasn't involved in it, so the powers that be allowed him to play in the NBA, where he was a very good player and a force for several years. I can only imagine what a player he could have been had they not blackballed him.

Julius Erving, who emulated Hawkins's moves to the basket, is one of the all-time great players. He was six feet seven and lean but strong, and he could really get up off the ground. I mean, he could soar and swoop in a very graceful way and throw down the most ferocious dunks. He could hang in the air and make all kinds of brilliant shots in close around the basket, holding the basketball in one of those huge hands of his. He could handle the ball and dribble and take the ball to the hole, had a good midrange jump shot, and could pass the ball well, too. He was one of those players I used to love to watch. I don't think too many players in the history of the game could outjump Dr. J. I mean, he could do spectacular moves high in the air and the fans just loved him.

I watched Bob Love develop as a player out in Chicago. He was another small-black-college player (out of Southern University in Baton Rouge, Louisiana) who didn't play a lot when he first came into the NBA with Cincinnati. Then I think he went to Milwaukee, where he didn't play much, before joining the Bulls in Chicago. It was there that he found a home with Norm Van Lier and Jerry Sloan and became a monster scorer. Everybody called him "Bean" because he was so slender. He was six eight and didn't have a lot of strength, but man could he shoot the ball! Jump shots from the top of the key to both corners. He could play forward and shooting guard. He was deadly. And he could score points in bunches. That was his strength: He could put up big numbers and carry a team on his back with his scoring.

Bob McAdoo was another great shooter. He understood how to score the ball. I mean, you talk about a three-point shooter and whatnot—I know McAdoo would have been really happy to be playing today, because he could hit that jumper from anywhere. He was a Kevin Durant–type player in terms of size, you know, six feet nine inches and real slender, but he could also run the floor. I have an interesting story about Bob McAdoo. He's from North Carolina and I was there when Coach Gaines tried to recruit him to Winston-Salem. But he chose to go to the University of North Carolina instead. So when he entered the league at Buffalo, I went up to him after we played them one night and said, "Bob, you turkey, man, I thought you were coming to play at Winston-Salem!"

And he said with a smile, "Earl, you know what happened? When I came for my visit with you and Coach Gaines, y'all served me salads. When I went over to the University of North Carolina, they served me steak and salad. So I went there."

Man, that shit cracked me up! You don't feed somebody and lose.

Another player who could really jump was Spencer Haywood, who was six feet eight, had a strong body, could run the floor, had a good turnaround jumper in the paint, and could really take the ball to the basket. When he was on, he was a great scorer. He's also important because, as I mentioned briefly in Chapter 15, he was the one who challenged the draft and made it possible for underclassmen to come into the league early, so he changed the game in that way also. He was a great talent, and from Detroit. Some people thought he was a selfish player, that he thought every play was for him. Still, Spencer could really play and it didn't hurt that he married the international super-model Iman.

Many people already know about Larry Bird because he was a great player. He wasn't the fastest guy in the world, or the highest jumper, but he could play the game real well because he was a student of basketball. His greatest strength was that he could shoot the ball so well that his defenders always had to come out to try and stop him. When they did that, he was able to go by them and get to the basket with an assortment of tricky shots and score. Larry's other biggest assets were his knowledge of the game and his feel for doing the right thing at the right time. He had that rocking thing, you know, he could rock in front of a player behind the three-point line, with the ball over his head in the shooting position, and if his defender didn't come out on him Larry would just shoot it and make a three pointer. Now, that really just started it off. Because if the defender came out after he'd made a couple of long shots, Larry would step in as the defender was coming out and fill up the space he'd just left and then, with the defender behind him, it would be all over. So he understood how to do things and how to make it happen for him. Plus, he was a great rebounder, and out in the open court he was a wonderful passer. He was just an all-around great player, one of the best ever.

Karl Malone, aka "the Mailman," was a tremendous player. Though he never won a championship ring, Malone was a champion talent over many years, the second-leading scorer in league history behind Kareem. He was a very big man, six feet nine inches and 250 pounds of muscle. But despite his weight, he could get up and down the floor, jump out of the arena, take the ball to the hole off the dribble, and shoot a nice little soft jumper from either side of the floor, and he was a ferocious dunker and could rebound with the best of them. Malone running the pick and roll with John Stockton, a tenacious little guard who could pass the hell out of the ball, was a thing of beauty to watch. I mean, those two worked that play almost to perfection. Karl Malone and Gus Johnson set the standard for what a power forward should be.

Another great player who doesn't get talked about a lot today is George Gervin, aka "the Iceman." The Iceman could have played anywhere, anytime, because he was just that cool of a player. He was another guy who could really put up big numbers on anybody. You couldn't stop him, you just had to hope he was off and had a bad game. He was great in the ABA and in the NBA too, where he led the league in scoring with the San Antonio Spurs four out of five years. He is one of the greatest shooting guards to ever play the game and was named one of the 50 greatest players of all time. Ice was another skinny guy at six feet seven inches and 185 pounds, but he could shoot the jumper from anywhere. He also perfected and popularized the finger roll (although Wilt's shot was called the funnel, the finger roll looked prettier), and he was another player who could put a team on his back and take them wherever they had to go. He was so smooth, could handle the ball and pass, and was one of those players I used to love to watch, even when I was playing against him.

Other forwards who I think deserve some notice are Gus Johnson, Dave DeBusschere, Chet Walker, Elvin Hayes, Jamaal Wilkes, James Worthy, and Bernard King, a tenacious player I once coached in a high school all-star game. I think he should be in the Hall of Fame also, and he probably would be if, like Ralph Sampson, he hadn't injured his knees.

All of those players, with the exception of George Gervin, a big shooting guard who could at times play the small forward position, were centers and forwards. Now I am going to turn my attention to pure shooting guards and point guards, though players like David Thompson, Magic Johnson, Michael Jordan, and Kobe Bryant all possessed the ability to play multiple positions.

But I want to begin with a player, Nate "Tiny" Archibald, who I think was the epitome of what I would call a true point guard and the prototype of the kind of player current NBA teams are looking for to play that position. They listed his height at six feet one, but he was probably shorter than that, maybe five eleven. Tiny was a player who could set up guys, was a leader, and could score points in a hurry and pass the ball like nobody's business. He's the only guy to lead the league in scoring and assists in the same year, averaging 34 points and more than 11 assists a game in 1972–1973. He had great peripheral vision and an innate ability to find his teammates when they were open for shots. He was super-quick, fast and shifty, and could blow past defenders and score all kinds of layups because of the way he positioned his body. Now, Tiny wasn't a great jumper, but he was so quick that he could charge at his opponents and with his speed, he'd have them back-pedaling. Then he'd pull up and hit his mid- to short-range jumper, which he shot with great accuracy. He was something else. Tiny was Allen Iverson, Kyrie Irving, Chris Paul, Damian Lillard, and Isiah Thomas decades before they came into the league. Then he changed his game when he joined the Celtics and basically became a playmaker, though he could still score points when he needed to.

The first time I saw my old Baker League sidekick Archie Clark play was at the Palestra in Philadelphia, when the University of Minnesota came to play the University of Pennsylvania or Temple or some other Big

Five school there, I think, in 1966. Anyway, Lou Hudson was the star of that team, but he was hurt and didn't play, so Archie Clark came in and really put on a show. I remember saying to myself, *Wow! Who is this guy?* Then he came into the league with the Lakers and was good out there, too. So now I knew who he was. Archie was six feet two inches and was the original shake-and-bake and crossover-dribble man. He would make opponents break their ankles trying to guard him, and then he would step back and shoot that great long jumper of his and score. But if you came out to get him after he made his shake-and-bake move and then stepped back as if he was going to shoot the jumper, he would go right by you because he still hadn't given up his dribble yet. That was his bread-and-butter move. Man, Archie was an original cat. He had his game down to a science. He understood the game, could really play, and was creative. That's why I liked playing with him, because he understood what you were doing and what he could do to make you better. He was one of the best at what he did, and he could have done the same thing today and been even more devastating.

Lou Hudson, Archie's old Minnesota teammate—man, I sure would like to have seen them play together—was just an out-and-out scorer. You couldn't really stop him from shooting his jumper because he got it off so quickly. "Sweet Lou" is what we called him, because he could shoot so well. He was six feet five and a classic shooting guard because he didn't handle the ball much. He was a really smooth player and a tremendous shooter. He knew how to move around the floor and get to where he needed to be. Plus, in most situations, the team he was on structured its offense around him, so that made it easier for him to score points. He played with Pete Maravich, Joe Caldwell, Bill Bridges, and Zelmo Beaty. But no matter who he played with, he would usually emerge as the leading scorer on the team. It wasn't that he was a gunner, he just hit a high percentage of his shots and was an out-and-out great player—another one who nobody hardly mentions today, which is a shame.

My old nemesis, Gail Goodrich, did everything on the court. He wasn't a great long jumper shooter, but he was deadly from about 15 to 18 feet and he could take it to the hole. He wasn't very big, only six one and 170 pounds, or very fast, but he understood the game and how to get his shot off. Gail was a reliable player. He could do pretty much whatever a team needed him to do offensively, and he meshed pretty well with Jerry West. Even at UCLA and when he first came into the league with the Lakers he was always a reliable scorer. He was left-handed, which I think caused problems for some people defensively. He had his way with me in the first final that I played against him. But I was hurt when we faced each other those times. But that takes nothing away from Gail: I think he was a very good player and I always give him his due.

Now, John Havlicek is another story. He was used to playing without the ball, and most of the time he only dribbled with his right hand, even when he went left. Hell, he probably couldn't dribble with his left hand. But he understood how to play the game. He would come off picks, get the ball, and if you were late getting there, he would shoot and score. Even if you were right there on him, he could still go by you and pull up and shoot the jumper, or go to the basket and put up a little left or right hook off the backboard, or shoot the ball off one leg. He was something else, very difficult to guard, a scorer who knew how to get his points and who was very reliable in the clutch. He was a great defensive player as well, and I think only Bill Russell and Sam Jones have won more NBA championships than him. John was one of the all-time great players.

Jo Jo White is another player that I think should be in the Hall of Fame. He was a quick-shooting guy and was also very quick getting up and down the floor. He was six feet three, could pull up and shoot the jumper really well, and could also drive by you. Jo Jo could take over a game just by coming down and shooting his deadly quick jumper.

Now, David Thompson was another truly great talent and player who had his career cut short because of injuries. Thompson was six four, and because he had a 44-inch vertical leap he was nicknamed Skywalker. I mean, today's game of alley-oop passes and high-flying dunks were preceded decades earlier by Monte Towe's (Thompson's backcourt teammate at North Carolina State) over-the-rim lobs, which the Skywalker converted into high-flying layups (college players couldn't dunk at that time because of the "Alcindor rule"). But Thompson's game wasn't only about jumping over opponents. He could shoot his jumper with accuracy from all over the floor, handle the ball, pass, play defense, block shots, and take his opponent to the hole off the dribble and score. He was a great college player on an equally great college team that went undefeated in 1973. In 1974, he led his team to victory over UCLA and Bill Walton in the NCAA semifinal game, ending the Bruins' streak of consecutive championships at seven, and then over Al McGuire's Marquette squad for the championship.

In the pros he was an all-star in both the ABA and the NBA. He had a memorable game in 1978 on the last day of the regular season, when he scored 73 points against Detroit. He barely lost the scoring championship that year to George Gervin, because Iceman scored 63 points later that same day and secured the title. But Thompson fell down some stairs at a New York nightclub and hurt his knee, and he was never the same player after that. David Thompson's high-flying approach to the game was an influence on Michael Jordan, and when Jordan was inducted into the Hall of Fame in 2009, he was introduced by the one and only Skywalker, which was a nod to Thompson's influence on His Airness's game.

Someone who I played against that I don't feel has gotten enough credit is Bobby Dandridge, probably because he played in the shadows of Kareem and Oscar Robertson. Bobby and I played in the CIAA Conference in college and always had big games against each other. I remember at halftime during one of our match-ups, Coach Ganies said, "God damn it, somebody else get Bobby Dandridge. It's like the two of 'em waltzing. He score, you score. He score, you score." So we had that type of rivalry, but became quite friendly when we both got into the pros— he in Milwaukee and me in Baltimore—as there weren't that many guys who had played in the CIAA, which definitely brought us closer. He was a helluva of player, won two rings, was a great teammate, and an integral member of that great Milwaukee Bucks team. I think he, as well as his teammate Bob Love, should both be in the Basketball Hall of Fame. The key was that Bobby could not only shoot but was a very good defender and gave them a strong presence on the court. He also gave them a lot of flexibility, as he could play both the off-guard and small forward positions. When we lost to them in the NBA Finals, one of the things I remember from that series—aside from us being completely devastated—was how solid Bobby played. Every time we get together, we still talk about our college days. One day he gave me a picture of a game at Norfolk State where I was in a corner and there were five of them around me. And I joke with him all the time, saying "this was the only way you could stop me." So he's been trying to get that picture back for thirty years!

I really feel that he is a Hall of Fame–type player because he fit so well into each system he played in. He made a difference in Milwaukee and especially in Baltimore, helping bring them a championship. I see a lot of guys going into the Hall of Fame that didn't have as much of an impact on a winning team as Bobby did. I really feel that he should get in, and I hope he eventually does.

Isiah Thomas was another player in the Tiny Archibald mold, only he had a much better outside jump shot and he was bigger. Isiah was an outstanding player, and I think his greatest strength was his desire to be the best and for people to know that he was the best. He was a very hard-nosed player who was a great leader on that Detroit team and a clutch shooter when the game was on the line; he also could play through injury. He could take the ball to the hoop and score inside against bigger players; he was fearless. He had the look of a nice young guy with a beautiful smile. But Isiah was an assassin, man. He was ruthless. He came to play hard every night, and he would fight if it came down to that. Isiah could jump, too, and would dunk on his defender if he relaxed. And he was a very good defensive player as well.

Magic Johnson was a player unto himself, and a really great one. I mean, he could see the whole court and make things happen in a blink. He knew where everyone was on the court, and man, did he have a handle. I mean, he was an incredible passer, and a great team leader and player, even as a rookie. He was the kind of player who made his teammates better, and you could tell how much they loved playing with him. It wasn't that Magic couldn't score a lot of points, because he could have, he just wasn't the kind of shooter a guy like Michael Jordan was. Magic always thought *Pass* first, getting his teammates involved in the flow of the game. In that way he was different from Michael Jordan, and any other player I can think of except LeBron James, who is a lot like Magic in the way he approaches the game.

Michael Jordan could also handle the ball and get to wherever he wanted to on the court and finish plays. If I had to give the ball to somebody to finish a play, I'd give it to Michael. But if I wanted to give the ball to somebody to make a play, I'd give it to Magic. Magic could play inside and outside, any position, and make it work for his team. He was a facilitator, just like LeBron is. But LeBron and Kobe Bryant are also finishers like MJ was, and that's a special gift, too. I mean, Magic brought excitement into the game, and he could run the fast break as well as anyone in the history of the game. Yeah, he was special, and he could have been a dominant player in any era, just like Larry Bird, or Michael Jordan, or Isiah Thomas could have been. Any of the players I mentioned above could have played in my era and been truly dominant players.

I would also place Allen Iverson in that category. Allen was a guy
with a lot of heart and ability. He played the game with attitude, which
made him even better because he was so fierce. Allen played the game
with a whole lot of ego because he believed he could do anything on the
court. He was one of the quickest guards I've ever seen, had a really good
jump shot, and could go to the hoop and dunk on you—as small as he
was—if he got the opportunity. He could handle the ball, pass, and run
the court in a flash. But it was his attitude and courage that pulled everyone on his team with him. He was a fearless player who got in the paint
and took it right to the big men. They would knock him down, but
Iverson, who had been an All-American high school quarterback in
Virginia, would just get back up and bring it to them again. He was relentless, talented, and tough as nails. In his prime he was a brilliant player.

Kobe Bryant was more of a Michael Jordan–type player—he always
tried to be like him. But they are both truly great players, fiery competitors. It's just a matter of what the situation calls for. I really liked Kobe
because I watched his game grow from the time he was a youngster in
Philadelphia, and he never disappointed. He was hard-nosed like Magic,
Michael, and Isiah—guys who wanted very badly to win championships—
were. That's a special attitude that some players just don't have.

Other really good guards were Lenny Wilkins, who we used to call
"the Quiet Assassin"; Dick Barnett; Geoff Petrie; Calvin Murphy; Norm
Van Lier; Jerry Sloan; and Jeff Mullins.

Now don't get me wrong, there have been other great players who
have played in the NBA over the years, but time and space don't allow me
to mention them all. I thought I would mention some of the really good
players that people don't often recall or mention today. After all, the NBA
has been built on star players, and it would be ludicrous for me to say that
the players I mentioned are the only ones who have had an impact on
the game. Yes, there are many more, and they know who they are.

LeBron James is the best player in the game today, with Kevin Durant a close second. I say this because I think LeBron can do anything he wants to on the basketball court. He can score whenever he wants, he sees the court well, and he is totally unselfish and a team player. He can really pass the ball and set up other players—just check out how many assists he gets every game—he can rebound, and he can really get out and run the floor. Even though he's a prolific scorer with the ability to take over games, he's a pass first–type player who looks to set up guys before he thinks to shoot the ball, which he can now do very well. When LeBron first came into the league, his jump shot was suspect and unreliable. And because he's such a big fella at six feet eight inches and 240 pounds—I think people forget he was an All-State wide receiver for his high school football team—and because he's so fast, he's just too much of a load for players to handle. Plus, he can really jump, get up off the floor and play that above-the-rim game. LeBron can take guys to the hole off the dribble—and he can really handle the ball, too—and jump over everyone and score. I mean, just watch how defenders get out of the way when he comes down on a fast break and throws down those ferocious dunks. Today he can hit the midrange jumpers and three-point shots as well as he can sink little finger rolls in the paint. So now he's got a complete game and a new attitude as a leader of his team. Before, he used to pout when things didn't go his way, but now he's more mature, and it's reflected in his game.

Kevin Durant is also a really great talent. He's definitely a finisher and can shoot the ball like nobody's business. I really love seeing him do that. But he's also a guy that doesn't have to take all the shots to make it happen. He's matured a lot, led the league in scoring, and is up there with the leaders this year also. But he knows and understands the game, knows he can get his points whenever he wants to, so he doesn't have to try to get his every time he comes down the floor. He can let everybody else get involved, which is the way I used to be. You see this a lot with what he's done since joining the Warriors. He plays within the system and rises to the moment when it calls for him to and helps facilitate when necessary. So we are going to be watching this matchup for years to come, and that's very good for the health of the game.

I like Russell Westbrook too, but sometimes I'm afraid of him. He's a guy with a lot of talent, but sometimes it's unharnessed. He's still growing as a player, and I can see that in his game this current season.

Tim Duncan was a special player, a leader on and off the court. He made everybody around him better because of the team-oriented way he played the game, leading by example and making the big shot or setting a pick to get one of his teammates free to score.

I think Chris Paul is the best pure point guard in the NBA today. I have always liked his game. He's a better shooter than I used to think, and he definitely has the knowledge of the game. He knows the pace of the game and how to run a team, and that's what sets him apart from all the other point guards. He understands the nuances of running a team. He is also fearless out there on the court, and he makes his teammates better just by being there and leading by example.

James Harden is another interesting young player. When I see him I think of Manu Ginobili, because their games mirror each other. They both play the same kind of game: Both have real good jumpers from anywhere on the floor and are adept at slashing to the basket. It doesn't matter if the defender knows they're going left, nobody's stopping them that much. They both have great energy and creativity with the ball in their hands, and they pass the ball and rebound as well. And while Ginobili often came off the bench, Harden has led as a starter.

Two other interesting young players today are Damian Lillard and Kyrie Irving. I think both of them are good, solid players who will only get better over time. I think Irving is more offense minded and Lillard is more an all-around player and I really like what I've seen from both of them.

The players of today who I think could have played well during my era, in no particular order, are LeBron James, Kevin Durant, James Harden, Chris Paul, Russell Westbrook, the Dirk Nowitzki of a couple of years ago, Kevin Love, Kawhi Leonard, Joel Embiid, Jimmy Butler, and Anthony Davis.

Some time ago I was watching either ESPN or NBA TV and the commentators were talking about who the top ten backcourts of all time were. They ranked Isiah Thomas and Joe Dumars as the number one backcourt of all time, Magic Johnson and Byron Scott the second best duo, and Walt Frazier and me as the third best. First of all, I don't think this kind of ranking serves any useful purpose because it only pits players against each in a sort of battle royal. But the networks seem to think they need to do these kinds of false comparisons to generate audience participation and excitement. The hype and media frenzy that began in the 1980s and treats talent like a product is full-blown today. It can also be seen in the entertainment-industry awards shows like the Oscars and the Golden Globes. It is not about who's really the best, but about who a small group of people think is the best product to commercialize in the marketplace. It's the same operative model in the world of sports today.

Media also plays a big part in players leaving/being traded. When the team wants to change things up, it's always leaked to the beat writer, who encourages the fans that this is not happening here, he's not fitting in, and then all of a sudden well, he should be traded, and eventually the trade happens. And the team itself remains unscathed by this whole thing. It's just something they had to do because of the bad publicity they were getting and how the fans felt. That's kind of how it all works. But, like I said before, the fact that guys have contracts and they're able to play out their contracts and do all the things that's expected of them during the course of them being there, then they deserve the opportunity to go someplace that they're going to be happy.

This national sports media hype began to hit on all cylinders, in my opinion, when Magic and Byron and Isiah and Joe arrived on the scene in the early '80s. Now, I will admit to the fact that because I played in Baltimore and Clyde played in New York, he received more media scrutiny than I did when we both first rose to prominence. The reason for this was because the Big Apple was one of the top media centers of the world, even back then. So he benefited from being in New York, but also had more pressure on him playing in this city, which I found out later when I came to play with the Knicks. When those other two duos came along, those players had to live up to the hype bestowed upon each of them once all that promotion, publicity, marketing, and commercialization kicked in. So, in my opinion, those players became more outward oriented in the things they had to do, like selling products for companies—becoming brand names, so to speak, in a way that wasn't as prevalent back in the early '70s. In the '80s, however, the hype was whether a talent was cool or not, or whether he was a winner—and you had to be a winner in order to sell products. That determined who was the best in any given sport.

But in response to that ranking of the best backcourts of the modern era, I will give you my ranking of the best three. First let me say that I know what I'm about to say will be disputed by some as not being objective, but I have thought about this deeply and I think fairly, and I would rank Walt Frazier and myself as the best NBA backcourt of all time, especially when we were both playing injury free. After us are Isiah Thomas and Joe Dumars of the Detroit Pistons and then Magic Johnson and Byron Scott of the Los Angeles Lakers.

The reason I rank Clyde and myself on top boils down to the fact that both of us were the leaders of our two different teams before we joined forces: Clyde with the Knicks and me with the Bullets. Now, I think that counts for something, because it was the meshing of two great talents—both of us in the top 50 NBA players of all time—when we came together in 1972. When looked at in this light, Isiah Thomas and Joe Dumars were both great talents, but Isiah was the leader of that duo. The same thing can be said for Magic Johnson and Byron Scott: Magic was the clear leader of that Lakers team. Also, both Clyde and I were amongst the originators of a style of play that was passed down to the other two duos.

Another factor is that Clyde and I came along at a time when the national media coverage had not yet reached the frenzy it evolved into when both Magic and Byron and Isiah and Joe came into prominence. What I mean by this is that before we became teammates, Clyde and I battled each other somewhat out of the national spotlight, because we played before the rise of ESPN and all the sports shows that now thrive on comparing and pitting athletes against each other. This symbiosis of media promotion, marketing, and the commercialization of talent—whether it's of athletes, movie stars, artists, whatever—was just beginning to form when Clyde and I entered the spotlight. Clyde and I didn't have to worry as much about being better than other players in the eyes of some critic or analyst who never played the game, because the era of frenzied hype had not yet arrived. So Clyde and I just went out and played basketball every night without worrying about what someone thought of us, about how we were being promoted and whatnot.

See, Clyde and I didn't have to be the best in the eyes of the media. What concerned us was how we felt about ourselves and each other and our reputations among the players and coaches in the league. Now, I'm not trying to take anything away from Magic and Byron and Isiah and Joe—they were all great players both individually and as two all-time great tandems. But I think Clyde and I were better, although I can say this much: if Clyde and I had played against those other two tandems, it would have been something to watch.

However, if I were to change this to the top four backcourts, I would have to include Steph Curry and his splash brother Klay Thompson. It's quite impressive what they've done to the game. Dunks are no longer the main highlight film, as their 3-point success is better than I've ever seen. And honestly, I think they are perhaps the greatest shooting duo of all-time.

In my opinion, the greatest teams of the last 60 or so years would have to be:

- The 1957 to 1969 Boston Celtics with Bill Russell, Bob Cousy, Bill Sharman, Frank Ramsey, Tommy Heinsohn, Sam Jones, K.C. Jones, and John Havlicek.

- The Saint Louis Hawks teams between 1958 and 1965 that had Bob Pettit, "Easy" Ed Macauley, and Cliff Hagan.

- The 1966–1967 Philadelphia 76ers team with Wilt Chamberlain, Hal Greer, Billy Cunningham, Chet Walker, and Wali Jones that went 68 and 13.

- The 1970–1971 Los Angeles Lakers with Jerry West, Wilt Chamberlain, Gail Goodrich, Happy Hairston, and Jim McMillian that won 33 straight games and the NBA championship.

- The New York Knicks teams of the early 1970s with Willis Reed, Walt Frazier, Dave DeBusschere, Bill Bradley, Dick Barnett, Jerry Lucas, and myself.

- The Baltimore Bullets from 1968 to 1971.

- The Milwaukee Bucks with Kareem Abdul-Jabbar, Oscar Robertson, and Bobby Dandridge from 1970 to 1972.

- Two other Lakers teams: The 80s-era squad led by Kareem Abdul-Jabbar, Magic Johnson, Byron Scott, Jamaal Wilkes, Norm

Nixon, and James Worthy, and the 2000 to 2002 squad led by Shaquille O'Neal and Kobe Bryant.

- The 1989–1990 Detroit Pistons team led by Isiah Thomas, Joe Dumars, Bill Laimbeer, Dennis Rodman, John Salley, Mark Aguirre, and Vinnie Johnson.

- The 1991 to 1998 Chicago Bulls led by Michael Jordan, Scottie Pippen, and Dennis Rodman.

- The 1994 and 1995 Houston Rockets, led by Hakeem Olajuwon and Clyde Drexler.

- The 1999 and 2003 San Antonio championship teams, led by David Robinson and Tim Duncan.

- The 2010 to 2013 Miami Heat, led by their big three of LeBron James, Dwayne Wade, and Chris Bosh.

- And the 2014 to present Golden State Warriors, led by Steph Curry and Klay Thompson, as well as the additions of Kevin Durant and veteran leadership of Andre Iguodala.

There are other great teams, like some of the New York Knicks teams that battled for championships during Patrick Ewing's career with Charles Oakley, John Starks, Greg Anthony, Anthony Mason, Charles Smith, and Doc Rivers. But these are my choices for the great teams over the past 60-some-odd years.

I would like to close by addressing a couple more topics, and the first one is what I'll call "the Golden Era of Basketball in the 20th Century." Now, things could change, but I have boiled it down to the 10 years between 1965 and 1975. Why those years, you might ask? I have picked that decade because if you look at all the players who played during that time, you will see that most of your Hall of Famers and the 50 greatest players of all time come from that era, that decade. There were no more than 17 teams playing in the league then, so you had a concentration of talent on squads, unlike what you have today. You had the great Boston, Saint Louis, New York, Philadelphia, Los Angeles, Baltimore, Milwaukee, and Golden State teams during that period. The competition every night was so very high, and the players were veteran players who knew the fundamentals of the game. Nobody could take a day off for fear of not only being embarrassed, but also of losing the game. So that's my reason for picking this decade.

The other thing that I have been thinking about is that we will ultimately have to expand the list of the 50 Greatest Basketball Players in NBA History to maybe 60, 75, or even 100. Because how else can you make room for Kobe Bryant, LeBron James, Kevin Durant, and all the other great young talent coming along today that will have to be included? So I think that list has to be expanded, and soon. I also think that the great coach John McLendon has to be inducted into the Basketball Hall of Fame as a coach, not as a contributor. What? Are you kidding me? Not having Coach McLendon in the Hall as a coach is not only insulting to his name and to the great legacy he left behind, but also to the integrity of the Hall of Fame. Because how can you have my Winston-Salem coach, Big House Gaines, in there as a coach and not have his mentor in there on the same level? He's the only one who was mentored by James Naismith, the inventor of the game. It's stupid and demeaning to John McLendon's name, memory, and legacy, and it must be addressed really soon, if not immediately.

I want to close this book with a postscript on what's happened in my life since 1973. First, after a long relationship, Tina and I mutually ended it in the 1980s. She has gone on with her life and I wish her well. As for me, Marita and I have been together since 1983. As you may recall, I met her at a party in the summer of 1972, while she was a student at Manhattanville College. After she finished law school in Washington, DC, she moved back to New York in 1976 and began doing legal work with me for the music production company I started. We live together in Harlem, New York. We were blessed with the birth of a daughter, Maya, who in December of 2011 blessed us again with the birth of her son and our grandson, Monroe, who is now the apple of all our eyes. My oldest daughter, Sandy, has two children of her own, Carlia and Harvey—we call him Champ—who now has a daughter, Madison. My other daughter, Danielle, has a daughter named Darian, who has a son of her own, Noah. My son, Rodney, doesn't have any children. So if you count them all up I have four grandchildren and two great-grandchildren, which is a total blessing.

My interest in music has grown over the years. Being in Philly and being around music was my entree into music. And when I left Baltimore and came to New York, I met two guys who were teenagers but were in Jimmy Hendrix's last band. They became the Aleem twins and had a career of their own. But I started managing them, and that's how I got into the music business. I started working with a company by the name of Spring Records. After that, I formed my own entertainment company that is involved with film production, brand marketing consulting, sports management and development, and technology, and I continue to be involved in music production.

One other thing I want to mention here is that I have had more than 40-plus operations mostly on my back, hips, feet, and knees because of my love of playing basketball over the years. So, being a professional athlete comes with a health cost a lot of the time. But as they say, that is the price of admission for playing a game I love. I wish the injuries hadn't happened, but they did, and as I have always said, "It is what it is," so I just deal with it. I have had, for the most part, a wonderful and blessed life. I don't think too much about regrets.

But the biggest of my few regrets, the one that hovers over my life even to this day, is that I truly wish my mother not only had lived to see me win an NBA championship in the year that she died, but also that she had been physically with me a lot longer. Because it was my mother who showed me every day, by her example, how to be strong. It was my mother who first made me believe in myself, and in my ability to make it. It was my Ma who gave me that little blue book when I was 14 and instructed me to cross off the names of my opponents as I improved and got better than them at playing the game of basketball. That lesson stayed with me for the rest of my life. It was she who sacrificed so much for me, who told me to stop whining and just go out and play. It was her wisdom that lifted me up so many times so I could persevere and help win that NBA championship. I just wanted to hear the joy in her voice had I been given the chance to call her from my Los Angeles hotel room that night in April 1973, after I had finally reached the NBA mountain-top. And later, too, when I would have gone down to Germantown to visit her, I wish I could have been able to see that beautiful smile of hers when she held me close and then looked at me with tears in her eyes and said, "I told you, Earl, you were going to win that championship." Those lost moments are my biggest regrets. Other than that, it's all good, and I'm looking into the future with optimism.

Life is good.

ACKNOWLEDGMENTS

I'D LIKE TO ACKNOWLEDGE the special efforts of those who helped make this book a reality: Jennifer Gates, my agent; our personal editor, Jane Rosenman; Mark Weinstein, our Rodale editor; Julie Ganz and Jason Katzman, our Skyhorse editors; and Margaret Porter Troupe. Also, I wish to thank Theresa Smith, Tijuana James Traore, Marita Green-Monroe, Sonny Hill, Lenny Clay, Ernie Browne, Sahib Abdulkabir, and Teddy Blunt for their contribution of additional content and George Kalinsky, the Winston-Salem State University Office of Athletic Media Relations, and the Washington Wizards/NBA Photos for the use of their photos.

No one succeeds by themselves. With that said, I'd like to acknowledge those who, in their own way, helped me on my journey. I'd like to start with the people who live on Alter Street in Philadelphia; my friends from South Philly, who helped me learn the game of basketball; my teammates at Audenried and Bartram; and those whom I played with and against in the playgrounds and leagues in Philly. Also, Coach Gaines and his wife, Clara, Claudette Weston, Sahib Abdulkabir, George Clisby, Edwin Wilkerson, John Anderson, Ronald Reese, Ernie Browne, Eugene Smiley, Joe Cunningham, James Reid, Bill English, John Lathan, Johnny Watkins, Donald Williams, Vaughn Kimbrough, David Green, and all my teammates, the faculty, and the administration during my stay at Winston-Salem State University.

My teammates on the Bullets: Gus Johnson, Wes Unseld, Kevin Loughery, Jack Marin, Fred Carter, Barry Orms, Bob Ferry, Stan McKenzie, Phil Chenier, Rich Rinaldi, Ray "Chink" Scott, Leroy Ellis, John Tresvant, as well as Skip Feldman, our trainer, and the others who played with me.

My teammates on the Knicks: Walt Frazier, Bill Bradley, Jerry Lucas, Willis Reid, Phil Jackson, Dave DeBusschere, Dick Barnett, Dean Meminger, Henry Bibby, John Gianelli, Luther Rackley, Hawthorne Wingo, Charlie Paullk, Eddie Mast, and others who played with me in New York. Also Danny Whelan, our trainer; Frankie Blauschild, our road secretary; and Jim Wergeles.

Special acknowledgment to my coach in Baltimore, Gene Shue, who allowed me to be me, and to Red Holzman, who taught me to be me.

There are a myriad of others that I could mention, but neither time nor space will allow me to do that. Hopefully, you all know who you are.

You all have been instrumental in my development as a basketball player and as a person, and I appreciate you all for being a part of my life!

—*Earl*

I'D LIKE TO OFFER special acknowledgment to my agent, Jennifer Gates, Jane Rosenman, and our editor, Mark Weinstein, for all of their efforts on behalf of this project.

I'd also like to acknowledge Teddy Blunt, Ernie Brown, Theresa Smith, Marita Gail Green, Sonny Hill, Sahib Abdulkhabir, Lenny Clay, Tijuana Traore, and Aaron Hill for their time and insights.

—*Quincy*

INDEX

An asterisk (*) indicates that photos are shown in the insert pages.

paper route, 48–49
playground games, 46–47, 51–52
poem in school newspaper, 34
racial tension noticed, 51
religious and moral beliefs, 41–42
three Es and downhill slide, 35–36

K

Kefalos, Chris, 72, 78
Kennedy, John F., 61, 112–13
Kennedy, Robert, 213
King, Bernard, 382
King, Martin Luther Jr., 101–2, 134, 204–5, 219, 239
Klores, Dan, 371

L

LaBelle, Patti, 76, 342
Leonard, Kawhi, 361, 392
Levane, Andrew, 375
Lillard, Damian, 383, 391
Littles, Gene, 150
Livingston, Shaun, 371
Lloyd, Earl, 180, 375
Logan, Henry, 159–60
Loughery, Kevin, 177, 182, 191, 196–97, 230, 245, 249, 252, 257–58, 271, 288, 311
Love, Bob "Bean," 267, 281, 288, 380, 387
Love, Kevin, 281, 360, 392
Lucas, Jerry, 202, 227, 295, 299, 315, 323, 326–27, 330, 351, 354, 355, 395

M

Malcolm X assassination, 132–33
Malone, Karl "the Mailman," 364, 381–82
Malone, Moses, 331, 354, 377
Manning, Ed "Razor," 175–78, 197, 200, 249
Maravich, "Pistol Pete," 267, 273, 281, 354, 356, 378, 384
Marin, Jack, 177, 181–82, 186, 197, 201, 224, 229, 255, 264, 271, 278–80, 288, 311, 331
Marshall, Thurgood, 165
Mayo, Melvin, 165
Mays, Willie, 44–46
McAdoo, Bob, 341, 380
McCloskey, Jack, 148
McLendon, John, 327, 376, 403
Media coverage, 192–93, 361, 392–94
Meminger, Dean, 299, 313–14, 325, 328–30, 345
Miles, Eddie, 189–90, 250, 264

Minnesota Timberwolves, 281
Mobley, Willie, 72, 73
Monroe, Ann (sister),* 3–5, 8, 31–32, 39, 59–60, 91, 120, 164, 335–36
Monroe, Earl "the Pearl".* See also Early years (1944–1956); High school years (1959–1962); Junior high school years (1956–1959); specific seasons
  admitting to being lucky, 135
  basketball statistics, 126, 137, 150, 235, 257, 288, 354
  on best backcourts, 392–95
  birth of, 3
  "Black Ben" nickname, 59, 60
  "Black Jesus" nickname, 145, 146, 181, 196, 266, 284, 286, 337, 348, 349
  Black Magic film produced by, 354, 370
  children and grandchildren of, 205–6, 234–35, 287, 398
  "Chocolate" nickname, 111–12
  competition enjoyed by, xv–xvi, 129
  credentials for opinions of, 353–56
  decision not to marry while pro, 179
  dinners with mother and father, 123
  "Duke of Earl" nickname, 60, 76
  in 50 Greatest Players list, 353–54
  first NBA Championship, 352
  on Golden Era of Basketball, 396
  on greatest NBA players, 371–92
  on greatest NBA teams, 395–96
  on international basketball, 355–56
  laxatives used by, 120
  life since 1973, 397–98
  Magic Johnson and, 371–73
  on media coverage, 367, 400
  music loved by, 31–32, 67, 342–43, 398
  paradigm shift in NBA due to, 355
  as part of best backcourt, 393–95
  "the Pearl" nickname, v, vii, 150, 155, 186, 196, 231, 266, 284, 286, 292, 337, 348, 349
  on pitfalls of success, 212
  playground style, 125–26, 128, 354–55
  practical approach of, xiii–xvi
  on referees' impact, 365–67
  reuniting with father, 119–23
  as Rookie of the Year, 202, 210
  on rule changes he'd like, 367–68
  "science of the game" approach, 58, 89–91, 210, 292, 296
  strengths and weaknesses known, xiv–xv
  on theatrics, 362
  "Thomas Edison" nickname, 60, 76